WOLVERHAMPTON COLLEGE

D0259592

12/2/02
1699
Wo1011478

CARE

S/NVQ

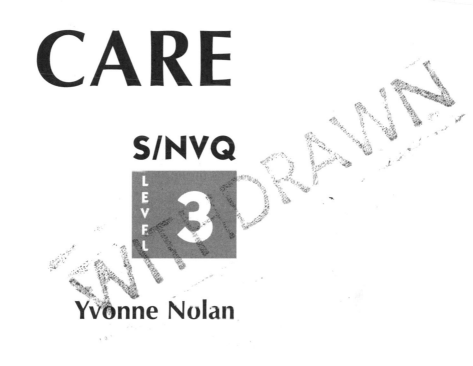

LEVEL 3

Yvonne Nolan

Heinemann

Candidate Handbook

Heinemann Educational Publishers
Halley Court, Jordan Hill, Oxford OX2 8EJ
a division of Reed Educational & Professional Publishing Ltd

Heinemann is a registered trademark of Reed Educational & Professional Publishing Limited

OXFORD   MELBOURNE   AUCKLAND   JOHANNESBURG   BLANTYRE
GABORONE   IBADAN   PORTSMOUTH (NH) USA   CHICAGO

Copyright © Yvonne Nolan 2001

First published 2001
2005   2004   2003   2002   2001
10 9 8 7 6 5 4 3

A catalogue record for this book is available from the British Library on request.

ISBN 0 435 45642 3

All rights reserved.

No part of this publication may be reproduced in any material form (including photocopying
or storing it in any medium by electronic means and whether or not transiently or incidentally
to some other use of this publication) without the written permission of the copyright owner,
except in accordance with the provisions of the Copyright, Designs and Patents Act 1988 or
under the terms of a licence issued by the Copyright Licensing Agency, 90 Tottenham Court
Road, London W1P 9HE. Applications for the copyright owner's written permission to
reproduce any part of this publication should be addressed to the publisher.

Designed by Wendi Watson

Typeset by TechType, Abingdon, Oxon

Printed and bound in Great Britain by The Bath Press Ltd, Bath

LEARNING CENTRE

3.62   NOL

'21 MAR 20 8770776

Tel: 01865 888058 www.heinemann.co.uk

Contents

Acknowledgements

To my family, John, Kate, Stewart and Patrick, thank you for being proud of me. To Linda for whom nothing is impossible and to Mary for her continued tolerance and faith in me.

The author and publishers would like to thank the following for permission to reproduce photographs:

A.P.A – page 310

John Birdsall Photography – page 142, 155

Collections/Anthea Sieveking – page 151

Empics – page 175

Format – page 166 (top right), 296

Robert Harding Picture Library – page 95

Peter Morris – page 317

Photodisc – page 365

S.P.L. – page 166 (bottom right0, 179, 199, 236

S.R.G. – page 20

Science Photo Library/Adam Hart-Davis – page 150

Every effort has been made to contact copyright holders of material published in this book. We would be glad to hear from unacknowledged sources at the first opportunity.

Dedication

To all those who give and receive care.

Unit 02

Promote people's equality, diversity and rights

WOLVERHAMPTON COLLEGE

This unit is one of the keys to working successfully in care at any level. You may have completed Unit O1 which is similar in content and will be referred to throughout this unit. If you have not completed Unit O1, then we strongly recommend that you read this unit in conjunction with that unit. It can be found in the companion book to this, entitled *NVQ Level 2 Care*, also by Yvonne Nolan. This unit will explore the issues in more depth and will consider some broader aspects of the significance of understanding the importance of equality, diversity and rights for all people who work in the health and care sector. As in Unit O1, the confidentiality of information is explored as a vitally important component of people's rights when they are receiving a service and care.

Element O2.1   Promote people's rights and responsibilities

WHAT YOU NEED TO LEARN

- The rights your clients have.
- How you can help people exercise their rights.

Clients' rights

Clients' rights are broadly divided into three categories. The first are basic human rights, the second are rights which are provided by legislation and the third are rights which are provided under charters, guidelines and policies. These rights are very different in their nature and in the way in which they are applied although, from October 2000 the basic human rights became law in this country for the first time. The **Human Rights Act** received the royal assent on 9 November 1998 and the majority of its provisions came into force on 2 October 2000. The effects of the Act are far-reaching and bring within UK jurisdiction the rights which were previously contained within the European charter of human rights and for the pursuit of which you had to go to the European Court of Human Rights in Strasbourg.

The Human Rights Act 1998

The Human Rights Act means that residents of the United Kingdom – this Act applies in Scotland, Wales and Northern Ireland – will now be entitled to seek redress (through the courts) in the United Kingdom if they believe that their human rights have been infringed by any public authority. The definition of public authority is very broad. It includes:

- government departments
- local authorities
- police
- benefits agencies
- the courts.

It also includes organisations which carry out any public function. The Act does not identify precisely what it means by a public function, but it is generally taken to mean:

- when an organisation performs or operates in the public domain as an integral part of a statutory system
- when it performs a duty which is of public significance
- when the rights or obligations of individuals are affected by the performance of the duty
- when a body is non-statutory but is established under the authority of government or local government
- when the body performs functions that the government or local government would otherwise perform
- when an individual may be deprived of some legitimate expectation in performance of the duty.

Organisations subject to the Human Rights Act 1998	
Residential homes or nursing homes	These perform functions which would otherwise be performed by a local authority
Charities	Again these may be providing functions which would otherwise be provided by a government or local authority
Voluntary organisations	Also in a similar capacity
Public service	This could include the privatised utilities, such as gas, electric and water companies, which will be affected by the provisions of this Act

This breadth of interpretation takes into account such bodies as the ones in the table below.

Within the health and care sector there are a great many organisations whose work will be covered by the Human Rights Act. Meals-on-wheels services, which are to a great extent provided by the voluntary sector, are likely to be seen as fulfilling part of the statutory duties of the local authority. As such they will have to ensure that they are not restricting anyone's human rights, for instance by failing to provide meals which meet somebody's religious dietary requirements. Similarly, home care services, many of which are run by the private sector, will also have to ensure that their services are provided within the requirements of the Act, and will have to ensure that all the carers are fully aware of the implications of the Act in their day-to-day work.

It is likely that anyone who works in health or care will be working within the provisions of the Human Rights Act. This Act is all about respect for, and the promotion and fostering of, the rights of individual people through all the functions of a public authority, or any organisation which is carrying out the role of a public authority. Under the Act everyone who works in a setting which is covered by the Act will have to interpret the legislation with which they work in a way which is compatible with the Human Rights Act. The workers will be required to act in accordance with the Human Rights Act. Under the Act the rights which are guaranteed are the following.

1   **The right to life.** Public authorities must not cause the death of any person and they have a positive obligation to protect life. There are particular situations where the Act defines a limited number of circumstances where it is not a contravention of the Act to take someone's life. But this only applies where the force used is no more than absolutely necessary, such as defending a person from attack or to effect a lawful arrest.

2   **The right to freedom from torture and inhuman or degrading treatment or punishment.** Torture is identified as the most serious kind of ill-treatment. Inhuman or degrading treatment is less severe than torture and may include physical assaults, inhuman detention conditions or corporal punishment. The ill-treatment relates to both mental and physical suffering. One of the factors which is taken into account under this right is the severity and duration of the torture, degrading or ill-treatment and the vulnerability of the victim.

3   **The right to freedom from slavery, servitude and forced or compulsory labour.** Slavery means that a person is owned by somebody else like a piece of property. Servitude is defined as a person not being owned by someone else but being in enforced service to them and unable to leave. There are some exceptions to this right, for example work which may be being carried out as part of a prison sentence.

4   **The right to liberty and security of person.** People have a right not to be arrested or detained except when the detention is authorised by law. This part of the Act does not just apply to police arrests but covers all aspects of detention, including for medical or psychiatric reasons. There are clearly defined circumstances under which people can be detained, such as after conviction by a court or where there are sufficient grounds to believe that they may have committed a crime.

5   **The right to a fair and a public trial within a reasonable time.** This right covers all criminal and most civil cases as well as tribunals and some internal hearings. People have a right to be presumed innocent until proven guilty and to be given adequate time and facilities to prepare their defence. The Act gives everyone a right to a trial in public so that justice can never be carried out behind closed doors.

6   **The right to freedom from retrospective criminal law and no punishment without law.** This right means that people cannot be convicted of an act which was not a criminal offence at the time it was committed, nor can they face a punishment which was not in place when the act happened.

7   **The right to respect for private and family life, home and correspondence.** This is one of the very far-reaching parts of the Human Rights Act. Public authorities may only interfere in someone's private life when they have the legal authority to do so. This covers matters such as the disclosure of private information, monitoring of telephone calls and e-mail, carrying out

searches, and imposes restrictions on entering a person's home. It also covers issues such as the right of families to live together or the right not to suffer from environmental hazards.

8 **The right to freedom of thought, conscience and religion.** Under this right people can hold whatever thoughts, positions of conscience or religious beliefs that they wish. They are guaranteed the right to manifest their religion or belief in worship, teaching, practice and observance.

9 **The right to freedom of expression.** Freedom of expression includes what is said in conversation or speeches, what is published in books, articles or leaflets, what is broadcast and what is presented as art or placed on the Internet. In fact, any means of communication.

10 **The right to freedom of assembly and association.** This includes the right of people to demonstrate peacefully and to join or choose not to join trade unions.

11 **The right to marry and found a family.** This part of the Act is particularly relevant to rules and policies concerning adoption and fostering. Public authorities will have to ensure that their policies in this regard, for example policies to do with age or race of applicants to become adoptive parents, are not contravening the Act.

12 **The prohibition of discrimination in the enjoyment of convention rights.** The Act recognises that not all differences in treatment are discriminatory, those that are discriminating are defined as those which have no objective or reasonable justification. For example, if a registry office was only to provide information about how to undertake a civil marriage in English only, then it is possible for this to be taken as affecting the human rights of someone who was unable to speak English and therefore unable to access the information they need. This could be said to be denying them the means to fulfil their human right to marry. This would probably be viewed as discriminatory because there is no objective or reasonable justification for failing to provide information in other languages. Take another case, that of a young person excluded from school and therefore unable to exercise their human right to receive an education. If it could be proved they were excluded because of their disruptive behaviour and not because of race or socio-economic circumstances, then this would not be discriminatory.

13 **The right to peaceful enjoyment of possessions and protection of property.** The Act defines many possessions as property, not just houses or cars, but things like shares, licences and goodwill. In some circumstances the right to engage in a profession can be regarded as a property right. Under the Act no one can be deprived of their property except where the action is permitted by law.

14 **The right of access to an education.** The right of access to education must be balanced against the resources available. This right may be relevant to the exclusion of disruptive pupils from schools, and may also prove to be very relevant for children with special needs.

15 **The right of free elections.** This part of the Act is about elections to whatever legislative bodies are relevant. They must be free and fair and be held at reasonable intervals. It is also likely to raise issues of participation and access and making sure that people with disabilities or those who are ill are still able to participate.

16 The right not to be subjected to the death penalty. This provision abolishes the death penalty.

What does the Human Rights Act mean in practice at work?

Under the Human Rights Act all other legislation that includes any Acts of Parliament or Regulations must be read, understood and used in a way which is compatible with the requirements of the Human Rights Act. Government advice is that this is a very strong provision and you must make every effort to interpret the legislation that you work with in a way which is compatible with the Human Rights Act. This means that if there are two possible interpretations of the provision under an Act, such as the Mental Health Act, the Children Act, or the Community Care Act, one which is compatible with the Human Rights Act and one which is not, then the one that is compatible must be followed.

Government guidance lays down that all public authorities have a positive obligation to ensure that respect for human rights is at the core of their day-to-day work. This guidance covers all aspects of activities including:

- drafting rules and regulations and policies
- internal staff and personnel issues
- administration
- decision making
- implementing policy and working with members of the public.

Active knowledge

Think about how the laws underpinning the policies and procedures in your workplace could be used better to build a culture of rights and responsibilities. This could be a useful area of discussion at a staff meeting or in a meeting with your line manager.

Quick check guide to how your work may be affected

Does my work involve making decisions concerning a person's private rights or deciding procedures for determining cases?

Unlikely.

It is unlikely that you will be involved in this area of work. This mainly concerns people who work within the law or in arranging tribunals, hearings or granting licences, making planning decisions and registering people with professional bodies. For example, when a nurse or midwife qualifies they are registered with the United Kingdom Central Council of Nurses and Midwives, and any nurse or midwife removed from this register means that they are no longer able to practise.

The nature of the health and care sector means that this provision of the Act is likely to apply to almost everything that you do. This is about the right under the Act which says that public authorities must not cause the death of any person and prohibits torture or degrading treatment. This provision is clearly very relevant when it comes to protecting and working with extremely vulnerable clients such as children or those who are confused or have learning disabilities.

The Act maintains that everyone has the right of respect to his or her private and family life, home and correspondence. This provision covers the requirements of confidentiality, and clients' rights of access to their own records and protection from intrusion into their family or private life. This could mean you cannot disclose important information about a client to their family if the client does not wish it.

This provision is largely concerned with people's rights to publish information, views and opinions and the role of the courts or other tribunals in seeking to prevent this.

This may affect the work you do. For example, the practice and policies of your organisation might prevent somebody from pursuing their religion, perhaps because you have failed to give them the assistance they need in order to observe their religion. An example would be not providing transport for an elderly disabled client to visit a Sikh temple.

This provision is mainly about those who work in situations where they could be depriving people of possessions, perhaps confiscating goods which have been gained through crime, or granting a compulsory purchase order against someone's property, or perhaps the removal of possessions, in order to satisfy a debt.

This part of the Act is an overarching clause which makes sure that you are not preventing anyone from exercising their rights through discrimination. The intention of the Act is to protect people from discrimination on any grounds, whether it be gender, race, colour, language, religion, political affiliations, national or social origin, association with a national minority, property, birth or other status. 'Other status' has been interpreted to mean sexual orientation, marital status, illegitimacy, military status and trade union status. For more details on discrimination, see page 18.

How to use the act

If someone believes that a public authority has breached their human rights they can take the authority to court or they can use their rights under the Act in any other proceedings such as a judicial review, a criminal trial, care proceedings or housing possession proceedings.

If the court finds in favour then it can award whatever remedy seems just and appropriate. It could include damages or may simply require the public authority to correct the human right which has been breached.

Proceedings under the Human Rights Act can only be brought by the victim of a breach of the Act. This means that interest groups will not be able to bring cases directly, however, under the Act they will be able to support victims who choose to pursue the route of legal redress.

Case study

P and J are both people with profound disabilities. They met while living in residential accommodation and have a close and happy marriage. Both P and J need wheelchairs for mobility. P was severely injured in a traffic accident when she was in her late teens and is completely dependent on 24-hour-a-day carers to meet all of her needs. J has a genetic degenerative condition and, like P, requires a wheelchair for mobility and 24-hour-a-day care. When they decided to marry following long discussions with local authority and support teams, they were able to obtain a specially adapted bungalow and a full-time team of carers in order to enable them to live as independent as possible.

P and J are now both in their late 20s. Through the use of technology and the Internet P has been able to continue her career as a highly successful finance advisor and dealer and J writes popular books. The couple are financially stable and are able to afford a good lifestyle within the limitations imposed by society because of their level of disability. After considerable thought and discussion, they decided they would like to start a family. Although P is physically capable of conceiving and carrying a child, conception would have to be achieved through an IVF intervention. However, J and P have been refused IVF treatment at all the clinics, both private and NHS, they have approached. And when they discussed the possibility of adoption with their local authority, the authority also felt unable to accept them as potential adopters. They now intend to pursue legal action on the grounds that their human right to found a family is being denied to them.

1 In this situation whose rights are paramount?
2 Does the potential unborn child have any rights?
3 What are the potential implications of this for the fertility service?
4 What are the potential implications of this for the adoption service?
5 Does the financial position of P and J have any significance in this case?

Human rights are a major issue world wide. In many parts of the world people's human rights are being flagrantly abused and disregarded daily in cases of serious torture, degradation, starvation and even death. Set against these horrific abuses of human rights, it may seem that the interpretation of some of the rights afforded by the Human Rights Act are relatively minor. However, it is the development of a culture and a society which respects human rights at all levels which is likely to prove the best source of protection against any society ever becoming involved in the major abuse of human rights of large parts of its population. The Human Rights Act 1998 should provide a major innovation in ensuring that the concept of people's rights are included as an integral part of the services provided by any public authority.

Other legislation

There are a number of other Acts of Parliament which are designed to protect and promote rights and responsibilities. Depending on your area of work, you are likely to work under the requirements of at least one of the following Acts:

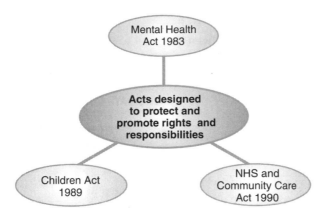

A care worker will work under conditions set down by one or more of these Acts

You will also need to know that there are provisions under a range of Acts of Parliament that protect and ensure the rights of specific groups of people. These Acts include:

Care workers need to know these Acts protect the rights of certain groups of people

For more details on these Acts, see Unit O1, in *NVQ 2 Care* .

Any work which is carried out under the provisions of Acts of Parliament is also going to be governed by the Human Rights Act. For example, under the Mental Health Act public authorities will need to consider carefully if any of their work affects the rights of patients who are compulsorily detained under the Mental Health Act or who are subject to guardianship under the Act or who are subject to any other limitations on their freedom of movement. Similarly, the Children Act will also have to be read in conjunction with the Human Rights Act to ensure that the provisions contained in that Act do not contravene the rights of people to found a family, and there may also be questions about rights of access to children. The NHS and Community Care Act covers a wide area of provision and affects the well-being, both physical and mental, of a great many people. It may also affect the way people are able to enjoy their home and possessions. It is therefore important that all public authorities consider very carefully how their work under the auspices of this Act may impinge upon human rights.

Promoting racial equality

Not all the Acts which have been designed to promote the rights of particular groups and to prevent **discrimination** are successful in doing so. There are many reasons for this, most of which are rooted in the way that society is structured and the factors which influence it and cause discrimination. For example, the Race Relations Act 1976 requires that there can be no discrimination either directly or indirectly against people in terms of employment. However, the employment figures for black and Asian people prove that the Act has not achieved its objective. For example, current figures from the Lord Chancellor's Department show that there are no black high court judges and only five black circuit court judges out of a total of over 550. Also ethnic minorities occupy only five part-time chairs of industrial tribunals out of almost 200 and only 11 part-time chairs of social security appeals tribunals out of almost 500, as you can see from the table.

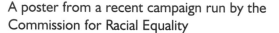

A poster from a recent campaign run by the Commission for Racial Equality

Post	Total	Ethnic minority post holders	%
High court judges	97	0	-
Circuit judges	553	5	0.9
Recorders	854	13	1.5
Assistant recorders	375	11	2.9
Assistant recorders in training	106	2	1.9
District judges	335	4	1.2
Family division district judges	18	0	-
Deputy district judges	740	12	1.6
Stipendiary magistrates	89	2	2.2
Acting stipendiary magistrates	84	4	4.8
Chairman of industrial tribunals (full time)	77	3	3.9
Chairman of industrial tribunals (part time)	195	5	2.6
Chairman of social security appeals tribunals (full time)	57	2	3.5
Chairman of social security appeals tribunals (part time)	497	11	2.2

Source: Lord Chancellor's Department

A similar picture occurs within the police. Despite a wide ranging and highly publicised examination of racism and its consequences within police forces, there has only been a minimal increase in the employment of black and Asian people as police officers. Between 1989 and 1995 the percentage of police officers from ethnic minorities only increased from 1.06 per cent to 1.75 per cent across all of the police forces in the UK. This represents an increase from 1,306 officers in 1989 to 2,223 officers in 1995. This was out of a force total of just over 122,000 in 1989 and just over 127,000 in 1995.

A similar picture occurs in the senior ranks of the police, as is shown in the table.

Ethnic minorities in 1995	Out of 2,223
Sergeants	158
Inspectors	36
Chief inspectors	8
Superintendents	1

Source: Commission for Racial Equality, 1997

Recently there have been several highly publicised cases of black or Asian members of the armed forces receiving compensation because they were racially abused. Figures for 1994 show that in all three of the armed services black and ethnic minority service personnel represented on average only about 1.3 per cent of the total. Only 13 per cent of black applicants were accepted by the Army, whereas approximately 25 per cent of white applicants were accepted. The table shows the percentage of black and ethnic recruits to each of the armed forces.

Forces	% Black and ethnic recruits
Royal Navy	1.1
Army	1.5
Royal Air Force	1.4

Source: Commission for Racial Equality, 1997

These figures show clearly that legislation alone is not sufficient to ensure that people are not discriminated against and that they are able to exercise their rights. Legislation will not be effective unless attitudes change along with it, and any change in attitude requires a long-term period of education, both formal and informal, before serious change actually occurs.

Many employers and a wide range of organisations claim to be non-racist and to have a policy of equal opportunities. However, the old saying, 'I cannot hear what you are saying, the things you do are speaking too loudly', is appropriate for many organisations in the UK today.

Active knowledge

Find out the local percentage of your population who are from black, Asian or other ethnic minority backgrounds and compare this to the number of people employed in your organisation. Check if the overall workforce reflects the makeup of your local population. Then check the number of people in senior management positions in your organisation and how many of them are from black, Asian or other ethnic minority backgrounds, and look at how this compares to the makeup of the overall work force. If your organisation compares unfavourably with the local population, what action could be taken to improve the ratio?

Promoting sexual equality

Other legislation which makes it illegal to discriminate against particular groups is the Sex Discrimination Act 1975. This legislation is also difficult to enforce and on its own can never achieve a truly non-discriminatory society with respect to gender. Women are particularly affected by sexual discrimination.

Women tend to work in predominately low paid occupations such as clerical, catering, hairdressing, caring and

A campaign against sexual discrimination run by the Equal Opportunities Commission

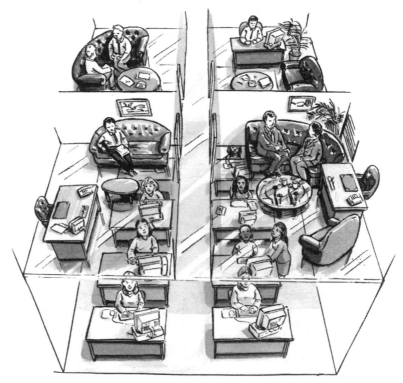

The 'glass ceiling' is a barrier to women in the workplace

other service industries. The 'glass ceiling' is an expression used to explain the barriers which exist to prevent women achieving promotion to senior positions. Many of these barriers are not obvious; they involve factors such as attitudes, working arrangements and working hours, balancing work and family, difficulties in mobility and the outdated attitude of some male senior managers.

The Hansard Commission reported in 1990 on the position of women in management. At that point less than 7 per cent of senior managers were women, by 1995 that had increased to just over 10 per cent. Within the legal and judicial system, women, like black and Asian people, are under-represented. Only 7 per cent of high court judges and 15 per cent of recorders are women. There are no women Law Lords and only one appeal court judge. In the police 16 per cent of the officers are women, but only 3 per cent are chief constables, in the armed forces there are only two women at the rank of brigadier or commodore and none above this rank. Even within the academic world women are not equally represented; at Oxford and Cambridge women represent an average of only 16 per cent of lecturers and 6.5 per cent of professors.

Just by providing women with rights in respect of employment the Sex Discrimination Act does not necessarily change attitudes. This is a long and protracted process, as is clear from the painfully slow progress that has been made over the 25 years that this Act has been in place.

The Equal Pay Act, which also relates to women and employment, has been in force since 1970, yet there are still major inequalities in the pay which women receive. In 1996 a study was carried out looking at low pay and women throughout the countries of the European Union. From this it emerged that 41 per cent of women in the UK received less than 66 per cent of the average wage which is considered to be low pay. This is the highest of all the European countries studied, followed by Germany at 33 per cent and Ireland and Spain at 29 per cent.

In 1998 the Equal Opportunities Commission showed that in real terms this meant:

Wage per hour	% of population	
	Women	Men
less than £3	10	5
less than £4	29	14
less than £4.50	40	20

Source: Equal Opportunities Commission, 1998

This should have been improved to some extent by the introduction of a national minimal wage, although this is only likely to affect those groups who were already earning less than £3 an hour. The inequalities in wages still remain.

Case study

K is the manager of a residential facility for children and young people. There are 15 children and young people in the facility, which provides a long-term stable environment, and there is a large staff group, many of whom have been working in the setting for several years. K is very much aware that amongst her staff there is a predominance of women; out of the 30 staff, 27 are women. The deputy officer in charge is male, as is the caretaker and one other care worker. K is concerned because (a) she feels that children and young people need to be exposed to positive male role models as many of them have only experienced poor quality or abusive relationships with men, and (b) she is concerned about her liability under equal opportunities legislation and guidelines and she is not sure if the Human Rights Act could also apply in her work setting. K finds that each time she advertises a position there is a relatively small number of men who apply. Also those men who have applied have not been as suitable as women who have applied for the same post. K is wondering what steps she can take to encourage the recruitment of men.

1 What steps do you think K could take to improve male recruitment?
2 Should K attempt to improve male recruitment?
3 Are there any advantages to having a gender-balanced staff group?
4 Do you think that K could be liable under any legislation?
5 Is so, what legislation?
6 Who would benefit most from additional recruitment of male staff:
   • the children
   • the staff group as a whole
   • unemployed male care workers?

Active knowledge

Check out the number of male and female employees in your organisation and the proportions. Compare this to the number of senior managers in your organisation and see if the proportions remain the same.

Promoting equality for the disabled

The Disability Discrimination Act 1995 has put in place new rights for people with disabilities concerning employment, access and land, property and housing. This still leaves a great deal to be desired in terms of changing attitudes towards people with disabilities because much of the Act is advisory and may not have adequate powers of enforcement. As with discrimination on the grounds of race or gender much remains to be done in terms of changing attitudes. There is an increasing movement amongst disabled people to educate society on the disabling environment and how disability is caused by the attitudes and restrictions of society rather than a specific or individual condition. The disabled people's movement would argue that in order for disabled people to function in society without discrimination, society must adapt to meet the needs of disabled people and not the other way around. Most disabled people are able to achieve most of their goals and aspirations provided that society makes it possible rather than expecting them to limit their dreams, hopes and aspirations as a result of their disability.

Rights under charters

One way in which the rights in respect of service provision are given to users of the provision is through a **charter**. Charters mean that those who use the service and those who support them know what they can expect and know when and how to complain if the service fails to meet the standards set out in the charter.

Did you know?

Did you know the government has an entire department which now deals with charters? It is part of the Cabinet Office and is called 'Service First'.

There are currently over 20 charters in the UK which outline the levels of public service which people can expect for a wide range of services – including the tax payers charter, the customs and excise charter, the job seekers charter, a courts charter and a higher education charter. The most important charters which relate to the area of health and social care are the patients charter, which informs patients about the levels of service they can expect within the National Health Service, and the long-term care charter, which lays down the standards that must be provided for both clients and their carers in the provision of long-term care. There is also a Benefits Agency customer charter which explains the standard of service provision which claimants can expect from the Benefits Agency.

You will need to make sure that you have read and understood any charters which provide people with rights and information about service levels which cover the services in which you work. Your employer should have trained you to know what the service levels are and how they are being achieved within your organisation.

The long-term care charter

The long-term care charter lays down the values which people can expect their local services, whether they be housing, health or social services, to be based on. They are:

- Treating people with courtesy, honesty and with respect for dignity.
- Helping people achieve and sustain the maximum possible independence.
- Working in partnership with people to provide the services they need.
- Involving people in decisions and giving them enough information to make informed choices.
- Helping people to give their views through advocacy and other representative organisations.
- Treating people fairly on the basis of need and not discriminating against them on the basis of age, sex, race, religion, disability or sexual orientation.
- Making sure that people feel able to complain about the standard of services they get and are not victimised because they complain.

It is interesting to note that all those values in the long-term care charter are covered by the units in the S/NVQ at levels 2 and 3 and are incorporated into the units and elements of the national occupational standards for care. The importance of putting those values into a charter means that people have a right to complain if they do not believe that the services with which they are provided are meeting the standards set out in those value statements. It is important for you as a worker in the health and care services to understand the contents and service levels identified in charters so that you can ensure that your own practice meets those requirements. It is also important that you understand how to access information on charters for a wide range of services so that you can ensure that your clients are getting service from any agency at the best possible level and that you have sufficient information to advise and if necessary assist them to complain if those services fall short. A full range of all the charters available can be obtained from 'Service First' at *www.cabinet.gov.uk* and will also be available from the agencies providing the service.

Case study

Mrs O has been receiving support from her local authority for the past five years. She is now 85 and her mobility and general health has become increasingly poor. When she began to have home care services her needs had been limited to some shopping and some housework support. However, over the years she has been able to do less so her need for home care has increased. She now has a considerable amount of personal care and requires a morning and put-to-bed service, along with bathing and other personal care.

Mrs O has recently had her care needs assessed and has been advised that owing to financial restrictions on her local authority the amount of care she receives will have to be reduced and that she can no longer have the level of service currently provided. This means that Mrs O will not be able to continue to live in her own home, but is likely to need a move into residential care. She has made an official complaint to her local authority and has contacted her MP complaining that the level of service that she is entitled to expect under the long-term care charter has not been provided. She feels that her ability to maintain her independence is being restricted by the decision of the local authority to reduce her service. She does not feel that the local authority has worked with her or involved her in making this decision.

1 What are Mrs O's rights in this situation?
2 What are Mrs O's expectations in this situation?
3 Has the local authority failed to comply with the long-term care charter?
4 Has the local authority failed to comply with any legislation?
5 How could this have been better approached?
6 Where could Mrs O go for support to make her complaint?

Active knowledge

Find the charter which covers the services in the area you work in. Make sure that you have read it and understand the levels of service required. Check that the services are being provided to the appropriate level in the area you work in. If you believe they are not, then you could raise this with your line manager.

Policies and guidelines

Most workplaces have their own policies and guidelines which are drawn up and agreed by their organisation. This usually covers matters such as equal opportunities, staff training and development, bullying, harassment, and **confidentiality**. Whilst these policies and guidelines may not necessarily confer specific rights upon clients they will certainly indicate the way in which they can expect the organisation to behave and would provide the basis for a complaint if those standards were not met.

How you can help people exercise their rights

Many people miss out on rights which they have either because they are unaware that they exist or because they have insufficient information or because they don't know how to properly complain when things go wrong. Many other people miss out on their rights because those rights simply fail to be enforced because of attitudes and ignorance. One of the most important roles which you can play in supporting people to exercise their rights is in raising awareness about discrimination and about inequality, which so many groups of people currently suffer. You can also refuse to be a part of discrimination yourself and should ensure that in your own practice you value the diversity and difference amongst the people you care for rather than allowing them to suffer disadvantage as a result of ignorance and fear. One of your most important roles is to ensure that you have all the information about the rights which apply to your clients and the services which they currently use. If you have sufficient knowledge of the existence of their rights and know where to obtain further information then you will be able to assist your clients in ensuring that they exercise the rights which have been provided for them under legislation, charters and guidelines.

Keys to good practice

- Hold regular staff meetings and have a regular item on your agenda about rights.
- Ensure that clients are fully aware of complaints procedures and know how to follow them.
- Make sure that your workplace has a series of policies and guidelines in place which will protect and promote people's rights.
- Ensure that you are updated and that you share with your colleagues updates on any information which relates to clients' rights.
- Make sure that you advise clients of their rights.
- Support clients in obtaining their rights if necessary.
- Never participate in or encourage discriminatory behaviour.

Active knowledge

Write a case study which describes a situation that you have been involved in or are aware of where it has been difficult to reach a balance between the rights of an individual client and the responsibility of the service provider to ensure a full range of service provision for all of those who need it.

Promote equality and diversity of people

WHAT YOU NEED TO LEARN

- The causes of inequality and discrimination.
- How to challenge the causes of inequality.
- How to support those who are subjected to discrimination and oppression.
- Recording information as part of anti-discriminatory practice.

Causes of inequality and discrimination

In Unit O1 you will have learned about many of the effects of **inequality** and failure to recognise and value people's **diversity**. Before you can actively promote and encourage the equal rights of everyone for whom you provide care and to work to ensure that the diversity of individuals is valued, you will need to understand how inequalities occur and the way in which society is structured.

Structure of society

The system by which people are grouped together and given status within all societies is called **social stratification**. The way in which this happens depends on the society. For example, in the American South before the American Civil War social stratification was carried out on the basis of racial grouping, whereby black communities existed only as slaves of white plantation owners. Many societies have used religion as a means of separating groups within society. In India a caste system separates social groupings on the basis of the caste into which each individual is born.

In most modern industrial societies social stratification is not governed entirely by a preordained group into which an individual is born or only by land ownership. Broadly, people are categorised according to their socioeconomic circumstances. This relates to their occupation, disposable income and housing. In Britain the government defines people according to their occupation. For many years this classification was referred to as the Registrar Generals Social Scale, however this has recently been replaced by a new occupational scale which classifies people on a scale of 1 (top) to 8 (bottom), as follows:

Social scale classification

1	Higher managerial and professional occupations
1.1	Employers and managers in larger organisations (e.g. company directors, senior company managers, senior civil servants, senior officers in police and armed forces)
1.2	Higher professionals (e.g. doctors, lawyers, clergy, teachers and social workers)
2	Lower managerial and professional occupations (e.g. nurses and midwives, journalists, actors, musicians, prison officers, lower ranges of police and armed forces)

3	Intermediate occupations (e.g. clerks, secretaries, driving instructors, telephone fitters)
4	Small employers and own account workers (e.g. publicans, farmers, taxi drivers, window cleaners, painters and decorators)
5	Lower supervisory craft and related occupations (e.g. printers, plumbers, television engineers, train drivers, butchers)
6	Semi-routine occupations (e.g. shop assistants, hairdressers, bus drivers, cooks)
7	Routine occupations (e.g. couriers, labourers, waiters and refuse collectors)
8	Those who have never had paid work and the long-term unemployed

Another way of dividing the population into different social groupings is one used by advertisers and market researchers, which is based on groupings A to E, and is divided as follows:

Group A	Professional workers – lawyers, doctors, etc., scientists, managers of large-scale organisations
Group B	Shopkeepers, farmers, teachers and white collar workers
Group C	Skilled manual workers – high grade, e.g. master builders, carpenters, shop assistants and nurses
	Skilled manual workers – low grade, e.g. electricians, plumbers
Group D	Semi-skilled manual workers, e.g. bus drivers, lorry drivers, fitters
Group E	Unskilled manual workers, e.g. general labourers, barmen, porters

It is interesting to note that this list does not include a category for those who are not in paid work or the long-term unemployed. This is primarily because advertisers and market researchers are only interested in those who are in an economic position to purchase the products that they are selling.

The government uses its scale 1 to 8 when it carries out research into the trends which are currently happening in society, and particularly once every 10 years when it carries out a count of the population in a census. This provides the government with information which it can use to plan for the services and infrastructure which it will need over the next 10 years and longer, in order to effectively meet the needs of the population.

Active knowledge

Think of two people you know of who come from the opposite ends of the occupational scale. For each, write down the main details of their socioeconomic circumstances, their likely income, housing, qualifications and education, possessions, etc. How do you think their circumstances affect their rights to equality?

Poverty, race, gender, disability

Many people in the lower socioeconomic group are likely to suffer hardships which are caused by **poverty**, either by living on state benefit or by working in jobs with low wages.

On a world-wide scale poverty is defined by the World Health Organisation as living on less than $1 a day. There is little doubt that in many Third World undeveloped countries there are millions of people who suffer great hardship and live in very real poverty. In a Western society, such as ours, poverty takes on a different meaning. The government definition of poverty within the UK is 'half the average income after housing costs' – this is known as the households below average income measure (HBAIM).

Some of the most obvious effects of poverty are poor housing and a poor neighbourhood

Individuals and families living in poverty are far more likely to experience the conditions which will lead to ill-health and a greater need for the health and care services than those higher on the occupational scale, who are likely to live in better conditions. Some of the most obvious effects of poverty are poor housing, a poor diet, the likelihood of living in a poor area or neighbourhood with poor quality local facilities. Socioeconomic factors are a major cause of inequality, as you can see from the following:

Socioeconomic factors and inequality

- Infant and childhood death rates are significantly higher amongst children whose fathers are unskilled and in social groups 7 and 8.

- Children from groups 7 and 8 are four times more likely to die in accidents as those from group 1.

- Children in poverty have poorer attendance records at school and are less likely to continue into further education – this also reduces their opportunity for social mobility.

- Highest incidents of mental health problems occur amongst people who live in poverty and are in groups 7 and 8.

- Nutrition and eating habits show that people in lower socioeconomic groups tend to eat less fruit and vegetables and less food which contains dietary fibre. There seems to be evidence that the diets of those in lower social groupings tend to lack choice and variety and often contain inappropriate foods such as crisps, sweets and soft drinks.

- Only 44 per cent of babies born to mothers in groups 7 and 8 are breast-fed compared with 81 per cent of babies born to mothers in group 1.

- Large numbers of the elderly population live on very low incomes. Over 30 per cent of pensioners entitled to higher levels of income through income support fail to claim it and as a result exist in a lifestyle of severe deprivation.

Poverty is not the only cause of inequality. It can also result from issues around race, gender or disability. For example, there are much higher rates of coronary heart disease and diabetes amongst the Asian population of the UK – the death rate from heart disease can be up to twice as high as that of the general population. There also seems to be a link between race and educational achievement. The Department for Education and Employment figures show that white and Indian students are twice as likely to obtain five or more passes at GCSE than those from Afro-Caribbean, black African, Bangladeshi or Pakistani backgrounds.

It is important that you assist in identifying within your workplace and work practice any processes or procedures which can contribute to discrimination or to reinforcing inequality.

The following table shows the number of people and children in poverty in the UK (including self-employed) – i.e. Those living on 50 per cent of average income after housing costs.

	People			Children		
	Total population (m)	Number in poverty (m)	% of total population	Total population (m)	Number in poverty (m)	% of total population
1979	54	5	9	13.8	1.4	10
1994/5	55.0	13.3	24	12.7	4	31
1998/9	56.6	14.3	25	12.8	4.5	35

Source: CPAG Poverty Facts and Figures

This table shows the risk and numbers in poverty by family type (including self-employed) – those living on 50 per cent of average income after housing costs.

	% of group in poverty			Number in poverty			% of total
	1979	1994/5	1998/9	1979	1994/5	1998/9	
Pensioner couples	21	23	25	1,020	1,219	1,350	9
Single pensioners	12	32	37	520	1,376	1,554	11
Couples with children	8	23	23	2,220	4,784	4,692	34
Couples without children	5	12	12	480	1,380	1,464	10
Single with children	10	55	62	480	2,310	2,914	20
Single without children	7	23	22	530	2,231	2,178	15

Source: CPAG Poverty Facts and Figures

socioeconomic deprivation is among the underlying causes of inequality in the UK, and makes people vulnerable to discrimination through race, sex and disability. While it is not always possible for workers in the health and social care sector to improve their clients' socioeconomic position, they can challenge discrimination and intervene actively to promote equality and diversity.

The pyramid of inequality below illustrates how inequality starts, how it is reinforced by attitudes and how it is allowed to go on.

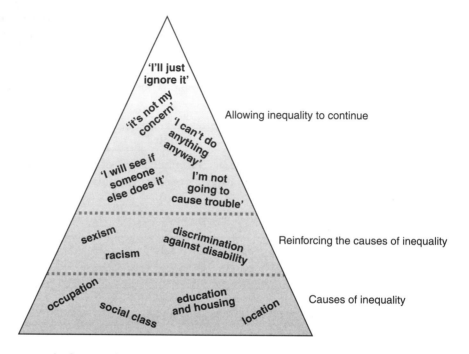

The pyramid of inequality

How to challenge the causes of inequality and discrimination

Challenging others on behalf of those who are discriminated against is often difficult and can mean confronting people about their attitudes and behaviour in a way which you may never have attempted before. The challenge is not only about individual behaviour, as you will have seen from the previous section. Inequality is caused by a great many other factors, many of which are easy to challenge on an individual basis.

However, challenging discriminatory attitudes and practices which reinforce the underlying inequalities is the responsibility of all of us who provide care and support. Although this is not easy, particularly where it involves colleagues or accepted ways of working, it is a challenge which you have a responsibility to undertake on behalf of those who are suffering from discrimination.

The following lists the types of discrimination you might encounter and ways of challenging these.

Type of discrimination	Ways to challenge
No provision for cultural or religious dietary requirements	Raise through management or in staff meetings
Inappropriate racist or sexist remarks or behaviour	Direct challenge to individual concerned. Seek support of colleagues and line manager. If necessary seek support through other channels such as supervisor or outside bodies. If behaviour results in somebody being physically at risk then the police should be contacted
Cruel or belittling and undermining behaviour or comments	Direct challenge to the individual, using the same support systems as above
Lack of knowledge amongst your work colleagues about cultural, religious or personal hygiene practices of those from ethnic minorities	Raise with your supervisor and through staff meetings and request that training is provided

Case study

G is a care worker in a residential setting for adults with disabilities. He is gay but had never discussed his sexual orientation at work or at the time of his appointment. His sexual orientation only became known when the parents of one of the residents spotted him in a picture of a gay pride event printed in a national newspaper. G had always been a popular member of staff and had an excellent work record, with appraisals which showed that his skills and abilities were developing and progressing. However, following the discovery that he was gay the atmosphere in the setting began to change. Two of the residents complained about being cared for by somebody who was gay and said they were not prepared to have G provide them with any personal care. Both these residents were young men in their late 20s. This action was supported by their parents, one of whom had spotted the photograph in the newspaper. Comments and gay jokes began to circulate within the setting, particularly when G was on duty. There would be snide comments about poofs and shirt lifters and warnings not to turn your back on him. The two residents concerned and their families had threatened to take the issue to the local press if G was not fired. The officer in charge felt that she had little choice but to ask G to leave. All the other residents, whilst they joined in with the jokes and comments about G, were happy to have their care provided by him and did not raise any objections. G felt that he was unfairly discriminated against and intended to obtain the support of his trade union.

1 What are G's rights in this situation?
2 What are his employer's rights?
3 What are the residents' rights?
4 Is the employer or the residents in contravention of any legislation?
5 How could G's trade union challenge what is happening to him?
6 What other sources of support may be available to G?

How to support those who are subjected to discrimination and oppression

In the same way as you support those who wish to make use of a complaints service and to challenge the quality and provision of services they receive, it is also important that you are able to support those who are the victims of discrimination. You have learned there are laws which provide a means of redress for those who have been discriminated against and it is essential that you ensure that you understand the broad provisions of these laws and the ways in which people may seek redress through them. This does not mean you offer legal advice, but you should be able to refer people to the right place to obtain that advice where this may be appropriate. If a client believes they have been the subject of discrimination then you should be able to advise them about the most appropriate sources of help. This could be a local advice centre, a legal aid centre or it could be a body such as the Commission for Racial Equality or the Equal Opportunities Commission. Whilst it is not your role to give detailed advice in these circumstances it is essential that you are able to give information and to support your client whilst they establish if they have any right of redress.

Not all discrimination and oppression is clear-cut, nor can all of it be acted upon through the law. Some may need to be challenged directly by the client and some may need to be referred to the police if it constitutes criminal activity. For example, an elderly person who is subject to threats and abuse from local gangs would need to be supported in making a complaint to the police.

The Sex Discrimination & Equal Pay Acts   Page 2

What are my rights?

Education

Co-educational schools, colleges and universities must not discriminate in the way they provide facilities or in the way they admit students. For example, all students should have equal access to the National Curriculum. The careers service must not discriminate between boys and girls in the way they provide advice and assistance. Single-sex schools may restrict admissions to boys or girls, but they must not restrict the types of subjects they teach as a result.

Housing, goods, facilities, and services

With a few exceptions, no one providing housing, goods, facilities or services to the public may discriminate against you because of your sex. For example, you must not be discriminated against when:

- applying for a mortgage or loan
- taking part in recreational activities
- buying or renting accommodation

Advertising

Advertisements must not show that the advertiser intends to discriminate unlawfully. The Equal Opportunities Commission can take legal action against advertisers who discriminate.

Victimisation

You are protected by the law in case you are victimised for trying to exercise your rights under the Sex Discrimination or Equal Pay Acts.

What should I do first?

To help you decide whether to start a case and to gather information on your claim to present your complaint in the best way you may send a Sex Discrimination Act questionnaire to the person you believe has discriminated against you. The questions and answers in this form can be used as evidence in a court or tribunal. The form, SD.74 is available from the EOC or from your trade union, professional association, local employment office, Jobcentre or unemployment benefit office.

Where do I take my complaint?

If you feel that you have been treated unfairly because of your sex, you can take your complaint to a county court, in England or Wales, or to sheriff court in Scotland. If your complaint is about employment or equal pay you go to an employment tribunal. If your complaint is about education in a state school, college or university you must first give the Secretary of State a chance to exercise the Secretary's powers under the Education Acts.

How soon must I take action?

You must present your complaint to a tribunal not later than three months (minus one day) after the act you are complaining about took place.

You may be able to take a complaint after this time if you can show a good reason that you could not make your complaint earlier.

Complaints about unequal pay can be presented to an employment tribunal at any time while in the job to which your claim relates and up to six months (minus one day) after leaving the job. If you are taking a case to a county or sheriff court you must begin your legal action not later than six months (minus one day) after the act you are complaining about took place.

Source: Equal Opportunities Commission

The Commission for Racial Equality and the Equal Opportunities Commission provide a wide range of leaflets and reports for those who are discriminated against

Active knowledge

Find out the names and addresses of your local organisations which can advise in the case of discrimination.

Recording information as part of anti-discriminatory practice

Much of the information in this unit has come from statistics collected by a wide range of organisations, many of which are government departments or organisations concerned with specific areas of our society such as Age Concern or CPAG (Child Poverty Action Group). Collection of data and statistics about the way in which our society is made up is an important way of being able to identify issues relating to equality and diversity and to establish where people are being discriminated against.

When you record information in your workplace it will be essentially used for two main purposes. The first and most important is to record information about the individual so that appropriate services can be provided. Second, and also important, you may be asked to record information which will be used to compile statistics which in turn will inform the government or your employer or a local or regional government, or any other interested agency, about the issues which affect your client group.

For example, you are likely to be asked to record the ethnic origin of any client with whom you deal. In this way it is possible for governments and other agencies to establish the way in which individuals from ethnic minorities use the health and care services and whether or not this is likely to meet identified needs. It is normal to record the age of any individual that you are working with. From this it is possible to establish information which, for example, shows that 15 per cent of all of the population and 24 per cent of those aged 75 and over have attended a casualty or out-patient department of a hospital, or that almost half a million households each week receive home help or home care services. It is important when people are thinking about their care as they get older that they are aware that statistically 1 per cent of the population between 65 and 74 are likely to live in a care home or long-stay hospital, and that 5 per cent of those aged between 75 and 84, and 22 per cent of those aged over 85 are likely to be receiving full-time residential care. The significance of this last set of figures shows that the need for services, even amongst those aged over 85, is overwhelmingly for domiciliary and support services in their own homes. Information is essential in helping us to understand the society we live in and in making sure that we plan properly to provide the right type and level of care.

The way in which information is recorded and the way in which it is obtained also plays an important part in anti-discriminatory practice and in ensuring that you are recognising and valuing the diversity of all individuals. It goes without saying that it is necessary to record information accurately and to ensure that you have taken as many steps as possible to obtain the correct information from your client, but you also need to ensure that the information which is *about the client* is accurate *from the client's point of view*. For example, many forms look like the one on page 26.

When you are completing this kind of form on behalf of a client it is important that you ask them what ethnic minority they see themselves as being from. It is not for you to make a decision on the basis of your own observations about the ethnic origins of any individual. There are many people who may appear to be white British

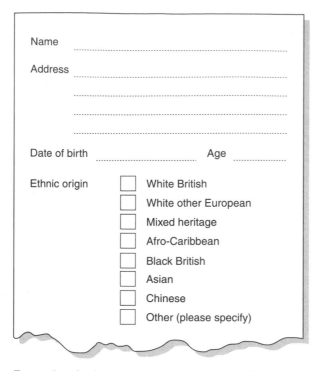

Name ....

Address ....

....

....

....

Date of birth .... Age ....

Ethnic origin

☐ White British

☐ White other European

☐ Mixed heritage

☐ Afro-Caribbean

☐ Black British

☐ Asian

☐ Chinese

☐ Other (please specify)

Example of a form which includes recording a person's ethnic identity

but who are in fact of mixed heritage and whose background, culture and experience is of Afro-Caribbean origin. They would rightly regard themselves as black, however an unknowing observer completing statistical information without asking may well conclude that they were white. Ethnic background is about much more than appearances, it involves culture, religion, values and the influences of the community in which an individual has grown up and developed. For example, there are many people living in the UK with Irish names but only a proportion of those would describe themselves as Irish if asked to give their racial background. The factors which are likely to influence the description will relate to family, culture and the value system of their family.

Many forms and recording requirements relate to the disability of an individual. It is essential to ask the individual concerned for their own view of their disability. It is for the individual to say whether they have a disability, or what the extent of their disability is. It is not for an observer to make those assumptions simply based on what they can see. Disability is often as much about attitude and response to disability as it is about the disability itself.

Now who is disabled?

Active knowledge

Collect together at least six different kinds of forms which are used by different agencies. You can include forms from your own workplace or from places such as the Benefits Agency, and application forms for a bank account or a mortgage or even a library ticket.

1 How many questions on each form would require you to make a judgement about somebody if you were filling it in on their behalf?
2 Think about different ways that the forms could be phrased to ensure that people's own views about themselves were included and not the images that others may have.

Element 02.3   People's right to the confidentiality of information

WHAT YOU NEED TO LEARN

- The legislation and guidelines which govern the keeping and retrieving of information.
- How to protect confidential information and the steps to take if you are concerned that confidential information is being misused.

Legislation and guidelines

In the fields of health and social care information is recorded and stored for a great many different purposes and by many different people. The information held can range from a patient's medical records, detailed personal information about relationships, information concerning child abuse or neglect to something quite simple, such as the means of transport used to take somebody to the luncheon club or day centre.

All people working in the fields of health and social care are expected to work within the bounds of confidentiality and to follow general ethical principles which ensure that people who receive care are able to have confidence that information about them will not be shared with those who do not have a legitimate reason to have the information.

There are extensive laws in the UK to protect information held about people and they have recently been considerably strengthened and extended. There is a generally established principle called the **common law duty of confidence** which states that in general **any personal information given or received in confidence for one purpose may not be used for a different purpose or passed to anyone else without the consent of the provider of the information**. Although this has been well established in law there are still arguments about how it applies in particular circumstances. However, recent developments in legislation and guidelines should clarify much of the uncertainty around using confidential information.

The Data Protection Act 1998

The major piece of legislation which covers confidential information is the **Data Protection Act 1998.** This has replaced the previous Data Protection Act 1984, the Access to Health Records Act 1990 and the Access to Personal Files Act 1987 (this was relevant to local authority health services departments). The new Act came into force on 1 March 2000. It sets rules for processing personal information and applies to some paper records as well as those held on computers. The Data Protection Act covers all data held in respect of any individual, including credit and financial information, membership of organisations, as well as medical, health and social services records. It is extremely relevant and will have significant implications for all those who work in health and care. The Act has eight principles which apply to data. The principles are:

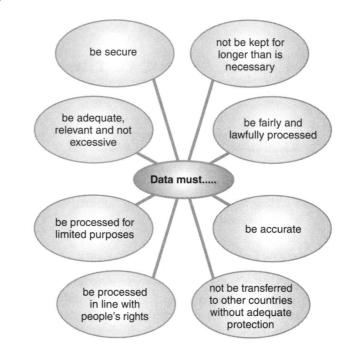

The principles of the Data Protection Act 1998

The data controllers in any organisation are required by law to work to these principles. Although the Act covers all data held by all types of organisations the implications for the National Health Service, for local authorities and for private care providers are clear. They must be able to satisfy the legal requirements in respect of keeping information.

The Data Protection Act will be further extended and is closely linked to the new Freedom of Information Bill which is currently going through the parliamentary process. When the Freedom of Information Bill becomes an Act of Parliament it will ensure that all information which is held by any public authority will, subject to certain exceptions, be available to the public. This will apply to individuals who request to see information held about themselves and there will be a provision for a 'third party access', though information will not be disclosed if that would breach the principles of data protection. It is likely that these two major pieces of legislation will make it far easier for individuals to access information contained in their own records, and the provisions should make it more difficult for information to be improperly used.

Information within the National Health Service is a huge issue. Broadly speaking the principles which apply within the National Health Service are appropriate for most other health and care settings. In 1997 the government published a report from a committee, chaired by Dame Fiona Caldecott, which had reviewed patient identifiable information within the National Health Service and which made a series of recommendations as to how this information should be handled. The recommendations of the Caldecott Committee were that each organisation should appoint an individual who would be responsible for maintaining and protecting patient information. This person has become known as a Caldecott Guardian. Every hospital and NHS organisation has to have a Caldecott Guardian. This person is normally a senior manager or a senior health professional within each organisation, however it is important that you are aware of who this person is and what their responsibilities are. The Caldecott Committee recommended a series of principles which apply to the handling of all patient identifiable information. These principles although developed for the National Health Service are sensible principles to apply in all work places.

The Caldecott Principles

Principle 1 – Justify the purpose
Every proposed use or transfer of patient identifiable information within or from an organisation should be clearly defined and scrutinised, with continuing uses regularly reviewed by an appropriate guardian.

Principle 2 – Don't use patient identifiable information unless it is absolutely necessary
Patient identifiable information items should not be used unless there is no alternative.

Principle 3 – Use the minimum necessary patient identifiable information
Where use of patient identifiable information is considered to be essential each individual item of information should be justified with the aim of reducing identifiability.

Principle 4 – Access to patient identifiable information should be on a strict need-to-know basis
Only those individuals who need access to patient identifiable information should have access to it and they should have access only to the information items that they need to see.

Principle 5 – Everyone should be aware of their responsibilities
Action should be taken to ensure that those handling patient identifiable information, both clinical and non-clinical staff, are aware of their responsibilities and obligations to respect patient confidentiality.

Principle 6 – Understand and comply with the Law
Every use of patient identifiable information must be lawful. Someone in each organisation should be responsible for ensuring that the organisation complies with legal requirements.

Active knowledge

Consider your own workplace and think about the ways in which data protection or freedom of information laws would apply in your own workplace. Note down all the different types of information which you keep about clients and the ways in which it is kept and then think about who has access to it.

Find out who your **Caldecott Guardian** is if you work for the National Health Service.

There are other Acts of Parliament which can affect the way in which information is used and the way in which information is shared between different organisations and agencies. For example, the Crime and Disorder Act 1998 introduces a number of measures to reduce crime and disorder, including the introduction of local crime partnerships which are based around local authority boundaries. Their role is to develop ways of reducing crime in the local area. This Act encourages exchange of information between local agencies, nonetheless it is essential that health and care agencies continue to observe the legal requirements concerning confidentiality of patient and client information. Other matters such as sexually transmitted diseases and infertility treatment are covered by specific pieces of legislation, even though the general rules on confidentiality still apply. The way in which information is used is the significant factor here. The Caldecott principles apply to patient identifiable information and similarly the Data Protection Act applies to information which can be identified as relating to a particular person.

For example, if you were to supply information which showed that Mrs Smith was receiving home help for three mornings a week because she was unable to manage

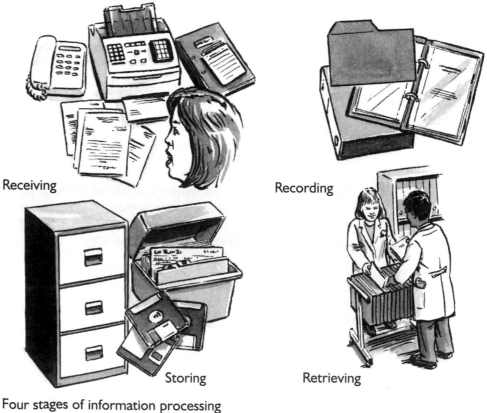

Receiving

Recording

Storing

Retrieving

Four stages of information processing

her shopping and housework and was making a financial contribution towards this because of the amount of money she had in the bank, then you would be quite rightly found to be in breach of the law. However, if you included the facts about Mrs Smith in a series of figures in a survey which showed that the home-help service in your local town was providing x number of hours per week service and y number of people were receiving that service because they were unable to cope with housework and shopping, and that z numbers of people were making a financial contribution because of their circumstances, then such information is quite legitimately allowed to be used. Mrs Smith is not identified as an individual in the survey and is simply there as one of the figures included in the report. It is also possible when compiling reports and giving information to use examples of individual circumstances provided those individuals cannot be identified. If you were providing examples as part of your survey it would be quite acceptable to say Mrs A received home-help service, and then to go on to explain Mrs Smith's circumstances provided that her identity was disguised.

How to protect confidential information

When any organisation aims to keep its information confidential one of its first considerations is to look at the ways in which information comes into the organisation. This could be from directly talking to patients or clients, it could be by letter, or fax, or telephone, or e-mail. The organisation then has to find ways to safeguard the confidentiality of the information at all the points at which it can enter the organisation. The next stage is to look at how that information is recorded, then to look at how it is stored, and the final stage is to look at how that information is retrieved from storage. At each of these stages it is possible for confidential information to be seen or heard or accessed by people who have no right or legitimate interest in knowing it.

Active knowledge

Make a list of the number of ways in which your workplace receives information on the patients or clients it cares for. You may be surprised to find out how many different ways there are to receive information. See if you can work out from your workplace procedures how information is protected at each stage.

You will have learned about the importance of not publicly discussing your clients or patients by name when the information could be overheard. You have also considered the importance of ensuring the safety and security of information which you record about individuals. But actively promoting confidentiality requires more than just being concerned about your own practice, it also requires that you are aware of the practices of your organisation and others who work inside it. You should be able to identify any potential weak points in the systems in your own workplace and raise these with your supervisor or manager.

There are several ways in which access to information can be restricted and controlled. There are physical barriers which can be placed to protect information. Medical records should always be kept in a locked room and the access to that should be limited to specific personnel. Most organisations will decide who should have access to particular information at any point in time. Access levels are very important and it should always be clear to everyone within the organisation who should have access and to what information.

Confidential information on computer can be protected by physical means

Information which is held electronically on computers is likely to require each user to have an identifier number user ID for their own use. This ensures that all activities on the computer system can be limited to the individual responsible and their access restricted by a password. Each level of access has to be carefully considered to ensure that all the procedures are within the law and within the guidelines. For example, it is not necessary for somebody who requires access to files in order to file them to have access to the contents of those files. A finance manager may need to know the numbers of people receiving a particular drug or requiring a particular type of dressing, but not necessarily any information

Another way of protecting confidential information is through a system of providing individual users with identifier numbers

about the individuals concerned. These types of access restrictions are probably easier to achieve with an electronic system than they are with paper files, thus allowing access at various levels through the user ID and password systems.

Safe havens

The idea of using **safe havens** has been adopted by many organisations as a useful way to control the flow of confidential information and to restrict the number of points within any organisation where information can be obtained. Safe haven procedures mean that each workplace or site within an organisation has one point which deals with information coming into and out of that part of the organisation. This means that confidential information is only disclosed or accepted through these designated safe haven contact points. The safe haven contact point will then ensure that when information is received, the access levels which are appropriate are applied so that only the relevant staff within the organisation can have access to the information. The idea behind this exchange through safe havens is that organisations can be confident that when information goes from their safe haven point to the safe haven point in another organisation the agreed protocols will govern the use of the information from that point on.

Ownership

Another system is to have 'ownership' of information or data. This means that each set of information, whether it is in a manual file or a set of electronically held information, is assigned an owner. The organisation has an up-to-date register of owners, who have responsibility for:

- identifying all the information or data which they hold
- identifying and explaining how the information can be used
- agreeing with the person responsible about who can access the information
- what type of access each user is permitted.

Every individual within a health and care workplace has a duty and a responsibility to ensure they are extremely careful not to disclose information which is confidential. They should also contribute to the organisation having procedures in place and adhering to those procedures which minimise the risk of confidential information falling into inappropriate hands.

Personal action to safeguard confidentiality

If you have doubts about the security of patient or client information within your workplace, then it is important that you raise these with your supervisor or line manager and explain the basis of your concern. It is not acceptable to allow any deliberate misuse of patient information to go unchallenged. It is also important that where the breach of confidentiality is not deliberate, but is through thoughtlessness or carelessness of a work colleague, that you point this out to them and make clear the steps they need to take in order to ensure that the breach of confidentiality is not repeated.

If you were to become aware of some very serious misuse of information you must report it immediately. For example, if you found out that a colleague was being paid to give information to a commercial company about elderly people who are becoming disabled and may be in the market to purchase items of equipment, this would be an extremely serious matter and an entirely inappropriate use of confidential information. On the other hand, if precisely the same information is being passed to the occupational therapy service in order that they can visit to assess the need to provide aids and adaptations for the individual concerned, and you are aware that the individual has given their permission for this information to be passed on, then this is an entirely right and proper use of confidential information. This is a clear example of the first of the Caldecott principles, which is about the purpose of confidential information. In the example above the identical information was being used for two entirely different purposes, one legitimate and one not. The difference is like giving information about vulnerable people living alone to the crime prevention officer in order that they are protected and giving the same information to a gang who intend to rob them. This may seem extreme, however it serves to show how important it is to consider the purpose of the information and to always be aware of the end for which that information will be used.

Whenever you have concerns you should always report them. If your concerns turn out to be unfounded, all you will suffer will be embarrassment. However, if your concerns are justified, then you will have prevented a serious misuse of confidential information. The Data Protection Act has put in place the Data Protection Commissioner as the person responsible for investigations into breaches of Data Protection Law throughout the country. The new Freedom of Information Bill will put in place a new officer, the Information Commissioner, who will oversee both the Freedom of Information Act and the Data Protection Act. In the meantime the Data Protection Commissioner is ultimately the person responsible for ensuring that individual records are adequately maintained and for investigating and taking action in any cases where the law has not been complied with. If you work for the National Health Service the Caldecott Guardian is the responsible person within your organisation, but they too are ultimately answerable to the Data Protection Commissioner for any breaches in the law found within their own particular organisation.

Unit test

1 How are human rights protected in the UK?

2 To what extent are health and care service providers required to observe human rights?

3 What are the main changes that the Human Rights Act is likely to bring about in health and social care workplaces?

4 What are the different ways of identifying social groupings in the UK?

5 List at least four different effects of social deprivation.

6 Identify three ways to challenge discrimination.

7 What is the major piece of legislation which protects confidentiality of information?

8 What are the main areas that all organisations need to consider when looking at how to protect information?

9 Give one acceptable and one unacceptable example of the use of confidential information.

Promote effective communication and relationships

In this unit you will look at how to deal with people in a way which takes account of their individuality. When time is short and demands are high, it is often easier to treat everyone in a group in the same way, to make plans for a whole group of people or to assume that what is good for one person will be good for all. You will learn how to avoid this.

Relationships are a part of communication and communication is a part of relationships. The two are linked so closely, that it is difficult to deal with one without the other. Working in a care setting means that you work with other human beings. Being able to make relationships and to communicate with them is a very basic requirement for doing your job. Each person you care for is an individual – completely different and unique. This may sound obvious but it is so important that it is worth repeating.

You will learn how to avoid making judgments about people which are based not on knowledge and understanding of that person, but on generally accepted stereotypes, often with little truth behind them.

The work you have chosen will involve you in relationships with other people all the time. Working in caring is different from other jobs. It is not only about having good working relationships with colleagues, although good teamwork is essential, it is also about the relationships you will make with the individuals you are caring for, and it is about understanding other relationships they have, with their friends and relatives.

Element CL1.1 — Develop relationships with people which value them as individuals

WHAT YOU NEED TO LEARN

- How to treat people as individuals.
- Knowing yourself and your prejudices.
- Behaviour which fails to value people.
- How to challenge unacceptable behaviour.

How to treat people as individuals

One in a million

One of the most effective ways you have of helping people is by recognising them as individuals. Learn never to make assumptions about people in groups.

Think about the number of ways in which people can be identified – they can be described by age, gender, eye colour, place of residence, job, and so on. This will remind you of the number of different aspects there are to any one individual.

The problem with 'labelling' people into particular groups for particular purposes is that it is very rarely accurate. It may be very convenient when planning care to decide that 'all individuals will want…' or 'this age group will benefit from…', but the number of individuals contained within any group means that any planning that starts with a generalisation is doomed to be unsatisfactory.

Active knowledge

Think of a way to describe yourself, starting with the most general – 'I am a woman' or 'I am a man'. So are many other people, so that does not describe you. 'I have brown hair' – so do a great many others. Continue thinking of ways to describe yourself, getting closer all the time to finding a description which is unique to you (i.e. which describes you, and no one else). Each time you think of another way to describe yourself, it will eliminate more and more people from the group, until finally you *may* (depending on how well you know yourself) come up with a description which applies to no one else but you.

Each time you are tempted to treat people as one of a group, remember how long this task took and how many descriptions you listed before you found a unique reference to you. Remember that everyone you deal with is unique – an *individual*.

You will say 'I'm not prejudiced'. Most people do, but the reality is that everyone has prejudices. They come from all kinds of previous experiences. You may be afraid of dogs because you were once bitten. Not every dog you meet is going to bite you, but that will not stop you judging all dogs from one experience. The way you have been brought up and the attitudes you grew up with will shape the kind of person you turn out to be.

What are stereotypes?

Prejudice is what makes people think in stereotypes and, equally, stereotypes support prejudice. Stereotypes are an easy way of thinking about the world. Stereotypes would suggest that all people over 65 are frail and walk with a stick, that all black young people who live in inner cities are on drugs, that all fat people are lazy, or that all families have a mother, father and two children. These stereotypes, or ways of looking at the world, are often reinforced by the media or by advertising. Television programmes will often portray violent, criminal characters as young and black.

Active knowledge

Next time you watch television, note down the number of adverts for household items that show a young, slim, white woman with one or two children, living in a nice house with a garden. This is referred to in the advertising world as the 'tart in the kitchen' scenario. The effect is to convince people that if they buy the product then they, too, will be young, slim, attractive and happy.

How many people do you know who are anything like the characters in the adverts?

How many do you know who wish they were?

What effect do stereotypes have?

The effect of stereotypes is to make us jump to conclusions about people. How many times have you felt uneasy seeing a young man with a shaved head walking towards you? You know nothing about him, but the way he looks has made you form an opinion about him. If you have a picture in your mind of a social worker or a policeman, think about how much that is influenced by the media – do they really all look like that?

1 What do you think each of these people does for a living?
2 What kind of place does each of them live in?
3 Why have you given the answers you have?

Accents can often evoke prejudice. Try to be aware of what regional accents mean – think about these stereotypes:

People from...	are known as...	are thought to be...
Liverpool	Scousers	work-shy, scroungers, funny
Birmingham	Brummies	slow, not very bright, boring
London	Cockneys	wheeler dealers, not trustworthy, clever
Glasgow	Glaswegians	aggressive, looking for a fight, drinkers
Newcastle	Geordies	warm, friendly, tough, 'salt of the earth'

The next time you find yourself making a judgement about somebody's character based on an accent, stop and think. Try to avoid a stereotype.

'Have you heard the one about...?'

Telling jokes at the expense of particular groups of people is similarly displaying prejudices. Stereotypes about people being mean or stupid because of their nationality fail to treat people as individuals and fail to recognise that there are individuals everywhere and that all people are different.

Active knowledge

Stop yourself every time you make a generalisation and look at the prejudice. Think about why you think the way you do, and do something about it. The next time you hear yourself saying 'Social workers never understand what is really needed', 'GPs always take ages to visit' or 'Our residents wouldn't be interested in that', stop and think what you are really doing.

It is probably quite correct that *some* social workers won't understand, maybe even all those you have met so far! But that does not necessarily apply to them all.

Perhaps most of your residents would not be interested in whatever was being suggested – a trip to the art gallery? a bike ride? or a naughty underwear party? – you cannot make that assumption. You need to ask.

Treating people as individuals

You should always consult the individual before you carry out any procedure, and explain everything you do. Even if the procedure is part of his or her plan of care and has been done many times before, you should never take a person's agreement for granted.

Everyone should be offered choices wherever possible. This may be about when, where or how their care is provided. In circumstances where a choice is not possible, either because of an individual's circumstances or a lack of resources, this should be explained.

These are examples of the kinds of choice you may be able to offer to people when you provide care:

Care service	Choices
Personal hygiene	Bath, shower or bed bath Assistance or no assistance Morning, afternoon or evening Temperature of water Toiletries
Food	Menu Dining table or tray Timing Assistance In company or alone

Clearly, the range of choices will vary depending on the circumstances, but the principal remains the same – that people should not have care imposed on them without them being able to be actively involved in the decisions about how and when care is delivered.

Did you know?

One of the fears most frequently expressed by people who need to be cared for, particularly older people whose health has deteriorated or people who have been disabled through an accident or illness, is that they will lose their independence and will no longer be regarded as a person of any value.

Part of valuing people as individuals is having respect for all of the people you deal with. Respect is usually something which develops as you form relationships. When you provide care for someone, you will get to know and talk to him or her, and a relationship will grow. This is not easy with all individuals you care for. When there appears to be no two-way communication, you may find that forming a relationship is difficult. If you work with people who do not appear to relate to you, perhaps because they are very confused, because they have a very low level of functioning or even because they are not conscious, then it is easy to forget that they are still individuals and need to be treated as such.

Keys to good practice

- Make sure that any service which you provide for someone is with their agreement. People have a right to choose the care which they receive and the way in which they receive it.
- You must make sure that each person you care for is treated in the same way, regardless of his or her ability to respond to you. This means talking to people who do not seem to understand you, and to people who may appear not to respond. You should explain everything you are doing and go through the details of any procedures you are carrying out.

Remember

• Everyone has the right to make choices about care.
• All people are different.

If you accept these points, you will never be guilty of making generalisations or making prejudiced judgements about people again.

If only it were that simple! Of course, you cannot suddenly stop doing and thinking things which you have been doing and thinking all your life, but you *can* develop an awareness of what you are doing and start to ask yourself questions about why you have acted in the way you have.

Once you realise how your own background and beliefs alter the way you think about people, you can begin to recognise the differences and see the value of other cultures and beliefs. It is inevitable that, by thinking carefully about what has influenced you, you will also consider what has influenced others with whom you come into contact.

You need to talk to people, whether they are colleagues or service users, about aspects of their culture or lifestyle you do not understand. As a care professional, it is your responsibility to make sure that you have considered the culture, beliefs and lifestyle of someone for whom you are providing care. It is not acceptable to expect that they will adapt to your set of cultural beliefs and expectations.

The diversity of the human race is what makes living in our society such a rich and varied experience. If you try to welcome this diversity, rather than resist, condemn or belittle the things you do not understand, you will find that your relationships with colleagues and service users will be much more rewarding and the quality of your care practice will be greatly improved.

Case study

H is from Somalia and is a devout Muslim. She had her first baby in hospital in the UK.

Following the delivery, H refused to get out of bed, and would press the buzzer every time she wanted anything, including asking staff to take her baby from the cot and give him to her to feed. This was in accordance with her own culture in which a new mother remains in bed for ten days after giving birth. During that time everything is done for her and her baby, and all she does is feed the baby. It is usually her mother-in-law or another female relative who takes control during this time.

The ward staff became resentful of the demands that H was making. They were not always as pleasant as they might be when they were called into her room. H became very distressed and was very agitated and nervous each time she needed assistance. She began to have problems feeding the baby and the staff were concerned about her. There was a great deal of concern about her refusal to get out of bed, and she was encouraged to do so. The midwives explained to her that she ran the risk of thrombosis or other circulatory problems if she continued to lie in bed.

A solution was eventually found by allowing her mother-in-law to remain with her in a side room to provide the care needed. But they still could not persuade her to

get out of bed. As she had been provided with all the information about possible consequences, and she had made an informed choice consistent with her own beliefs, her decision to stay in bed had to be respected.

1 What were the problems presented by H's beliefs?
2 Why is this situation difficult to deal with?
3 Do you think it was handled correctly?
4 What would you have done?
5 What do you think would have happened if the situation had continued as it was?

Remember

- Stereotypes can influence how you think about someone.
- Don't rush to make judgements about people.
- Don't make assumptions.
- Everyone is entitled to his or her own beliefs and culture. If you don't know about somebody's way of life – ask.

Knowing yourself and your prejudices

'To see ourselves as others see us'

It is vital, if you are to help anyone effectively, that you understand how you affect any situation. Human beings do not react in the same way to everyone. You have all experienced meeting someone who makes you feel relaxed and at ease – you find it easy to talk to them and feel as if you had known them for a long time. Equally, there are other people you meet and find it much harder to talk to – they make you feel nervous, or unsure; you can't think of anything to say and feel generally uncomfortable. You are still the same person, but you have reacted in a totally different way to two different people. This is called **interaction** and describes what takes place between human beings. To be a good practitioner in caring, you have to learn to understand how people react to you and the way in which your own beliefs, background and prejudices will influence and alter the outcome of an interaction.

It is essential that you understand about interaction if you are working in caring. It is not always easy to understand how it works. It may help if you think about it as a fairground mirror – all of the reflections look different, some are short and fat, some long and thin, some are wavy and curved; it all depends on the mirror. You are still the same, but the mirror makes everything appear different. It is the same with people. The same person will behave in a different way – interact – depending on the person they are talking to.

Active knowledge

Try this out for yourself at work. Pick two different people and tell them both the same thing. For example, you could ask to leave early on the next shift, explain why a particular person needs a change in their plan of care, or explain where the new delivery of equipment is – in fact, anything at all. Note down how you carried out the task with each person and how you felt. Make sure you note the differences in your behaviour and feelings. Try to work out how, and why, each of them made you feel different.

Working in caring makes huge demands on people. The most important attribute you bring to the job is your own personality. This is why it is so important that you know yourself, and know what you bring to the job. You will have to learn to recognise your own prejudices and what effect they will have in the workplace.

Learning about yourself is not an easy task. Everyone thinks they know themselves so well – or do they? Often you never take the time to examine your own behaviour in depth. It is often a shock when someone else points out something you are doing, or a way you have of behaving, which you had not realised before.

Keys to good practice

- If you intend to be effective as a carer, then you will need to spend some time looking at your own behaviour and try to look in the mirror of others' reactions. You will never really know how you look in a physical way to others because you can only ever see a mirror image of yourself. If you think about looking at the world through a mirror, you will realise that it always looks slightly different to how you see it first-hand. However, you can judge how your actions and behaviour affect others by using them as your 'mirror' and being sensitive to their reactions.

Mirror, mirror on the wall...

- If you are talking to someone and he or she suddenly seems to close down the conversation, or appear unsure, try to think back to the point at which the atmosphere changed. Be honest with yourself. Did you react to something he or she said? What did you say? Was it a little thoughtless? Did you laugh? Maybe he or she thought you were laughing at him/her? Or did he or she begin to back away when you looked at your watch, or spoke briefly to someone else who wanted your attention?
- Do some individuals seem to find it easier to talk to you than others? Do you find it easier to talk to some individuals than others? Of course, there are bound to be some people you like more than others, but when you are working as a professional carer it is not enough just to acknowledge that. You have to know 'why' in order to make sure that it does not result in individuals being treated differently.
- Only you can work at examining your own behaviour. If you have a manager or colleague to work with you, that is a great help, but essentially, no one can do it for you. You will need to be able to ask yourself a series of questions, and be prepared to answer them: Which people do you find it hard to deal with? Can you work better with women than men? Do you find it hard to talk to young people? or to older people? or to people of a particular social class? or to people of particular races? or to anyone with a different accent?
- Do you find that you have less patience with some people? Can you identify which people? Is there a pattern? You may not always like the answers you come up with, but until you can work out how you behave towards others and why, you will never be able to make any adjustments to your responses.

- You will need to look at your own culture and beliefs. You may have grown up surrounded by people who believed that it was unthinkable to owe a penny to anyone, so you may find it difficult to offer empathy and support to someone who is desperate because he or she is in massive debt. If you have lived in a culture which holds older family members in high regard and accords them respect, you may find it hard to relate to the family of someone who hardly ever visits and does not appear interested in his or her welfare. Nevertheless, in your role as a carer you have to be aware of how your own background may influence you and to ensure that you include that factor in the analysis of any situation.

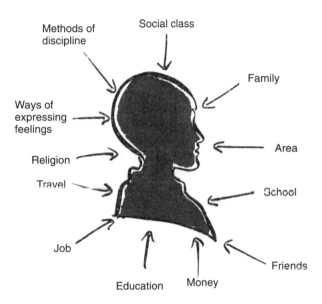

Influences on who you are

- Don't be too hard on yourself. Acknowledging your own prejudices is to go more than halfway to overcoming them. Just being able to understand *why* you behave in the way you do is more than most people achieve in a lifetime! So don't worry if it takes a while before you feel that you are really thinking about what you do and how you affect others. It may seem unlikely, but knowing how people respond to you and making allowances for that will, eventually, become second nature.

Behaviour which fails to value people

Practising a policy of equal opportunities in the workplace is one part of recognising and welcoming diversity. There are several pieces of legislation which address equal opportunities for various groups, and they are covered in depth in Unit O1 (in *NVQ Level 2 Care*), but whether or not any of those principles are put into practice is influenced by how much people are valued as individuals in any care setting.

There is little point in having legislation unless it is generally observed, and any breaches of the law are dealt with. Legislation gives rights to certain groups of people which should ensure that they are not discriminated against, but individual workers have to be prepared to defend and uphold those rights for themselves and others.

However, valuing people and welcoming the fact that everyone is diverse is about more than just upholding the law, although that is very important. Workers must be prepared to recognise when someone is subjected to behaviour which infringes their rights.

Generally you can define behaviour as unacceptable if:

- it is outside what you would normally see in that situation
- it does not take into account the needs or views of others
- people are afraid or intimidated
- people are undermined or made to feel guilty
- the behaviour is likely to cause distress or unhappiness to others.

Examples of unacceptable behaviour include:

- threatening violence
- subjecting someone to unwelcome sexual harassment
- playing loud music in a quiet area, or late at night
- verbal abuse, racist or sexist taunts
- spreading malicious gossip about someone
- attempting to isolate someone.

All of these types of behaviour are oppressive to others and need to be challenged. You can probably think of many other situations in your own workplace which have caused unhappiness. You may have had to deal with difficult situations, or have seen others deal with them, or perhaps you have wished that you had done something to challenge oppressive behaviour.

You may come across unacceptable and oppressive behaviour in your colleagues or other professionals in your workplace. Behaviour which is actually abusive is dealt with in Unit Z1. While you may see or hear a colleague behaving in a way which is not abusive as such, it may be oppressive and unacceptable. This can take various forms such as:

- speaking about clients in a derogatory way
- speaking to clients in a rude or dismissive way
- humiliating clients
- undermining people's self-esteem and confidence
- bullying or intimidation
- patronising and talking down to people
- removing people's right to exercise choice
- failing to recognise and treat people as individuals
- not respecting people's culture, values and beliefs.

In short, the types of behaviour which are unacceptable from workers in care settings are those which simply fail to meet the standards required of good quality practitioners. Any care worker who fails to remember that all people they care for are individuals and that all people have a right to be valued and accepted, is likely to fall into behaving in an oppressive or inappropriate way.

Active knowledge

Ask three colleagues in your workplace to state one behaviour that they would find unacceptable in (a) a service user and (b) a colleague. Compare the six answers and see if they have anything in common. Find out from your supervisor about the type of behaviour that is challenged in your workplace, and that which is allowed.

How to challenge unacceptable behaviour

Steps to dealing with difficult situations

Step 1 Consider all the people involved in the situation

If you have some knowledge of an individual's background, culture and beliefs, it may be easier to see why he or she is behaving in a particular way. This does not make it acceptable, just easier to understand. For example, men in some cultures, such as in Arab countries, are far more likely to touch other men (hugging and kissing as a sign of friendship), than men from the UK, where such physical contact (except between footballers!) is not generally acceptable. An individual who has been in a position of wealth or power may be used to giving people instructions and expecting to have immediate attention, and may be quite rude if it does not happen. This type of attitude is obviously not going to be tolerated, but approaching the situation with some understanding allows people to maintain their dignity whilst adapting their behaviour.

Step 2 Be aware of everyone's needs

If you are in a work situation, it can be complicated by the fact that the person whose oppressive behaviour you are challenging may also be one of your service users. In this case, it is important to ensure that you challenge the behaviour without becoming aggressive or intimidating yourself, and that you do not undermine the individual.

Step 3 Decide on the best approach

How you decide to deal with an incident of unacceptable behaviour will depend on:

- whether the behaviour is violent or non-violent – if the behaviour is violent, what the potential dangers of the situation are, who may be in danger and what needs to be done to help those in danger
- who is involved, how well you know them and know how to deal with them
- whether you need help, and who is available to help you
- whether the cause is obvious and the solution is easy to deal with.

Clearly, you will need to weigh up the situation quickly, in order to deal with it promptly. You will, no doubt, feel under pressure, as this is a stressful situation to be in, whether you are experienced or not. Try to remain calm and think clearly.

Step 4 Deal with non-violent behaviour

If the behaviour you have to deal with is not physical aggression or violence, then you will need to deal with it by ensuring that you make the challenge in a situation which provides privacy and dignity. You should challenge without becoming aggressive, remain calm and quietly state what you consider to be unacceptable about their behaviour. Do not try to approach it from various angles, or drop hints. Be clear about the problem and what you want to happen.

For example, 'Bill, you have been playing your radio very loudly until quite late each night. Other residents are finding it difficult to get to sleep. I would like you to stop playing it so loudly if you want to have it on late.' You may well have to negotiate with Bill about times, and the provision of headphones, but do not be drawn into an argument and do not be sidetracked into irrelevant discussions. For example:

> Bill: 'Who's been complaining? No one's complained to me. Who is it?'
>
> You: 'Bill, this is about your radio being too loud. The issue is not about who complained, but about the fact that it is upsetting residents and I want you to stop doing it.'

By the end of this discussion, Bill should be very clear about what is being required of him and be in no doubt that his behaviour will have to change.

Step 5 Attempt to calm a potentially violent situation

It is always better to avoid a violent situation than to respond to one, so you need to be aware of the signals which may indicate that violence could erupt. Be on the lookout for verbal aggression; raised volume and pitch of voice; threatening and aggressive gestures; pacing; quick, darting eye movements; prolonged eye contact.

Try to respond in ways least likely to provoke further aggression:

- Use listening skills, and appear confident (but not cocky).
- Keep your voice calm and at a level pitch.
- Do not argue.
- Do not get drawn into prolonged eye contact.
- Attempt to defuse the situation with empathy and understanding. For example, 'I realise you must be upset if you believe that George said that about you. I can see that you're very angry. Tell me about what happened.'

Be prepared to try a different approach if you find you are not getting anywhere. Always make sure that an aggressor has a way out with dignity, both physically and emotionally.

Did you know?

There is a technique which is recommended for use in situations which become violent. It is called 'Breakaway' and is approved by the Home Office for use in all types of care settings. It provides you with methods for dealing with a physical threat or attack without causing injury. Ask your employer to arrange for you to attend a course with an approved trainer.

Step 6 Deal with aggressive or violent behaviour

Be aware of the situation you are in and take some common-sense precautions: make sure that you know where the exits are, move so that the aggressor is not between you and the exit; notice if there is anything which could be used as a weapon, and try to move away from it; make sure that the aggressor has enough personal space, and do not crowd him or her.

If you are faced with a violent situation, you should try to remain calm (even though that is easier said than done!) and not resort to violence or aggression yourself.

It is often the case that a simple technique like holding up a hand in front of you, as if you were directing traffic, and shouting 'Stop' may deflect an attacker, or stop him or her long enough for you to get away. You should remove yourself from the situation as speedily as possible.

If there are other, vulnerable people at risk, you must decide whether you can summon help more effectively from outside or inside the situation.

If you decide to remain, you must summon help at once. You should do one of the following:

- Press a panic alarm or buzzer, if one is provided.
- Shout 'help!' very loudly and continuously.
- Send someone for help.
- Call the police, or security, or shout for someone else to do so.

Do not try to be a hero – that is not your job.

Active knowledge

Your workplace should have a policy on dealing with aggression and violence. Ask to see it and make sure that you read it carefully.

Remember

- Everyone is different and will react differently to each situation.
- You are the factor that makes the difference.
- Learn to know yourself before you think you can know about others.
- Each person should be valued as a unique individual.

Element CL1.2 | Establish and maintain effective communication with people

WHAT YOU NEED TO LEARN

- Ways in which people communicate.
- Barriers to communication.
- How to listen.
- How to communicate clearly.

Ways in which people communicate

This element is about how people reach out to each other. Communication is much more than talking. It is about how people respond to each other in many different ways: touch, facial expression, body movements, dress, position – and this is before you start on written communication, telephone, cyberspace, message in a bottle or pigeon!

Remember

You are the most important tool you have for doing your job. Carers do not have carefully engineered machinery or complex technology – your own ability to relate to others and to understand them is the key you need!

More than talking

Any relationship comes about through communication. In order to be an effective care worker, you must learn to be a good communicator. But communication is about much more than talking to people!

People communicate through:

* speaking
* facial expression
* body language
* position
* dress
* gestures.

You will have to know how to recognise what is being communicated to you, and to be able to communicate with others without always having to use words.

Active knowledge

Do this with a friend or colleague.

1 Write the names of several emotions (such as anger, joy, sadness, disappointment, fear) on pieces of paper.
2 One of you should pick up a piece of paper. Your task is to communicate the emotion written on the paper to your partner, without saying anything.
3 Your partner then has to decide what the emotion is and say *why*.
4 Then change places and repeat the exercise. Take it in turns, until all the pieces of paper have been used. Make sure that you list all the things which made you aware of the emotion being expressed.
5 Discuss with your partner what you have discovered about communication as a result of this exercise.

Key to good practice

When you carried out the last exercise, you will have found out that there are many things which told you what your partner was trying to communicate. It is not only the expression on people's faces which tells you about how they feel, but it is also the way they use the rest of their bodies. This area of human behaviour is referred to as **non-verbal communation**. It is very important for developing the ability to understand what people are feeling. If you understand the importance of non-verbal communication, you will be able to use it to improve your own skills when you communicate with someone.

Recognising the signals

Look at a person's facial expression. Much of what you will see will be in his or her eyes, but the eyebrows and mouth also contribute.

Notice whether someone is looking at you, or at the floor, or at a point over your shoulder. Lack of eye contact should give a first indication that all may not be well. It may be that they are not feeling confident. They may be unhappy, or feel uneasy about talking to you. You will need to follow this up.

Look at how a person sits. Is he or she relaxed and comfortable, sitting well back in the chair, or tense and perched on the edge of the seat? Is he or she slumped in the chair with the head down? Posture can indicate a great deal about how somebody is feeling. People who are feeling well and cheerful tend to hold their heads up, and sit in a relaxed and comfortable way. An individual who is tense and nervous, who feels unsure and worried is likely to reflect that in the way he or she sits or stands.

Observe hands and gestures carefully. Someone twisting his or her hands, or playing with hair or clothes is a signal of tension and worry. Frequent little shrugs of the shoulders or spreading of the hands may indicate a feeling of helplessness or hopelessness.

Case study

Mr J has just been admitted to a residential care home. He has severe arthritis and his mobility is very poor. He has some incontinence of urine. The arthritis in his hands, elbows and shoulders means that he is not able to carry out basic domestic tasks, but he can wash and dress, although he is slow and sometimes cannot manage the buttons. He had been cared for at home by his wife until last week, when she suffered a massive stroke and died. Mr J has one son who lives 200 miles away. His son came at once when his mother died, and has stayed all week with his father. However, he now has to return to work and has arranged for his father to be admitted into residential care as a matter of urgency.

1 What would you expect Mr J's facial expression to be?
2 Allowing for his physical difficulties, how do you think he would be sitting?
3 What do you think he would be doing with his hands?
4 What emotions and feelings is Mr J likely to be expressing through his body language?

Did you know?

Research shows that people pay far more attention to facial expressions and tone of voice than they do to spoken words. For example, in one study, words contributed only 7 per cent towards the impression of whether or not someone was liked, tone of voice contributed 38 per cent and facial expression 55 per cent. The study also found that if there was a contradiction between facial expression and words, people believed the facial expression.

Giving out the signals

Being aware of your own body language is just as important as understanding the person you are talking to.

Keys to good practice

- Make sure that you maintain eye contact with the person you are talking to, although you should avoid staring at them! Looking away occasionally is normal, but if you find yourself looking around the room, or watching others, then you are failing to give people the attention they deserve.
- Be aware of what you are doing and try to think why you are losing attention.
- Sit where you can be comfortably seen. Don't sit where someone has to turn in order to look at you.
- Sit a comfortable distance away – not so far that any sense of closeness is lost, but not so close that you 'invade their space'.
- Make sure that you are showing by your gestures that you are listening and interested in what they are saying – sitting half-turned away gives the message that you are not fully committed to what is being said.
- Folded arms or crossed legs can indicate that you are 'closed' rather than 'open' to what someone is expressing.
- Nodding your head will indicate that you are receptive and interested – but be careful not to overdo it and look like a nodding dog!

- Lean towards someone to show that you are interested in what they are saying. You can use leaning forward quite effectively at times when you want to emphasise your interest or support. Then move backwards a little at times when the content is a little lighter.
- Using touch to communicate your caring and concern is often useful and appropriate. Many individuals find it comforting to have their hand held or stroked, or to have an arm around their shoulders.
- Be aware of a person's body language which should tell you if they find touch acceptable or not.
- Always err on the side of caution if you are unsure about what is acceptable in another culture. Later in this chapter, and in many other places throughout the book, you will look at issues about cultures in which touch is unacceptable.
- Think about age and gender in relation to touch. An older woman may be happy to have her hand held by a female carer, but may be uncomfortable with such a response from a man.
- Ensure that you are touching someone because you think it will comfort him or her, and not because you feel helpless and can't think of anything to say.

Active knowledge

Do this with at least one other person – two or three is even better.

1. Think of an incident or situation which is quite important and significant to you. Stand still in the middle of a room and begin to tell your partner about your significant incident.
2. Your partner should start at the edge of the room and slowly move closer and closer to you.
3. At the point where you feel comfortable talking to your partner, say 'Stop'. Mark this point and measure the distance from where you are standing.
4. At the point where you feel that your partner is too close, say 'Stop'. Mark this point and measure the distance from where you are standing.
5. Change places and repeat the exercise.

You may find that you and your partner(s) will have different distances at which you feel comfortable, but it is likely to be in the range of 3–5ft.

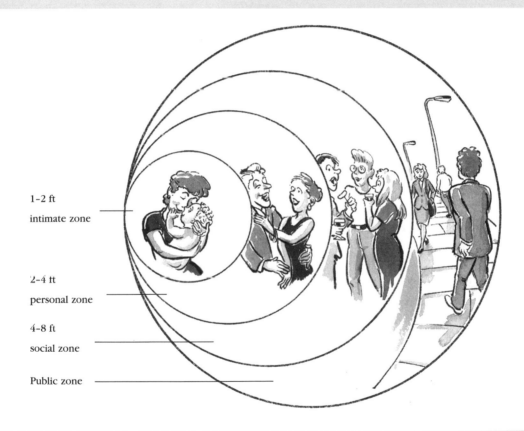

1–2 ft
intimate zone

2–4 ft
personal zone

4–8 ft
social zone

Public zone

Remember

- You can often learn as much by observing as by listening.
- Learn to 'listen with your eyes'.
- *Your* body sends out as many messages as the person you are talking to.
- Be aware of the messages you give to others.

Barriers to communication

Not getting through?

There are many factors which can get in the way of good communication. You will need to understand how to recognise these and to learn what you can do to overcome them. Until you do this, your communication will always be less effective than it could be. It is easy to assume that everyone can communicate, and that any failure to respond to you is because of someone's unwillingness rather than inability. There are as many reasons why people find communication difficult as there are ways to make it easier.

Remember

You need to understand the things which can get in the way so you can make sure they don't!

Active knowledge

Choose two different ways in which you communicate with people, for example talking, writing, telephone – you can probably think of others. Consider the most important element in each one. For example, for talking it could be language, for telephone, hearing, and so on. Now think about how you would manage that communication without that important element. List the problems you would have and the ways you could try to overcome them. Do you begin to see how difficult it can be sometimes for people to communicate?

Checklist
Practical difficulties ✓
Cultural difficulties ✓
What words mean ✗
Physical barriers ✓

Thinking about the obstacles

Never assume that you can be heard and understood and that you can be responded to, without first thinking about the individual and his or her situation. Check first to ensure you are giving the communication the best possible chance of success by dealing with as many barriers as possible.

Practical difficulties

If you need to communicate with someone who has a known disability, such as hearing loss, impaired vision, mobility problems

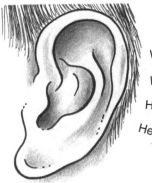

Level of hearing?

Is a signer needed?

Hearing aid needs cleaning?

Hearing aid working properly?

or speech impairment, you must consider the implications for your communication.

If someone is profoundly deaf, you will need to establish what sort of assistance he or she needs. If he or she communicates by signing, you will need to have a sign language interpreter available. Do not assume that you can do this yourself – it is highly skilled and people train for a long time to do this. If someone uses a hearing aid, consider that it may not be operating efficiently if you seem to be having communication problems.

Consider the level of someone's hearing. Many people are hard of hearing, but this may not be a profound hearing loss. It can mean that they have difficulty hearing where there is background noise and other people talking.

If someone has a physical disability, you will need to consider whether this is likely to affect his or her non-verbal communication. Also, his or her body language may not be what you would expect.

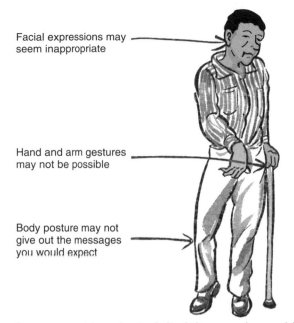

Facial expressions may seem inappropriate

Hand and arm gestures may not be possible

Body posture may not give out the messages you would expect

Someone with a physical disability may be unable to communicate in the expected non-verbal way

Case study

Mr T lives alone. For many years he had been well known in the neighbourhood. He was never particularly chatty, but always said a polite 'Good Morning' on his way to the shops, and had a smile and a kind word for the children. His wife died about fifteen years ago. They had only had one son, and he was killed in the war. Recently, however, Mr T's health has begun to deteriorate. He has had a bad winter with a chest infection and a nasty fall in the snow. This has seemed to shake his confidence, and he has accepted the offer of a home care assistant twice a week.

Neighbours began to notice that Mr T no longer spoke to them, and he failed to acknowledge the children. His outings to the shops became less frequent. Jean, his home care assistant, was worried that he hardly responded to her cheerful chat as she worked. She realised that Mr T's hearing was deteriorating. After medical investigations, Mr T was provided with a hearing aid. He began to be much more like his old self – he spoke to people again, smiled at the children and enjoyed his visits to the shops.

1 How do you think Mr T felt when he began to have problems hearing people?
2 Why do you think he reacted in the way he did?
3 What other factors might Jean have thought were causing Mr T's deterioration?
4 How are people likely to have reacted to Mr T?

Individuals who have visual impairment to any significant degree will need to be addressed with thought and care. Do not rely on your facial expressions to communicate your interest and concern – use words and touch where appropriate. Remember to obtain any information they may need in a format they can use. Think about large print books, braille or audio tapes. If you need any further information, the Royal National Institute for the Blind (RNIB) will be able to advise you about local sources of supplies.

The way you address people who have an impairment needs to be done with thought and care

Make sure that you know what language an individual is comfortable with – do not assume it is the same as yours without making certain! Find out if you need to provide any translation facilities, or written information in another language. If translation is needed, your team leader or manager should be able to help you to arrange it. Your local social services department will have a list of interpreters, as will the police or the consulate or embassy of their country. Many organisations provide information about where specialised assistance can be obtained.

Did you know?

The Benefits Agency produces a catalogue of its leaflets, posters and information. This lists which items are available in other languages, braille, large print or on audio tape. Many other agencies and organisations do the same. Always make sure you ask if information is available in the format your client needs. Being given information in an accessible format is far better than having to receive it 'second-hand'.

Cultural difficulties

You will need to be aware of cultural differences between you and the person you are talking to. For example, using first names or touching someone to whom you are not related, or a very close friend, can be viewed as disrespectful in some cultures. Talking familiarly to someone of a different gender or age group can be unacceptable in some cultures. For example, some young Muslim women believe they should not talk at all to men to whom they are not related.

Many older men and women consider it disrespectful to address people by their first names. You will often find older people with neighbours they have known for fifty years, who still call each other 'Mrs Baker' or 'Mrs Wood'.

Remember

The golden rule when you are communicating with someone from a different culture is to *find out*. Do not assume that you can approach everyone in the same way. It is your responsibility to find out the way to approach someone.

What words mean

Be aware that the words you use can mean different things to different people and generations – words like 'web', 'chip' or 'gay'. Be aware of particular local words which are used in your part of the country, which may not mean the same to someone from another area.

Think carefully about the subject under discussion. Some people from particular cultures, or people of particular generations, may find some subjects very sensitive and difficult to discuss. These days, it is not unusual amongst a younger age group to discuss personal income levels. However, people of older generations may consider such information to be highly personal.

Physical barriers

Communication can be hindered by physical and environmental factors. This may seem obvious, but they need to be considered when planning communication.

Always provide a private situation if you have personal matters to discuss. It is rarely the case that the best which can be arranged is to pull the curtains around a bed.

You need to think about the surroundings. People find it difficult to talk in noisy, crowded places. A communal lounge with a television and other people is not going to produce good communication.

Remember the temperature – make sure that it is comfortable. Think about lighting. Is it too dark or too bright? Is the sun in someone's eyes? Make sure that you do not sit with your face in shadow. It is very disconcerting not to be able to see someone's face when talking to him or her – remember the previous section on non-verbal communication.

It is important when communicating with someone that they see your face and that you hear what they are saying

Remember

- Never take communication for granted.
- Not everyone communicates in the same way.
- It is *your* responsibility to ensure that the individual is able to communicate.
- As far as possible, plan ahead and think what you will need to take into account.

How to listen

So far you have looked at some of the factors which assist effective communication, and some of the barriers which can hinder it. Now it is time to look at the key areas of listening and talking. You may think that this comes naturally to most people. Not so. You can learn some basic skills which will improve your communication significantly.

Remember

- To hear what someone is really telling you, you have to be a *good listener*.
- To help someone understand what you are saying and tell you what he or she wants to say, you have to be a *good communicator*.

Active listening

Active listening is about doing much more than simply hearing the words which an individual is speaking. It is the way you encourage someone to talk to you, the way you let him or her know that you are interested, concerned and supportive, and the way you allow him or her the space, time and attention to express feelings and concerns.

Active knowledge

This really needs to be done with a friend or colleague. Begin to tell your partner about something simple and straightforward – about your holiday, what you did last Saturday, a planned shopping trip – anything at all. Your partner's job is to look around the room, to look at you but not nod or make any sound, to examine his or her nails – in short to fail to respond to you in any way. You should stop talking when you feel uncomfortable. Then change places. During this exercise you will begin to see how difficult it is to keep talking when you do not get a positive response.

The way in which you listen to someone can make all the difference to how easy he or she finds it to talk to you. When someone is talking to you, keep encouraging him or her by responding – nodding and 'mm' or 'I see' are often all that is needed. There is nothing worse than talking to someone who gives you no response.

Sometimes people find it difficult to express what they want to say and need some encouragement. You can help by repeating back to them what they have been saying, not in a 'parrot style', but in an encouraging way, such as:

Client: 'My family are very busy, I don't see them much, they all have important jobs…' [silence].

You: 'So your children don't have much time to come here because they all work so hard…'

Paraphrasing what someone has told you can also be a useful way of showing that you have understood what he or she is saying. In paraphrasing you take what someone has been saying and repeat it in a slightly different way.

This can be used effectively to clarify what someone has said. For example, if an individual has just told you about feelings ranging from sadness and anger to relief at coming into residential care, a reply of something like 'so your feelings are very mixed – that's very understandable' demonstrates that you have heard what he or she said and also offers reassurance that this reaction is normal and only to be expected.

How to communicate clearly

How you talk to someone matters a great deal. You can ask 'open' or 'closed' questions. Which questions you use makes a difference to the response you will get:

- Closed questions are those which allow people to answer 'Yes' or 'No'. For example, 'Are you worried about the tests tomorrow?' This may get only a one-word response. If you then want to find out any more, you have to ask another question. If you are not careful, individuals can then end up feeling like they are on 'Twenty Questions'.
- Open questions are those which do not allow a one-word response. So, if you rephrase the previous question it becomes 'How do you feel about tomorrow's tests?' The difference is obvious, and there is a far greater chance that the person you are talking to will feel able to express his or her feelings.

Advice

There will be occasions when you are asked to give advice. Sometimes this is appropriate. If, for example, someone asked whether he or she would be able to carry on claiming a particular benefit whilst in residential care, it would be pretty silly to say 'Well, do you think that you will continue to need that benefit?' Clearly, there are three possible answers: 'Yes', 'No' or 'I'm not sure, but I'll find out'. These sorts of request for factual advice are quite different from a situation where someone is dealing with personal or emotional issues.

What you say

Make sure that you are not the one doing all the talking. Be careful not to tell someone what *you* think and keep giving *your* opinions. Telling someone 'If I were you I would...' is not good practice and is not good communication.

Do not *ever* say 'That's silly' or 'Oh you shouldn't feel like that'. That effectively dismisses people's feelings or tells them that they have no right to feel that way.

How you say it

Think about the speed and volume of what you say. We often fail to realise how quickly we speak. It can often be difficult for someone who has some impairment of hearing or poor eyesight to catch what you say, if you speak too fast.

Think about your accent, and the individual you are talking to. Local accents can be difficult to understand, if they are unfamiliar.

Active knowledge

You may not know how strong your own accent is. Try making a tape recording and listening to yourself. Or ask a friend or colleague to advise you honestly about the strength of your accent and the speed at which you talk.

Volume is also important. There is no need to shout – it simply distorts what you say and plays havoc with your facial expression! You should, however, make sure that you speak clearly and at a reasonable level. Generally, speaking too softly can make it hard for you to be understood.

There are some occasions when you may have to balance the volume of what you say with the need to maintain someone's privacy. It may be worth having to repeat yourself a few times, if it helps to keep a discussion private.

Stages of an interaction

As you spend time in communication with someone, the nature of the interaction will go through changes.

*   *Stage 1:* Introduction, light, general. At first, communication may be light and general with very little content of any significance. This is the stage at which both parties decide if they want to continue the discussion, and how comfortable they feel. Body language and non-verbal communication are very important at this stage.
*   *Stage 2:* Main contact, significant information. The middle of any interaction is likely to contain the 'meat' and this is where you will need to use active listening skills to ensure that the interaction is beneficial.
*   *Stage 3:* Reflect, wind up, end positively. People often have the greatest difficulty in knowing how to end an interaction. Ending in a positive way where all participants are left feeling that they have benefited from the interaction is very important. You may find that you have to end an interaction because of time restrictions, or you may feel that enough has been covered – the other person may need a rest, or you may need a break!

At the end of an interaction you should always try to reflect on the areas you have covered, and try to offer a positive and encouraging ending, for example, 'I'm glad you have talked about how unhappy you have been feeling. Now we can try to work at making things better.'

Even if the content of an interaction has been fairly negative, you should encourage the individual to see the fact that the interaction has taken place as being positive in itself.

If you get called away before you have had a chance to properly 'wind up' an interaction with an individual, make a point of returning to end things in a positive way. If you say 'I'll be back in a minute', make sure that you do go back.

Written communication

Written communication may not be something you do very frequently. You may not write many formal letters, but as a care worker you will have to write information in records which could prove to be of vital importance.

The golden rule of good communication is to consider its *purpose*. If you are completing a care plan or record for an individual, then that information needs to be there in order to inform the next carer who takes over.

Think about the sort of information you would need to know. What things are important when handing over care?

You need to record accurately any distress or worries you have tried to deal with, any physical signs of illness or accidents. You may need to record fluid balances or calorie intake charts. It may be important to record visitors, or any medical interventions. The purposes of records and the systems are dealt with in detail in Unit CU5 in NVQ Level 2 Care, but the importance in this context is the usefulness of what you write in terms of communication.

Written communication is useless unless it is legible. There is no point in scribbling something unreadable in someone's notes. It is actually worse than not writing anything, because colleagues waste time trying to decipher what is there, and have to deal with the concerns raised by the fact that there was clearly something worth recording, but they have no idea what it was.

You also need to convey the message in a clear and concise way. People do not want to spend time reading a lengthy report when the main points could have been expressed in a paragraph. Equally, you need to make sure that the relevant points are there. Often bullet points can be useful in recording information clearly and concisely. Look at the examples on page 60.

Mrs P had a bad night.

Too little information

Mrs P had a bad night. It began when I found her crying about 10 p.m. She said she had been thinking about her husband. I thought she seemed a bit hot, so I made her a cup of tea and got her to sit in the lounge for a while before she went to bed. After about half an hour, I managed to get her to go to her room and I went with her . . .

Too much irrelevant information

Mrs P had a bad night because:
a) she was distressed about her husband
b) she wandered out of her room about 2 a.m. crying again
c) unable to settle despite further cocoa
d) wandered into Mr W's room at 5.30 believing he was her husband
She will need to be closely observed today. Any further confused episodes should be logged.

Clear, helpful. Gives a short picture of problems overnight, and suggests action for next day

Records should be accurate, clear and concise

Remember
- Communication is a two-way process.
- Barriers have to be removed for communication to work.
- You have to recognise the barriers before you can remove them.
- Communication is about more than talking.

Unit test

1. How can your personality affect how you work?
2. Is there any point in talking to someone who clearly doesn't understand you? Give reasons for your answer.
3. How does society reinforce stereotypes?
4. Why do you have to challenge oppressive behaviour?
5. Why is body language important?
6. What factors can affect the way people will respond to you?
7. List some examples of unacceptable behaviour and say how you would challenge each.
8. Name three possible barriers to communication. How would you deal with each of them?
9. What environmental factors do you need to consider when planning communication?
10. What is the difference between an open question and a closed question? Name situations where you would use each type of question.

Unit CU1 Promote, monitor and maintain health, safety and security in the workplace

This unit is about the way you can contribute to making your workplace a safe, secure and healthy place for people who need care. Workplace, in this unit, means a home environment or any other facility which provides a health or care service. In the first element you will need to learn about what needs to be done to ensure a safe workplace environment. In the second element you will be looking at how you may need to adapt the way you work and become more safety conscious. The third element in this unit is about how to respond in an emergency.

Element CU1.1 Monitor and maintain the safety and security of the work environment

WHAT YOU NEED TO LEARN

- How to maintain safety.
- How to maintain security.
- The legal framework.
- Dealing with hazardous waste.

How to maintain safety

It sounds very simple and straightforward: make sure that the place in which you work is safe and secure. However, when you start to think about it – safe for whom? from whom? safe from tripping over things? or safe from hazardous fumes? safe from infection? safe from intruders? safe from work-related injuries? You can begin to see that this is a wide and complex subject. It may help if you think about safety and security in respect of the areas of responsibility shown in the table on the next page.

Responsibilities for safety and security in the workplace

Employer's responsibilities	Employee's responsibilities	Shared responsibilities
Planning safety and security Providing information about safety and security Updating systems and procedures	Using the systems and procedures correctly Reporting flaws or gaps in the systems or procedures when in use	Safety of individuals being cared for Safety of the environment

Safety of the environment

You share the responsibility with your employer for the safety of all the people in your care. There are many hazards which can cause injury to people, even more so if they are old, ill or disabled. You need to be aware of:

- *environmental hazards,* such as:
  - wet or slippery floors
  - cluttered passageways or corridors
  - re-arranged furniture
  - worn carpets or rugs
  - electrical flexes

- *hazards to do with equipment and materials,* such as:
  - faulty brakes on beds
  - worn or faulty electrical or gas appliances
  - worn or damaged lifting equipment
  - worn or damaged mobility aids
  - incorrectly labelled substances, such as cleaning fluids
  - leaking or damaged containers
  - faulty waste disposal equipment

- *hazards connected with people,* such as:
  - visitors to the building
  - handling procedures
  - intruders
  - violent and aggressive behaviour.

Your responsibility to contribute to a safe environment is more than simply being aware of these potential hazards. You must take steps to check and deal with any sources of risk.

You can fulfil your role in two ways:

- by dealing directly with the hazard, which means that you have taken individual responsibility. This will probably apply to obvious hazards such as:
  - trailing flexes – roll them up and store them safely
  - wet floors – dry them as far as possible and put out warning signs
  - cluttered doorways and corridors – remove objects and store them safely or dispose of them appropriately. If items are heavy, use assistance or mechanical aids

- visitors to the building – challenge anyone you do not recognise. 'Can I help you?' is usually sufficient to establish whether a person has a good reason to be there or not
- fire – by following the correct procedures to raise the alarm and assist with evacuation

• by informing your manager, which means that it becomes an organisational responsibility. This applies to hazards which are beyond your role and competence to deal with, such as:
  - faulty equipment – fires, kettles, computers, etc.
  - worn floor coverings
  - loose or damaged fittings
  - obstructions too heavy for you to move safely
  - damaged or faulty aids – hoists, bed brakes, bathing aids, etc.
  - people acting suspiciously on the premises
  - fire.

Manual handling

Handling and moving clients is dealt with in detail in Unit Z7, but the implications for the safety of both the care worker and the client are examined in this unit.

Did you know?

Lifting and handling individuals is the single largest cause of injuries at work in health and care settings. One in four workers take time off because of a back injury sustained at work.

The Manual Handling Operations Regulations 1993 require employers to avoid all manual handling where there is a risk of injury 'so far as it is reasonably practical'. Everyone from the European Commission to the Royal College of Nurses has issued policies and directives about avoiding lifting.

There is almost no situation in which manual lifting and handling could be considered acceptable.

Remember

• Always use lifting and handling aids.
• There is no such thing as a safe lift.
• Use the aids which your employer is obliged to provide.

On the rare occasions when it is still absolutely necessary for manual lifting to be done, the employer has to make a 'risk assessment' and put procedures in place to reduce the risk of injury to the employee. This could involve ensuring that sufficient staff are available to lift or handle someone safely, which can often mean that four people are needed.

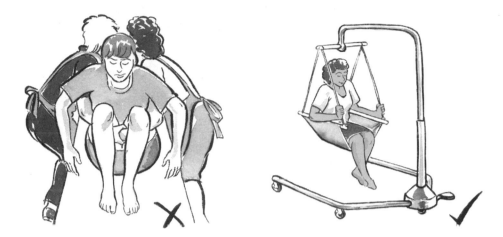

Use the aids which your employer is obliged to provide

Remember

- Many workers in care still lift people manually – it seems quicker and easier than going to all the trouble of using a hoist – *it isn't.*
- Manual lifting is now actively discouraged throughout the profession.
- Manual lifting presents unnecessary and unacceptable risks to the client and to you.
- Don't forget, a back injury can end your career. It's not worth the risk.

Your employer should arrange for you to attend a lifting and handling course. You must attend one each year, so that you are up-to-date with the safest possible practices.

Fire safety

Your workplace will have procedures which must be followed in the case of an emergency All workplaces must display information about what action to take in case of fire. The fire procedure is likely to be similar to the one shown below.

Fire Safety Procedure

1 Raise the alarm.

2 Inform telephonist or dial 999.

3 Ensure that everyone is safe and out of the danger area.

4 If it is safe to do so, attack fire with correct extinguisher.

5 Go to fire assembly point (this will be stated on the fire procedure notice).

6 Do not return to the building for any reason.

- Make sure that you know where the fire extinguishers or fire blankets are in your workplace, and that you know where the fire exits are.
- Your employer will have installed fire doors to comply with regulations – *never* prop them open.
- Your employer should provide fire lectures each year. You must attend and make sure that you are up-to-date with the procedures to be followed.

Which for what?

There are specific fire extinguishers for fighting different types of fire. It is important that you know this. You do not have to memorise them as each one has clear instructions on it, but you do need to be aware that there are different types and make sure that you read the instructions before use.

Did you know?

All new fire extinguishers are red. Each one has its purpose written on it. Each one also has a patch of the colour previously used for that type of extinguisher.

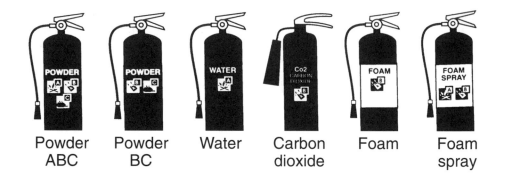

| Powder ABC | Powder BC | Water | Carbon dioxide | Foam | Foam spray |

Remember

- Read the fire extinguisher instructions before tackling the fire. The extra few seconds will be well spent making sure you are using the correct equipment. This is even more important with the new extinguishers which are predominately red.
- Check that you have the right extinguisher for the blaze you are tackling. Check the colour labels:
    - red – water, used for paper, wood and general fires
    - cream – foam, used for liquid oil fires, fat, petrol, oil, etc.
    - blue – dry powder, used for fuel oil, and can be used on electrical fires
    - black – carbon dioxide, used for electrical, wiring fires
    - green – BCF, used for electrical and most other fires, but not used in most workplaces because of high cost.
- Only tackle a fire if you can do so safely – otherwise leave the building and wait for help to arrive.

Evacuating buildings

You may be involved in evacuating buildings if there is a fire, or for other reasons, such as:

- a bomb scare
- the building has become structurally unsafe
- an explosion
- a leak of dangerous chemicals or fumes.

The evacuation procedure you need to follow will be laid down by your workplace. The information will be the same whatever the emergency is: the same exits will be used and the same assembly point. It is likely to be along the following lines:

- Stay calm, do not shout or run.
- Do not allow others to run.
- Organise people quickly and firmly without panic.
- Direct those who can move themselves and assist those who cannot.
- Use wheelchairs to move people quickly.
- Move the bed with the person in, if necessary.

How to maintain security

Most workplaces where care is provided are not under lock and key. This is an inevitable part of ensuring that people have choice and that their rights are respected. However, they also have a right to be secure. Security in a care environment is about:

- security against intruders
- security in respect of their privacy and decisions about unwanted visitors
- security against being abused
- security of property.

Security against intruders

If you work for a large organisation, such as an NHS trust, it may be that all employees are easily identifiable by identity badges with photographs. Some of these even contain a microchip which allows the card to be 'swiped' to gain access to secure parts of the building. This makes it easier to identify people who do not have a right to be on the premises.

In a smaller workplace, there may be a system of issuing visitors' badges to visitors who have reasons to be there, or it may simply rely on the vigilance of the staff.

Keys to good practice

- Be aware of everyone you come across. Get into the habit of noticing people and thinking, 'Do I know that person?'
- Challenge anyone you do not recognise.
- The challenge should be polite. 'Can I help you?' is usually enough to find out if a visitor has a reason to be on the premises.

If a person says that he or she is there to see someone:

- Don't give directions – escort him or her.
- If the person is a genuine visitor, he or she will be grateful. If not, he or she will disappear pretty quickly!

The more dependent individuals are, the greater the risk. If you work with babies, high-dependency or unconscious patients, people with severe learning difficulties or multiple disabilities or people who are very confused, you will have to be extremely vigilant in protecting them from criminals.

Remember

If you find an intruder on the premises, don't tackle him or her – raise the alarm.

Protecting people

If very dependent individuals are living in their own homes, the risks are far greater. You must try to impress on them the importance of finding out who people are before letting them in. If they are able to use it, the 'password' schemes from the utilities (water, gas and electricity companies) are helpful. Information record cards like those provided by the 'Safe as Houses' scheme can be invaluable in providing basic information to anyone who is involved in helping in an emergency.

Remember

- Every time you visit, you may have to explain again what the individual should do when someone knocks on the door.
- Give the individual a card with simple instructions.
- Obtain agreement to speak to the local 'homewatch' scheme and ask that a special eye is kept on visitors.
- Speak to the local police and make them aware that a vulnerable individual is living alone in the house.

People also have a right to choose who they see. This can often be a difficult area to deal with. If there are relatives or friends who wish to visit and an individual does not want to see them, you may have to make this clear. It is difficult to do, but you can only be effective if you are clear and assertive. You should not make excuses or invent reasons why visitors cannot see the person concerned. You could say something like: 'I'm sorry, Mr P has told us that he does not want to see you. I understand that this may be upsetting, but it is his choice. If he does change his mind we will contact you. Would you like to leave your phone number?'

Do not allow yourself to be drawn into passing on messages or attempting to persuade – that is not your role. Your job is to respect the wishes of the person you are caring for. If you are asked to intervene or to pass on a message, you must refuse politely but firmly: 'I'm sorry, that is not something I can do. If your uncle does decide he wants to see you, I will let you know right away. I will tell him you have visited, but I can't do anything else.'

Abuse is dealt with in depth in Unit Z1, but it can never be repeated often enough that individuals have a right to be protected from abuse, and you must report immediately any abuse you see or suspect.

Active knowledge

You need a colleague or friend to try this. One of you should be the person who has come to visit and the other the care worker who has to tell him or her that a friend or relative will not see them. Try using different scenarios – angry, upset, aggressive, and so on. Try at least three different scenarios each. By the time you have practised a few times, you may feel better equipped to deal with the situation when it happens in reality.

If you cannot find anyone to work with you, it is possible to do a similar exercise by imagining three or four different scenarios and then writing down the words you would say in each of the situations.

Security of property

Property and valuables belonging to individuals in care settings should be safeguarded. It is likely that your employer will have a property book in which records of all valuables and personal possessions are entered.

There may be particular policies within your organisation, but as a general rule you are likely to need to:

- make a record of all possessions on admission
- record valuable items separately
- describe items of jewellery by their colour, for example yellow metal not 'gold'
- ensure that individuals sign for any valuables they are keeping, and that they understand that they are liable for their loss
- inform your manager if an individual is keeping valuables or a significant amount of money.

Active knowledge

Find out where the property book is in your workplace, and how it is filled in. Check who has the responsibility to complete it. If you are likely to have to use the book at any time, make sure you know exactly what your role is. Do you have to enter the property in the book, then give it to someone else to deal with the valuables? Do you have to make sure the valuables are safe? Do you have to give the individual a copy of the entry in the book? Ask the questions in advance – don't leave it until you have to do it.

It is always difficult when items go missing in a care setting, particularly if they are valuable. It is important that you check all possibilities before calling the police.

Action stages when property goes missing

The legal framework

The settings in which you provide care are generally covered by the Health and Safety at Work Act 1974 (HASAWA). This Act has been updated and supplemented by many sets of regulations and guidelines, which extend it, support it or explain it. The regulations most likely to affect your workplace are shown in the diagram on page 71.

The effect of the laws

There are many regulations, laws and guidelines dealing with health and safety. You do not need to know the detail, but you do need to know where your responsibilities begin and end.

The laws place certain responsibilities on both employers and employees. For example, it is up to the employer to provide a safe place in which to work, but the employee also has to show reasonable care for his or her own safety.

Employers have to:
- provide a safe workplace
- ensure that there is safe access to and from the workplace
- provide information on health and safety
- provide health and safety training.

The Health and Safety at Work Act is like an umbrella.

Workers must:
- take reasonable care for their own safety and that of others
- co-operate with the employer in respect of health and safety matters
- not intentionally damage any health and safety equipment or materials provided by the employer.

Both the employee and employer are jointly responsible for safeguarding the health and safety of anyone using the premises.

Each workplace where there are five or more workers must have a written statement of their health and safety policy. The policy must include:
- a statement of intention to provide a safe workplace
- the name of the person responsible for implementing the policy
- the names of any other individuals responsible for particular health and safety hazards
- a list of identified health and safety hazards and the procedures to be followed in relation to them
- procedures for recording accidents at work
- details for evacuation of the premises.

Active knowledge
Find out where the health and safety policy is for your workplace and make sure you read it.

Risk assessment

The Management of Health and Safety at Work Regulations 1992 states that employers have to assess any risks which are associated with work activities. This means *all* activities, from walking on wet floors to dealing with violence. Having carried out a risk assessment, the employer must then apply *risk control measures*. This means that actions must be taken to reduce the risks, for example alarm buzzers may need to be installed or extra staff employed, as well as steps like extra training provided for staff or written guidelines produced on how to deal with a particular hazard.

Risks in someone's home

Of course, the situation is somewhat different if you work in an individual's own home. Your employer can still carry out risk assessments and put risk control measures in place, such as a procedure for working in twos in a situation where there is a risk of violence. What cannot be done is to remove environmental hazards such as trailing electrical flexes, rugs with curled up edges, worn patches on stair carpets or old equipment. All you can do is to advise the person whose home it is of the risks, and suggest how things could be improved. You also need to take care!

Remember

- It may be your workplace, but it is the person's home. If you work in an individual's home or long-term residential setting, you have to balance the need for safety with the rights of people to have their living space the way they want it.
- Both you and the individuals receiving care are entitled to expect a safe place in which to live and work, but remember their rights to choose how they want to live.

Control of Substances Hazardous to Health (COSHH)

What are hazardous substances? There are many substances hazardous to health – nicotine, many drugs, even too much alcohol! In this context, however, COSHH applies to substances which have been identified as being toxic, corrosive or irritant. This includes cleaning materials, pesticides, acids, disinfectants and bleaches. Workplaces may have other hazardous substances which are particular to the nature of the work carried out.

Every workplace must have a COSHH file. This file lists all the hazardous substances used in the workplace. It should detail:

- where they are kept
- how they are labelled
- their effects
- the maximum amount of time it is safe to be exposed to them
- how to deal with an emergency involving one of them.

Hazardous substances are not just things like poisons and radioactive material, they are also substances like cleaning fluids and bleach.

Active knowledge

Ask to see the COSHH file in your workplace. Make sure you read it and know which substances you use or come into contact with. Check in the file what the maximum exposure limits are. Your employer must include this information in the COSHH file.

If you have to work with hazardous substances, make sure that you take the precautions detailed in the COSHH file – this may be wearing gloves or protective goggles, or it may involve limiting the time you are exposed to the substance or only using it in certain circumstances.

The COSHH file should also give you information about how to store hazardous substances. This will involve using the correct containers as supplied by the manufacturers. All containers must have safety lids and caps, and must be correctly labelled.

Never use the container of one substance for storing another, and *never* change the labels.

These symbols, which warn you of hazardous substances, are always yellow.

The symbols above indicate hazardous substances. They are there for your safety and for the safety of those you care for. Before you use *any* substance, whether it is liquid, powder, spray, cream or aerosol, take the following simple steps:

* Check the container for the hazard symbol.
* If there is a hazard symbol, go to the COSHH file.
* Look up the precautions you need to take with the substance.
* Make sure you follow procedures, which are intended to protect you.

If you are concerned that a substance being used in your workplace is not in the COSHH file, or if you notice incorrect containers or labels being used, report it to your supervisor. Once you have informed your supervisor, it becomes his or her responsibility to act to correct the problem.

Reporting of Injuries, Diseases and Dangerous Occurrences (RIDDOR)

Diseases

There are certain diseases and groups of infections which are 'notifiable'. In other words, you must report them to the appropriate authorities, usually the Environmental Health Department of your local council. The list of notifiable diseases and infections is a long one, ranging from food poisoning and measles to rabies and yellow fever. Your employer, or an individual's own doctor, will have procedures in place for making the notification, but it is useful for you to know what the more common ones are, and if there is any role you have to play, such as recording or passing on any information.

The most common notifiable diseases are:

acute encephalitis	malaria	smallpox
acute poliomyelitis	measles	tetanus
anthrax	meningitis	tuberculosis
cholera	mumps	typhoid
diphtheria	plague	viral hepatitis
dysentery	rabies	whooping cough
food poisoning	rubella (German measles)	yellow fever
leprosy	scarlet fever	

Injuries and dangerous occurrences

You are, however, much more likely to be involved in reporting and recording accidents or dangerous incidents which occur in your workplace. If accidents or injuries occur at work, either to you or to an individual you are caring for, then the details must be recorded. For example, someone may have a fall, or slip on a wet floor. You must record the incident regardless of whether there was an injury.

Your employer should have procedures in place for making a record of accidents, either an accident book or an accident report form. This is not only required by the RIDDOR regulations, but also, if you work in a residential or nursing home, by the Registered Homes Inspectors.

Make sure you know where the accident report forms or the accident book are kept, and who is responsible for recording accidents. It is likely to be your manager.

You must report any accident in which you are involved, or have witnessed, to your manager or supervisor.

Any medical treatment or assessment which is necessary should be arranged without delay. If an individual has been involved in an accident, you should check if there is anyone he or she would like to be contacted, perhaps a relative or friend. If the accident is serious, and you cannot consult the individual – because he or she is unconscious, for example – the next of kin should be informed as soon as possible.

Complete a report, and ensure that all witnesses to the accident also complete reports. You should include the following in any accident report (see the example on the next page):

- date, time and place of accident
- person/people involved
- circumstances and details of exactly what you saw
- anything which was said by the individuals involved
- the condition of the individual after the accident

- steps taken to summon help, time of summoning help and time when help arrived
- names of any other people who witnessed the accident
- any equipment involved in the accident.

Date: *24.3.01*   Time: *14.30 hrs*   Location: *Main lounge*

Description of accident:

PH got out of her chair and began to walk across the lounge with the aid of her stick. She turned her head to continue the conversation she had been having with GK, and as she turned back again she appeared not to have noticed that MP's handbag had been left on the floor. PH tripped over handbag and fell heavily, banging her head on a footstool.

She was very shaken and although she said that she was not hurt, there was a large bump on her head. P appeared pale and shaky. I asked J to fetch a blanket and to call Mrs J, deputy officer in charge. Covered P with a blanket. Mrs J arrived immediately. Dr was sent for after P was examined by Mrs J.

Dr arrived after about 20 mins and said that she was bruised and shaken, but did not seem to have any injuries.

She wanted to go and lie down. She was helped to bed.

Incident was witnessed by six residents who were in the lounge at the time: GK, MP, IL, MC, CR and BQ.

Signed: _   Name: _ _ _ _ _ _ _ _ _ _ _ _ _ _ _ _ _

An example of an accident report

Active knowledge

Your manager has asked you to design a new incident/accident report form for your workplace. She has asked you to do this because the current form does not provide enough information. The purpose of the new form is to provide sufficient information to:

- ensure the individual receives the proper medical attention
- provide information for treatment at a later date, in case of delayed reactions
- give information to any inspector who may need to see the records
- identify any gaps or need for improvements in safety procedures
- provide information about the circumstances in case of any future legal action.

Think about how you would design the new report form and what headings you would include. Use the list above as a checklist to make sure you have covered everything you need.

Dealing with hazardous waste

As part of providing a safe working environment, employers have to put procedures in place to deal with waste materials and spillages. There are various types of waste, which must be dealt with in particular ways. These are summarised in the table below.

Types of hazardous waste and methods of disposal

Type of waste	Method of disposal
Clinical waste – used dressings	Yellow bags, clearly labelled with contents and location. This waste is incinerated.
Needles, syringes, cannulas ('sharps')	Yellow sharps box. *Never* put sharps into anything other than a hard plastic box. This is sealed and incinerated.
Body fluids and waste – urine, vomit, blood, sputum, faeces	Cleared and flushed down sluice drain. Area to be cleaned and disinfected.
Soiled linen	Red bags, direct into laundry, bags disintegrate in wash. If handled, gloves must be worn.
Recyclable instruments and equipment	Blue bags, to be returned to the Central Sterilisation Services Department (CSSD) for recycling and sterilising.

Remember

- Other people will have to deal with the waste after you have placed it in the bags or containers.
- Make sure it is properly labelled and in the correct containers.

Active knowledge

Look carefully around your workplace. Try to identify six potential hazards, or risky activities. When you have chosen them, check through the Health and Safety Manual and find the risk control measures and provisions made for each of them. If you believe that you have noticed a potential risk which your employer has not covered, you should discuss it with your manager or supervisor immediately.

Element CU1.2 — Promote standards of health and safety in working practice

This element is about what you *do* when you are working. In the previous element, you looked at the procedures and policies which have to be put in place to protect workers and people who use the service, and the laws which govern health and safety. Now you need to learn about the steps you should be following to ensure that the laws and policies actually work in practice.

WHAT YOU NEED TO LEARN

- How to promote a safe work environment.
- How to contribute to infection control.
- How to maintain personal safety.
- How to lift and handle safely.

How to promote a safe work environment

It is important that you develop an awareness of health and safety risks and that you are always aware of any risks in any situation you are in. If you get into the habit of making a mental checklist, you will find that it helps. The checklist will vary from one workplace to another, but could look like the one below.

Checklist for a safe work environment	
Hazards	*Check*
Environment	
Floors	Are they dry?
Carpets and rugs	Are they worn or curled at the edges?
Doorways and corridors	Are they clear of obstacles?
Electrical flexes	Are they trailing?
Equipment	
Beds	Are the brakes on? Are they high enough?
Electrical or gas appliances	Are they worn? Have they been safety checked?
Lifting equipment	Is it worn or damaged?
Mobility aids	Are they worn or damaged?

Checklist for a safe work environment (*cont.*)

Hazards	Check
Substances such as cleaning fluids	Are they correctly labelled?
Containers	Are they leaking or damaged?
Waste disposal equipment	Is it faulty?
People	
Visitors to the building	Should they be there?
Handling procedures	Have they been assessed for risk?
Intruders	Have police been called?
Violent and aggressive behaviour	Has it been dealt with?

One of the other factors to consider in your checklist may be what your colleagues do about health and safety issues. It is very difficult if you are the only person following good practice. You may be able to encourage others by trying some of the following options:

- always showing a good example yourself
- explaining why you are following procedures
- getting some health and safety leaflets from your trade union or environmental health office and leaving them in the staffroom for people to see
- bringing in any information you can about courses or safety lectures
- asking your supervisor if he or she can arrange a talk on health and safety.

What you wear

You may not think that what you wear has much bearing on health and safety, but it is important. Even if your employer supplies, or insists on you wearing, a uniform, there are still other aspects to the safety of your work outfit.

There may be restrictions on wearing jewellery or carrying things in your pocket which could cause injury. This can also pose a risk to you – you could be stabbed in the chest by a pair of scissors or ball-point pen!

Many workplaces do not allow the wearing of rings with stones. Not only is this a possible source of infection, but they can also scratch people or tear protective gloves.

High-heeled or poorly supporting shoes are a risk to you in terms of foot injuries and very sore feet! They also present a risk to individuals you are helping, because if you overbalance or stumble, so will they.

What you wear in the workplace has an important bearing on health and safety. What problems can you see in this picture?

Key to good practice

Simple precautions can often be the most effective in reducing the risk. Always look for the risk and take steps to reduce it.

THINK RISK ⟶ ASSESS ⟶ REDUCE ⟶ AVOID

How to contribute to infection control

The very nature of work in a care setting, means that great care must be taken to control the spread of infection. You will come into contact with a number of people during your working day – an ideal opportunity for infection to spread. Infection which spreads from one person to another is called 'cross-infection'. If you work in the community, cross-infection is difficult to control. However, if you work in a residential or hospital setting, infection control is essential. There are various steps which you can take in terms of the way you carry out your work (wherever you work), which can help to prevent the spread of infection.

You do not know what viruses or bacteria may be present in any individual, so it is important that you take precautions when dealing with everyone. The precautions are called 'universal precautions' precisely because you need to take them with everyone you deal with.

Wear gloves

- *When?* Any occasion when you will have contact with body fluids (including body waste, blood, mucus, sputum, sweat or vomit), or when you have any contact with anyone with a rash, pressure sore, wound, bleeding or any broken skin. You must also wear gloves when you clear up spills of blood or body fluids or have to deal with soiled linen or dressings.

- *Why?* Because gloves act as a protective barrier against infection.

- *How?* Check gloves before putting them on. Never use gloves with holes or tears. Check that they are not cracked or faded. Pull gloves on, making sure that they fit properly. If you are wearing a gown, pull them over the cuffs. Take them off by pulling from the cuff – this turns the glove inside out. Pull off the second glove whilst still holding the first so that the two gloves are folded together inside out. Dispose of them in the correct waste disposal container and wash your hands.

Wash your hands

- *When?* Before and after carrying out any procedure which has involved contact with an individual, or with any body fluids, soiled linen or clinical waste. You must wash your hands even though you have worn gloves. You must also wash your hands before you start and after you finish your shift, before and after eating, after using the toilet and after coughing, sneezing or blowing your nose.

- *Why?* Because hands are a major route to spreading infection. When tests have been carried out on people's hands, an enormous number of bacteria have been found.

- *How?* In running water, in a basin deep enough to hold the splashes and with either foot pedals or elbow bars rather than taps, because you can re-infect your hands from still water in a basin, or from touching taps with your hands once they have been washed. Use the soaps and disinfectants supplied. Make sure that you wash thoroughly, including between your fingers.

Wear protective clothing

- *When?* You should always wear a gown or plastic apron for any procedure which involves bodily contact or is likely to deal with body waste or fluids. An apron is preferable, unless it is likely to be very messy, as gowns can be a little frightening.

- *Why?* Because it will reduce the spread of infection by preventing infection getting on your clothes and spreading to the next person you come into contact with.

- *How?* The plastic apron should be disposable and thrown away at the end of each procedure. You should use a new apron for each individual you come into contact with.

Tie up hair

- *Why?* Because if it hangs over your face, it is more likely to come into contact with the individual you are working with and could spread infection. It could also become entangled in equipment and cause a serious injury.

Clean equipment

- *Why?* Because infection can spread from one person to another on instruments, linen and equipment just as easily as on hands or hair.

- *How?* By washing large items like trolleys with antiseptic solution. Small instruments must be sterilised. Do not shake soiled linen or dump it on the floor. Keep it held away from you. Place linen in proper bags or hampers for laundering.

Deal with waste

- *Why?* Because it can then be processed correctly, and the risk to others working further along the line in the disposal process is reduced, as far as possible.

- *How?* By placing it in the proper bags. Make sure that you know the system in your workplace. It is usually:

  clinical waste – yellow
  soiled linen – red
  recyclable instruments and equipment – blue.

Take special precautions

- *When?* There may be occasions when you have to deal with an individual who has a particular type of infection that requires special handling. This can involve things like hepatitis, some types of food poisoning or highly infectious diseases.

- *How?* Your workplace will have special procedures to follow. They may include such measures as gowning, double gloving or wearing masks. Follow the procedures strictly. They are there for your benefit and for the benefit of the other individuals you care for.

Active knowledge

Make notes of three ways in which infection can be spread. Then note down three effective ways to reduce the possibility of cross-infection.

There is always an element of risk in working with people. There is little doubt that there is an increase in the level of personal abuse suffered by workers in the health and care services. There is also the element of personal risk encountered by workers who visit people in the community, and have to deal with homes in poor states of repair and an assortment of domestic animals!

However, there are some steps which you can take to assist with safety.

Keys to good practice

- If you work alone in the community, always leave details of where you are going and what time you expect to return. This is important in case of accidents or other emergencies, so that you can be found.
- Carry a personal alarm, and use it if necessary.
- Ask your employer to provide training in techniques to combat aggression and violence. It is foolish and potentially dangerous to go into risky situations without any training.
- Try to defuse potentially aggressive situations by being as calm as possible and by talking quietly and reasonably. But, if this is not effective, leave. There is more detail on how to deal with potentially violent situations in Units CL1 and Z1.
- If you work in a residential or hospital setting, raise the alarm if you find you are in a threatening situation.
- Do not tackle aggressors, whoever they are – raise the alarm.
- Use an alarm or panic button if you have it – otherwise yell – very loudly.

Case study

K was a home-care assistant on her first visit to a new client, Mr W. She had been warned that his house was in a poor condition and that he had a large dog. She also knew that he had a history of psychiatric illness and had, in the past, been admitted to hospital compulsorily under the Mental Health Act.

When K arrived on her first morning, the outside of the house was in a very poor state – the garden was overgrown, and it was full of rubbish and old furniture. The front door was half open and she could see that half the floor boards in the hallway appeared to be missing – there were simply joists and a drop into the cellar below. Mr W's dog was at the top of the hallway growling and barking, and Mr W was at the top of the stairs shouting 'Who are you? You won't get me out of here – I'll kill you first!'

1 **Q** What should K do?
  A Leave! She should leave the house at once and report the situation to her manager.
2 **Q** When should she go back?
  A Only after a risk assessment has been carried out.
3 **Q** What sort of risks need to be assessed?
  A a Mr W's mental health and whether any treatment or support is required.
    b The safety of the house. Mr W will have to be consulted about whether he is willing for his house to be made safe and the floorboards repaired.
    c The dog and whether it is likely to present a risk of attack on a visitor to the house.

4 Q If Mr W refuses to allow a risk assessment, or his house to be repaired, should K go back in anyway?

A No. K's job is to provide care, but not at the risk of her own safety.

5 Q Who should carry out the risk assessment?

A K's employer.

How to lift and handle safely

In the previous element you found out about the regulations which govern lifting and handling. Unit Z7 will give you detailed information about using lifting and handling equipment safely.

You will know that your employer is required to carry out a risk assessment of any lifting and handling which is necessary and to supply the necessary equipment, and sufficient people, to carry out the lift.

All lifting and handling should be carried out using appropriate aids and sufficient people. Manual lifting is not something to be undertaken in the normal course of events and you should use mechanical lifting aids and hoists wherever possible.

Remember

Your employer has a statutory requirement to install lifting equipment, but it is your responsibility to use the equipment that is there.

If you do have to lift, what should you do?

Encourage all individuals to help themselves – you would be surprised how much 'learned helplessness' exists. This is largely brought about by care workers who find it is quicker and easier to do things themselves rather than allowing a person to do it for him or herself! Does this sound familiar?

There is more detailed information in Units Z6 (in the level 2 book) and Z7 about maintaining mobility and helping people to move themselves.

Keys to good practice

On the rare occasions when you have to lift, take the following precautions:

* Never lift without an assessment and the right number of people.
* Never lift alone.
* Never lift a dead weight.
* Never lift someone vertically from the floor.
* Always keep your back straight.
* Bend your knees and lift with the weight on your legs.
* Never lift with your spine twisted.
* Never stretch and lift.
* Never lift with your arms outstretched.
* Attend a lifting and handling course – your employer should allow you to do this every year, as part of your workplace manual handling policy.

Minimise the risks arising from health emergencies

This element is about first aid, and helping you to understand the actions you should take if a health emergency arises. This is not a substitute for a first aid course, and will only give you an outline of the steps you need to take. Reading this unit will not qualify you to deal with these emergencies. Unless you have been on a first aid course, you should be careful about what you do, because the wrong action can cause more harm to the casualty. It may be better to summon help.

WHAT YOU NEED TO LEARN

- What you can safely do.
- How you can help the casualty in a health emergency.
- Other ways to help.
- How to deal with witnesses' distress – and your own.

What you can safely do

Most people have a useful role to play in a health emergency, even if it is not dealing directly with the ill or injured person. It is also vital that someone:

- summons help as quickly as possible
- offers any assistance to the competent person who is dealing with the emergency
- clears the immediate environment and makes it safe – for example, if someone has fallen through a glass door, the glass must be removed as soon as possible before there are any more injuries
- offers help and support to other people who have witnessed the illness or injury and may have been upset by it. Clearly this can only be dealt with once the ill or injured person is being helped.

Remember

Only attempt what you know you can safely do. Do not attempt something you are not sure of. You could do further damage to the ill or injured person and you could lay yourself and your employer open to being sued. Do not try to do something outside your responsibility or capability – summon help and wait for it to arrive.

How you can help the casualty in a health emergency

It is important that you are aware of the initial steps to take when dealing with the commonest health emergencies. You may be involved with any of these emergencies when you are at work, whether you work in a residential, hospital or community setting. Clearly, there are major differences between the different work situations:

- If you are working in a hospital where skilled assistance is always immediately available, the likelihood of your having to act in an emergency, other than to summon help, is remote.

- In a residential setting, help is likely to be readily available, although it may not necessarily be the professional medical expertise of a hospital.
- In the community you may have to summon help and take action to support a casualty until the help arrives. It is in this setting that you are most likely to need some knowledge of how to respond to a health emergency.

This section gives a guide to the recognition and initial action to be taken in a number of health emergencies:

- severe bleeding
- cardiac arrest
- shock
- loss of consciousness
- epileptic seizure
- choking and difficulty with breathing
- fractures and suspected fractures
- burns and scalds
- poisoning
- electrical injuries.

Severe bleeding

Severe bleeding can be the result of a fall or injury. The most common causes of severe cuts are glass, as the result of a fall into a window or glass door, or knives from accidents in the kitchen.

Symptoms

There will be apparently large quantities of blood from the wound. In some very serious cases, the blood may be pumping out. Even small amounts of blood can be very frightening, both for you and the casualty. Remember that a small amount of blood goes a long way, and things may look worse than they are. However, severe bleeding requires urgent medical attention in hospital. Although people rarely bleed to death, extensive bleeding can cause shock and loss of consciousness.

Aims

- To bring the bleeding under control.
- To limit the possibility of infection.
- To arrange urgent medical attention.

Action

1 You will need to apply pressure to a wound that is bleeding. If possible, use a sterile dressing. If one is not readily available, use any readily available absorbent material, or even your hand. Do not forget the precautions (see 'Protect yourself' below). You will need to apply direct pressure over the wound for ten minutes (this can seem like a very long time) to allow the blood to clot.

2 If there is any object in the wound, such as a piece of glass, *do not* try to remove it. Simply apply pressure to the sides of the wound.

3 Lay the casualty down and raise the affected part if possible.

4 Make the person comfortable and secure.

5 Dial 999 for an ambulance.

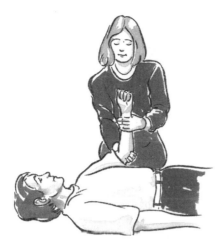

Lay the casualty down and raise the affected part

Protect yourself

You should take steps to protect yourself when you are dealing with casualties who are bleeding. Your skin provides an excellent barrier to infections, but you must take care if you have any broken skin such as a cut, graze or sore. Seek medical advice if blood comes into contact with your mouth, nose or gets into your eyes. Blood-borne viruses (such as HIV or hepatitis) can be passed only if the blood of someone who is already infected comes into contact with broken skin.

- If possible, wear disposable gloves.
- If possible, wash your hands thoroughly in soap and water before and after treatment.
- If this is not possible, cover any areas of broken skin with a waterproof dressing.
- Take care with any needles or broken glass in the area.
- Use a mask for mouth-to-mouth resuscitation if the casualty's nose or mouth is bleeding.

Cardiac arrest

Cardiac arrest occurs when a person's heart stops. Cardiac arrest can happen for various reasons, the most common of which is a heart attack, but a person's heart can also stop as a result of shock, electric shock, a convulsion or other illness or injury.

Symptoms

- No pulse.
- No breathing.

Aims

- To obtain medical help as a matter of urgency.
- It is important to give oxygen, using mouth-to-mouth resuscitation, and to stimulate the heart, using chest compressions. This procedure is called cardio-pulmonary resuscitation – CPR. You will need to attend a first aid course to learn how to resuscitate – you cannot learn how to do this from a book. On the first aid course you will be able to practise on a special dummy.

Actions

1 Check whether the person has a pulse and whether he or she is breathing.
2 If not, call for urgent help from the emergency services.
3 Start methods of resuscitation *if* you have been taught how to do it.
4 Keep up resuscitation until help arrives.

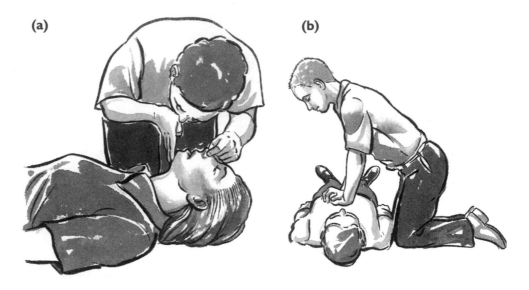

(a)   (b)

Mouth-to-mouth resuscitation (a) and chest compressions (b)

Shock

Shock occurs because blood is not being pumped around the body efficiently. This can be the result of loss of body fluids through bleeding, burns, severe vomiting or diarrhoea, or a sudden drop in blood pressure or a heart attack.

Symptoms

The signs of shock are easily recognised. The person:

- will look very pale, almost grey
- will be very sweaty, and the skin will be cold and clammy
- will have a very fast pulse
- may feel sick and may vomit
- may be breathing very quickly.

Aims

- To obtain medical help as a matter of urgency.
- To improve blood supply to heart, lungs and brain.

Actions

1 Call for urgent medical assistance.
2 Lay the person down on the floor. Try to raise the feet off the ground to help the blood supply to the important organs.
3 Loosen any tight clothing.
4 Watch the person carefully. Check the pulse and breathing regularly.
5 Keep the person warm and comfortable, but *do not* warm the casualty with direct heat, such as a hot water bottle.

Do not:

- allow casualty to eat or drink
- leave the casualty alone, unless it is essential to do so briefly in order to summon help.

Raise the feet off the ground and keep the casualty warm

Loss of consciousness

Loss of consciousness can happen for many reasons, from a straightforward faint to unconsciousness following a serious injury or illness.

Symptom

A reduced level of response and awareness. This can range from being vague and 'woozy' to total unconsciousness.

Aims

- To summon expert medical help as a matter of urgency.
- To keep the airway open.
- To note any information which may help to establish the cause of the unconsciousness.

Action

1 Make sure that the person is breathing and has a clear airway.
2 You need to maintain the airway by lifting the chin and tilting the head backwards.

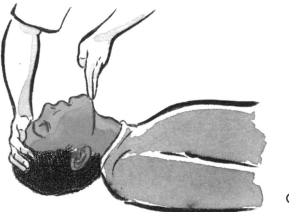

Open the airway

3 Look for any obvious reasons why the person may be unconscious, such as a wound or an ID band telling you of any condition they may have. For example,

many people who have medical conditions which may cause unconsciousness, such as epilepsy or diabetes, will wear special bracelets or necklaces giving information about their condition.

4 Place the casualty in the recovery position (see below), *but not if you suspect a back or neck injury*, until the emergency services arrive.

Do not:

- attempt to give anything by mouth
- attempt to make the casualty sit or stand
- leave the casualty alone, unless it is essential to leave briefly in order to summon help.

The recovery position

Many of the actions you need to take to deal with health emergencies will involve you in placing someone in the recovery position. In this position a casualty has the best chance of keeping a clear airway, not inhaling vomit and remaining as safe as possible until help arrives. This position should *not* be attempted if you think someone has back or neck injuries, and it may not be possible if there are fractures of limbs.

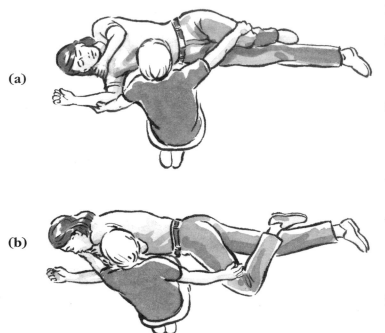

(a)

(b)

(c)

1 Kneel at one side of the casualty, at about waist level.

2 Tilt back the person's head – this opens the airway. With the casualty on his/her back, make sure that limbs are straight.

3 Bend the casualty's near arm as in a wave (so it is at right angles to the body). Pull the arm on the far side over the chest and place the back of the hand against the opposite cheek (**a** in diagram opposite).

4 Use your other hand to roll the casualty towards you by pulling on the far leg, just above the knee (**b** in the diagram). The casualty should now be on his or her side.

5 Once the casualty is rolled over, bend the leg at right angles to the body. Make sure the head is tilted well back to keep the airway open (**c** in diagram).

The recovery position

Epileptic seizure

Epilepsy is a medical condition that causes disturbances in the brain which result in sufferers becoming unconscious and having involuntary contractions of their muscles. This contraction of the muscles produces the fit or seizure. People who suffer with epilepsy do not have any control over their seizures, and may actually do themselves harm by falling when they have a seizure.

Aims

- To ensure that the person is safe and does not injure him or herself during the fit.
- To offer any help needed following the fit.

Action

1 Try to make sure that the area in which the person has fallen is safe.
2 Loosen all clothing.
3 Once the seizure has ended, make sure that the person has a clear airway and place in the recovery position.
4 Make sure that the person is comfortable and safe. Particularly try to prevent head injury.
5 If the fit lasts longer than five minutes, or you are unaware that the casualty is a known epileptic, call an ambulance.

Do not:

- attempt to hold the casualty down, or put anything in the mouth
- move the casualty until he or she is fully conscious, unless there is a risk of injury in the place where he or she has fallen.

Choking and difficulty with breathing (in adults and children over 8 years)

This is caused by something (usually a piece of food) stuck at the back of the throat. It is a situation which needs to be dealt with, as people can quickly stop breathing if the obstruction is not removed.

Symptoms

- Red, congested face at first, later turning grey.
- Unable to speak or breathe, may gasp and indicate throat or neck.

Aims

- To remove obstruction as quickly as possible.
- To summon medical assistance as a matter of urgency if the obstruction cannot be removed.

Action

1 Try to get the person to cough. If that is not immediately effective, move on to step 2.
2 Bend the person forwards. Slap sharply on the back between the shoulder blades up to five times (**a** in diagram on page 90).
3 If this fails, stand behind the person with your arms around him/her. Join your hands just below the breastbone. One hand should be in a fist and the other holding it (**b** in the diagram).
4 Then sharply pull your joined hands upwards and into the person's body at the same time. The force should expel the obstruction.
5 You should alternate backslaps and abdominal thrusts until you clear the obstruction.

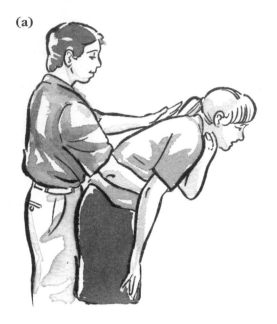

Dealing with an adult who is choking

Fractures and suspected fractures

Fractures are breaks or cracks in bones. They are usually caused by a fall or other type of injury. The casualty will need to go to a hospital as soon as possible to have a fracture diagnosed correctly.

Symptoms

- Acute pain around the site of the injury.
- Swelling and discoloration around the affected area.
- Limbs or joints may be in odd positions.
- Broken bones may protrude through the skin.

Action

1 The important thing is to support the affected part. Help the casualty to find the most comfortable position.
2 Support the injured limb in that position with as much padding as necessary – towels, cushions or clothing will do.
3 Take the person to hospital or call an ambulance.

Do not:

- try to bandage or splint the injury
- allow the casualty to have anything to eat or drink.

Support the injured limb

Burns and scalds

There are several different types of burn; the most usual are burns caused by heat or flame. Scalds are caused by hot liquids. People can be burned by chemicals or by electrical currents.

Symptoms

- Depending on the type and severity of the burn, skin may be red, swollen and tender, blistered and raw or charred.
- Usually severe pain and possibly shock.

Aims

- To obtain immediate medical assistance if the burn is over a large area (as big as the casualty's hand or more) or is deep.
- To send for an ambulance if the burn is severe or extensive. If the burn or scald is over a smaller area, the casualty could be transported to hospital by car.
- To stop the burning and reduce pain.
- To minimise possibility of infection.

Action

1 For major burns, summon immediate medical assistance.
2 Cool down the burn. Keep it flooded with cold water for 10 minutes. If it is a chemical burn, this needs to be done for 20 minutes. Ensure that the contaminated water used to cool a chemical burn is disposed of safely.
3 Remove any jewellery, watches or clothing which are not sticking to the burn.
4 Cover the burn if possible, unless it is a facial burn, with a sterile or, at least, clean dressing. For a burn on a hand or foot, a clean plastic bag will protect it from infection until it can be treated by an expert.

Cool the burn with water

5 If clothing is on fire, remember the basics: *stop, drop, wrap* and *roll* the person on the ground.

Do not:

- remove anything which is stuck to a burn
- touch a burn, or use any ointment or cream
- cover facial burns – keep pouring water on until help arrives.

Remember

If a person's clothing is on fire, STOP – DROP – WRAP – ROLL
- *Stop* him or her from running around.
- Get him/her to *drop* to the ground – push him/her if you have to and can do so safely.
- *Wrap* him/her in something to smother the flames – a blanket or coat, anything to hand. This is better if it is soaked in water.
- *Roll* him/her on the ground to put out the flames.

Poisoning

People can be poisoned by many substances: drugs, plants, chemicals, fumes or alcohol.

Symptoms

Symptoms will vary depending on the poison.
- The person could be unconscious.
- There may be acute abdominal pain.
- There may be blistering of the mouth and lips.

Aims

- To remove the casualty to a safe area if he/she is at risk, and it is safe for you to move him/her.
- To summon medical assistance as a matter of urgency.
- To gather any information which will identify the poison.
- To maintain a clear airway and breathing until help arrives.

Action

1 If the casualty is unconscious, place him/her in the recovery position to ensure that the airway is clear, and that he/she cannot choke on any vomit.
2 Dial 999 for an ambulance.
3 Try to establish what the poison is and how much has been taken. This information could be vital in saving a life.
4 If a conscious casualty has burned mouth or lips, he or she can be given small frequent sips of water or cold milk.

Do not try to make the casualty vomit.

Electrical injuries

Electrocution occurs when an electrical current passes though the body.

Symptoms

Electrocution can cause cardiac arrest and burns where the electrical current entered and left the body.

Aims

- To remove the casualty from the current when you can safely do so.
- To obtain medical assistance as a matter of urgency.
- To maintain a clear airway and breathing until help arrives.
- To treat any burns.

Action

There are different procedures to follow depending on whether the injury has been caused by a high or low voltage current.

Injury caused by high voltage current

This type of injury may be caused by overhead power cables or rail lines, for example. What you need to do.

1 Contact the emergency services immediately.
2 *Do not* touch the person until all electricity has been cut off.
3 If the person is unconscious, clear the airway.
4 Treat any other injuries present, such as burns.
5 Place in the recovery position until help arrives.

Injury caused by low voltage current

This type of injury may be caused by powered kettles, computers, drills, lawnmowers, etc. What you need to do.

1 Break the contact with the current by switching off the electricity at the mains if possible.
2 It is vital to break the contact as soon as possible, *but* if you touch a person who is 'live' (still in contact with the current) you too will be injured. If you are unable to switch off the electricity, then you must stand on something dry which can insulate you, such as a telephone directory, rubber mat or a pile of newspapers, and then move the casualty away from the current as described below.
3 Do not use anything made of metal, or anything wet, to move the casualty from the current. Try to move him/her with a wooden pole or broom-handle, even a chair.
4 Alternatively, drag him/her with a rope or cord or, as a last resort, pull by holding any of the person's dry clothing which is *not* in contact with his/her body.
5 Once the person is no longer in contact with the current, you should follow the same steps as with a high voltage injury.

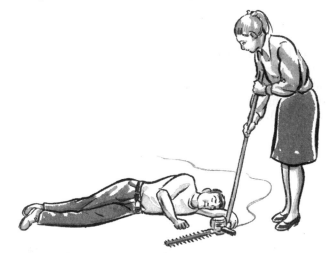

Move the casualty away from the current

Other ways to help

Summoning assistance

In the majority of cases this will mean telephoning 999 and requesting an ambulance. It will depend on the setting in which you work and clearly is not required if you work in a hospital! But it may mean calling for a colleague with medical qualifications, who will then be able to make an assessment of the need for further assistance. Similarly, if you work in the residential sector, there should be a medically qualified colleague available. If you are the first on the scene at an emergency in the community, you may need to summon an ambulance for urgent assistance.

If you need to call an ambulance, try to keep calm and give clearly all the details you are asked for. Do not attempt to give details until they are asked for – this wastes time. Emergency service operators are trained to find out the necessary information, so let them ask the questions, then answer calmly and clearly.

Follow the action steps outlined in the previous section whilst you are waiting for help to arrive.

Assist the person dealing with the emergency

A second pair of hands is invaluable when dealing with an emergency. If you are assisting someone with first aid or medical expertise, follow all his or her instructions, even if you don't understand why. An emergency situation is not the time for a discussion or debate – that can happen later. You may be needed to help to move a casualty, or to fetch water, blankets or dressings, or to reassure and comfort the casualty during treatment.

Make the area safe

An accident or injury may have occurred in an unsafe area – and it was probably for precisely that reason that the accident occurred there! Sometimes, it may be that the accident has made the area unsafe for others. For example, if someone has tripped over an electric flex, there may be exposed wires or a damaged electric socket. Alternatively, a fall against a window or glass door may have left shards of broken glass in the area, or there may be blood or other body fluids on the floor. You may need to make the area safe by turning off the power, clearing broken glass or dealing with a spillage.

It may be necessary to redirect people away from the area of the accident in order to avoid further casualties.

Maintain the privacy of the casualty

You may need to act to provide some privacy for the casualty by asking onlookers to move away or stand back. If you can erect a temporary screen with coats or blankets, this may help to offer some privacy. It may not matter to the casualty at the time, but he or she has a right to privacy if possible.

Make accurate reports

You may be responsible for making a report on an emergency situation you have witnessed, or for filling in records later. Concentrate on the most important aspects of the incident and record the actions of yourself and others in an accurate, legible and complete manner.

How to deal with witnesses' distress - and your own

People who have witnessed accidents can often be very distressed by what they have seen. The distress may be as a result of the nature of the injury, or the blood loss. It could be because the casualty is a friend or relative or simply because seeing accidents or injuries is traumatic. Some people can become upset because they feel helpless and do not know how to assist, or they may have been afraid and then feel guilty later.

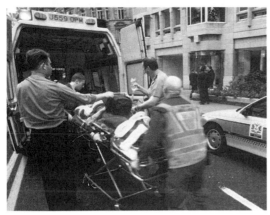

Witnessing accidents is often distressing

You will need to reassure people about the casualty and the fact that he or she is being cared for appropriately. However, do not give false reassurance about things you may not be sure of.

You may need to allow individuals to talk about what they saw. One of the commonest effects of witnessing a trauma is that people need to repeat over and over again what they saw.

What about you?

You may feel very distressed by the experience you have gone through. You may find that you need to talk about what has happened, and that you need to look again at the role you played. You may feel that you could have done more, or you may feel angry with yourself for not having a greater knowledge about what to do.

There is a whole range of emotions which you may experience. Unit Z1 covers in detail the different ways to cope with these feelings, but you should be able to discuss your feelings with your supervisor and use any support provided by your employer.

If you have followed the basic guidelines in this element, you will have done as much as could be expected of anyone at the scene of an emergency who is not a trained first aider.

Unit test

I Name three aspects of safety which you could deal with in your workplace: List the actions you would take in each of the three situations you have identified.

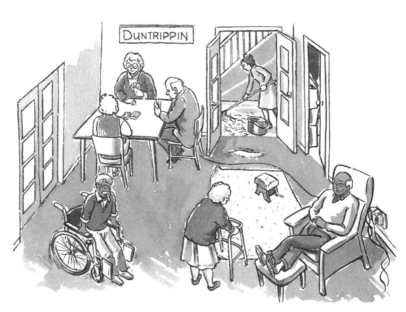

DUNTRIPPIN

2 Look at the picture on page 95. How many possible hazards and risks can you find in the picture?
   a   List at least six.
   b   Which of these are the responsibility of the employer?
   c   Which should you do something about?
3 What are the employer's responsibilities in respect of hazardous substances? What are the employee's responsibilities for hazardous substances?
4 What should you do if you see someone in your workplace whom you do not recognise?
5 What are the different ways of disposing of waste?
6 What should you do if you find an intruder on the premises?
7 You should always attempt first aid because it is always better to do something. True or false? What is the single most important act for an untrained person to do in a health emergency? List three tasks you can carry out at the scene of an emergency which do not necessarily involve first aid.
8 How would you talk to a casualty while you waited for help? What would you say to others who had witnessed the incident?
9 Imagine you are just about to start work in a new day-care facility for older people.
   a   What kinds of substance would you expect to see in the COSHH file?
   b   Which tasks would you expect to find in the risk assessment file?
   c   Would you expect to see any specialised care equipment in the centre?
   d   What type of equipment?
   e   What basic precautions will you expect to follow?
   f   Do you think there will be an expectation about how you dress? What do you think it will be?
   g   What training courses would you expect to undertake?
   h   List at least three security precautions you think the setting may take.
10 Now imagine that you are about to start working in a residential home for teenagers. Answer the same questions. Which of your answers are different and which remain the same?

Unit CU7

Develop one's own knowledge and practice

The knowledge and skills you will learn about in this unit are the key to working effectively in all aspects of your practice. Understanding yourself and the factors which have influenced your attitudes and beliefs is an essential part in shaping the way you work. The care sector is constantly benefiting from new research, new developments, policies and guidelines. In order to offer the best possible level of service to those you care for, you need to make sure that you are up to date in work practices and knowledge and aware of current thinking. The information in this unit will help you to identify the best ways to develop and update your own knowledge and skills.

Element CU7.1 Reflect on and evaluate one's own values, priorities, interests and effectiveness

WHAT YOU NEED TO LEARN

- How to explore your own values, interests and beliefs.
- How your values, interests and beliefs influence your practice.
- How to use feedback and support to improve your practice.

How to explore your own values, interests and beliefs

Everyone has their own values, beliefs and preferences. They are essential to making you who you are. What you believe in, what you see as important and what you see as acceptable or desirable are as much a part of your personality as whether you are shy, outgoing, funny, serious, friendly or reserved.

People whose work involves caring for others need to be more aware than most as to how their work can be affected by their beliefs.

Active knowledge

If you work in a library people will still continue to borrow and read books that you consider boring, poorly written or distasteful. With the exception of a small number of those who might ask your advice, most of the people for whom you provide a service will remain unaware of your beliefs, interests or values. However, if you work providing care for others and your work involves forming relationships with vulnerable people and carrying out tasks which affect their health and well-being, then your own attitudes, values and beliefs are very important.

The way in which you respond to people is linked to what you believe in, what you consider important and the things that interest you. You may find you react positively to people who share your values and less warmly to people who have different priorities. When you develop friendships it is natural to spend time with people who share your interests and values, that is those who are on your 'wave length'.

Choosing your friends and meeting with others who share your interests is one of life's joys and pleasures, however the professional relationships you develop with people you care for are another matter. As a professional carer you are required to provide the same quality of care for all, not just for those who you can identify as sharing your views and beliefs. This may seem obvious, but knowing what you need to do and achieving it successfully are not the same thing.

You may believe that everyone should be treated in the same way, however there are differences in approach or attitude you may be unaware of. For example, you may not be aware you are spending more time with someone who is asking your advice about a course of action which you think is sensible than you are with someone who wanted to do something you thought inadvisable. There are many other ways in which your beliefs, interests and values can affect how you relate to people. Some of these are listed in the table.

Your beliefs/values/interests	Situation	Possible effect
People have a responsibility to look after their health	You are caring for someone with heart disease who continues to smoke and eats a diet high in fried foods and cream cakes	You find it difficult to be sympathetic when they complain about their condition and you make limited responses
War and violence are wrong and people who fight should not be glorified as heroes	An elderly client constantly recalls tales of his days as a soldier and wants you to admire his bravery and that of his comrades	You try to avoid spending time chatting with him and limit your contact to providing physical care
Modern chart and disco music	You visit a client who constantly plays country and western music very loudly	You find it hard not to ask her to turn it down or off. You hurry through your work and your irritation shows in your body language

There is nothing wrong, or unusual in behaving differently towards different people – in fact the only way to behave identically towards everyone is to be a robot! However, it is important that you are aware of it, because it could make a difference to the quality of your work. Being aware of the factors that have influenced the development of your personality is not as easy as it sounds. You may feel you know yourself very well, but knowing *who* you are is not the same as knowing *how* you got to be you.

Unravelling these influences is never easy, and you are

Getting to know yourself

Active knowledge

Step I

Take a range of items from a newspaper, about six or seven. Make a note of your views on each of them: say what your feelings are to each one – does it shock or disgust you, make you sad, or angry, or grateful that it hasn't happened to you?

Step 2

Try to think about why you reacted in the way you did to each of the items in the newspaper. Think about what may have influenced you to feel that way. The answers are likely to lie in a complex range of factors, including your upbringing and background, experiences you had as a child and as an adult, and relationships you have shared with others.

not being asked to carry out an in-depth analysis yourself – simply to begin to realise how your development has been influenced by a series of factors.

Factors which influence our development

Everyone's values and beliefs are affected to different degrees by the same range of factors. These include:

Various factors affect the way we develop

Each of us will be influenced to a greater or lesser degree by some or all of those factors. As each individual is different the combination of factors and the extent of their influence will be different for each person. It is therefore important that you have considered and reflect on those factors which have influenced your development so that you have an understanding of how you became the person you are.

Life stages and development

One of the most significant influences is the **life stage** which people are at. Most people who are working in care are likely to fall into the young or middle adult group, so if you look at those columns in the chart below, you should be able to see the stages of development which apply to your age group. The chart will have other important uses in helping you to understand the life stages which your clients are either at, or have experienced.

Developmental stages and chronological age					
	Intellectual	**Social/emotional**	**Language**	**Gross motor**	**Fine motor**
Infant Birth – 1 year	Learns about things by feeling with hands and mouth	Attaches to parent(s), begins to recognise faces and smile; at about 6 months begins to recognise parent(s) and expresses fear of strangers; plays simple interactive games like peekaboo	Vocalises, squeals and imitates sounds, says dada' and 'mama'	Lifts head first then chest, rolls over, pulls to sit, crawls and stands alone	Reaches for objects and rakes up small items, grasps rattle
Toddler 1–2 years	Learns words for objects and people	Learns that self and parent(s) are different or separate from each other, imitates and performs tasks, indicates needs or wants without crying	Says some words other than 'dada' and 'mama', follows simple instructions	Walks well, kicks, stoops and jumps in place, throws balls	Unbuttons clothes, builds tower of 4 cubes, scribbles, uses spoon, picks up very small objects
Preschool 2–5 years	Understands concepts such as tired, hungry and cold, recognises colours, becomes aware of numbers and letters	Begins to separate easily from parent(s), dresses with assistance, washes and dries hands, plays interactive games like tag	Names pictures, follows directions, can make simple sentences of two or three words, vocabulary increases	Runs well, hops, pedals tricycle, balances on one foot	Buttons clothes, builds tower of 8 cubes, copies simple figures or letters
School age 5–12 years	Develops understanding of numeracy and literacy concepts, learns relationship between objects and feelings, acquires knowledge and understanding	Acts independently, but is emotionally close to parent(s), dresses without assistance, joins same sex play groups and clubs	Defines words, knows and describes what things are made of, vocabulary increases	Skips, balances on one foot for 10 seconds, overestimates physical abilities	Draws person with 6 parts, copies detailed figures and objects

Developmental stages and chronological age					
	Intellectual	**Social/emotional**	**Language**	**Gross motor**	**Fine motor**
Adolescent 12–18 years	Understands abstract concepts like illness and death, develops understanding of complex ideas	Experiences rapidly changing moods and behaviour, interested in peer group almost exclusively, distances from parent(s) emotionally, concerned with body image, likely to have first sexual relationship	Uses increased vocabulary, understands more abstract concepts like grief	May appear awkward and clumsy while learning to deal with rapid increases in size due to growth spurts	Fully developed
Young adults 18–40 years	Fully developed, continues to develop knowledge base related to school or job	Becomes independent from parent(s), develops own lifestyle, and career, social and economic changes, develops interests, chooses a partner, becomes a parent	Fully developed	Fully developed	Fully developed
Middle age 40–65 years	Fully developed	Builds social and economic status, is fulfilled by work or family, children grow and nest leave nest, deals with ageing parents, copes with the death of parents	Fully developed	Begins to experience physical changes of ageing, changing hair colour, lack of elasticity in skin, women experience menopause, reduction in muscular flexibility	Fully developed
Older adult 65+ years	Fully developed	Adjusts to retirement, adjusts to loss of friends and relatives, copes with loss of spouse, adjusts to new role in family, copes with dying	Fully developed	Experiences more significant physical changes associated with ageing	Begins to experience physical changes associated with ageing

Other key influences on development

The following are some of the key influences on your growth and development and on your current values.

Aspects of the environment which affect us

You should be able to begin to see from this how the environment in which you developed may have affected many of your attitudes. You may also have been affected by the social class to which you belonged and the relationships and emotional bonds you have formed. This can affect your life in various ways:

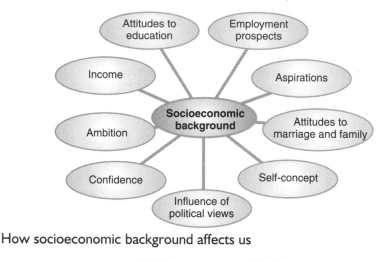

How socioeconomic background affects us

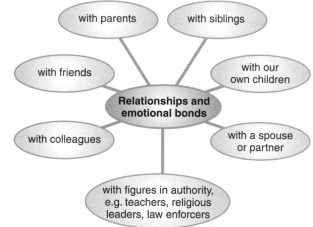

How relationships and bonds affects us

Active knowledge

Construct spider diagrams for each of the factors on page 99 which have influenced your development and from those begin to identify which factors have exercised the greatest influence on your development. This exercise should help you to be able to identify what has affected the development of your own personality and abilities and how this may affect the way in which you work.

How your values, interests and beliefs influence your practice

Once you have begun to identify the major factors which have influenced your development, the next stage is to look at how they have affected the way in which you work and relate both to clients and colleagues. This is the basis of developing into a '**reflective practitioner**'. Working in care requires that in order to be an effective practitioner and to provide the best possible service for those you care for, you need to be able to reflect on what you do and the way you work and to identify your strengths and your weaknesses. It is important that you learn to use reflection on your own practice in a constructive way. Reflection should not be used to undermine your confidence in your own work, rather you should use it in a constructive way to identify areas which require improvement. The ability to do this is not an indication of poor practice, it is an indication of excellent practice. Any worker in care who believes that they have no need to improve their practice or to develop and add to their skills and understanding is not demonstrating good and competent practice, but rather an arrogant and potentially dangerous lack of understanding of the nature of work in the care sector.

You need to think about how you can improve work practices to become more effective

Becoming a reflective practitioner is not about torturing yourself with self-doubts and examining your weaknesses until you reach the point where your self-confidence is at zero! But it is important that you examine the work that you have done and identify areas where you know you need to carry out additional development. A useful tool in learning to become a reflective practitioner is to develop a checklist which you can use, either after you have dealt with a difficult situation or at the end of each shift or day's work, to look at your own performance.

Reflective practice checklist

1 How did I approach work?
2 Was my approach positive?
3 How did the way I worked affect the client?
4 How did the way I worked affect my colleagues?
5 Did I give my work 100%.
6 Which was the best aspect of the work I did?
7 Which was the worst aspect of the work I did?
8 Was this work the best I could do?
9 Are there any areas in which I could improve?
10 What are they?

How to use feedback and support to improve your practice

The most important method is the one which we have already discussed, that of regularly examining your own work and considering the ways in which it could have been improved and the strengths and weaknesses of your own practice. However, this is very hard to do without any support from others and without using **feedback** from colleagues in your workplace. **Support networks**, whether they be formal or informal, are one of the most effective means of identifying areas of your own practice which need further development.

Formal networks

These are networks of support put in place usually by your employer. They are likely to consist of your immediate supervisor and possibly other more senior members of staff on occasions. You are likely to have a regular system of feedback and support meetings, or appraisal sessions with your supervisor. These could be at differing intervals depending on the system in your particular workplace, but is unlikely to be less frequent than once a month. These systems are extremely useful in giving you the opportunity to benefit from feedback from your supervisor who will have been fully aware of the work that you have been undertaking, and will have been able to identify areas of practice which you may need to improve and areas in which you have demonstrated strength. The appraisal or supervision system in your workplace may also be the point at which you identify a programme of development which you will undertake over the next period of time. Some employers identify this at six-monthly or twelve-monthly intervals, and some more frequently. This is likely to take the form of your supervisor identifying training and development programmes which are going to be available over the next period of time and which appear particularly appropriate to the development areas of your practice which have been identified.

Getting the most out of a supervision/appraisal section

You need to make sure that you are well prepared for these sessions in order that you can get the maximum benefit from them. This will mean bringing together the reflections you have carried out on your own practice, and using examples and client case notes where appropriate. You will need to be able to demonstrate to your supervisor that you have reflected on your own practice and that you have begun the process of identifying areas for development. If you can provide evidence through case notes and records to support your identification of development areas this will assist your supervisor greatly. You will also need to be prepared to receive feedback from your supervisor. Whilst feedback is likely to be given in a positive way this does not mean that it will be uncritical. Many people have considerable difficulty in accepting criticism in any form, even where it is intended to be supportive and constructive. If you are aware that you are one of the people who has particular difficulty in accepting criticism then you should begin to prepare yourself to view feedback from your supervisor as valuable and useful information which can add to your ability to reflect effectively on the work which you are doing.

Active knowledge

Ask a friend or a member of your family to offer some constructive criticism of something you have undertaken. It is unlikely to be helpful in the first instance to ask them to criticise aspects of your personality. If you do not react well to criticism then a major family crisis could be provoked. However, you could begin by requesting feedback on a simple practical activity that you have undertaken, such as cooking a meal, or work you have undertaken in the garden or in the house.

If you can get accustomed to receiving feedback on doing something which is relatively unthreatening, such as the quality of your cooking or decorating abilities, then you could use the same approach for receiving feedback on your working practices. Your response to negative feedback should be not to immediately defend yourself or to reject the validity of the feedback, but to accept it, perhaps using the phrase, 'Thank you, that's very helpful, I can use that next time to improve.' Using this technique for your supervisor/appraisal session can be extremely valuable, in that you are likely to make the maximum use of opportunities to improve your practice.

On the other hand, if any criticism undermines your confidence and makes it difficult for you to value your strengths, then you should also benefit from doing the exercise above. However, you should not only ask your friends or relatives to identify the areas in which you did well, but also those that need improvement. You would then be more likely to respond to negative feedback in a positive way.

Accepting criticism

Training and development sessions

One of the other formal and organised ways of assisting with reflection on your own practice and in identifying strengths, weaknesses and areas for development is during training and development opportunities. On a course, or at a training day, you may find that aspects of practice and areas of knowledge which are new to you are discussed, which will often open up avenues for you that you had never considered before. Apart from gaining new knowledge and understanding, this is one of the major benefits from making the most of the training and education opportunities which may be available to you.

Learning styles

One of the best ways to make sure that you get the most out of any training or feedback opportunity, whether in a formal training session or in informal networking with colleagues, is to extend the reflection on your own practice to include reflection on the way you learn. Just as there are differences in the way each of us work and what factors have influenced us, so each of us is different in the way we learn best. You may be the sort of person who never remembers anything you read in a textbook, but remembers everything you were taught by your supervisor when they worked alongside you. If this is the case, then when you take up a training opportunities you should particularly look for those which give you the chance to become actively involved in exercises and workshops and don't just require you to sit and listen to a lecturer. However, you may be the sort of person who likes to study a textbook or find information on the Internet, who enjoys making notes, finding out new information and then discussing how to apply it to your work. If this is the case, you should look for training courses where you will be given plenty of written handouts to back up the day and where you can listen to lectures from which you can make your own notes.

You may be the sort of person who absorbs information better from visual communication. If so, then you should try to get access to video and television documentaries and learning materials which are likely to be the most effective method of helping you to remember new information. A simple checklist will help you to identify the way in which you learn best.

Checklist to identify the way you learn best

1 Which training do I enjoy most?

2 Who has given me the most information about my work?

3 Do I enjoy reading books about health and care?

4 Do I watch television documentaries about health and care when they are on?

5 Do I fall asleep in lectures?

6 Do I find it easy to see how the information in a textbook could be used in my job?

7 Do I like to watch someone else in order to learn?

Informal networks

Informal networks are likely to consist of your work colleagues. These can be major sources of support and assistance. Part of the effectiveness of many teams in many workplaces is their ability to support each other and to provide useful informal ideas for improving practice and support when things go badly.

Informal networks can be major sources of support and assistance

Some staff teams will simply provide a completely informal and ad-hoc support system. This provides advice, guidance and support, as and when necessary. Other teams, however, will organise this on a more regular basis and they may get together to discuss specific situations or problems which have arisen for members of the team during recent practice. You need to be sure that you are making maximum use of the opportunities offered, both formal and informal, to gain support, advice and feedback on your practice.

Active knowledge

Identify formal and informal support networks in your workplace. Note down the ways in which you use the different types of network and the way in which they support your development. If you identify any gaps or areas where you feel unsupported you should discuss this with your supervisor or manager.

Element CU7.2 | # Synthesise new knowledge into the development of one's own practice

WHAT YOU NEED TO LEARN

- How to keep aware of new developments in your own area of practice.
- How to understand and interpret the latest research.
- How to ensure that your practice is current and up-to-date.

How to keep aware of new developments

There is a range of ways in which you can ensure that you keep up to date with new developments in the field of care, and particularly those which affect your own specialist area of work. However, you should not necessarily assume that your workplace will automatically inform you about new developments, changes and updates which affect your work – you must be prepared to actively maintain your own knowledge base and to ensure that your practice is in line with current thinking and emerging new theories. The easiest way to do this is to incorporate an awareness of the need to constantly update your knowledge of practice into all your work activities. If you restrict your awareness of new developments to specific times, for example, on the third Friday of each month you go to the library, or you make sure that you take a training course at least once every six months, you are likely to miss out on many new and emerging theories.

Sources of information

Fortunately the area of health and care is one which is topical, so it is relatively easy to find out information in respect of new studies and research. You will need to be aware when watching television and listening to radio news programmes of new developments, legislation, guidelines and reports which are being reported in relation to health and care clients and workers.

Active knowledge

For one week keep a record of every item which relates to health and care services which you hear on a radio news bulletin, see in a television programme, or read in a newspaper article. You are likely to be surprised at the very large number of references that you manage to find.

Articles in newspapers and professional journals are excellent sources of information. When reporting on a recently completed study they tend to give information at the end of the article as to where you can obtain a copy of the study or report. Professional journals are also where you will find advertisements for conferences and training opportunities. You may also find information about such opportunities circulated to your workplace. There is often a cost involved in attending these events, so it may not be possible within the training budget of your workplace. However, if the information about conferences or seminars which are of interest is passed on, it may be within the budget to send one person who could then pass on the information gathered (e.g. papers and handouts) to others in the workplace. The development of information technology, and in particular the **Internet**, has provided a vast resource of information, views and research. There are clearly some limitations to using the Internet; for example, many people are reluctant to use it because they are not sufficiently confident in

The Internet can be a useful source of information to help you keep up to date with developments in your field of work

using computers and modern technology. However, the use of computers in the health and care sector is becoming increasingly widespread and important in many ways. Computers are being used for more than just accessing information, though this is their major use.

If you have access to a computer and are able to use it then accessing the Internet is essentially a simple process. However, you will need to be wary of the information that you obtain on the Internet. Unless it is from accredited sources, such as a government department, a reputable university or college, or an established research establishment, then you should make every effort to check out the validity of what you are reading. The concept of the **World Wide Web**, which provides free and unregulated access to vast amounts of information, is a wonderful and enlightened idea which forms an essential part of modern society. However, there is a downside to such an unregulated environment. Anyone can publish information on the Internet and there is no requirement for it to be checked or approved through any central agency. This means that people can communicate their own views and opinions, which may not be based on fact. These views and opinions from a wide range of people are valuable and interesting in themselves, but be careful that you do not assume anything to be factually correct unless it is from a very reliable source. Taken with that 'health warning', the Internet can prove to be one of the speediest and most useful tools in maintaining high levels of up-to-date information.

Never overlook the obvious. Some of the most useful sources of information, and easily accessible, are your own workplace supervisor and colleagues. They may have many years of experience and knowledge which they will be happy to share with you. They may also be updating their own practice and ideas and may have information that they would be willing to share.

Sources of information for keeping up to date

How to understand and interpret the latest research

Reading and hearing about new studies and pieces of research is all very well, but you must understand what it is that you are reading and it is important that you understand how new theories are developed and how research is carried out. There are specific methods of carrying out research to make it *reliable* and *valid*. So you need to be able to satisfy yourself that reports which you read are based on reliable and valid research. When research is reliable this means that if somebody else were to carry out the same piece of research, the results would be exactly the same. To be valid means that the conclusions that have been drawn from the research are consistent with the results, consistent with the way the research was carried out and consistent with the way the research information has been interpreted. You will need to understand certain key processes involved in research in order to get the most out of information you find.

The research process

You will need to understand some of the basic terms used when discussing research in any field.

Primary sources/data – refers to information or data which is obtained directly as a result of carrying out research. The information is original, it has not been taken from books or previously published work, but has been obtained directly through any of the research methods for obtaining information.

Secondary sources/data – refers to information which is obtained from books, previously published research and reports, CD-ROMs, the Internet, etc. Essentially this refers to any information which is obtained from work carried out by others. For example, if you were asked to write an assignment for your NVQ you are most likely to find the information from secondary sources, for example from textbooks or from the Internet, rather than carrying out a research project yourself in order to establish the information that you need.

The information obtained from research is often referred to as **data**. Data is information in the form of numbers or words. There are two broad areas of approach to research and they determine both the way in which the research is carried out and the type of results that are obtained. The first is referred to as **quantitative method**, the second is **qualitative method**.

Quantitative approach

This approach or method is based upon scientific research and has developed from the way in which scientists carry out laboratory experiments. It produces and is based on information which is statistical and numerical. It provides hard facts and figures and uses statistics and numbers to draw conclusions and to make an analysis. There are many researchers in the field of health and care who use quantitative approaches and produce quantitative data. They may carry out 'experiments' in order to provide their research data. These are based on those carried out in the scientific world, although obviously not under the same conditions as in a laboratory, but many of the rules of scientific investigation are followed during the process. In general, if you are reading research which provides you with statistics and numerical information and is based purely on facts, then you are likely to be reading the results of research which has used one of the quantitative approaches. The easiest way to find examples of quantitative research is to look at government publications with statistics. These statistics may be in relation to the National Health Service, where they are compiled to determine, for example, the numbers of patients on waiting lists, the numbers of a particular operation carried out, or the numbers of residents in nursing homes throughout the country.

Qualitative approach

The qualitative approach, as used in health and care, is more likely to investigate, for example, the feelings of people who are on the waiting list for treatment, or to explore people's attitudes towards residential care, or examine the relationships between those in residential care and those who care for them. Generally, qualitative research produces qualitative data in the form of words rather than figures, as in quantitative data, and will consist of descriptions and information about peoples lives, experiences and attitudes. Within these two approaches there are many other more detailed methods which dictate how particular research is carried out, but for the purposes of understanding the research which you read it is sufficient to be able to identify the kind of data that you are reading and to be able to recognise whether it is quantitative or qualitative data.

Presenting data

The data resulting from any research can be presented in a variety of ways. Most researches will use tables and graphs to present statistical information, as in these examples.

January	21
February	45
March	69
April	112
May	136
June	151

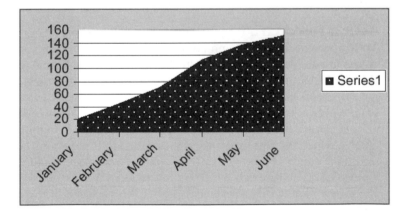

It is also possible to show the data in terms of charts and pie diagrams, as in these cases.

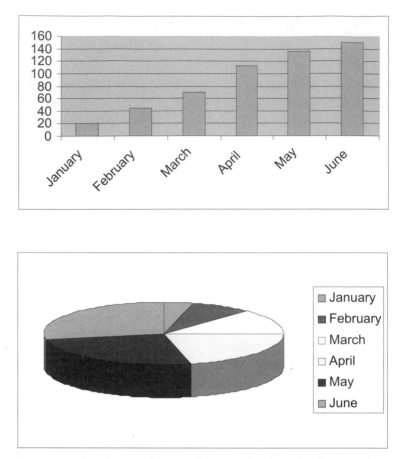

Demonstrating data in this visual way makes it easier for people to understand the implications of the data which is being presented. However, these types of presentation must be accompanied by a detailed written report which explains the way in which the research was carried out and the results and the implications of those results. Many large research projects can fill an entire book with their results.

Action research

Action research is the commonest form of research which you are likely to come across in your day-to-day work. Although the scientific formal research which we have looked at is carried out on a wide national scale to look at trends and developments in health and care, action research is often carried out on a smaller scale within organisations or even within workplaces. It is very different in that the people involved in the research are also those who are committed to the action or change which the research is usually designed to bring about. For example, a plan to introduce a new key worker system within a workplace could well be as the result of a piece of action research which set out to identify how many different carers one client may have during a seven-day period. As the result of this exercise and piece of research with its commitment to change and improvement, the work setting has not only introduced a more effective system, it has also added to the overall body of knowledge, in both the workplace and the whole sector, about the quality of care which is currently provided and the extent to which that falls short of the ideal. Action research by its nature provides both an addition to the overall knowledge of the sector and the solution to an immediate problem.

Active knowledge

By using any of the methods for finding up-to-date information, i.e. newspapers, journals, reports, television, Internet, textbooks or your own workplace, find two pieces of research carried out within the last two years. One should be quantitative, one qualitative and one should be action research. Read the results of the pieces of research and make a note of the differences in the type of information which is provided by the different approaches.

How to ensure that your practice is current and up to date

There is little point in reading, watching and attending training days if your work practice is not updated and improved as a result. With the enormous pressures on everybody's time in the health and care services it is often difficult to find the time to keep up to date and to change practices which you are used to. Any form of change takes time and is always a little uncomfortable or unusual to begin with. So when we are under pressure because of the amount of work we have to do it is only normal that we tend to stick with practices, methods and ways of working which are comfortable, familiar and we can do swiftly and efficiently.

Changes in work practice may need time to become effective

You will need to make a very conscious effort to incorporate new learning into your practice. Your personal development plan should include time for updating your practice and knowledge, and should include time for incorporating that into your practice. You could try the following ways to ensure that you are using new knowledge that you have gained.

How to make sure you use new knowledge

1   Plan out how you will adapt your practice on a day-to-day basis, adding one new aspect each day. Do this until you have covered all the aspects of the new information you have learned.

2   Discuss with your supervisor and colleagues what you have learned and how you intend to change your practice and ask for feedback on how it is going.

3   Write a checklist for yourself and check it at the end of each day.

4   Give yourself a set period of time, for example one month, to alter or improve your practice and review it at the end of that time.

New knowledge is not only about the newest and most exciting emerging theories. It is also often about mundane and day-to-day aspects of your practice and knowledge which are just as important and can make just as much difference to the quality of care which you provide for your clients.

Case study 1

J is a health care support worker in a large hospital. She works on a busy medical ward and was very aware of the fact that she lacked assertiveness in the way she dealt with both her colleagues and with many of her clients. J was always the one who would agree to do additional duties and to fulfil requests from colleagues to run errands and to cover additional tasks which often they should have been doing themselves. She knew that she ought to be able to say no, but always felt that she never could and then became angry and resentful because she felt she was doing far more work than many others on her team.

Her supervisor raised the issue during an appraisal and supervision session and suggested that J should consider attending assertiveness training. Although initially reluctant J decided to take the opportunity when she saw a local class advertised. After six weeks of attending classes and working with the supportive group that she met there, J found that she was able to deal far more effectively with unfair and unreasonable requests from her colleagues and to deal in a firm but pleasant assertive way with her clients. Overall, J's practice improved significantly because of her own increase in confidence and her ability to deal with her colleagues and clients more effectively.

1   Have you ever said 'yes' to extra work or additional responsibility when you wanted to say 'no'?

2   How did this make you feel?

3   What could you have done about it?

Case study 2

P was a support worker in a young person's unit run by the local authority youth justice team. He was providing support for young people who were involved with the criminal justice system but were still living in the community, who occasionally needed time out in the unit and attended regularly as part of the requirements of the court. P was aware that his knowledge of the legislation relating to young people and to the criminal justice system was not as comprehensive as it ought to be. He often felt unsure when some of his colleagues were quoting Acts of

Parliament by short-hand names or by simply quoting dates, and he felt uncertain in answering some of the queries that the young people put to him.

P raised this issue with his line manager who immediately identified that there were training days coming up shortly within the local authority that P could attend and have a chance to learn about the relevant legislation. Following his training days P felt far more confident, as not only had he learnt a great deal during the course itself, he had also been given a lot of handouts and several useful textbooks had been identified. He made sure that he spent some of his own time, in addition to the training days, to read and re-read the handouts and the textbooks until he felt that his knowledge was sufficient to enable him to practice in a way which would be of the greatest benefit to the young people using the centre.

1 Are you confident about your knowledge of your own work setting?
2 If not, what steps are you taking to improve it?

Case study 3

T is a support worker working with a young woman in the community who suffers from multiple sclerosis. T's work enables the young woman to live an independent life. T spent many years working in a residential setting and is very experienced in dealing with people with disabilities. However, her knowledge of multiple sclerosis was limited. One day she noticed an advertisement for a conference which was describing the outcome of the latest research into multiple sclerosis, so she arranged to get cover for a day while she went to the conference and found out a great deal more about potential new treatments and ways in which symptoms of MS could potentially be eased. She was able to discuss this in detail with the young woman that she worked with and with her agreement she discussed it with her doctor. As a result some new plans for treatment were developed and tried out.

What difference is T's new knowledge likely to make to a) her client b) herself?

Case study 4

W worked as a home carer in part of a large team. She was very experienced and an extremely good carer, and was keen to apply for promotion when a team manager's job became available. However, when she received the job description and person specification for the job role it was obvious that the person appointed would be undertaking a considerable amount of administration and would have to have a working knowledge of computers and a range of standard software packages. W did not even know how to turn a computer on! She realised that if she was ever to achieve promotion she would need to understand information technology and overcome her fear of computers and all things technological. W signed up for an 'Introduction to Computers' evening class at her local college and spent a year developing new skills. At the end of the year she was able to achieve her Key Skills in information technology and successfully applied for promotion to team manager. W now uses computer technology as a part of her job every day and can't imagine a time when she did not know how to use it.

1 What other ways could W have responded to the job description information?
2 What are the benefits of her responding as she did?
3 Who gains from W's new skills?

Active knowledge

Think about an occasion when you have been able to reflect on an area of your own practice or knowledge which needed improvement and what necessary steps you took to achieve the improvement. Record what you actually did and the steps you took and also how you incorporated the new knowledge into your practice. Once you have identified this and recorded it in detail you should keep this and include it in your NVQ portfolio as part of the evidence that you will need to produce to achieve this unit.

Unit test

1 What are the factors that can influence the way people work in health and care?

2 What is the key difference between working in health and care and working in most other jobs?

3 Identify the differences in social and emotional aspects of development between a pre-school child, an adolescent and an older adult?

4 What are the most effective ways of reflecting on your own practice?

5 Describe the differences between formal and informal support networks.

6 How would you ensure that you gain the maximum benefit from a supervision session?

7 Name five sources of information where you could find new learning to improve your practice?

8 What are the basic forms of research?

9 What is the information called which is obtained by research?

10 How would you ensure that you have incorporated new learning into your practice?

Contribute to the protection of individuals from abuse

In this unit you will look at some of the most difficult issues that you will face as a care professional. You need to know how society handles abuse, how to recognise it, and what to do about it. It is a tragic fact that almost all disclosures of abuse are true – and you will have to learn to *think the unthinkable*. If you can learn always to consider the possibility of abuse, always to be aware of potentially abusive situations and always to *listen* and *believe* when you are told of abuse, then you will provide the best possible protection for people in your care.

This unit refers to 'children and young people', and deals with children between 8 and 18 years. Work with very young children (under 8 years) is not covered by the NVQ Care qualification. If this is the age group you work with, you should look at an NVQ in Early Years Care and Education.

Element Z1.1 — Contribute to minimising the level of abuse in care environments

WHAT YOU NEED TO LEARN

- What is meant by abuse in care environments.
- How the law affects what you do.
- How you can contribute to the minimising of abuse.
- How to report and to record information.

What is meant by abuse in care environments

What is a care environment?

The obvious answers are residential care and hospitals, but people are cared for in many other situations: children are cared for by their parents, by a childminder, in school, in a youth group or in foster homes. Vulnerable adults can be cared for in supported living schemes, at home with informal carers or professional carers, with relatives and in day care, as well as in residential or nursing homes.

What is abuse?

Abuse is more than being hit or sexually assaulted. Of course, they are the most violent and obvious forms of abuse, and they may be the ones which are easier to identify. But there are other ways in which people can be abused, as the diagram on the next page shows.

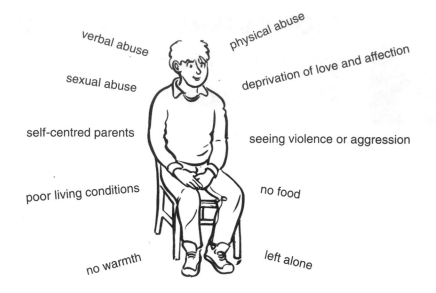

verbal abuse

physical abuse

sexual abuse

deprivation of love and affection

self-centred parents

seeing violence or aggression

poor living conditions

no food

no warmth

left alone

Ways in which children can be abused

Children can be abused:

- emotionally, by being deprived of love or physical contact
- verbally, by being constantly shouted at
- by having to witness violent or aggressive scenes at home
- by being parented by people who are unable to put their child's needs before their own
- by being physically neglected, by living in filthy conditions
- by being deprived of food, warmth or shelter
- by being left without adult protection, to fend for themselves
- at the hands of other children, by being bullied at school or in the local neighbourhood.

Remember

Child abuse can be:

- physical
- sexual
- emotional
- neglect.

Did you know?

About 10,000 calls are made each day to Childline, the helpline for children who are being abused. Of those, only around 3,000 actually get through because the lines are so busy.

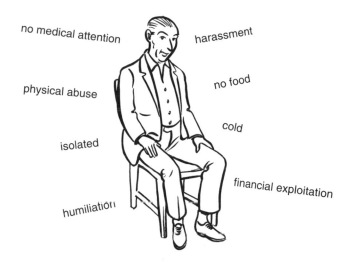

no medical attention

harassment

physical abuse

no food

cold

isolated

financial exploitation

humiliation

Ways in which older people can be abused

Abuse of older people is described in the government guidelines 'No Longer Afraid' as:

> 'physical, sexual, psychological or financial: intentional or unintentional or the result of neglect; causing harm or distress to the older person either temporarily or over a period of time.'

This definition could be usefully applied to abuse of all adults, not just older people. As with children, abuse of older people can take many forms:

- physical – hitting, slapping, pushing, restraining
- psychological – blaming, swearing, humiliating or harassing
- neglect, where people are deprived of food, warmth, comfort or medical attention
- forcible isolation, where a carer may deny someone access to the outside world
- sexual
- financial – theft of money or property, or exploitation.

Abuse can also be self-inflicted, for example through the use of substances or self-harming behaviours. Individuals in such a position may also be regarded as at risk.

Remember
Adult abuse can be:
- physical
- sexual
- psychological
- financial
- neglect
- isolation.

Active knowledge

How many types of abuse does your workplace have guidelines to deal with? Look at the policy and procedures for dealing with abuse. See how many types of abuse are listed and what the procedures are. Ask your supervisor if you cannot find any information.

Who can abuse?

Abuse can take place at home or in a formal care setting. At home, it could be an informal carer who is the abuser, although it could be a neighbour or regular visitor. It can also be a professional care worker who is carrying out the abuse. This situation can mean that abuse goes undetected for some time because of the unsupervised nature of a carer's visits to someone's home.

In a formal care setting, abuse may be more likely to be noticed, although some of the more subtle forms of abuse, such as humiliation, can sometimes be so commonplace that it is not recognised as abusive behaviour.

Abuse is not only carried out by individuals; groups, or even organisations can also create abusive situations. It has been known that groups of carers in residential settings can abuse individuals in their care. Often people will act in a different way in a group than they would alone. Think about teenage 'gangs' which exist because people are prepared to do things jointly which they would not think to do if they were by themselves.

Abuse in a care setting may not just be at the hands of members of staff. There is also abuse which comes about because of the way in which an establishment is run, where the basis for planning the systems, rules and regulations is not the welfare, rights and dignity of the residents or patients, but the convenience of the staff and management. This is the sort of situation where people can be told when to get up and go to bed, given communal clothing, only allowed medical attention at set times and not allowed to go out.

No dear, you can't go out now, you nearly slipped last time. You can't go on your own and I don't have anyone to send with you – can't you see how busy we all are?

Remember

Abusers can be:
- individuals
- groups
- organisations.

Case study

Meadow View was a 40-bed EMI (Elderly Mentally Infirm) unit. The residents were all suffering various forms of dementia – some wandered, many were aggressive and several residents were violent. Over 75 per cent of the residents were incontinent. There was no formal continence management programme, but staff would toilet residents at regular intervals throughout the day. Following a regular visit from the Registered Homes Inspector, the staff were surprised to find that they were considered to have been abusive towards their residents. The inspector reported that she had heard staff talking loudly to residents in the lounge with such phrases as 'Come on Mary, time for a tinkle or we'll have another puddle like we did this morning' and 'Oh Charlie, my little pooh machine – you've done it again!'

1 Do you agree that the behaviour of the staff amounted to abuse?
2 If you do, why was it abusive?
3 If you do not think that this was abusive, why not?
4 How could Mary and Charles have been treated differently?

Up to this point, consideration has been given to abuse by carers, whether parents, informal or professional. But, do not forget that in residential or hospital settings, abuse can occur between residents or patients, and it can also happen between visitors and residents or patients. People can also abuse themselves.

As a carer whose role is to reduce the risk of abuse wherever you can, you need to be very much aware of abuse between individuals you are caring for and to take action whenever you suspect that this is happening. Bear in mind the types of behaviour which are abusive and be alert to any signs of those behaviours.

Visitors can also behave abusively, and if the care team considers that they pose a risk to the health or well-being of an individual, then a plan will be developed for how the visitor should be dealt with. You must ensure that you follow the plan of care, and always check with your supervisor if you are unsure about access.

Did you know?

Some of the most difficult places to make secure are hospitals and residential homes. The large number of visitors makes it almost impossible to have a secure system of identifying everyone on the premises at any given time.

The one abuser it is very hard to protect someone from is him or herself. Individuals who self-harm will be identified in their plan of care, and responses to their behaviour will be recorded. You must ensure that you follow the agreed plan for provision of care for someone who has a history of self-harm. It is usual that an individual who is at risk of harming him or herself will be closely supported and you may need to contribute towards activities or therapies which have been planned for the individual.

How the law affects what you do

Much of the work in caring is governed by legislation, but the only group where legislation specifically provides for protection from abuse is children. Older people, people with learning difficulties, disabilities or mental health problems have service provision, restrictions, rights and all sorts of other requirements laid down in law, but no overall legal framework to provide protection from abuse. The laws which cover your work in the field of care are summarised in the table below.

There are, however a number of sets of guidelines, policies and procedures in respect of abuse for client groups other than children, and you will need to ensure that you familiarise yourself with policies for your area of work and particularly with those policies which apply in your own workplace.

Active knowledge

Ask your supervisor about the procedures in your workplace for dealing with abuse. There should be a written policy and guidelines to be followed if abuse is suspected. Ask if there are any laws or guidelines which are related to the way you work. Check with experienced colleagues about situations they have dealt with and ask them to tell you about what happened.

A summary of the laws you work with

Client group	Laws which govern their care	Protection from abuse?
Children	Children Act 1989	Yes
People with mental health problems	Mental Health Act 1983	No
Adults with learning difficulties	Mental Health Act 1983	No
Adults with disabilities	Chronically Sick and Disabled Persons Act 1986 Disability Discrimination Act 1995	No
Older people	National Assistance Act 1948 NHS and Community Care Act 1990	No

Government guidelines

The most influential set of government guidelines which lay down practices for inter-agency co-operation is called 'Working Together'. It was published along with the Children Act 1989, and forms the basis for present child protection work. This guideline ensures that information is shared between agencies and professionals, and that decisions in respect of children are not taken by just one person.

There is a similar set of guidelines published by the government about older people, called 'No Longer Afraid'. These guidelines state that older people have specific rights, which include being treated with respect, and being able to live in their home and community without fear of physical or emotional violence or harassment.

What does the law say about protecting children?

The Children Act 1989 requires that local authority social services departments provide protection from abuse for children in their area. This Act gives powers to social services departments to take legal steps to ensure the safety of children.

What happens in an emergency?

In an emergency, a social worker, or an NSPCC officer, can apply to a magistrate for an order to look after a child. This is an Emergency Protection Order (known as an EPO). The police are also able to take immediate steps to protect children in an emergency situation. (This is a Police Protection Order, or PPO.) These orders require evidence which shows that there is reasonable cause to believe that a child may suffer 'significant harm'. They are short-term orders, usually for 3–7 days, and are followed by a court hearing where more detailed evidence is produced and the parents are represented.

Not all investigations into abuse are emergencies, and not all involve legal proceedings. Some abusive, or potentially abusive, situations are dealt with by working with the family, usually by agreeing a 'contract' between social services and the family.

The three agencies able to protect children

What does the law say about protecting older people?

The Acts of Parliament which are mainly concerned with provisions for older people are the National Assistance Act 1948 and the NHS and Community Care Act 1990. They do not specifically give social services departments a 'duty to protect' but, of course, older people are protected by the law. If an older person is abused and that abuse is considered to be a criminal offence, then the police will act. It is sometimes thought that because someone is confused, that a prosecution will not be brought – this is not so. One of the rights specified in 'No Longer Afraid' is the right to have an advocate or representative to act on behalf of the older person, if necessary.

Some older people suffer abuse in residential or hospital settings. These settings are ultimately controlled by legislation. Hospitals have complaints procedures and arrangements for allowing 'whistleblowers' who have concerns about abuse to come forward. Residential homes and nursing homes have to be registered either with social services or with the health service. Both run registration and inspection units which will investigate allegations of abuse and can ultimately close an unsatisfactory residential home or nursing home.

What happens in an emergency?

Many social services departments now have procedures in place similar to those for protecting children. There will be an investigation of the alleged or suspected abuse, followed by a case conference where information will be shared between all the professionals concerned and a plan of action worked out. The older person concerned and/or a friend or advocate will also be invited to take part in the conference if he or she wishes.

What does the law say about adults with mental health problems or learning difficulties?

The Mental Health Act 1983 forms the framework for service provision for people with mental health problems and people with learning difficulties. There are provisions within this legislation for social services departments to assume responsibility for people who are so 'mentally impaired' that they are not able to be responsible for their own affairs. This is called guardianship. However, like all other adults, there is no overall duty to protect people from abuse.

What does the law say about adults with disabilities?

Whilst the Chronically Sick and Disabled Persons Act and the Disability Discrimination Act provide disabled people with rights, services and protection from discrimination, they do not provide any means of comprehensive protection from abuse.

As with all vulnerable groups, there is a long and tragic history to the physical and emotional abuse suffered by people with disabilities and learning difficulties. The public humiliation and abuse of those with mental health problems is still visible today, so it is hardly surprising that abuse on an individual level is still all too commonplace.

These vulnerable groups have not benefited from the high level of public awareness of child abuse, or the growing recognition of abuse of older people. Few workplaces will have specific procedures in place, although exactly the same guidelines should apply.

What if a professional carer abuses?

There are special procedures in place for investigating abuse which is inflicted by care workers or foster carers. It is investigated by an outside agency and immediate steps are taken to remove the suspected abuser (often called the 'perpetrator') from contact until the investigation has been completed.

These issues are well publicised at the moment as many cases of systematic and long-term abuse by care workers are coming to light. Later, this unit will make sure that you know how to deal with a situation where you know, or suspect abuse in your workplace.

How you can contribute to the minimising of abuse

One of the key contributions you can make towards limiting abuse is to be aware of where abuse may be happening. It is not easy to accept that abuse is going on, and it is often simpler to find other explanations.

Be prepared to *think the unthinkable.* If you know about the circumstances in which abuse has been found to occur most frequently, then you are better able to respond quickly if you suspect a problem.

It is not possible accurately to predict situations where abuse will take place – a great deal of misery could be saved if it were. It is possible, though, to identify some factors which seem to make it more likely that abuse could occur. This does not mean that abuse will definitely happen – neither should you assume that all people in these circumstances are abusers – but it does mean that you should be aware of the possibility when you are dealing with these situations.

Situations when child abuse can happen

Child abuse can happen in situations where:

- parents are unable to put a child's needs first
- parents or carers need to show dominance over others
- parents or carers have been poorly parented themselves
- parents or carers were abused themselves as children
- families have financial problems (this does not just mean families on low incomes)
- families have a history of poor relationships or of use of violence.

Situations when adults may be abused at home

Adults may be abused at home in situations where:

- carers have had to change their lifestyles unwillingly
- the dependent person has communication problems, has had a personality or behaviour change, such as dementia, rejects help or is aggressive
- there is no support from family or professional carers
- carers are becoming dependent on drugs or alcohol
- carers have no privacy
- the dependent person is difficult and inconsiderate.

Active knowledge

Think about the clients you deal with. Make a list of how many of them fit into the circumstances outlined. Now resolve to keep a particular eye on those clients and watch for any signs that abuse may be happening. Be prepared to *think the unthinkable.*

Situations when abuse can happen in a care setting

Abuse can happen in a care setting when:

- staff are poorly trained or untrained
- there is little or no management supervision or support
- staff work in isolation
- there are inadequate numbers of staff to cope with the workload

- there are inadequate security arrangements
- there is no key worker system and good relationships are not formed between staff and residents.

Active knowledge

Look at your workplace. Do any of the above points apply? If any of these are the case in your workplace, you need to be aware that people can be put under so much stress that they behave abusively. Remember that abuse is not just about physical cruelty. If none of these things happen in your workplace, then try to imagine what work would be like if they did. Sit down with a colleague, if you can, and discuss what you think the effects of any two of the items in the list would be. If you cannot do this with a colleague, you can do it on your own by making a list.

If you want to be effective in helping to stop abuse you will need to:

- believe that abuse happens
- recognise abusive behaviour
- be aware of when abuse can happen
- understand who abusers can be
- know the policies and procedures for handling abuse
- follow the individual's plan of care
- recognise likely abusive situations
- report any concerns or suspicions.

Your most important contribution will be to be *alert*. For example, an individual's plan of care or your organisational policy should specify ways in which the individual's whereabouts are constantly monitored – and if you are alert to where a vulnerable person is, and who he or she is with, you can do much to help avoid abusive situations.

There are many factors involved in building protection against abuse

Remember

Either in a care setting or in an individual's own home, it is important to establish that callers are genuinely entitled to see the individual. Any doubts about rights of access should be cleared up immediately.

How to report and record information

Information about abuse you suspect, or situations you are working with which are 'high risk', must be recorded after being reported to your supervisor. Your supervisor will be responsible for passing on the information, if necessary.

Sometimes your information may need to be included in a client's plan of care or personal records, particularly if you have noticed a change in the way he or she is cared for, or if his/her behaviour could be an 'early warning' that the care team need to be especially observant. Your workplace may have a special report form for recording 'causes for concern'. If not, you should write your report, making sure you include the following:

- what happened to make you concerned
- who you are concerned about
- whether this links to anything you have noticed previously
- what needs to happen next.

> P. was visited by her son this afternoon. She was very quiet over tea, did not join in conversation or joke with anyone. Just said she was tired when asked what was wrong. Went to her room without going into lounge for the 'seconds evening'. Said she thought the clothes were too expensive and she couldn't afford them. Unusual for her. Similar to incident about a month ago when she said she couldn't afford the hairdresser - again after a visit from her son.
>
> Needs to be watched. Is he getting money from her? For discussion at planning meeting.

An example of a written report on possible abuse

Discuss your report and your concerns with your supervisor and colleagues.

You must report anything unusual that you notice, even if you think it is too small to be important. It is the small details which make the whole picture. Sometimes, your observations may add to other small things noticed by members of the team, and a picture may start to emerge. Teamwork and good communication are vitally important.

Case study

One family support worker had a nickname – he was known as 'Cecil', short for Cecil B. de Mille the film director. Cecil was known for regularly phoning the schools, social workers and GP surgeries of the families he visited every time there was any event, incident or change with the families he visited. Cecil always started his conversation with 'I'm just keeping you in the picture' hence the nickname! However, with the G family, it was thanks to being 'kept in the picture' by Cecil that the social worker was made aware of the mother's new boyfriend. When his details were checked out, it was discovered that he had lived with another family where the children were on the Child Protection register. When this information was put together with the teacher noticing that one of the children had become much quieter recently, alarm bells began to ring and the children were carefully monitored, both at home and school.

1 What was Cecil doing which was important?
2 What might have happened if the information had not been passed on?
3 Why was Cecil in a good position to keep everyone informed?

Keeping professional carers informed of possible abuse is importaant

Did you know?

If you were to take one piece from a jigsaw puzzle, it would be very difficult to guess from it what the complete picture is – if not impossible. It would be easy to guess wrongly! You would need quite a few pieces before you could begin to draw a conclusion. The same applies to identifying the true picture in cases of abuse.

Remember
- Care environments are not just in residential homes and hospitals.
- Abuse is about far more than physical or sexual assault.
- Vulnerable adults and children can be abused by carers, other patients or service users or by organisations.
- Children are the only client group specifically protected by the law.
- You need to be alert to the situations where abuse can occur.
- You must share information.
- You must record information clearly and accurately.

lement Z1.2   Minimise the effects of abusive behaviour

WHAT YOU NEED TO LEARN
- Indications of abuse.
- How to respond to disclosure of abuse.
- How to deal with abusive behaviour.
- The effects of abuse on all those concerned.

Indications of abuse
This is not a comprehensive list of all the indicators of abuse. It is not possible to be exhaustive, neither does the existence of one of these signs mean that abuse has definitely occurred. Each is an *indicator,* which needs to be used alongside your other skills, such as observation and listening. It is a further piece of evidence – often the conclusive one – in building a complete picture.

Physical signs of abuse in children
- Bruising, or injuries which the child cannot explain.
- Bruises in the shape of objects – belt buckles, soles of shoes, etc.
- Handmarks.
- Bruises in lines.
- Injuries to the frenulum (the piece of skin below the tongue), or between the upper and lower lips and the gums.
- Black eyes.
- Bruising to ears.
- Burns, particularly small round burns which could have come from a cigarette.
- Burns or scalds to buttocks and backs of legs.
- Burns in lines, like the elements of an electric fire.

Emotional signs of abuse in children
- Sudden change in behaviour, becoming quiet and withdrawn.
- Change to overtly sexual behaviour, or an obsession with sexual comments.
- Problems sleeping or onset of nightmares.
- A sudden unwillingness to change clothes or participate in sports.

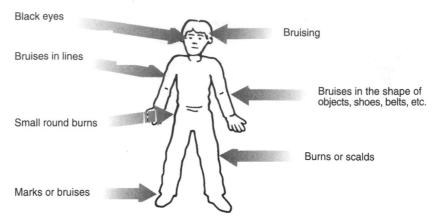

Physical signs of abuse in children

- Complaints of soreness or infections in the genital/anal area.
- Frequent complaints of abdominal pain.
- Deterioration of personal hygiene.
- Finding excuses not to go home.
- Appearing tense or frightened with a particular adult.

Physical signs of abuse in adults

- Series of unexplained falls or injuries.
- 'Pepperpot' bruising – a covering of small bruises, usually on the chest and caused by poking with a finger or tightening of clothing.
- Finger marks.
- Bruising in unusual areas, such as inside arms or thighs.
- Burns in unusual areas.
- Marks to wrists, arms or legs which could show use of physical restraint.
- Ulcers or bed sores, rashes caused by wet clothing.
- Unusual sexual behaviour.
- Recurrent genital infections.
- Blood or marks on underclothes.

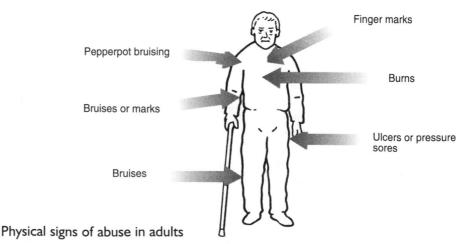

Physical signs of abuse in adults

Emotional signs of abuse in adults

- Changes in behaviour, becoming withdrawn or anxious.

- Unusually expressing feelings of hopelessness and depression.
- Change in eating pattern, loss/gain in weight.
- Sleep problems.
- Fear of making decisions or choices.
- Difficulty for care professionals to gain access to individual – be concerned if there is always a reason why the person cannot be seen.
- Sudden apparent change in financial circumstances.
- Disappearance of bank account records or pension books.
- Unusual level of interest by carer or others in finances and assets.
- Financial arrangement which the individual has not understood or has not willingly agreed to.
- Excessive requests for repeat prescriptions.
- Insistence by carer on being present at interviews.
- References to the dependent person in a derogatory way by the carer.

Active knowledge

Think of three clients you have worked with in the past month. Look carefully at the list of indications of abuse, and write down any which could apply to the clients you have selected. If there are none, that is fine. If you have noticed any signs, the first thing to do is to report this to your supervisor. Then go back to the previous element and look at the list of *circumstances* in which abuse is likely to occur. Do any of those fit? If so, you should also discuss this with your supervisor and develop a plan to monitor the situation.

How to respond to disclosure of abuse

If abuse is disclosed to you by someone you are caring for, you should deal with it in the same way whether it is a child or adult. First you must *listen* and *believe*. Make sure that you communicate, both by words and by body language, that you believe the person.

Did you know?

Being abused is terrible, and not being believed makes that abuse ten times worse. Don't be the second abuser – always *listen* and *believe*.

Do not ask any questions which could possibly be leading questions, for example 'and then did he hit you again?' The only questions you should ask should be to prompt the individual to continue his or her disclosure, such as 'and then what happened?'

You may well be asked to promise not to tell anyone – *never make that promise,* as it is not one you can keep. If you are asked 'If I tell you something, will you promise not to tell anyone?' you must always make it clear that you cannot make that promise. You must say something like, 'I can't say that until I know what you are going to tell me'.

Following disclosure, you must make it clear that you have to tell others about what you have been told, but you should also make it clear that the information is confidential within the group of people who need to know in order to protect. The answer to 'I don't want people to know' is to say something like 'The only people who will know are those who will make you safe'.

Remember

- People who disclose abuse do so because they want to be protected.
- They tell you because they want the abuse to stop.
- You are the first step to that protection.
- You have a responsibility to ensure that the information is passed on.

How to deal with abusive behaviour

Most of the time, your role in dealing with abuse will be the vital one of being aware of the possibility of abuse, reporting and recording any concerns you have, or reporting any disclosure made to you.

However, there may be occasions when you have to intervene in order to prevent an abusive situation developing. The abuse can be physical, verbal or behavioural. This is most likely to happen in a hospital, residential or day-care setting between patients or service users. If you work in the community, you could be in the situation of having to deal with abusive behaviour from a carer. If you do have to act directly to prevent abuse, you need to take the following steps:

- Always prevent a situation if you can. If you know, for example, that two people regularly disagree violently about everything from politics to whether or not it is raining, try to arrange that they are involved in separate activities and, if possible, have seats in separate lounges! Alternatively, you may decide to deal with the situation by talking to them both, and offering to help them to try to resolve their disagreements.
- Deal with abusive behaviour in the same way as aggression – be calm and be clear. Do not get drawn into an argument and do not become aggressive, but make it very clear that abusive behaviour will not be tolerated.
- You should only intervene directly if there is an immediate risk. You will need to use your communication skills to ensure that you handle the situation in a way that does not make things worse and will ensure that you protect the person at risk.
- If there is not an immediate risk, you should report the incident and get assistance as soon as possible.
- If you do have to intervene in an abusive situation, you will need to behave assertively. Do not shout, panic or get into an argument. State firmly and clearly what you want to happen – 'Mary, stop hitting Enid now!' You can deal with the consequences a little later, but the key action is to stop the abuse – 'Lee, stop calling Mike those names and move away from him now!' There must be no mistake about what has to happen. This is not the time to discuss it, this is the time to stop it – the discussion comes later.
- If you have witnessed, or intervened in, an act of abuse which may constitute a criminal offence, you must *not* remove any possible evidence until the police have examined the scene.

Rules for dealing with abusive behaviour
1. *Avoid it if possible.*
2. *Try to get people talking.*
3. *Keep calm. Be clear.*
4. *Be assertive, never aggressive.*

Active knowledge

Think of a situation where you have had to act to stop abuse or likely abuse. Make a note of how you handled it. Could you have dealt with it in a better way? What else could you have done? Would it have turned out differently? If you have never had to act in such a situation, ask an experienced colleague to tell you about an incident he or she has had to deal with.

Then answer the same questions, based on what your colleague has told you. Remember – your colleague may not want to hear the answers you come up with!

Once the immediate risk has been averted, you must then report the incident to your manager, and the correct procedures for dealing with abuse must be followed. You are not in a position to take a decision about what is and what is not serious enough to be followed up. That is a decision which will be taken after discussion between the agencies involved.

Where there are injuries, or the possibility of physical evidence, as in sexual abuse, then a medical examination must be carried out. If an adult has been abused, he or she must consent to an examination before one can be carried out. In the case of a child, the parents must consent, unless they are the suspected abusers.

Recording an incident

It is also important that you write a report of the incident as soon as possible. You may think that you will never forget what you saw or heard, but details do become blurred with time and repetition. Your workplace may have a special form or you may have to write a report. If there is a reason why writing a report is not possible, then you should record your evidence on audio tape. It is not acceptable practice to pass on the information verbally – there must be a record which can be referred to. Your evidence may be needed by the social workers who will investigate the situation. It may be useful for a doctor who will conduct an examination, or it may be needed for the case conference or for court proceedings.

Active knowledge

Think about the children's game of Chinese Whispers. The players sit in a circle and a message is whispered from one person to the next around the circle. The last player speaks the message aloud. It has usually changed quite a lot as it has been passed around the circle!

So it is easy to see how verbal information can become distorted, or messages lose their emphasis, as they are retold. Always make sure you record information as soon as you can.

When risk situations occur in the community, you may be in a position to intervene directly or to report to your supervisor and offer suggestions about ways to reduce risks.

No one can guarantee to prevent abuse from happening – human beings have always abused each other in one form or another. However, using the information you have about possible abusive situations, you are now able to work towards preventing abuse by recognising where it can happen.

Try to ensure that people in potentially abusive situations are offered as much support as possible. A carer, whether of a child or an adult, is less likely to resort to abuse if he or she feels supported, acknowledged and appreciated. Showing caring and understanding of a person's situation can often defuse potential explosions. A care worker could express this by saying, 'It must be so difficult caring for your mother. The demands she makes are so difficult. I think you are doing a wonderful job.' Such comments can often help a carer to feel that he or she does have someone who understands and has some interest in supporting him or her. So many times the focus is on the individual in need of care and the carer is ignored.

Did you know?

There is a saying that 'The best way to keep on caring *about* someone is not to have to care *for* them'. There are many thousands of carers looking after relatives who would testify to the truth of that saying.

Some situations require much more than words of support, and giving practical, physical support to a carer or family may help to reduce the risk of abuse. The extra support provided by a professional carer can do this in two ways: firstly, it can provide the additional help which allows the carer to feel that he or she is not in a hopeless never-ending situation; and secondly, it can provide a regular opportunity to check an individual where abuse is suspected or considered to be a major risk.

When resources are provided within the community rather than at home, this also offers a chance to observe someone who is thought to be at risk. Day centres, training centres, schools, after school clubs and youth centres also provide an opportunity for people to talk to staff and to feel that they are in a supportive environment where they can talk about any abuse they have suffered and they will be believed and helped.

Remember
- Preventing abuse is better than dealing with it.
- Support may make all the difference to a carer under stress.
- Only intervene directly if there is an immediate risk.
- Act assertively to stop any abusive behaviour.

The effects of abuse on all those concerned

Abuse devastates those who suffer it. It causes people to lose their self-esteem and their confidence. Many adults and children become withdrawn and difficult to communicate with. Anger is a common emotion amongst people who have been abused. It may be directed against the abuser, or at those people around them who failed to recognise the abuse and stop it happening.

One of the greatest tragedies is when people who have been abused turn their anger against themselves and blame themselves for everything which has happened to them. These are situations which require expert help, and this should be available to anyone who has been abused, regardless of the circumstances.

In an earlier section of this chapter you learned about the indications of abuse. Some of the behaviour changes which can be signs of abuse can be almost permanent, or certainly very long-lasting. There are very few survivors of abuse whose personality remains unchanged, and for those who do conquer the effects of abuse, it is a long, hard fight.

The abuser, often called the 'perpetrator', also requires expert help, and this should be available through various agencies depending on the type and seriousness of the abuse. People who abuse, whether their victims are children or vulnerable adults, receive very little sympathy or understanding from society. There is no public recognition that some abusers may have been under tremendous strain and pressure, and abusers may find that they have no support from friends or family. Many abusers will face the consequences of their actions alone.

Did you know?

Prisoners who are serving sentences for child abuse, or for abuse of vulnerable adults, have to be kept in separate areas of the prison for their own safety. If they were allowed to mix with other prisoners, they could be seriously assaulted or even killed.

Care workers who have to deal with abusive situations react in different ways. There is no 'right way' to react. Everyone is different and will deal with things in his or her own way. If you have to deal with abuse, these are some of the ways you may feel, and some steps you can take which may help.

- You may feel quite traumatised by the abusive incident. It is quite normal to find that you cannot get the incident off your mind, that you have difficulty concentrating on other things, or that you keep having 'flashbacks' and re-enact the situation in your head. You may also feel that you need to keep talking about what happened.

- Talking can be very beneficial, but if you are discussing an incident outside your workplace, you must remember rules of confidentiality and *never* use names. You will find that you can talk about the circumstances just as well by referring to 'the boy' or 'the father' or 'the daughter'. This way of talking does become second nature, and is useful because it allows you to tell others about things which have happened at work whilst maintaining confidentiality.

- These feelings are likely to last for a fairly short time, and are a natural reaction to shock and trauma. If at any time you feel that you are having difficulty, you must talk to your manager or supervisor, who should be able to help.

- Alternatively, the situation may have made you feel very angry, and you may have an overwhelming urge to inflict some serious damage on the perpetrator of the abuse. Whilst this is understandable, it is not professional and you will have to find other ways of dealing with your anger. Again, your supervisor or manager should help you to work through your feelings.

- Everyone has different ways of dealing with anger, such as taking physical exercise, doing housework, punching a cushion, writing feelings down and then tearing the paper up, crying or telling your best friend. Whatever you do with your anger in ordinary situations, you should do the same in this situation (just remember to respect confidentiality if you need to tell your best friend – miss out the names). It is perfectly legitimate to be angry, but you cannot bring this anger into the professional relationship.

- The situation may have made you distressed, and you may want to go home and have a good cry, or give your own children or elderly relatives an extra hug. This is a perfectly normal reaction. No matter how many years you work, or how many times it happens, you may still feel the same way.

- Some workplaces will have arrangements in place where workers are able to share difficult situations and get support from each other. Others may not have any formal meetings or groups arranged, but colleagues will offer each other support and advice in an informal way. You may find that work colleagues who have had similar experiences are the best people with whom to share this type of experience.

- There is, of course, the possibility that the situation may have brought back many painful memories for you of abuse you have suffered in your own past. This is often the most difficult situation to deal with, because you may feel as if you should be able to help because you know how it feels, but your own experience has left you without any room to deal with the feelings of others. There are many avenues of support now available to survivors of abuse. You can find out about the nearest support confidentially, if you do not want your workplace colleagues or supervisor to know.

- There is no doubt that dealing with abuse is one of the most stressful aspects of working in care. There is nothing odd or abnormal about feeling that you need to share what you have experienced and looking for support from others. This is a perfectly reasonable reaction and, in fact, most experienced managers would be far more concerned about a worker involved in dealing with abuse who appears quite unaffected by it, than about one who comes looking for guidance and reassurance.

Remember

- Feeling upset is normal.
- Talk about the incident if that helps.
- Being angry is OK, but deal with it sensibly – take physical exercise, do the housework, cry.
- Do not be unprofessional with the abuser.
- If you are a survivor of abuse and you find it hard to deal with, ask for help.

Contribute to monitoring individuals who are at risk from abuse

WHAT YOU NEED TO LEARN

- How to share information.
- Ways of assessing risk.
- What to do if you suspect abuse in your own workplace.

How to share information

Sharing information between different agencies and organisations can often be a vital way of ensuring that people at risk are protected.

There are often several care and other professionals involved with any child or adult considered to be at risk. One of the most important features of work with people at risk is co-operation between agencies.

Teamwork is vital, both with other involved professional care workers and within your own team. Information is always clearer and more comprehensive when it is shared, and you may find that different members of the team have observed slightly different aspects and so the picture will become more complete.

It may also be possible that people will have different views on any allegations or incidents which have taken place. It is important that all these views are taken into account. Some of the professionals involved may be working with the person alleged to be the abuser and they may have a different perspective to add to any discussions. Remember that there is always more than one story to be told, even though it may not always be easy to take account of the alleged abuser's perspective.

Did you know?

Every report (called Fatal Case Inquiry) into child deaths from abuse in the past twenty-five years has highlighted the need for agencies to co-operate, work together and share information.

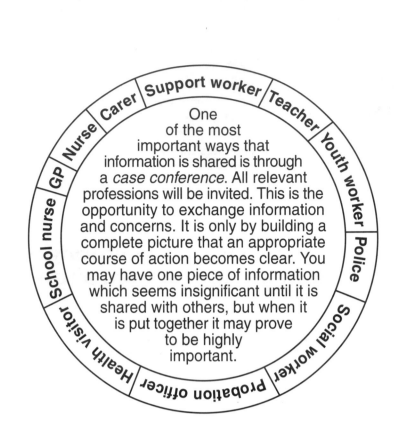

One of the most important ways that information is shared is through a *case conference*. All relevant professions will be invited. This is the opportunity to exchange information and concerns. It is only by building a complete picture that an appropriate course of action becomes clear. You may have one piece of information which seems insignificant until it is shared with others, but when it is put together it may prove to be highly important.

Sharing information

Each local area has an Area Child Protection Committee (ACPC), which includes representatives of all relevant professionals: social workers, health professionals, teachers, police, and so on. The ACPC meets to lay down procedures which must be followed where child abuse is suspected or confirmed. It also ensures that a register of children who have been abused, or are at risk of abuse, is maintained by the social services department.

The Child Protection Register is a record of all the children about whom there are concerns. The register is held and maintained by social services, but the information can be shared with other relevant professionals. There are four main categories in the register: physical abuse, sexual abuse, neglect and emotional abuse.

There is no similar register for adults considered to be at risk.

Did you know?

Anyone, including a child, who has been abused by someone who has been tried in court and found guilty, can receive Criminal Injuries compensation. It is also possible for cases to be brought even where there is no criminal trial. It is vital that anyone who has been abused in any way should have a solicitor to act in his or her interests.

Ways of assessing risk

Decisions about abuse of adults are different from those about children because, ultimately, it is the adult him or herself who will make the decision about how to proceed. Clearly there are some situations where this is not possible, but such circumstances are provided for under the law. If an adult has been abused, but he or she decides to remain in the abusive situation, then there are generally no legal steps which can be taken to prevent that.

Case study

Mrs C is 75 years old. She is quite fit, although increasingly her arthritis is slowing her down and making her less steady on her feet. She has been a widow for fifteen years and lives with her only son, R, who is 51. When R was 29, he was involved in a motorcycle accident which caused brain damage, from which he has never fully recovered. His speech is slow and he sometimes has problems in communication. His co-ordination and fine motor skills have been affected, so he has problems with buttons, shoelaces and writing. R also suffers from major mood swings and can be aggressive. Mrs C is R's only carer. He has never worked since the accident, but he goes to a day centre three days each week. Mrs C takes the opportunity to go to a day centre herself on those three days because she enjoys the company, the outings and activities.

Recently, Mrs C has had an increasing number of injuries. In the past two months she has had a grazed forehead, a black eye, a split lip and last week she arrived at the day centre with a bruised and sprained wrist. She finally admitted to the centre staff that R had inflicted the injuries during his periods of bad temper. She said that these were becoming more frequent as he became more frustrated with her slowness.

Despite being very distressed, Mrs C would not agree to being separated from R. She was adamant that he didn't mean to hurt her. She would not consider making a complaint to the police. Finally, Mrs C agreed to increasing both her and R's attendance at their day centres, and to having some assistance with daily living.

1 What do you think Mrs C should have done?
2 Can she be left with R?
3 Why do you think Mrs C will not take any action against R?

This kind of situation may cause a great deal of concern and anxiety for the care workers, but there are limits on the legal powers to intervene and there is no justification for removing Mrs C's right to make her own decisions.

Care workers faced with an abusive situation which cannot be resolved must assess the risks and work out ways of minimising the likelihood of further abuse. A 'risk assessment' will be carried out. Your workplace will have procedures about the way in which a risk assessment is carried out and how decisions are made. Many workplaces will have a system where decisions about level of risk are taken by a case conference. In others, decisions may be made by a team manager, who would need to be in possession of all the available facts. At no time would any worker be expected to make such judgements and decisions alone, or to accept full responsibility for this type of assessment.

Did you know?

This type of shared responsibility and decision-making has only developed over the past twenty years or so in the case of children, and far more recently in the case of adults. Prior to that, workers were often left to make decisions without any support, and took the full weight of blame if things went wrong.

A risk assessment will consider all the elements in a situation and try to reach a judgement about potential dangers and what can be done. Clearly, the options are far more limited in respect of adults, because there is no overall legislation offering protection. It is also very rarely possible to act against the will of an adult, even where it may be in his or her best interests.

What to do if you suspect abuse in your own workplace

Blowing the whistle

One of the most difficult situations to deal with is when you believe that abuse is happening in your workplace. It is often hard to accept that the people you work with would abuse, but if you have evidence or good grounds for concern, then you will have to take action.

- The first step is to report the abuse to your manager.
- If you suspect that your manager is involved, or will not take action, you must refer it to the most senior manager who is likely to be impartial.
- If you do not believe that it is possible to report the abuse to anyone within your workplace, you should contact social services (or the NSPCC, if you prefer, for children).
- If you work for the NSPCC, social services or the health service and you are concerned about abuse, you should still follow the same steps, although you may need to contact a senior manager who is not directly involved with your workplace.
- There are organisations which provide helplines offering support and advice to workers concerned about abuse. You may find that a good starting point.
- You could also contact your trade union if you belong to one.

Remember

- Consider all possibilities when there are any suspicions about the care of a vulnerable person.
- Abuse may be the last thing you would expect in a particular situation.
- Think the unthinkable – *listen* and *believe*.
- That does not just mean listening to what you are told: *listen* to what you see and *believe* what you feel.

Keys to good practice

- Always listen and believe those who tell you they have been abused.
- Be prepared to accept the possibility of abuse where you don't expect it.
- Know the procedures and follow them strictly.
- Never underestimate the importance of sharing information.
- Protecting the vulnerable is your first priority.
- Never allow abusive behaviour to go unchallenged.
- Remember that people who disclose abuse want it to stop.
- You could make the difference – always be aware of the possibility of abuse.
- Do not try to deal with abuse alone.
- Use the support available for those who work with abusive situations.

The last word

Much of this unit may sound as though the field of dealing with abuse is full of rules and procedures. It is – and for very good reasons. Abuse is very serious – it is potentially life-threatening. Systems and rules have been developed by learning from the tragedies that have happened in the past. Many of these tragedies occurred because procedures were either not in place, or were not followed. You must make sure that you know what the procedure is in your workplace and follow it to the letter.

Unit test

1 Abuse can happen when people are being cared for. Name the circumstances which make this more likely.
2 Look back to the case study on page 121. Write a report on this situation, making sure you include the main information points.
3 Make a list of the people in your workplace with whom you would need to share information. Say why each of them is on your list.
4 Make notes about the way you would behave if someone told you he or she had been abused.
5 If you consider an abusive incident to be minor and unimportant, what should you do?
6 What effects might abuse have on a child?
7 What reactions would you expect to see in a care worker who had dealt with an abusive situation?
8 What should you do if you suspect abuse in your workplace?
9 Are there different factors to consider when dealing with abuse of adults or children? If so, what are they?
10 What are the two key things to do when someone discloses that he or she has been abused?

Promote communication with individuals where there are communication differences

Communicating in normal circumstances is dealt with in Unit CL1. This unit deals with communication where there are differences between the worker and an individual which can cause problems.

It is important that you, as a health or care worker, understand how to communicate with people even though the differences may make that quite difficult. Communication is not just about talking to people when it is easy, it is also about managing to make contact with those people for whom it is much harder.

There are many ways in which you can help to make communication more effective, not just by talking, but by the actions that you take in making the environment better for communication or by making sure that communication is handled appropriately for the particular individual and that proper records are kept on the best way of communicating with each individual for whom you provide care.

It is important that you understand how to communicate with the people in your care.

Determine the nature and scope of communication differences

WHAT YOU NEED TO LEARN

- What communication differences are and their effects.
- How to find out about likely communication problems.
- How to record information.

What communication differences are and their effects

Communication differences

Communication differences include:

- people speaking different languages
- either the worker or the individual having a sensory impairment
- distress, where somebody is so upset that he or she is unable to communicate
- a physical illness or disability, such as a stroke or confusion
- cultural differences.

Language

Where an individual speaks a different language from those who are providing care, it can be an isolating and frustrating experience. The individual may become distressed and frightened as it is very difficult to establish exactly what is happening and he or she is not in a position to ask or to have any questions answered. The person will feel excluded from anything happening in the care setting and will find making relationships with carers extremely difficult. There is the possibility that confusion and misunderstanding will occur.

Hearing loss

A loss or reduction of ability to hear clearly can cause major differences in the ability to communicate.

Communication is a two-way process, and it is very difficult for somebody who does not hear sounds at all or hears them in a blurred and indistinct way to be able to respond and to join in. The result can be that people become withdrawn and feel very isolated and excluded from others around them. This can lead to frustration and anger. People may present some quite challenging behaviour.

Profound deafness is not as common as partial hearing loss. People are most likely to suffer from loss of hearing of certain sounds at certain volumes or at certain pitches, such as high sounds or low sounds. It is also very common for people to find it difficult to hear if there is background noise – many sounds may jumble together, making it very hard to pick out the voice of one person. Hearing loss can also have an effect on speech, particularly for those who are profoundly deaf and are unable to hear their own voices as they speak. This can make communication doubly difficult.

Visual impairment

Visual impairment causes many communication difficulties. Not only is an individual unable to pick up the visual signals which are being given out by someone who is speaking, but, because he or she is unaware of these signals, the person may also fail to give appropriate signals in communication. This lack of non-verbal communication and lack of ability to receive and interpret non-verbal communication can lead to misunderstandings about somebody's attitudes and behaviour. It means that a person's communications can easily be misinterpreted, or it could be thought that he or she is behaving in a way that is not appropriate.

Physical disability

Depending on the disability, this can have various effects. People who have suffered strokes, for example, will often have communication difficulties, not only in forming words and speaking, but they often also suffer from dysphasia, which is the inability to understand and to express meaning through words. That is, they lose the ability to find the right words for something they want to say, or to understand the meanings of words said to them. This condition is very distressing for the individual and for those who are trying to communicate. Often this is coupled with a loss of movement and a difficulty in using facial muscles to form words.

In some cases, the communication difficulty is a symptom of a disability. For example, many people with cerebral palsy and motor neurone disease have difficulty in controlling the muscles that affect voice production, and so speaking in a way which can be readily understood becomes very difficult. Other disabilities may have no effect at all upon voice production or the thought processes that produce spoken words, but the lack of other body movements may mean that non-verbal communication may be difficult or not what you would expect.

Learning difficulties

These may, dependent upon their severity, cause differences in communication in terms of the level of understanding of the individual and his or her ability to respond appropriately to any form of communication. This will vary depending on the degree of learning disability of the individual, but broadly the effect of learning disabilities is to limit the ability of an individual to understand and process information given to him or her. It is also likely that individuals will have a short attention span, so this may mean that communications have to be repeated several times in an appropriate form.

Dementia/confusion

This difficult and distressing condition is most prevalent in older people and people who suffer from Alzheimer's disease. The confusion can result ultimately in the loss of the ability to communicate, but in the early stages it involves short-term memory loss to the extent of being unable to remember the essential parts of a conversation or a recent exchange. It can necessitate the constant repetition of any form of communication.

Cultural differences

People's communication differences can result from differences in culture and background. Culture is about more than language – it is about the way that people live, think and relate to each other. In some cultures, for example, children are not allowed to speak in the presence of certain adults. Other cultures do not allow women to speak to men they do not know.

Some people may have been brought up in a background or in a period of time when challenging authority by asking questions was not acceptable. Such people may find it very hard to ask questions of doctors or other health professionals and are unlikely to feel able to raise any queries about how their care or treatment should be carried out.

Remember
Communication differences can result as much from differences in attitude as they can from differences in language.

Active knowledge
Try renting a video in a language other than your own, or watch a subtitled film on TV, covering the lower half of the TV screen where the subtitles are. Try to make sense of what is shown in the film. Note how difficult it is to understand what is happening and how frustrating it is. Notice how quickly you lose interest and decide that you will not bother to watch any more. Imagine how that feels if you are ill or in need of care, and everyone around you is speaking in a language you do not understand.

General effects of communication differences
The most common effect of communication differences is for the person receiving care to feel frustrated and isolated. It is an important part of your job to do everything in your power to reduce the effect of communication differences and to try to lessen the feelings of isolation and frustration that people experience.

Case study
D is from a small town just outside Athens. He speaks little English. While in England on an exchange visit to a university, he has been involved in a road accident. As a result of the accident, he has spinal injuries and is likely to be in hospital for several weeks. His injuries mean that his movements are limited and he is restricted to lying flat. The other students in his group visited during the first two weeks of his hospitalisation, but they have now all returned to Greece. His family cannot afford to travel to England to visit him.

1 How do you think D is feeling?
2 What would you do as a first step to communicating?
3 If you were D's key worker, who else would you involve?
4 What effect could a lack of communication have on his overall condition?

How to find out about likely communication problems
You can discover likely communication problems by simply observing an individual. You can find out a great deal about how a person communicates and what the differences are between his or her way of communicating and your own.

Observation should be able to establish:
- which language is being used
- if the client experiences any hearing difficulties or visual impairment
- if there is any physical illness or disability
- if there are any learning difficulties.

Any of these factors could have a bearing on how well a person will be able to communicate with you, and what steps you may need to take to make things easier. Observation will give you some very good clues to start with, but there are other useful sources of information for establishing exactly what a particular individual needs to assist communication. You may consider:

- asking the individual where this is possible – he or she is likely to be your best source of information
- discussing with colleagues who have worked with the individual before and who are likely to have some background information and advice
- consulting other professionals who have worked with the individual and may have knowledge of means of communication which have been effective for them
- reading previous case notes or case histories
- finding out as much as you can about an individual's particular illness or disability, where you have been able to establish this – the most useful sources of information are likely to be the specialist agencies for the particular condition
- talking to family or friends. They are likely to have a great deal of information about what the differences in communication are for the individual. They will have developed ways of dealing with communication, possibly over a long period of time, and are likely to be a very useful source of advice and help.

How to record information

There would be little point in finding out about effective means of communication with someone and then not making an accurate record so that other people can also communicate with that person.

You should establish your employer's policy on where such information is to be recorded – it is likely to be in the client's case notes.

Be sure that you record:

- the nature of the communication differences
- how they show themselves
- ways which you have found to be effective in overcoming the differences.

Information recorded in notes may look like this:

Mr P has communication difficulties following his stroke. He is dysphasic, with left side haemaplaegia. speech is slurred but possible to understand with care. Most effective approaches are:

a) allow maximum time for communication responses
b) modify delivery if necessary in order to allow understanding
c) speak slowly, with short sentences
d) physical reassurance (holding and stroking hand) seems to help while waiting for a response
e) can use flashcards on bad days (ensure they are placed on the right-hand side)

Keys to good practice

- Check what the differences in communication are.
- Remember they can be cultural as well as physical.
- Examine the effects of the communication differences for a particular individual.
- Use all possible sources to obtain information.

ement CL2.2 Contribute to effective communication where there are communication differences

- How to communicate appropriately.
- How to respond to communication and check understanding.

How to communicate appropriately

Overcoming language differences in communication

Where you are in the position of providing care for someone who speaks a different language from you, it is clear that you will need the services of an interpreter for any serious discussions or communication.

- Your work setting is likely to have a contact list of interpreters.
- Social services departments and the police have lists of interpreters.
- The embassy or consulate for the appropriate country will also have a list of qualified interpreters.

You should always use professional interpreters wherever possible. It may be very tempting to use other members of the family – very often children have excellent language skills – but it is inappropriate in most care settings. This is because:

- their English and their ability to interpret may not be at the same standard as a professional interpreter and misunderstandings can easily occur
- you may wish to discuss matters which are not appropriate to be discussed with children, or the individual may not want members of his or her family involved in very personal discussions about health or care issues.

It is unlikely that you would be able to have a full-time interpreter available throughout somebody's period of care, so it is necessary to consider alternatives for encouraging everyday communication.

Be prepared to learn words in the individual's language which will help communication. You could try to give the person some words in your language if he or she is willing and able to learn them.

There are other simple techniques that you may wish to try which can help basic levels of communication. For example, you could use flashcards and signals, similar to those which you would use for a person who has suffered a stroke. This gives the person the opportunity to show a flashcard to indicate his or her needs. You can also use them to find out what kind of assistance may be needed.

Some of the flashcards you may use

The suggestions shown above are not exhaustive and you will come up with many which are appropriate for the individual and for your particular care setting. They are a helpful way of assisting with simple communication and allowing people to express their immediate physical needs.

The most effective way of communication with a person who speaks a different language is through non-verbal communication. A smile and a friendly face are understood in all languages, as are a concerned facial expression and a warm and welcoming body position.

However, be careful about the use of gestures – gestures which are acceptable in one culture may not be acceptable in all. For example, an extended thumb in this culture would mean 'great, that's fine, OK', but in many cultures it is an extremely offensive gesture. If you are unsure which gestures are acceptable in another culture, make sure that you check before using any which may be misinterpreted.

Overcoming hearing difficulties in communication

- Ensure that any means of improving hearing which an individual uses, for example a hearing aid, is working properly and is fitted correctly, that the batteries are fresh and working, that it is clean and that it is doing its job properly in terms of improving the individual's hearing.
- Ensure that you are sitting in a good light, not too far away and that you speak clearly, but do not shout. Shouting simply distorts your face and makes it more difficult for a person with hearing loss to be able to read what you are saying.

Some people will lip read, while others will use a form of sign language for understanding. This may be BSL (British Sign Language) or MAKATON, which is a simplified form of sign language. They may rely on a combination of lip reading and gestures.

Remember

If you are able to learn even simple signing or the basic rules of straightforward spoken communication with people who have hearing loss, you will significantly improve the way in which they are able to relate to their care environment.

Other services which are extremely helpful to people who have hearing difficulties are telecommunication services, such as using a minicom or typetalk service. These allow a spoken conversation to be translated in written form using a form of typewriter, and the responses can be passed in the same way by an operator who will relay them to the hearing person. These services have provided a major advance in enabling people who are hard of hearing or profoundly deaf to use telephone equipment. For people who are less severely affected by hearing impairment there are facilities such as raising the volume on telephone receivers to allow them to hear conversations more clearly.

Did you know?

Although humans use language to communicate, most forms of life have some means of communication. Bees dance in a particular pattern to show each other where the nectar is; elephants communicate with sounds which are so low pitched that humans cannot hear them; monkeys and chimpanzees are thought to use body language to communicate.

Overcoming visual difficulties in communication

One of the commonest ways of assisting people who have visual problems is to provide them with glasses. You need to be sure that these are clean and that they are the correct prescription. You must make sure that people have their eyes tested every two years and that their prescription is regularly updated. A person whose eyesight and requirements for glasses have changed will obviously have difficulty in picking up many of the non-verbal signals which you will be giving out when you are communicating with him or her.

For people with more serious loss or impairment, you will need to take other steps to ensure that you minimise the differences that will exist in your styles of communication.

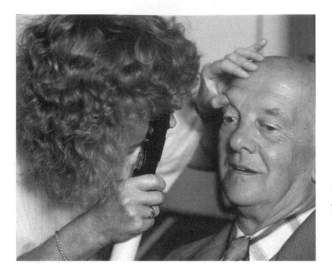

People should have their eyes tested every two years and their prescription should be regularly updated

Keys to good practice

When communicating with people who have visual impairment:

- Do not suddenly begin to speak to someone without first of all letting him or her know that you are there by touching and saying hello.
- Make sure that you introduce yourself when you come in to a room. It is easy to forget that someone cannot see. A simple 'Hello John, it's Sue' is all that is needed so that you don't 'arrive' unexpectedly.
- You may need to use touch more than you would in speaking to a sighted person, because the concerns that you would normally be expressing through your face and your general body movements will not be seen. So, if you are expressing concern or sympathy, it may be appropriate to touch someone's hand or arm, at the same time that you are saying you are concerned and sympathetic.
- Ask the individual what system of communication he or she requires – do not impose your idea of appropriate systems on the person. Most people who are visually impaired know very well what they can and cannot do, and if you ask they will tell you exactly what they need you to do.
- Do not decide that you know the best way to help. Never take the arm of somebody who is visually impaired to help him or her to move around. Allow the person to take your arm, to ask for guidance and tell you where he or she wishes to go.

Overcoming physical learning disabilities in communication

Physical disability or illness has to be dealt with according to the nature of the disability or the illness. For example, if you were communicating with somebody who had a stroke you would have to work out ways of coping with his or her dysphasia. This is best dealt with by:

- using very simple, short sentences, speaking slowly and being prepared to wait while the individual processes what you have said and composes a reply

- using gestures – they are helpful in terms of making it easier for people to understand the idea that you are trying to get across
- using very simple, closed questions which only need a 'yes' or 'no' answer. Avoid long, complicated sentences with interrelated ideas. For example, do not say 'It's getting near tea time now, isn't it? How about some tea? Have you thought about what you would like?' Instead say, 'Are you hungry? Would you like fish? Would you like chicken?' and so on, until you have established what sort of meal the individual would prefer.

Other illnesses, such as motor neurone disease or cerebral palsy, can also lead to difficulties in speech, although not in comprehension.

- The individual will understand perfectly what you are saying to him or her but the difficulty will be in communicating with you.
- There is no need for you to speak slowly, although you will have to be prepared to allow time for a response owing to the difficulties that the individual will have in producing words.
- You will have to become familiar with the sound of the individual's voice and the way in which he or she communicates. It can be hard to understand people who have illnesses which affect their facial, throat or larynx muscles.

Many people with learning disabilities are able to communicate on a physical level more easily than on a verbal level

Overcoming learning disabilities in communication

Where people have learning disabilities, you will need to adjust your methods of communicating to take account of the level of disability that they experience. You should have gathered sufficient information about the individual to know the level of understanding that he or she has – and how simply and how often you need to explain things and the sorts of communication which are likely to be the most effective.

Many people with learning disabilities respond well to physical contact and are able to relate and communicate on a physical level more easily than on a verbal level. This will vary between individuals and you should be prepared to use a great deal of physical contact and hugs when communicating with people who have learning difficulties.

Overcoming cultural differences in communication

Communication is about much more than words being exchanged between two people – it is influenced by a great many things. The way in which people have been brought up and the society and culture that they live in has a great effect on the way in which they communicate.

For example, some cultures use gestures or touch much more than others. In some cultures it is acceptable to stand very close to someone, whereas in others people feel extremely uncomfortable if others stand too close. You need to find out about the person's background when you are thinking about how you can make communication work for him or her. To find out the information you need, you could:

- look in the person's records
- speak to a member of the family or a friend, if this is possible
- ask someone else from the same culture, either a colleague or through the country's cultural representatives (contacting their embassy or consulate and asking for the information) – alternatively you could try a local multicultural organisation
- use reference books, if necessary.

It is also important that you communicate with people at the correct intellectual level. Make sure that you communicate with them at a language level which they are likely to understand, but not find patronising. For example, older people and people who have disabilities have every right to be spoken to as adults and not patronised or talked down to. One of the commonest complaints from people with physical disabilities is that people will talk to their carers about them rather than talk to them directly – this is known as the 'does he take sugar' approach.

Never treat disabled people as if they are incapable of being talked to

Active knowledge

Find out the policy in your workplace for checking on people's cultural preferences. Ask who establishes the information about the cultural background of people who use your service, and what the policies are to ensure their needs are met.

Case study

A Russian teacher accompanied a group of students on a visit to England. All of the party were staying with host families and the teacher was placed with a woman of similar age (early forties) who was a single parent with a teenage son. Neither woman spoke any of the other's language.

On the first morning the organiser of the trip spoke to the host family on the telephone and asked how the two women had got on the previous evening. He was amazed to be told that, despite not speaking a word of each other's language, they had spent the evening sitting either side of the fire with a bottle of wine and that both knew each other's life stories. They had managed to tell each other of their marriages, divorces and problems with their children. They had laughed and cried together, and had achieved all of this by using family photographs, gestures and facial expressions, and by speaking in their own language had managed to communicate their entire life histories. The two women had ended the evening firm friends and this continued throughout the rest of the visit.

1 How do you think the women managed to communicate?
2 What methods of communication would you have used if you were in that situation?
3 Do you think it is significant that they were both middle-aged women with no disabilities? Why?
4 Can you think of a situation in your workplace which has any similarities to this?

How to respond to communication and check understanding

Although it is unacceptable to talk down to people, it is pointless trying to communicate with them by using so much jargon and medical terminology that they don't understand anything you have said. You must be sure that your communication is being understood. The most straightforward way to do this is to ask someone to recap on what you have discussed.

You could say something like: 'Can we just go over this so that we are both sure about what is happening – you tell me what is happening tomorrow', or you can rephrase what you have just said and check with the individual that he or she has understood. For example:

'The bus is coming earlier than usual tomorrow because of the trip. It will be here at eight o'clock instead of nine – is that OK?'

'Yes.'

'So, you're sure that you can be up and ready by eight o'clock to go on the trip?'

Communication through actions

For many people, it is easier to communicate by actions than by words. You will need to make sure that you respond in an appropriate way by recognising the significance of a touch or a sudden movement from somebody who is ill and bedridden, or a gesture from somebody who speaks a different language. A gesture can indicate what his or her needs are and what sort of response the person is looking for from you. You may be faced with a young person with challenging behaviour who throws something at you – this is a means of communication. It may not be a very pleasant one, but nonetheless, it expresses much of the person's hurt, anger and distress. It is important that you recognise this for what it is and respond in the same way you would if that person had been able to express his or her feelings in words.

Remember

If you are planning communication with somebody who has a sensory impairment or who has a learning disability, you will need to take account of this and adjust your communication so that it is at a level he or she is are able to understand and make sense of. The single most important factor in communicating is that you are understood.

Encouraging communication

The best way to ensure that somebody is able to communicate to the best of his or her ability is to make the person feel as comfortable and as relaxed as possible. There are several factors to consider when thinking about how to make people feel confident enough to communicate. They are summarised in the table below.

Ways of encouraging communication

Communication difference	Encouraging actions
Different language	• Smile • Friendly facial expression • Gestures • Use pictures • Warmth and encouragement – repeat their words with a smile to check understanding
Hearing impairment	• Speak clearly, listen carefully, respond to what is said to you • Remove any distractions and other noises • Make sure any aids to hearing are working • Use written communication where appropriate • Use signing where appropriate and understood • Use properly trained interpreter if high level of skill is required
Visual impairment	• Use touch to communicate concern, sympathy and interest • Use tone of voice rather than facial expressions to communicate mood and response • Do not rely on non-verbal communication, e.g. facial expression or nodding head • Ensure that all visual communication is transferred into something which can be heard, either a tape or somebody reading
Confusion or dementia	• Repeat information as often as necessary • Keep re-orientating the conversation if you need to • Remain patient • Be very clear and keep conversation short and simple • Use simple written communication or pictures where they seem to help
Physical disability	• Ensure that surroundings are appropriate and accessible • Allow for difficulties with voice production if necessary • Do not patronise • Remember that some body language may not be appropriate

Communication difference	Encouraging actions
Learning difficulties	• Judge appropriate level of understanding • Make sure that you respond at the right level • Repeat things as often as necessary • Remain patient and be prepared to keep covering the same ground • Be prepared to wait and listen carefully to responses

Use signing where it is appropriate and understood

Active knowledge

Take some of the ideas from the table on pages 154-155 and discuss them with your supervisor. Ask him or her to give you other ideas and methods which have been found to be effective in your workplace.

Key to good practice

The single most important thing that you need to remember is that you must tailor your response to the individual not the condition.

Unit test

1   What would you expect to be the effects of partial hearing loss on someone's style of communication?

2   What sort of steps could you take to improve communication with someone following a stroke? List three.

3   What would you expect to be the cultural differences between an 80-year-old woman brought up in an industrial town and the 25-year-old son of an Indian consultant cardiac surgeon, who is working as a care assistant in the care home she lives in?

4   What is one of the most important ways of communicating with someone who speaks a different language?

5   An inability to communicate will not affect the rate of recovery or standard of physical care. True or false?

6   What factors would you take into account when judging the best way to communicate with somebody from a different country?

7   What common mistake is made in talking to older people?

8   What do you need to do to encourage somebody with visual impairment to feel confident about communicating?

9   What is the most important purpose of communication?

10 Collect information about different cultures and the gestures which are used in communication.

11 Imagine you have to devise methods of communicating with:
   - a blind French teenage girl
   - an older man from Pakistan who is hard of hearing.
   a   What would be the problems you would expect to face?
   b   What are the likely differences in their communication needs?

Unit CU2 Prepare and maintain environments for clinical procedures

In order to ensure that the environments in which clinical procedures take place are as free from infection risk as possible it is important that you understand the process of how infection develops and can pass from one person to another. An understanding of the basic principles of infection will help you to work more effectively in combating it.

Your own role in terms of your personal hygiene practice is also vitally important and will make a major contribution to the reduction of the spread of infection. Good quality practice which makes hygiene and infection control central will deliver enormous benefits for all clients for whom you provide care.

Element CU2.1 Prepare environments for clinical procedures

WHAT YOU NEED TO LEARN

- The causes of infection and cross-infection.
- How to ensure your own hygienic practice.
- Ways to clean, disinfect and sterilise the environment.
- How to prepare the equipment and paperwork.

Causes of infection and cross-infection

Infection in humans is caused by micro-organisms. They are too small to be seen by the naked eye and have to be seen under a microscope, either a light microscope or, in the case of viruses, an electron microscope. There are billions of micro-organisms in our environment, the vast majority of which are harmless to humans. These harmless micro-organisms are called **non-pathogenic**. The micro-organisms which cause disease and infection in humans are called **pathogenic** micro-organisms.

Broadly, pathogenic micro organisms, or **pathogens**, fall into four categories:

1 Viruses
2 Bacteria
3 Fungi
4 Protozoa.

The first two are the ones with which you will need to be concerned. There are relatively few human diseases and infections which you are likely to come into contact with caused by fungi and protozoa.

Viruses

Viruses are the smallest living organisms. They are up to ten times smaller than bacteria and can only be seen under an electron microscope. However, considering their size, viruses cause some major human diseases and are responsible for the most prevalent and common ones. Viruses cause diseases such as:

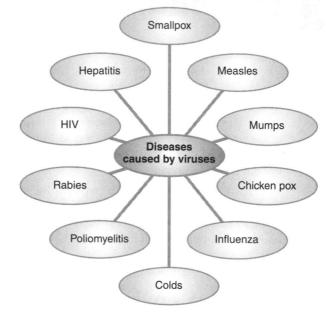

Viruses are the smallest living organisms, but they cause some serious diseases

Although diseases such as smallpox are virtually eradicated in the Western world, common diseases such as colds and influenza regularly occur. Influenza is known to cause a large number of deaths in vulnerable people each year. In such cases viruses enter the human body through various routes:

- **Respiratory route**. This is when people breathe in through the nose or mouth droplets of moisture in the air which have been infected by other people with the virus coughing or sneezing. Many of you may remember some years ago a health promotion advertising campaign reminding us that 'Coughs and sneezes spread diseases, trap your germs in your handkerchief.'

  Viral infection can also be carried in the air in dust which has been shaken from infected bedding or clothing. When smallpox was prevalent it was often carried in this way.

- **The digestive route**. Viruses can be introduced into the body by swallowing infected food or water. A common way of contracting poliomyelitis was by swallowing infected river or sea water.

- **The placenta route**. Viruses can pass from the mother to an unborn child through the placenta. The most common and well-known is rubella, or German measles.

  Viruses cannot penetrate unbroken skin. However, they will if the skin has been damaged. For example, a rabid dog cannot pass the rabies virus to humans unless it bites someone.

Bacteria

Bacteria are far larger than viruses but still too small to be seen with a naked eye. There are many millions of bacteria but only a very few are pathogenic. Bacteria are mostly harmless and some are beneficial to the environment because they break down and recycle waste material. The few bacteria which are pathogenic cause a range of serious and even fatal diseases in human. It is also bacteria which infect wounds, sores, ulcers and surgical sites, and which are the most common cause of infection in clinical environments.

Some of the diseases caused by bacteria are:

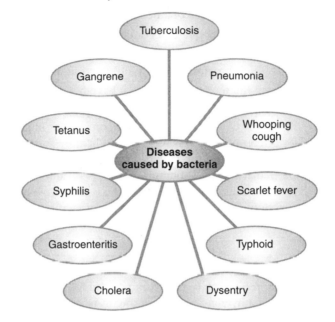

Bacteria cause serious diseases, some of which can be fatal

The bacteria entry routes into the human body are the same as viruses. They can either be inhaled through the respiratory tract, swallowed into the digestive tract or introduced through broken skin. Unlike viruses, most bacteria cannot be passed to a foetus through the placenta, however the syphilis and tuberculosis bacteria can cross the placenta and can be passed to an unborn child.

Fungi

The fungi most of us are familiar with are mushrooms, toadstools, yeasts and moulds. Indeed these comprise the vast majority of the hundred thousand or so varieties of fungi. Like bacteria, most are harmless or even beneficial to humans and very few are pathogenic. Few serious fungal diseases occur in the UK, so you are highly unlikely to come across any that can cause serious illness in humans. You are more likely to come across the more common superficial fungal infections such as:

- athlete's foot
- thrush
- ringworm.

Protozoans

Protozoans are minute animals consisting of just a single cell. They cause diseases such as amoebic dysentery, sleeping sickness and malaria. You are unlikely to come into contact with diseases spread by protozoans. They are not common in the UK, although people who have been to countries where they are common may return to the UK with the disease. In such cases special protocols are put in place for caring for these people in order to limit the potential for spread of the infection.

Cross-infection

Cross-infection is the term which describes the passing of infection from one person to another. This can occur in a range of ways, such as:

- from the hands of a health or care worker moving from one client or patient to another
- from the clothes of a health or care worker
- through inadequate decontamination of instruments or equipment between use from one client or patient to another
- through breathing in droplet infection or dust infection from the air
- from linen or surfaces which have been inadequately cleaned.

It is important to remember that people who are already vulnerable, because they are ill, elderly or very young or have some other illness or infection, are far more likely to be infected than somebody who is healthy and fit. You need to take extra care because most of the clients you are dealing with are likely to be those who are particularly susceptible to infection. The aim of cleaning, disinfecting and sterilising an environment is to minimise the risk of cross-infection. Your personal hygiene practice is one of the most significant factors in reducing the risk of infection being spread.

How to ensure your own hygienic practice

If you refer back to the work you did for Unit CU1 you will recall the importance of personal hygiene when working in health or care. Take time to review that work and implement it with your work for this unit.

Hand washing

Hand washing is the single most important procedure for preventing the spread of infection within health or care settings. Units X13 and X19 contain details of hand-washing procedures, however for ease of reference they are repeated here.

- Hands should be thoroughly wet before applying soap. Ideally this should be liquid soap as soap bars have a tendency to retain bacteria if they sit in water.
- The surfaces of both hands should be vigorously massaged with the lather, special attention being paid to the finger tips, thumbs and between the fingers. If you wear a wedding ring you should wash underneath it.
- Rinse your hands well under running water and dry them with a paper towel.

The hand-washing process should take no less than 30 seconds.

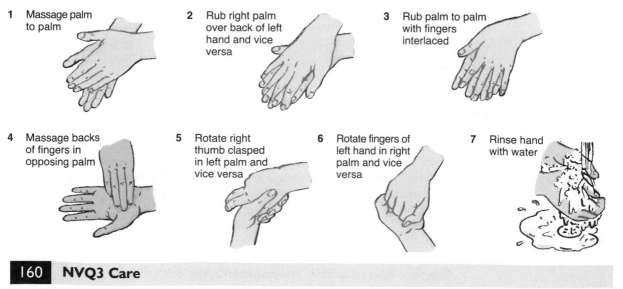

1 Massage palm to palm

2 Rub right palm over back of left hand and vice versa

3 Rub palm to palm with fingers interlaced

4 Massage backs of fingers in opposing palm

5 Rotate right thumb clasped in left palm and vice versa

6 Rotate fingers of left hand in right palm and vice versa

7 Rinse hand with water

Hand washing is important because the micro-organisms which live on the skin can cause infection, particularly in patients or clients who are very vulnerable following surgery, or in any of the other particularly vulnerable categories. Although most of the micro-organisms which live on skin are harmless and not pathogenic, the pathogens which you may have picked up from other infected clients or patients can be passed on if hands are not adequately washed and can cause serious infections.

Did you know?

The only major study ever carried out on hand washing was done in 1978. No major research into the importance and effectiveness of hand washing as a means of reducing cross-infection has been done since that time.

The research was carried out by blindfolding a group of nurses and asking them to wash their hands as if they were going on duty. The cleanser which was used contained a coloured dye which remained on the areas of the hand that were reached by the cleanser. The results of the research are shown below.

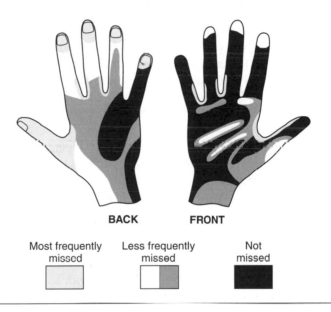

BACK　　**FRONT**

Most frequently missed	Less frequently missed	Not missed

As you can see from the pictures above, in many cases the hand-washing technique was not adequate. It is easy to miss parts of your hands unless you diligently follow a process like the one shown in the illustration on page 160. Depending on where you work, you may carry out hand washing with soap or liquid soap or you may use a specific hand-washing solution such as Betadine, Aquasept or Manusept. These contain different types of antiseptic and disinfectant solution properties.

Alcohol hand rub

Alcohol hand rubs can be very useful as they are simple to use and do not require you to wash your hands. However they can only be used if you have clean hands. You can use them if you are moving between clients or patients and are not near to a source of water to wash your hands, provided you have not touched any contaminated material or any articles or instruments which have blood or body fluids on them. A small amount of alcoholic hand rub should be rubbed well into the hands, particularly around the finger tips, between the fingers and on the nails. You should continue to rub your hands until the alcohol hand rub has completely dried.

Your own health

You should never go into work if you are suffering from an infectious disease or from diarrhoea or vomiting. If you have any cuts or broken skin you must ensure they are covered with a dressing. This is to ensure you are not a risk to your clients in passing on pathogens from your own infections. When you know that your workplace will be short-staffed and if you have a strong commitment to the clients you care for, it is often difficult not to go in when you are feeling ill. If you have diarrhoea and vomiting or a respiratory infection or any other infectious disease, do not be tempted to go into work and take the risk of passing on the infection to people who are already vulnerable and at high risk. Not only are they more likely to develop an infection as a result of your pathogens, but the effects of that infection could be extremely serious for someone who is already vulnerable. You may feel guilty about not going to work, but you will feel a great deal more guilty if you cause serious illness or even worse to somebody you are supposed to be caring for.

Likewise, if you are responsible for other care staff and you see that they are unwell, you should send them home immediately.

Blood-borne viruses

Although most of your work for this unit is concerned with ensuring that you do not pass on infection or transmit infection from one person to another, there is one area of health care practice where the greatest risk of transmission is not from the health care worker to patient or client but from the patient or client to the health care worker. This involves blood-borne viruses, in particular HIV (Human Immunodeficiency Virus), hepatitis B (HBV) and hepatitis C (HCV).

There are some basic rules designed to minimise the risk of a blood-borne virus being passed to you whilst you are working. These rules are called **universal precautions** because they should be followed in all circumstances. The most important principle of universal precautions is:

'All blood tissues and most body fluids should be regarded as potentially infectious.'

You should take precautions because of the possibility of being exposed to blood and body fluids. This is why they are called universal precautions. You start by assuming that everyone is potentially infected with a blood-borne virus. This maximises the effectiveness of the precautions by ensuring that you are not unwittingly exposed to infection from a patient or client when you do not expect to be. Also it does not discriminate against those who are infected with a blood-borne virus by treating them in a different way or taking additional precautions to those which you apply to everyone that you deal with.

HIV and hepatitis are most commonly passed from one person to another by unprotected sexual intercourse with an infected person, or by the inoculation of infected blood. The latter mainly results from drug abusers sharing injecting equipment and through the placenta of an infected mother who passes the virus to her unborn child. However, it is possible for both hepatitis and HIV to be passed to health care workers from infected patients or clients and it is important that you take the necessary steps to minimise that risk. Hepatitis B is the only blood-borne virus for which there is a vaccine to provide protection. This is effective in up to 90 per cent of people who receive it. While immunisation is not a substitute for good infection control practice, it is likely to provide you with effective protection against hepatitis

B if combined with following universal precautions. It will not however protect against hepatitis C or against HIV. Most workplaces have a programme of immunising health care employees against hepatitis B. If this is not the case in your workplace, then you should arrange to be immunised by your GP.

Active knowledge

Check whether you have been immunised against hepatitis B. If not, enquire from your line manager whether your occupational health service has an immunisation programme and ask to be immunised. If there is no programme within your workplace then contact your GP to arrange to have a hepatitis B immunisation. **DO IT NOW**.

The commonest way of blood-borne viruses being transmitted in health and social care settings is through '**percutaneous exposure**' to a patient or client's blood. In other words, this is a needle stick or sharp injury, in which a needle or other sharp instrument contaminated with the blood of an infected person penetrates your skin. In such a case, the risk of the infected blood being transmitted to you is around 1 in 3 for hepatitis B, around 1 in 30 for hepatitis C, and around 1 in 300 for HIV. These are the official risk figures from the Department of Health. They show that the risk of infection of hepatitis B is very significant and that the risks of hepatitis C and HIV are significant. It is important that you follow universal precautions and have an effective policy in your workplace to avoid being injured by sharps.

The other common way blood-borne viruses are transmitted is through contaminated mucus membranes. This most usually occurs when infected body fluid is splashed into the eye. This is called a '**mucocutaneous exposure**'. It presents a significantly lower risk than infection through broken skin, however it is important that steps are taken to minimise the risk of splashes of body fluids into the eyes, and that steps are taken to deal with them if this occurs.

Remember, not everyone with a blood-borne infection may have had their infection diagnosed. It has to be stressed that all blood and body fluids and tissues are potentially infectious and that you should follow the general measures, known as universal precautions, in order to minimise the risk.

Universal precautions checklist

- Wash hands before and after contact with each patient/client and before putting on and after removing gloves.

- Change gloves between dealing with different patients or clients.

- Cover any wounds or breaks in skin with waterproof dressings. If you have extensive broken skin on your hands through eczema or other skin problems, then wear gloves all the time.

- Wear gloves when you anticipate you may have contact with blood or other body fluids.

- Exercise great care in the handling and disposal of sharps, including scalpels, needles, scissors, etc.

- Do not wear open footwear in situations where blood or other body fluids may be spilt or where sharp instruments or needles are handled. Wear footwear which encloses your feet and does not leave them exposed to injury from falling instruments or from being splattered with blood or body fluids.

- Clear up any spills of blood or body fluid promptly and disinfect the area.

- Wear gloves when cleaning equipment, before sterilisation or disinfection and when cleaning up spillages.

- Follow safe procedures for the disposal of any contaminated waste. These should be applied in every workplace where there is a risk of coming into contact with blood or body fluids.

- Where there is a potential for blood or body fluids to splash and splatter then protective eyewear should be used. Eye wash should be readily available in all treatment areas and it should be used immediately if there has been any accidental exposure.

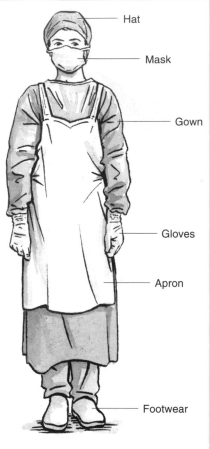

Protective clothing

Active knowledge

Check out the universal precautions which operate in your workplace. Find out how staff are told about these – whether through the induction process or through written instructions readily available to staff. If these precautions are not being followed, you may wish to raise this with your line manager.

There are new safety devices becoming available, such as needleless intravenous systems for setting up drips, syringes which have needle guards, safety needle holders and gloves which indicate when they have been punctured.

Male health care workers may be more at risk from blood or body fluids which splash onto the face as they are more likely to have small cuts and nicks on their faces from shaving. Additional care should be taken and consideration given to using face masks.

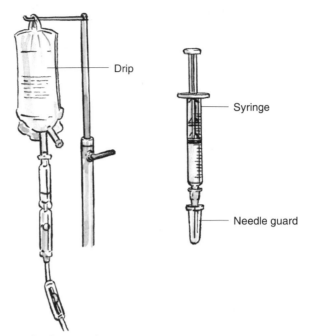

Safety devices used in medical procedures

Ways to clean, disinfect and sterilise the environment

Just as infections can be passed from person to person, they can be passed from object to person and environment to person. To limit the risk of transmission of pathogenic micro-organisms between the surrounding environment and an individual you will need to know how to disinfect and sterilise the environment. Cleaning, sterilisation and disinfection are part of the same process, but all achieve different results. Also each are appropriate to different circumstances.

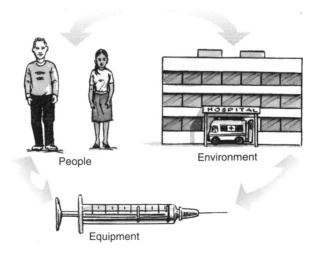

How infection can be transmitted

System for cleaning and disinfecting

Most workplaces will have a system for disinfecting and cleaning general areas which is likely to involve disposing of the cloths used and pouring away the water, with or without chemicals added, down the sluice. It is not good practice to use the same water or cloth for wiping or cleaning surfaces in a different area or for a different patient or client. Some workplaces may have a system of using different buckets to mop floors and walls in different areas. For example:

- Red buckets used for mopping and cleaning blood or any bodily fluids.
- Yellow buckets used to mop corridors and floors.
- Blue buckets used in special environments such as operating theatres.

How to clean

Cleaning is designed to remove rather than to kill micro-organisms. It usually refers to the physical removal of dirt or other organic material from objects, surfaces or instruments. This is usually done by using water with or without detergents. Cleaning is the first stage of any process of ensuring that there is no contamination of an environment and cleaning will precede any disinfection or sterilisation that has to be done.

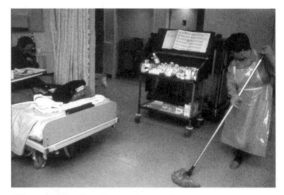

Cleaning is the first stage of any process to ensure there is no contamination

How to disinfect

Disinfection is an intermediate measure between cleaning and sterilisation. It is usually done by using a range of chemicals which can inactivate most of the serious pathogens. However, disinfection is not the same as sterilisation. It will not achieve the complete destruction of micro-organisms. Disinfection is used on floors, surfaces and other equipment and objects which make up the environment the patient or client is in. However, it will not come into invasive contact with them.

Disinfection can be carried out by simply immersing clean instruments in boiling water and leaving for five minutes. This can only be done effectively in a purpose-made instrument boiler, which has a shelf with a handle for raising and lowering items into and out of the boiling water and has it's own water heater. This will effectively disinfect instruments which are not required to be fully sterile.

Most areas which require disinfection are not likely to require sterilisation or boiling, for example floors, surfaces, and so on. These areas will need to be disinfected using chemical disinfection. There are chemicals which are effective against most pathogens. The chemicals are available under different commercial names, however they consist mainly of hydrochloride. Floors and surfaces are normally cleaned with different concentrations of sodium hydrochloride (bleach), or sodium dichlorisocyanurate. This comes in tablets or granules and tends to be used for disinfecting most surfaces. This needs to be at a higher concentration for surfaces that are contaminated with blood or for mopping up blood spillage. You may know this under the name of 'Clorhexadine'.

The chemical glutaraldehyde is sometimes used for disinfecting more delicate items which would be corroded by using bleach. Glutaraldehyde itself is listed as a hazardous substance as it can cause severe skin or respiratory irritation. Its use is controlled and you should comply with any instructions before using it. You may know it under the name of 'Cidex' or 'Totacide'. Some workplaces will also use alcohol wipes for cleaning equipment which comes into external contact with patients or clients, such as scales, stethoscopes, and so on.

How to sterilise

Sterilisation is the destruction of all micro-organisms. It can be achieved through a range of different processes and is used for instruments or equipment which will come into internal contact with an individual.

Equipment or instruments which are used to penetrate the skin and to enter inside the body must be sterilised before use. Instruments can be reused time and again provided that they are sterilised between each use. Normal sterilisation procedures use heat, either steam or hot air. The minimum temperatures recommended for sterilising in steam sterilisers are 134°C for 3 minutes (if a lower temperature is used then it must be maintained for a longer period, for example 125°C for 10 minutes) and 121°C for 15 minutes (or 115°C for 30 minutes). If a hot air steriliser is used the temperatures are even greater. This requires a temperature of 180°C for 30 minutes or 160°C for 2 hours. All hospitals and many other community resources and nursing homes now have sterilising equipment. It is possible to sterilise through other methods but the commonest is steam sterilisation. Obviously because of the temperatures, this cannot be used for plastic with low melting points. It is possible to sterilise plastic using gas or chemicals.

Hospital autoclave ovens sterilise surgical instruments and ward equipment using high-pressure steam

Categories and processes of decontamination			
Example	**Process**	**Method**	**Notes**
Sterilised in the health or care setting	Surgical instruments and devices, trays and sets	1 Thoroughly clean objects and wrap or package for sterilisation 2 Sterilise using appropriate protocol for steriliser type 3 Inspect package for integrity and for exposure of sterility indicator before use	Sterilisation processes are designed to have a wide margin of safety. Maximum safe storage time of items processed in steriliser varies according to type or package or wrapping materials used. Follow manufacturer's instruction for use and storage times

(cont. opposite page)

Example	Process	Method	Notes
		4 Use before maximum safe storage time has expired, if applicable	
Purchased as sterile	Intravenous fluids, irrigation fluids, normal saline, trays and sets	1 Store in safe clean area 2 Inspect package for integrity before use 3 Use before expiry date if one is given	Contact your line manager if contamination is suspected
May be subjected to disinfection rather than sterilisation process	Respiratory therapy equipment and instruments that will touch mucous membranes. Floors, tables, surfaces or walls in environments such as operating theatres	1 Sterilise or follow a protocol for high-level disinfection 2 Bag and store in safe, clean area	Bacterial spores may survive after disinfection, but these usually are not pathogenic
Usually contaminated with some bacteria	Bedpans, crutches, rails, EKG leads, etc. Floors, walls, surfaces	Follow a protocol for cleaning and disinfection process	Remaining micro-organisms not usually pathogenic

Active knowledge

Check on the cleaning and disinfectant materials and the chemicals which are used in your workplace. By reading the labels establish what is the chemical content of the particular brand of disinfectant used. Make a note of which grades and concentrations of chemicals you use to disinfect or clean particular areas of your workplace.

How to prepare the equipment and paperwork

It is important to check any environment in which clinical procedures are to be carried out to ensure that there are no safety hazards to the person receiving the treatment or to those carrying it out. You should refer back to your work in Unit CU1 for details of the safety hazards which can exist if equipment is not regularly checked to make sure it is working correctly. Lighting should be clear and bright in any area where treatments are to be undertaken and there should not be gloomy or shadowy areas. This is extremely important to enable the person carrying out the treatment to effectively see what they are doing and also to ensure that areas which may be contaminated or dirty cannot be missed.

Your workplace may have a system which requires you to sign a record to show that an area has been thoroughly prepared for any clinical treatments. If this is the case, it is likely to have sections for confirming that areas that require cleaning or disinfection have been cleaned and disinfected, that any safety checks on equipment have been made and that the package containing instruments or equipment which are sterile have been checked to ensure the expiry date has not passed or there are no obvious signs of them being torn, wet or dirty.

All workplaces in which clinical procedures are carried out, including **primary** and **secondary clinical environments**, will have to develop a system by early 2002 which allows instruments which have been used for invasive procedures to be checked through the process of decontamination and to be identified against the individual for whom they have been used. This is to ensure that if a risk factor is subsequently identified then the relevant individuals can be traced. Records are important in establishing that correct procedures have been followed and that individuals have not been exposed to any risk. They are equally important for being able to trace if there has been a particular risk and to take action to counteract or reduce the effects of the risk. As with all records it is important that they are completed accurately, promptly and clearly and in line with the practices in your own workplace.

Checklist of how to prepare an environment

- Check equipment and furniture – is it ready and prepared?
- Adjust heating and ventilation
- Clean/sterilise/disinfect area
- Prepare paperwork, e.g. forms for patient to fill in
- Prepare those taking part, e.g. with gowns and gloves

Element CU2.2 Maintain environments following clinical procedures

WHAT YOU NEED TO LEARN

- How to clean areas and equipment and dispose of waste safely.
- How to follow safe procedures for sending specimens to the laboratory.

How to clean areas and equipment and dispose of waste safely

Regardless of whether you are preparing an area or clearing away following a clinical procedure you should carefully follow the universal precautions outlined in Element CU2.1. Any waste products of clinical procedures have the potential to transmit infection and you should ensure you do not expose yourself to unnecessary risks.

Spillages

The first priority is to deal with any spillage of blood or other body fluids. It is important to deal with these as they can represent a serious infection hazard, are potentially a slip risk and can easily be trodden into other areas. Blood spills should be dealt with by completely covering the spill with sodium dichlorisocyanurate granules. Alternatively, the spillage can be covered with disposable towels and then treated with a strong (ten thousand parts per million) solution of sodium hypochlorite. If the waste or blood spillage is mopped up with disposable towels then they must be handled with care using gloves

Spillages can be an infection hazard and need to be cleaned up immediately

and following all the universal precautions. They should then be placed inside the appropriate disposal bag, which is likely to be a yellow bag for clinical waste. You must be sure when you place soiled disposable towels, or any other soiled articles, inside a yellow clinical waste bag that the outside of the bag is not contaminated by any of the fluid or waste leaking from the towels. If the outside of the bag is contaminated in any way it is not sufficient to simply wipe the bag clean. It must be placed inside another bag. If you fail to do this you are placing the people handling these bags for disposal at considerable risk. After clearing the blood or body fluid spillage the area should be cleaned using the correct cleaning equipment and correct disinfectant as identified in Element CU2.1.

Other clinical waste

The next stage after clearing away any blood or body fluids is to deal with any other clinical waste in the treatment area. This could be:

- used and dirty dressings
- needles or other sharps
- instruments, both single use and reusable
- wipes
- used linen
- medicines or prescription only drugs.

You will need to deal with each of these in the following way.

Used and dirty dressings	These are categorised as clinical waste and should go into a yellow clinical waste bag, bearing in mind the same concerns about not contaminating the outside of the bag as with the disposable towels.

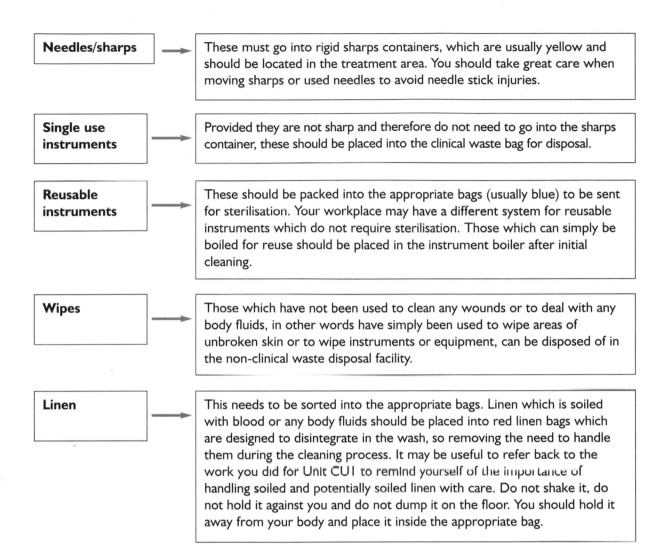

Needles/sharps	These must go into rigid sharps containers, which are usually yellow and should be located in the treatment area. You should take great care when moving sharps or used needles to avoid needle stick injuries.
Single use instruments	Provided they are not sharp and therefore do not need to go into the sharps container, these should be placed into the clinical waste bag for disposal.
Reusable instruments	These should be packed into the appropriate bags (usually blue) to be sent for sterilisation. Your workplace may have a different system for reusable instruments which do not require sterilisation. Those which can simply be boiled for reuse should be placed in the instrument boiler after initial cleaning.
Wipes	Those which have not been used to clean any wounds or to deal with any body fluids, in other words have simply been used to wipe areas of unbroken skin or to wipe instruments or equipment, can be disposed of in the non-clinical waste disposal facility.
Linen	This needs to be sorted into the appropriate bags. Linen which is soiled with blood or any body fluids should be placed into red linen bags which are designed to disintegrate in the wash, so removing the need to handle them during the cleaning process. It may be useful to refer back to the work you did for Unit CU1 to remind yourself of the importance of handling soiled and potentially soiled linen with care. Do not shake it, do not hold it against you and do not dump it on the floor. You should hold it away from your body and place it inside the appropriate bag.

Laundry

If you work in a community or a residential setting, which does not have full-scale clinical laundry facilities, then any laundry which has been contaminated or stained with blood or any other body fluids, and is to be reused, must be washed with detergent using a hot wash cycle to a temperature of at least 80°C. Alternatively, it can be dry cleaned at high temperatures, or it can be dry cleaned cold but then must be steam pressed.

If the linen is not to be reused but to be disposed of, then it must be incinerated. If you are dealing with soiled linen in a setting where you have no alternative but to hand wash it, then this must be done using household grade rubber gloves.

Medicines and drugs

Your workplace will have a strictly controlled process for disposing of prescription-only medicines and drugs which you must follow. Clinical waste is defined by the Health and Safety Advisory Committee as 'waste arising from medical, nursing, dental, veterinary, pharmaceutical or similar practice, investigation, treatment, care, teaching or research, which by nature of its toxic infections or dangerous content may prove a hazard or give offence unless previously rendered safe and inoffensive. Such waste includes human or animal tissue or excretion, drugs and medical products, swabs and dressings, instruments or similar substances and materials.'

Did you know?

NHS Trusts produce about 200,000 tons of clinical waste per year. This is equalled by the amount of waste produced in total by all the other sources, such as private hospitals, GPs, dentists, nursing homes, etc., making a total of around 400,000 tons per year of clinical waste. The Health and Safety Executive provides detailed guidelines for all employers on the disposal of clinical waste.

Areas and equipment

Finally, you should ensure that all the surfaces, instruments and equipment in the area meet the necessary standard of cleanliness or disinfection required and that fresh linen is in place where necessary. You will need to ensure that instruments and equipment that have been used are replaced with fresh, sterile or newly cleaned or disinfected ones. It is also important to check equipment after each use to make sure it is functioning correctly and to report any faults.

Some of these procedures may seem lengthy and cumbersome but they are an essential part of protecting yourself and the patient or client from the risk of infection and disease.

How to follow safe procedures for sending specimens to the laboratory

If the clinical procedures have resulted in any specimens which need to be sent to a laboratory for testing, then they need to be appropriately labelled and prepared for transport. You need to know that the person responsible for handling specimens which can be potentially hazardous has a duty under the Health and Safety at Work Act and the Control of Substances Hazardous to Health Regulations to conduct the work in a safe way. Where the specimens have been taken from people who have known or suspected blood-borne virus infections, such as HIV or hepatitis, then the specimens must be conspicuously labelled or marked DANGER OF INFECTION. Any paperwork which accompanies them should also have DANGER OF INFECTION written on it clearly. However, in order to protect patient confidentiality the diagnosis of infection, whether known or suspected, should not be included. Specimens taken to the laboratory should be sealed in individual transparent plastic bags. Only one sample should be placed in each plastic bag and there should be a means of attaching the request forms stating the tests needed, either a pocket or some other way of attaching the form to the bag. However, some bags have a facility for sliding a request form in a separate bag inside the plastic bag which will be sealed. There must be no possibility of the request form becoming detached from the specimen. Unit X13 provides information on the importance of correct labelling of specimens.

After the specimens and the request forms are placed in the proper container for transportation, they should be taken to the collection point or handed to the person who is to take them to the laboratory.

Did you know?

Clinical material or samples can be sent by post within the UK. However they have to meet very strict conditions laid down by the Royal Mail. Clinical samples cannot be sent through the post by any member of the public, they can only be sent a medical practitioner, a dentist, a vet, a registered nurse, a registered midwife or a recognised laboratory.

Unit test

1   What causes infection?

2   What are pathogens?

3   What is the commonest way that cross-infection happens?

4   What are universal precautions?

5   Why is hand washing important?

6   What are the main groups of micro-organisms which cause infections?

7   Describe how infection can spread

8   Name three ways in which equipment can be sterilised

9   What is the difference between cleaning, disinfecting and sterilising?

10 What is the chemical most commonly used for disinfection?

Unit CU9 Contribute to the development and effectiveness of work teams

Most of the work that is done in caring for others involves working as part of a team. You will either be working as part of a team within a residential establishment, within a hospital, or within a supported living environment, or you could be working as part of a more broadly based team if you support people in the community. In order for your clients to benefit from the best quality care that you can provide you need to work effectively as part of your team and a team needs to be clear about the service it is providing and the best way of organising to provide it.

This unit is designed to be generally applicable to anyone who works as part of a team but does not carry overall responsibility for the functioning of the team and is not in a management role.

Element CU9.1 Contribute to effective team practice

WHAT YOU NEED TO LEARN

- How to communicate constructively with other team members.
- How a team can work effectively.
- How to help resolve issues or difficulties that arise in the team.

How to communicate constructively

You will have developed good communication skills through your work in Units CL1 and CL2, but communicating well and working effectively in a team means that you need to develop those communication skills even further. Teams are essentially groups with a purpose and, as such, people communicate within teams in the same way as they do in groups. So you will need to use your group communication skills and to recognise the way your team is operating within those identified ways in which groups perform.

Teams and groups form for many different purposes. It could be to form:

- a family group
- a group of friends
- a support group
- a group with a common interest, such as a club
- an educational group.

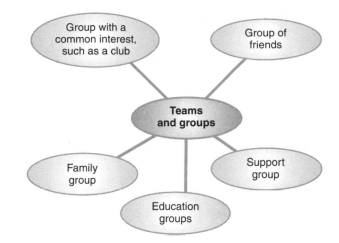

Groups and teams form for many different purposes

The list of groups is large. The circumstances in which groups can form are almost endless. However, if a group has a specific aim, objective or range of aims and objectives which it is setting out to achieve, then that group becomes a team. For example, a group of friends who are a group because they all drink in a particular pub become a team when they enter the annual tug-of-war contest and attempt to win. This is the way a quiz team develops or a football team develops.

A team, however it is formed, is a group which shares the same aims and objectives

A team = a group with a purpose

In order to work well and effectively and communicate constructively in a team you need to understand how it operates. Two of the most important key things that you need to understand about a team are its **aims** and **objectives**.

The aims and objectives of a team can be:

- set by the organisation which employs the team
- decided by the members of the team
- focused on those who receive the service provided by the team.

Hopefully any of these aims and objectives will be shared by all those involved. Where they are different, serious problems can arise in the effectiveness and the working of the team.

A team is more likely to be effective if the members share the same aims and objectives

Active knowledge

Make three lists.

1 The aims and objectives of the organisation you work for. This should be contained in your organisation's mission statement or policy documents or possibly a public plan or charter that your organisation has developed.

2 Make a list of your own aims and objectives in your work. Although they may appear to be different from those of your organisation, they may include things like wanting to give the best possible service to people, wanting to be of use to the people you provide a service for, or possibly wanting to improve your skills and understanding of the area you work in. When you have completed this list you should check how well it fits with the aims and objectives of your organisation. Do not compare simply the words on the list but look at the overall effect of what it is you want to achieve and your organisation wants to achieve and see how far they match.

3 Ask the service users what they want from the service and what their aims are in terms of their own achievement and how they see the service that you provide can assist them.

When you have completed all three lists compare them and see to what extent they match in what they are setting out to achieve.

Communication in teams

If you work on the basis that a team is simply a group with a purpose, then you need to understand how groups operate. Some understanding of this will help you to see how communication works inside a team. There are many theories about communication in groups, the roles of individuals within groups and how people respond to group situations in very different ways. One of the major theories about groups and their formation and behaviour is that they go through certain stages of development in their lifetime.

These are:

Forming

The forming stage, as you might expect, is the early stage of the group. It occurs when a team has just begun to work together. New teams can be formed from scratch, out of reorganisation, or when team members have changed. You need to remember that a change in team members produces a new team, even though some members are still part of it. A different member makes a different team.

During the forming stage people are getting to know each other, getting to understand the way in which each other works and establishing what the team is about. It is during this stage that teams need to work out what their aims and objectives are and to make plans for the way in which they will work together. This is when the team plans work rotas and off duty periods, how the work is allocated and when individuals assume particular roles within the team. The roles within a team are not just those which are allocated by an employer. The employer may decide the job description and working tasks of the individuals in the team, however there are other roles which people will take up depending on their individual personality.

For example:

- There may be a *natural organiser*, who may take a lead role in planning and organising the team.

- There is likely to be someone who is a *peace maker*, who is always keen to settle disagreements and arrange for people to compromise.

- Someone else may take on the role being a *team jester*, keeping everyone amused and always seeing the funny side of things.

- Somebody else may be the *finisher*, who makes sure the group achieves the tasks it sets out to complete.

- The team may have a *bully*, somebody who is aggressive and challenges others constantly.

- There may be someone who is an *innovator*, who always thinks up new plans and new ideas and makes sure that the team stays up to date.

There are a wide range of different roles that people will assume in the team. If you take time to look at the way in which your team operates, you may be surprised to find that particular roles are not necessarily fulfilled by the people who hold the job titles for those roles.

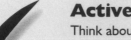

Active knowledge

Think about the team you work in. If you work in a hospital or residential setting it is far easier to think about a work team. If you work in the community as a support worker where you spend much of your time working alone with clients, then your team may not be as close. However you should think about the colleagues with whom you have regular contact and the way in which that team is structured and how it operates. Make a list of the roles that people have assumed within your group. You can call them any names you wish (try not to use rude ones!). The names should describe the way in which they behave in the team. When your list is complete you should be able to see how each individual within your team assumes a particular role. Do this immediately following a team meeting when you have had a chance to observe people's behaviour in the meeting.

Storming

The second stage of the development of effective teams is the storming stage. This is when teams seem to do nothing but argue. This is because after the first stage the team members feel more confident with each other and each individual fights to establish what they believe to be the best way forward for the team. This is when you may see particular individuals engaging in what may seem to be a power struggle, where one or two people may be fighting to take control of the team. This can be a distressing and worrying stage for many people in the team as they feel that everything is going wrong and that every team meeting involves conflict and disagreement.

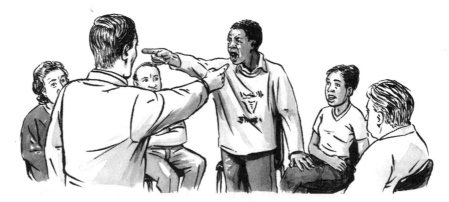

Arguing with one another is part of the storming stage of team development

Storming is part of the development of a strong and effective team and can be valuable in establishing the way in which the team will operate and in the forming of strong bonds and relationships between the members. However, it is important at the storming stage that debate, discussion and argument within the team does not become destructive. Whilst challenge and disagreement are a normal part of this stage, this should not degenerate into aggression, bullying, intimidation or an attempt to split and divide the team. If the team becomes aware of individuals who are becoming potentially destructive in their behaviour, then this should be openly challenged at a team meeting. Alternatively, the issues could be raised with a manager or whoever is responsible for running team meetings, who would be asked to raise the issues at meetings. Storming is a valuable and important stage of developing a strong team, however it is also the most potentially dangerous time, when a team can degenerate into cliques and factions who are each following their own aims and objectives. If it is used constructively to air issues and to plan a way forward in a robust and mature way then storming has achieved its purpose.

Norming

Norming is when the team begins to settle down and people firmly adopt the roles identified in the forming stage. The points at which these different stages occur will vary greatly, depending on the individuals in the team, the way it is structured, how often it meets and the way it is managed. The transaction from one stage to the next may almost be unnoticeable unless you are carefully charting the progress of your particular team. You are 'norming' as a team when you have stopped the storming stage and people have settled down and are working together, beginning to accept each others' roles, and becoming more tolerant of them. This can happen almost before you realise it and it may be only on reflection that you will recognise this stage of development.

This stage of team formation also establishes the rules for behaviour in the group and the general acceptance of the way people will behave towards each other and to the clients. The sets of rules that were considered at the forming stage and battled over at the storming stage have by the norming stage begun to settle down and be accepted as the 'normal' ways of behaving within that particular team. By the time the team is norming, the team members should be effectively working together. They should be able to openly share ideas, constructive criticism and suggestions at team meetings. Any unacceptable behaviour should be openly challenged and be established within the norms of group behaviour as unacceptable.

Performing

The ultimate aim of any team development is that after progressing through the first three stages, the team finally reaches the stage where it is delivering an effective service – that is, performing. This is the stage of team development which is the most satisfactory because the aims and objectives should be being achieved, people should be gaining satisfaction from their own roles in the team and the client group that you provide a service for should be feeling the benefits. If

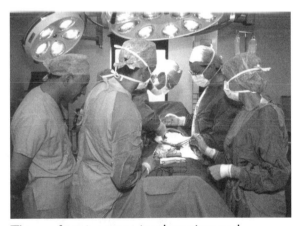

The performing stage is when aims and objectives should be being achieved

there are no changes to team members then teams can reach the performing stage and remain there for a considerable period of time. There is no reason why a team which works well when it first begins to perform effectively should not continue to do so, provided all of the factors remain the same. But there are many things which influence a team's ability to continue to perform: change of team members, change of workplace or work practices, change in the level of resources available to the team. All these have the potential to affect the team's ability to perform. It is important to be aware of the changes that can be brought about by any of these factors and the way in which they can influence the behaviour of your team. If teams are aware of the changes and the way that this can affect their ability to deliver a service, then it is more likely that a well formed strong team will be able to discuss the effects of the changes and to plan for how they will meet them without an overall deterioration in performance.

How a team can work effectively

One important way to maintain good team performance is to keep the team motivated. Much research has been carried out on the **motivation** of people at work. Clearly, in industry and manufacturing the profitability of companies depends on the motivation of the employees. This has led to a considerable amount of work being done by industrial psychologists in examining the concept of motivating people at work.

Having a purpose and new challenges

The first stage in motivating any team, and maintaining that motivation, is to make sure that the team has a purpose and that it is one that meets each member's personal aims and objectives. This takes us back to the exercise on aims and objectives on page 176. In many ways this is the same as the concept of purpose. Every so often you should look at whether your role is continuing to provide you with the sort of purpose which meets your own wants, needs and aspirations. Sometimes when the team appears to be losing its motivation and people are becoming disheartened and demoralised it can help to set a smaller challenge – a purpose within a purpose in your own work setting. For example, your overall purpose, aim and motivation may be to provide a caring service for the young people with disabilities who are in the residential establishment you work for, or it may be to provide support, personal care and protection for the group of frail, confused, elderly residents that you care for. However, these broader aims alone may not be sufficient to maintain good team performance because they may not maintain people's

To be motivated, the team and each member of it must have a purpose

motivation. So your team may decide to undertake a new and specific task for the benefit of the client group you work with. This could take the form of developing a new type of service or developing further the skills and abilities of some of the team members. This approach helps to maintain motivation and also provides challenges, another key factor in maintaining a sense of purpose and providing a challenge. Research has shown that the teams which tend to be most effective are those which continually set themselves new challenges.

However, teams do not want to face challenges every day – many who work in caring services say that this is a sufficient challenge for anyone! But challenges are important as even the most difficult job can become hum drum eventually. As individual team members become more skilled and confident in their own area of work the challenge decreases, so it is important that the team recognises when this stage is being reached and that all members share and contribute in developing new ideas and innovative ways of working.

Camaraderie

One of the other keys to successful team performance is the way team members relate to each other. The camaraderie of team members and the support that they give each other are vital components in the continuous quality performance of a successful team. The ways in which team members relate to each other can often be the difference between a successful and an unsuccessful team. In all the best teams there is a genuine warmth, concern and caring between team members. They are loyal to each other and to the team and genuinely care about and like each other. Of course, it is not possible to like every individual with whom you come into contact, neither is it possible to work only with people who share your own interests, values and beliefs. However, applying all the principles you have learned about valuing individuals, recognising the effects on individuals of their background, culture and beliefs, will encourage the workings of a successful team if each member of the team is genuinely respected and valued.

Camaraderie is one of the keys to a successful team

Active knowledge

Make a list of members in your team and honestly make a note of those you like and those you dislike. This is unlikely to be straightforward, as there are always degrees in who you like or dislike, and other considerations. You will find that there are people who you consider to be perfectly pleasant but with whom you have nothing in common, and there will be others who you genuinely like and would be happy to form a personal friendship with. There may be others in the team you find extremely difficult to deal with and whose attitudes and beliefs you find unpleasant or totally opposed to yours. It is important that you are aware of these feelings and that you take time to consider what may be behind them and how you can approach them.

Responsibility

One of the other factors likely to maintain the motivation, and therefore the performance, of a team is responsibility. Responsibility for the outcome of the team's work is often a very important factor in motivating the team. If you have developed challenges and plans for your own team and are able to see and be responsible for the outcome of this, rather than have to hand over responsibility to another level in the management chain, then this is far more likely to provide the team members with the challenge and motivation necessary to maintain good team performance. For your team to be able to accept responsibility for its actions it will also need to have the authority to carry out the plans it has made. The team may need to approach management in order to gain this authority, and it may only be for specific events or plans that this is possible. However, the research evidence into effectively performing teams shows that those with both responsibility and the authority to carry out their plans and actions tend to maintain motivation over longer periods of time.

Responsibility, however, can be demotivating if the consequences of error or failure are too great. For example, if the organisation has a history of punishing mistakes then the giving of responsibility could be viewed as a negative factor in the performance of the team. The short-term performance may be good (fear is a motivator), but long-term motivation is likely to be difficult to sustain because it is hard for teams to maintain a good performance over a period of time when the major motivation is the fear of the consequences of failing to deliver.

Personal development

The other major influencing factor in helping teams to perform well is the development of the individual within the team and the team as a whole. When people feel that they are moving forward in their own personal career goals, learning new concepts, adding to their skill base and stretching their minds, motivation is likely to remain high. Personal growth enhances self-

Major factors that contribute to the good performance of teams

esteem and self-worth, and a team member who is feeling self-confident and believes that their own personal goals are being achieved is likely to contribute effectively to the work of the team.

How to help resolve issues and difficulties

When you start considering your relationship with the individuals in your team you will need to work out how you will deal with any problem relationships. It's inevitable that some members in any team will not get on with each other. Bear in mind that a working relationship does not require the same commitment, sharing of ideals, values and understanding as a personal friendship. In order to work with someone it is sufficient that you recognise and value their contribution to the team performance and that you always communicate effectively and courteously when working with them. It is not necessary that you socialise with your work colleagues, although many team members do socialise with one another. However, this is not an essential requirement for a successful team. The loyalty and camaraderie which is built up amongst good team members can be purely based on their performance at work and does not involve their personal lives. It is not uncommon to hear the comment, 'I can't stand the women personally but you have to hand it to her she is brilliant at her job'. The important part of this statement is the valuing of people's contribution to the work of the team. This is an essential part of developing the loyalties which are the characteristics of effective teams.

Thinking positively checklist

If you have to work with people with whom you feel you have little in common try following the guidelines in this checklist in order to view them in a more positive light.

1 Tick off all the positive things and only the positive things about your colleague. For example:

- Do they have a nice smile? ☐
- Are they very good with the clients? ☐
- Do they have a particular skill in one area of practice? ☐
- Are they good in a crisis? ☐
- Are they willing to accommodate swaps in rotas? ☐
- Are they good at organising? ☐
- Do they make good coffee? ☐

2 Make a positive comment to your colleague at least once each day. This could range from 'Your hair looks nice today' to 'I have learned such a lot from watching you deal with Mrs.'

3 Ask questions about your colleague and try to find out more about them. This does not have to be on a personal level. Questions could be about their professional skills. You could try something like, 'Where did you learn to move patients so well?' Or take the trouble to find out their opinions on current issues. Perhaps you could ask, 'What do you think about the new set of proposals for the shift rotas?'

---

4 Pick up on any comments which may lead to areas of common interest. For example, your colleague may comment about something they have done over the weekend, or they may make a reference to reading something or seeing a film or a play that you know something about. You should follow up on any of these potential leads which may allow you to find out more about the individual.

5 Learn what you can about your colleague, either by listening to others or by asking questions about the person's background, and look at where their ideas and influences have come from. If you understand their culture, their beliefs and values it will be easier to see how and why they hold the opinions and views that they do.

6 Make a list of the positives that this particular colleague brings to the team.

Active knowledge

After looking at your list of team members and those who you like and dislike, it will be useful to set out an action plan of how you will tackle the issues raised by those team members that you find it more difficult to relate to. You may decide that you will concentrate on looking at the quality of their work and appreciating and valuing their contribution, or you may consider their personal circumstances and develop an understanding of why they may act as they do. If your team has reached the stage where you feel confident enough to openly share your concerns about the behaviour of another, then you should do so in a team meeting, provided that you can do this in a constructive way.

Be careful before you share views about somebody's personal behaviour that you are not making statements which can be hurtful and destructive. Make sure that any aspects of behaviour that you challenge is behaviour which genuinely affects the quality of the work or the functioning of the team. You do not have a right to challenge somebody's behaviour simply because you personally do not like it. You should only challenge behaviour which is damaging others or the work of the team.

Communication styles

So how can you contribute towards the self-confidence and success of your team?

Everything which you have learnt so far about the development of teams makes it clear that without good communication it is not possible to have an effective team. Each team member may have a different style of communication but it is important that all the team members are able to relate to each other, even if the style of communication is different. Some people communicate openly and are happy to share their feelings and concerns with others, but others may find it harder to discuss feelings and will need encouragement and support within the team to enable them to do that. The different styles of communication that you may see amongst team members could be:

- Open, sharing and clear.
- Secretive, unwilling to share information.

Individual style of communication can have an effect on the performance of the team

- Aggressive, dominating, wanting to override the views of others and to impose their own views on the workings of the team.

- No confidence, someone who finds it difficult to express any of their views, who is unassertive and although they may have ideas and suggestions which are valuable they are unable to share them with the team.

- Manipulative, someone who may try to control the team in a less obvious way than the aggressive person.

- Negative, someone who can only see the problems in every situation, who is never able to offer a constructive idea or suggestion but simply identifies the problems.

You will need to recognise the value of each different style of communication within your team and to appreciate that every team member, regardless of the way in which they communicate, will have something valuable to bring to team meetings. It will be important for the effectiveness of the team that your meetings and communications take account of the range of ways in which people function within the team. Also you need to make sure that information is shared in a way that each different member is able to use it best and that all members of the team are able to make a contribution in the way in which they feel comfortable. For example, if the team is discussing ideas for a new project or how a particular event will be organised and take place, then contributions should be asked for from team members in a way which is going to allow everyone to contribute. If there are people in the team who tend to be unassertive and quiet in team meetings, then the request for ideas and contributions could be posted on the staff notice board some days before. Contributions and suggestions could be asked for in writing or at the meeting. This will give an unassertive team member the chance to make some notes which can then be circulated to other team members. If there is a team member who tends to be dominant and take over group discussions, then this will have to be challenged if it is damaging the functioning of the team. Remember that not all teams are damaged by having a dominant member. It may suit the structure of some teams, and there may be team members who are happy to allow someone else to take that leading role and to make their own contribution to the work of the team in other ways. However, this is unusual and in most teams the attempted domination by an individual is unlikely to be welcome. Similarly, any aggressive behaviour in team meetings must be challenged.

In the work you did for Unit Z1 you learned about challenging inappropriate and unacceptable individual behaviour. However challenging this in a group situation can be far more threatening and more difficult to achieve. Conversely, if you are confident that you have the support of other team members it can be easier than making a challenge on a one-to-one basis, as you know that you will be supported by other members. Challenges to the behaviour of an individual in a team must be made in a constructive way. These are some ways to do it:

Team member	Response
Dominant team member	'Carol, you have some brilliant ideas for how we can run this event but it would be really helpful if you could give the rest of us a chance to comment on them and to see what we have got to add to your ideas.'
Aggressive/rude/bullying team member	'Jim, I don't think there is any need to be so aggressive to make your point. We all appreciate what you are saying, you don't need to shout.'
Unassertive – unwilling to contribute team member	'Leslie, could you explain to the rest of the team those ideas you were telling me about over coffee the other day.'
Manipulative team member	'Nancy, are you intending to make everyone feel guilty or hadn't you realised what you were doing?'

The Apollo syndrome

One of the greatest difficulties in team operation arises when there is more than one dominant individual or when teams are composed of a group of high-powered, often highly intelligent members. It is often assumed that if you form a team of real high flyers that they will achieve great things. This situation, known as the **Apollo syndrome**, is often not the case. In fact it is often the reverse and the teams with the highly intelligent, high-flying members often achieve far less than other teams.

Too many high-flyers in a team can make it impossible for the team to perform effectively

The Apollo syndrome was identified in 1981 by Dr Meredith Belbin, who has done a great deal of research into team development and team building. What he established in his identification of the Apollo syndrome was that teams formed of people with high mental ability showed the following characteristics:

- They spent excessive time in abortive or destructive debate trying to persuade other team members to adopt their own view and demonstrating a flair for spotting weaknesses in others' arguments.

- They had difficulties in decision making and the decisions they did reach lacked coherence.

- They tended to pursue their own interests without taking account what other members were doing, so effectively they worked as a group of individuals and not as a team.

- They are likely to be people or individuals who have an overly important view of their own role within a team.

This work has been extremely useful in helping to identify the sorts of problems which can arise within teams and helps to clarify the view that everybody working at the same time is not necessarily the same thing as everybody working together.

Case study

Tom, Jane, Rose and Natalia were all members of the support worker team at a small mental health hostel. Sue had just arrived as a new team member to fill a long-standing vacancy. Jane was the senior support worker and had been in the post for about four months. Tom, Rose and Natalia had all worked at the hostel since it opened six years previously.

The first staff meeting following Sue's appointment was to discuss new rotas and the staff development programme planned for the coming year. Jane announced the first item on the agenda, which was the new staff rotas. She began by briefly outlining the hours which they had now been asked to cover and the number of staff who would need to be available on sleep-in cover. At this point Tom said that he had organised the rotas and produced a chart showing when everybody would be working. He said that he had explored all the options and had discussed them with one of the senior managers. He had also contacted workers in other hostels to ask how they had adapted the new system, but he felt that the system he had developed was probably the one which would work most effectively. Sue was a little surprised that there was no discussion about the issue and that the other members of staff and herself did not appear to have been consulted about whether or not these rotas were suitable, but she did not feel that she could make a stand, given it was the first item of her first staff meeting.

Jane then moved on to the next item on the agenda, which was the staff development plans for the coming year. She explained the budget which had been allocated for staff development for mental health support workers. At this point Tom interrupted to say that he had been speaking to the staff at the local university who were running some excellent courses which he felt were entirely appropriate for the staff to attend. He had accordingly booked people to attend a series of courses which reflected the needs of the particular hostel and the skill mix that people had. He said that he had the information pack with details of the courses and he would leave it in the staff room for people to look at. At this point Sue said that she felt that the selection of training courses should be a matter for the individual members of staff and not have the choice made on their behalf by a colleague. She said that she would welcome the opportunity to look at the pack and when she had done so she would advise Jane if she was interested in any of those courses. She added that she would also bring in some information she had about courses which were being run by a local voluntary organisation, and which were extremely relevant to the needs of the workers in the mental health hostel.

1 How do you think Tom will react to Sue's intervention?

2 How would you expect Rose and Natalia to react?

3 What are Jane's feelings likely to be?

4 Who should have resolved this situation?

5 How should it have been approached?

6 What alternatives are there for Tom to behaving in this way?

7 Suggest what Sue's feelings may be following the meeting.

Keys to good practice

To be a team member in a successful team you will need to check that you are contributing to the following:

- ☐ Agreeing and sharing a common purpose, aims and objectives.

- ☐ Working on building relationships which value and respect all team members.

- ☐ Contributing to the planning process for all the team activities.

- ☐ Making sure that all team members are involved in decision making.

- ☐ Respect and value the diversity of each team member.

- ☐ Value working together and recognise the difference between working at the same time and working together.

- ☐ Support the goals which have been agreed by the team.

- ☐ Praise and give credit to the work of all team members.

- ☐ Use your communication skills effectively when working with other members of the team.

- ☐ Ensure the team has dialogue and not debate.

- ☐ Work to identify and resolve conflicts within the team.

- ☐ Examine the way the team is operating and don't be afraid to initiate constructive and supportive criticism.

- ☐ Contribute to the growth and development of the team as a whole, the members of the team and yourself as an individual.

Active knowledge

Teams are good for us?

The *Lancet* medical journal reported that research showed that people who work in effective teams have a lower risk of coronary heart disease. The research found that people who had low control felt frustrated and unhappy, were not motivated in their work setting, and were more likely to suffer coronary heart disease than those who were able to exert more control over their working environment. One of the ways of achieving more control is by working in an effective team.

Element CU9.2 Contribute to the development of others in the work team

WHAT YOU NEED TO LEARN

- How to support other members of your team effectively.
- How to communicate in a way that increases understanding.
- How to disseminate information to other team members.

How to support team members

Supporting people is a very general term and it can mean a great many things depending on the context and the purpose for which the support is offered. In the context of supporting a work colleague in a team, support could mean:

- Recognising when somebody is having difficulty in a particular area of work.
- Recognising when somebody is having difficulty in their personal life which may be affecting their work.
- Recognising and acknowledging when a colleague has worked particularly well.
- Noticing when people are overloaded with jobs to do and offering to lend a hand.
- Telling colleagues about information you have discovered or something you have seen or read which you know would be of interest to them.
- Making sure colleagues know of opportunities for training courses which you think are likely to interest them.
- Noticing when a colleague is nervous or unsure of a new task or procedure and offering help and encouragement.
- Noticing if a colleague is being made uncomfortable by the way in which they are being spoken to or treated by another colleague or client and offering to help if it is needed.

This list and any additional items which you can add to it will make a contribution towards the support and development of other members of your team. If your team is working well, your colleagues will be doing the same thing for you and supporting you in your development.

Active knowledge

Keep a calendar for a week or two or even a month. On each day draw a stick figure which represents yourself and at the end of each working shift draw arrows out from you for support which you have given to others in your team and draw inward facing arrows for the occasions when support has been offered to you. None of the support may be major, however a series of small actions of support are what is likely to contribute most effectively to

successful teams. At the end of each week count up the arrows inward and the arrows outward. They should be in proportion to the people who work on the team and you should be giving and receiving support in equal measure. If there are more arrows in than out then you need to explore for yourself additional ways in which you can support colleagues. If there are more arrows out than in then this is an item that could be placed on the agenda for discussion at a team meeting.

Ways to offer support

Giving support to other team members can sometimes be misinterpreted. So you will need to ensure that you use all your communication skills in order to offer the support, advice or encouragement in a way which is not seen as patronising or implying some kind of criticism of your colleague. Every team is different in nature, some are quite formal in the relationships between team members, others are very casual and relaxed. The communication style of your team should always be the approach which you use when you are offering support to any colleagues. If your team works on a casual, friendly basis and you notice a colleague struggling, it would be normal practice to cheerfully say, 'Want a hand?' However, if your team has a more formalised relationship, with lines of responsibility and seniority carefully observed, then the same kind of offer of help would be approached quite differently. Perhaps, 'You look busy Mrs M…, can I help with that?' The way in which help is offered can often be the key to whether or not it is accepted. If you are offering advice, support or information with a genuine desire to assist your colleagues then you are unlikely to offend.

Case study

Sandy Court is a large purpose-built day centre which caters for 60 older people with varying ranges of mobility and levels of confusion. Most of the staff have worked in the day centre for the past three years since it was opened. Val is the officer in charge, Sharan is the deputy officer in charge and Margaret, Maureen and Hyacinth are the care team. Elaine and Louise, who is a trainee, work in the kitchen and a new member of staff, Sarah, has just started work at the centre. Margaret has been asked to look after Sarah and support her during her first few weeks. She has introduced Sarah to all the regular users of the centre.

On the second day, Sarah went to join one of the groups after lunch and suggested that they may begin to do some story telling and to recall the things that used to go on in the local area in the past. Margaret was quick to explain that this group was the card-playing group and that talking was not something that they wanted to do, or would have enjoyed. She carefully explained to Sarah that it wasn't her fault, it was just that she was new and obviously she would get to know these things as she gained more experience. Later that same afternoon Sarah was assisting Mrs B to the toilet when Margaret came across and said, 'Oh, it's much better to put Mrs B in a wheelchair, she gets there a lot quicker that way and we don't have any accidents. Don't worry Sarah, you will soon get used to it, it just takes a bit more knowledge.'

At the end of Sarah's first fortnight, Val, the officer in charge, spoke to Margaret to ask her views about how Sarah was progressing. Margaret said that she was sure that the girl had potential, but she didn't seem to know very much and that she wasn't sure how quickly she was learning things because she still seemed not to be able to undertake any tasks for herself.

1 What do you think Sarah's response will be when Val asks her how she has got on in her first two weeks?

2 What is the possible motivation behind the way Margaret is dealing with Sarah?

3 Are there any advantages for Sarah in this kind of approach?

4 Are there any advantages for Margaret in this kind of approach?

5 Can Sarah do anything to improve this situation, if so what?

6 What should Val do?

7 What should the rest of the team do?

How to communicate in a way that increases understanding

Every group of people has its own way of communicating. This is particularly true of teams who work in particular settings. It is also true in many situations in life, as in the case of people in a particular age group or class who use certain phrases and terminology common to their age group or class and which identifies them to others.

For example, you would be advertising yourself as coming from fairly high up the social ladder if you were to refer to:

- a sitting room or drawing room rather than a lounge.
- a napkin rather than a serviette.
- a toilet rather than a loo or lavatory.

You would be clearly identified as being of an older generation if you were to use such phrases as: 'Before the war we may not have had much money, but we did see life'; and 'We had a wireless.'

Terminology can also define people's occupational background. For instance, if you heard somebody saying that they had a 'nasal discharge' rather than a 'runny nose', you might be likely to assume that that person worked in the medical field. If you were to overhear somebody explaining that their 'galanthus nivalis had looked wonderful under the ilex aquifolium', then you would

You need to communicate to others in a language they will understand

be correct in assuming that this was a gardener telling you that their snowdrops had looked wonderful under the holly bush.

The words used by this person identifies her as someone with specialised knowledge of gardening. She is saying that 'snowdrops look wonderful under the holly bush'

This is no less true of people who work in the care sector. For example, if you were to read a set of medical case notes and a set of case notes for a child being looked after by the local authority you may find the initials B/O in both of them. In the medical notes it would mean 'bowel open', in the child's case notes it would refer to the child being 'boarded out', that is placed with foster parents. Similarly, if you talked about CPD in a social work or early year setting, people would understand you to be talking about 'continuous professional development'. In other words, ensuring that their practice was current and up to date. On the other hand, if you were part of a team working in a maternity unit, this would refer to 'cephra pelvic disproportion', which means that a woman has a pelvis which is too small to fit a baby through.

It is always important to check that the terminology that you are using is the terminology which your work colleagues use and that you all understand to mean the same thing. This is particularly important if you are working in a multi-disciplinary team, or have moved to a new team in a slightly different setting.

Active knowledge

Translate the following paragraph and rewrite it or explain it verbally to a brand new member of staff.

'I'm not happy about signing off this NVQ. I am not convinced that the PCs have been covered and I don't think the IV has assessed it yet. It is going to have to be ready for the EV and I think I will ask her advice. If you look at the latest QCA guidance it seems to argue and say the opposite to the guidance from DfEE. But I saw information the other day from the NTO that indicated that not all the PCs on the EARS had to be recorded, so I want some guidance before I make a decision.'

If you have a problem with translating this ask your assessor and your internal verifier for help. If you have had a problem, think about how you felt and remember how new members of staff feel when jargon is being used which they may not understand.

How to disseminate information

One of the valuable roles of all team members is to share information they have. This may be information that you picked up from a meeting or a training day that you attended, or it may have come from a documentary that you saw on TV, or an article you read, or information that you found on the Internet. One of the important contributions that you can make to your team and to the development of all the team members is to make sure that such information is shared and that you do not keep it to yourself and fail to let others know about it. There is an old but true saying 'that knowledge is power', and there are people who will hold onto information in the hope that it will give them an edge or an advantage over their own team members. This means they are not functioning well as members of their team and having difficulty in accepting the basic requirements of contributing to team effectiveness.

If there is a member of your team who tends to behave in this way then the team will need to consider some strategies to deal with that person. One effective way might be to suggest that at each team meeting a different team member makes a presentation about some new or emerging information they know about which will be of value to others. It could be suggested that the team member who is causing difficulties is the first one to make this presentation and the team could then praise and encourage them for the valuable contribution they have made. This might help the team member to see that there is more to be gained from sharing information with others than keeping it to oneself.

There is little point in sharing information and updates with your colleagues unless you do it in a way they can understand and accept. Placing an interesting article on a notice board may be one way of letting people see it, however notice boards tend to be like wallpaper, in that people don't always notice what's on them. Also, it isn't easy to stand and read a whole article if it is pinned on a notice board. If you have an interesting article which you would like to share with team members, the best way might be to ask your manager if you can photocopy the article and distribute it to

Information   knowledge

In organisations information and knowledge can 'cascade' to others

team members. If you have been to a particularly valuable or useful meeting or training day you may want to copy and share any of the handouts with your colleagues. Or it may be possible to arrange a short presentation at a team meeting so you can share the information you have gained. This is called '**cascading**' and is used by many organisations as a cost-effective way of sharing information across a wide range of staff.

Active knowledge

Think of an occasion when some useful or interesting information was passed on to you by a fellow team member. How did it make you feel?

Element CU9.3   Develop oneself in own work role

WHAT YOU NEED TO LEARN

- How to make a development plan.
- How to make use of feedback.
- How to monitor and evaluate your own development.

How to make a development plan

Development plans can take many forms, the best ones likely to be those developed in conjunction with your manager or the workplace supervisor. You need to carefully consider your 'areas of competence' and understand which you need to develop for your work role. You will have to make judgements about yourself in respect of those. You need to identify each one as either an area in which you feel fully confident, or one where there is room for improvement and development, or where you have very limited current ability. In the table below the headings in the columns are suggestions only, however if you do this exercise yourself the headings will need to broadly reflect those three different areas.

Once you have completed your table you can then identify the areas on which you need to concentrate. You should set some goals and targets and your line manager should be able to help you ensure they are realistic. For example, if you were to decide that you needed to achieve competence in managing a team and you were to identify your goal as being fully competent in six months time, this would be unrealistic and unachievable. You would inevitably fail to meet your target and would therefore be disappointed and likely to become demoralised and demotivated. Alternatively, if your target was to attend a training and development programme on team building during the next six months and to lead perhaps two team meetings by the end of the next six months, those goals and targets would be realistic and you would be likely to achieve them.

Only in conjunction with your line manager can you examine the areas of competency and skills which you need to achieve. There are no rights or wrongs,

Development plan

Development area:	Goals
Time management and workload organisation	Learn to use computer recording and information systems
Skills development, including time scale and how skill improvement has been measured	
Action plan: Attend two-day training and use study pack. Attend follow-up training days. Use computer instead of handwriting reports	Improvement
Review date: 3 months	
Professional development – priorities My priorities for training and development in the next 6 months are:	IT and computerised record systems.
My priorities for training and development in the next 6-12 months are:	As above and NVQ assessor training.
Repeat this exercise in 6 months and review the areas of competency and priorities.	

this is very much a personal development programme for you, and you must be sure it reflects not only the objectives of your organisation and the job roles they may want you to fulfil, but also your own personal ambitions and aspirations. After you have identified the areas in which you feel competent and have chosen your target areas for development, you will need to include other pages in your personal development log which will enable you to keep a record of your progress in achieving your goals. The pages can be put together in any way that you find effective, however the suggestions in the table on page 195 of things to include may be helpful.

The types of things you may wish to include can be as varied as developing a particular skill, for example learning sign language or learning a particular technique for working with clients with dementia. Or it could be developing your skills as a potential manager, for example, learning about organisational and human resources skills. It could also include some areas of personal professional development, such as time management and stress management. All these are legitimate areas for inclusion in your own personal and professional development plan.

How to make use of feedback

Feedback is one of the most valuable ways of ensuring that you are continuing to work towards your targets. If some of the targets you have set yourself involves the acquisition of particular skill levels you will not know whether or not you have achieved them if you do not receive feedback from colleagues and line managers. You should make arrangements to include feedback from your line manager at the review stages of your personal development plan and you should also set aside time to ask colleagues and, if appropriate, clients to provide you with some feedback on your progress. When you have received feedback you should make sure that you make good use of it. You could use it to improve the skills and practice you are intending to develop.

How to monitor and evaluate your own development

Use your personal and professional development plan as a means of recording ongoing monitoring of your progress towards your goals and targets. If you find that you are moving too slowly towards your target, you will need to consider whether you have set your goal or target too high, or if there is anything that you can or should be doing in order to speed up progress. Many things can get in the way of achieving goals, for example your employer may have reduced the resources available for training and development and so your plans to attend a particular number of training days may no longer be possible. Where you meet this type of difficulty you should explore alternative means of obtaining the information that you would have had, such as using textbooks, the Internet and gathering information from colleagues and others who have previously attended such training days. The review and evaluation process is essential to the successful progress and achievements of your own career goals. Your development plan should be a working document which you use on an ongoing basis year on year, and each time you review and evaluate you should update your targets and alter them to fit any changed circumstances or changed ambitions or aspirations which you may develop. A development plan can move with you if you change job roles or settings and you will need to undertake a major review at that point.

If you value your own career development sufficiently to take the time and effort to ensure that you plan it and follow the plan to achieve your goals then you are more likely to be an effective and valuable member of a team. You will also better understand the importance of supporting and encouraging others to achieve their own goals, aspirations and ambitions and thus contribute to a team which performs enthusiastically and well and provides a high-quality service for those for whom you care.

Unit test

1   What are the stages of development of teams?

2   Identify the characteristics of each of the stages?

3   What is the Apollo syndrome?

4   How can you deal with the Apollo syndrome?

5   What are the main characteristics of effective teams?

6   What steps can you take to ensure that your team is effective?

7   Suggest three different sources of information which could be shared with the team?

8   Consider likely methods of disseminating information to team members.

9   What is the importance of a personal development plan?

10 What are the important elements to be included in a personal and professional development plan?

Unit SC8

Contribute to the development, provision and review of care programmes

Services are provided by a wide range of agencies in many different ways. These could be as different as providing a hospital bed for somebody who is acutely ill, providing residential accommodation for a homeless young person or providing large print books for somebody who has visual impairment. One of the most important aspects of the provision of service is to ensure that it is meeting the needs of the client.

Clients' needs are not about what the agency or the care worker believes is needed, they are about what the client understands their own needs to be. One of the most important roles of a care worker is to find out from the client about the type of service they need and then to work alongside them and with their family, and any other carers, to ensure that the maximum effective level of service is provided and that it meets the needs of all those concerned. It is also important that the worker understands the limitations of the service that is provided by their own agency. Sometimes it is necessary to explain this to the client, even though it may be disappointing not to provide them with exactly what they had hoped for.

In this unit you will learn about the best ways to ensure that you have the maximum possible information about your client, about how you can work with them and make sure that they are happy about the service they are getting. You will also learn about the importance of continually looking at the service which is provided for your client together them to make sure that it continues to meet their needs.

Element SC8.1 — Obtain information about clients and their needs

WHAT YOU NEED TO LEARN

- How to understand and explain the role that you play in the assessment process.
- How to obtain information from the client.
- How to obtain information about the client from other sources.
- How to organise recorded information for easy access.

Your role in the assessment process

Many different care workers undertake the role of obtaining information about clients and what services they need. You could be assessing people for domiciliary services while they remain in their own homes, you could be assessing the needs which people may have once they leave a hospital or a residential care setting, you could be talking to a teenager or a young person about the needs they have either for residential or other support services – the possibilities are very broad. However, whatever role you have as a worker and regardless of which agency you are working for and the kind of services that your agency provides, there are some basic principles which apply to the work you will do. One of these is that you must carefully explain to the client your role in the whole process. However, before you can clearly explain your role to someone else in a way that they can understand, you must ensure that you understand your own role.

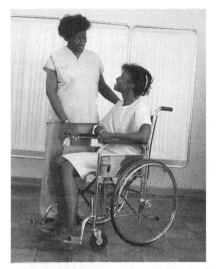

One of your roles as carer is to provide the client with as much information as you can about the service that will be provided

In these circumstances it is not necessarily your role to speak on behalf of your client.

Your role is to ensure that:

- what your client wants and needs is clearly explained to those providing the service
- as much information as possible is obtained from the client
- you also provide the client and their carers and family with as much information as you can about the nature of the service that will be provided.

This helps to avoid misunderstandings which can occur through lack of information and through lack of clear explanation about exactly what a client can expect from the agency that is providing the service.

There are also other matters you need to deal with in your role in providing a care service.

1 You will also need to explain to a client exactly what service your agency provides. It can sometimes be helpful to explain how your agency is funded and what the limitations may be on the types of services that can be provided.

2 You might find that clients or their families have an unrealistic expectation and will ask for services which are simply not available – either because of lack of funding or other resources or lack of trained personnel, or simply that this service is not one which is currently available in your area or through your agency. Explaining this can be difficult to handle. You may feel as if you have 'let down' the client, and in some way that it is your responsibility.

3 It is important to realise that it is not your personal responsibility or any personal failing of yours if your agency is unable, through lack of funding or any other resources, to provide a specific service at the level or with the frequency that a client is looking for.

4 You should not let this influence or affect the way in which you are able to relate to the client, neither should you over-commit your agency or make promises that simply cannot be fulfilled. It is far worse for a client to feel let down and

disappointed because you told them or led them to expect that something can be provided which later proves to be impossible.

Before visiting a client it may be helpful to make a list of exactly what your role is and the limitations of that role. You can then check off the points on the list, either on the list, or in your head, and in that way be sure that you have covered all the important information points.

Remember

- To give all possible information about your role and the role of your agency.
- That you may have to repeat this several times if there are several family members or other people who are involved in your client's care.
- That if your client has hearing, understanding, or learning difficulties you may have to repeat the information or write it down or make it available in some other accessible format.
- That information is very important and that it empowers people. You will fail to properly empower your client to make informed choices if you fail to give them sufficient information.

How to obtain information from the client

Developing a relationship with the client

The importance of the relationships which you develop with your clients cannot be stressed enough. There is no substitute for an effective worker/client relationship in the assessment delivery and review of services. In Unit CL1 you will have learned the basic communication skills involved in building working relationships with clients and you will need to use all those skills when you are working with clients in order to establish their needs and expectations of a service. The information that you gather should be based on much more than the answers your client has supplied to a set of questions. It should also include your observations, what you know about your clients' values and beliefs and the factors which have influenced their development. All of these are important in assessing the kind of service which will be appropriate for any particular individual. It is through using effective communication skills to develop a working relationship with your client that you will be able to best contribute towards providing a service which will meet their individual needs.

Case study

Elizabeth G is 85 years old. She lives alone and has recently become increasingly frail. She has no memory difficulties but finds shopping, cooking and coping with housework increasingly difficult. Elizabeth had never married and during her professional life had been head teacher of a large primary school. She has one brother, who emigrated to New Zealand over 50 years ago and never returned to live in England. Since her retirement she enjoyed travelling abroad and visited many countries, including New Zealand to see her brother. She always travelled alone, or occasionally with another teacher from her school. Elizabeth had never been particularly religious and attended her local Anglican church only on formal occasions, such as the marriage of friends, baptisms or funerals. She has always enjoyed gardening but recently been unable to do it, so her once lovely garden had now become overgrown.

Elizabeth reluctantly contacted social services to ask for help with the preparation and cooking of meals and some basic housework. She no longer had the money to pay for the private provision of any of these services, and she was aware she felt it inappropriate for her to be asking for help from social services. The help provided was in the form of a home help once a week to do some shopping. The person carrying out the assessment of Elizabeth's needs also decided she needed some company. It was decided that the best way for her to get a regular meal and some company would be to attend a local luncheon club. The worker dealing with Elizabeth arranged transport for her to do this, in the hope that Elizabeth would enjoy socialising with the others at the luncheon club. Elizabeth attended the luncheon club once. When transport arrived for her the following day she told them that she would not be going again and then contacted social services to cancel all the other arrangements that had been made for her. She said that she had re-thought her needs and decided that she could manage quite well and that there was no need for them to take up services which could be of more use to someone else.

1   From what you know of Elizabeth's background would you expect her to be happy with a group of strangers?

2   Given her background what would you expect her interests to be?

3   What sort of social situations would you expect Elizabeth to feel comfortable in?

4   What do you know about Elizabeth's feelings about asking for help?

5   What do you think Elizabeth's reaction would be to any problems in the provision of her service?

6   How do you think Elizabeth's feelings about asking for help should be approached?

7   Do you think that the services provided were appropriate for Elizabeth?

8   If not, why not?

9   Were Elizabeth's background and influences taken into account?

10 What services would be appropriate provision for Elizabeth?

11 What would you do to re-establish contact with Elizabeth?

In addition to considering the cultural and developmental influences on your client you should never forget the influence that your presence and your relationship has on the way in which your client will describe their own needs. It is always extremely difficult for us to assess what affect we have on others, however it is possible to take this into account when you are considering someone's response. If you have done some of the exercises in Unit CL1, where you began to look at the affect you have on others, then you should apply what you learned from those exercises to the situation of establishing client needs and expectations. Remember that if a client believes you expect them to minimise their complaints and to always be cheerful, then they are less likely to tell you the true extent of their needs and are far more likely to minimise their requirements. It is normal for any of us to seek approval from others by doing what they expect us to do.

You need to think carefully about the way you can influence clients. It is not only your own personal style of communication which influences them, it is also the way you explain the possibilities of service provision. So you will need to be aware of pushing clients and their families into a particular solution, simply because you happen to believe that it is the best one. Clients will ask for your advice and will ask the question 'What would you do?' You will have to learn to avoid answering the client directly, as it is not for you to give direct advice about a course of action that a client can take, nor is it for you to explain what you would do if you were them. You are not them, you

It is difficult for us to see how much we influence others

are not in their circumstances and never will be, therefore it is not possible for you to answer in any helpful way the question, 'What would you do if you were me?'

What you can usefully do is provide information about the services and empower your client to make their own decisions. However, you should be very careful not to direct or influence your client in making those decisions, simply provide unbiased, accurate and clear information and then follow that by supporting them to achieve the outcome of the decision they have made.

Putting clients in control

Throughout the process of obtaining information you should make sure you constantly check back with the client that they are fully aware of everything that is happening and feel they are in control of the process. One of the problems with the way services are provided, regardless of whether they are services for health, for social care provision or provision for children and young people, is that many clients feel they play only a passive role in the services they receive. It is easy to see how this can happen. Agencies and service providers have well-organised systems which can often involve filling in a great many forms, attending meetings and working through the bureaucracy. If you work regularly for such an organisation these things are a day-to-day part of your working life. They do not represent a threat to you and they do not represent something which is frightening, confusing or difficult to understand. However, you need to remind yourself that many of the clients you deal with will not be as familiar with all of the workings of your agency and that they may not feel confident enough to question or to challenge what is happening. There are several steps you can take at each stage of the process to ensure that clients feel that they are in charge of providing the information that is required for their service.

1   Clients should make clear who needs to be involved in the process of thinking about and planning their service provision.

    You may need to prompt your client to think about the people that they would like to be involved. Sometimes it is helpful to make some suggestions or to ensure that your client has considered all the possibilities. For example, you could ask 'What about your neighbour Mrs S, the one who pops in with your dinner. Might it be a good idea to ask her?' Or, 'You know your niece Susan, she might have some ideas about the sort of services that you could use.'

If you are meeting your client for the first time and you have little knowledge of their background or family, you will need to ask some questions to establish the people who are significant in their lives and who should be involved in planning their care. You could prompt your client by asking, 'Is there anyone else who pops in to see you? Does anyone help with your shopping or take you out? Is there anyone amongst your friends, family or neighbours who helps with cooking or providing meals?'

2   At each stage of the process you should check with the client that they are in agreement with the steps which have been taken so far. You should do this by using the means of communication which is most effective with your client and to go over what you have already discussed with them and any arrangements which you have put in hand. For example, if your normal means of communication is to talk to your client, then you could have a regular review with them where you would explain, 'Right Mr F... so far you have decided that you would like a home-help and I have arranged for that to start next week. And you said that you would like to have meals on wheels delivered. They will be able to start next Thursday. Is this alright with you, or do you want anything different?' Alternatively, if you have a client who has any form of hearing impairment then your means of communication may be written. If this is the case you could provide a short list of what has so far been arranged and check that they are still happy with that.

3   The use of any additional sources of information, for example previous records or other agencies who may be involved with your client, must be agreed with the client in advance before you approach the sources for the information.

4   It is important you do not take this agreement for granted and that you establish an agreement with your client and make sure that they understand. You will need to explain exactly what it is you intend to do so your client is clear what they are agreeing to. You could say, 'Mrs J, it would be helpful if we could talk to your doctor to find out exactly the kind of help that we can give you to make sure that you are not putting your health at risk. Are you happy for us to do this? It will mean me telephoning your doctor and asking her exactly how much you are able to do without aggravating your heart condition. Do you understand the sort of information that I am going to ask for?'

You should make sure that you record your client's agreement to approaching other people for information. Many agencies will require written confirmation of your client's agreement to provide information about them. You will need to establish this at the agency concerned and if necessary complete their authorisation form with your client, ensuring that you explain to them what the implications of signing the form are. If at any point during your initial assessment and checking of information your client withdraws their consent for you to approach a particular agency or individual, then you must respect that and not pursue that particular source of information.

How to obtain information from other sources

We have already looked at the information you can obtain directly from the clients themselves and also considered the information which you will gain by observing your client and from what you know about their background, culture and beliefs, however there are other sources of information which are extremely useful. Once you have ensured you have your client's agreement to do so, you may wish to consider accessing a range of other sources to complete the picture you have of your client and the way in which they can most benefit from the services that your agency provides. Examples of to the sources are:

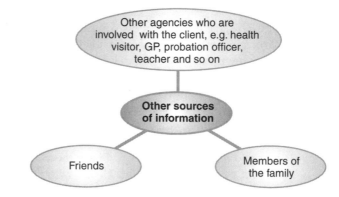

A care worker may need access to other sources of information to get a fuller picture of what services a client needs

Bear in mind that information that you gain, particularly from other professional sources, may be restricted by:

- the bounds of confidentiality under which that professional operates
- the legal restrictions as to how information may be passed on.

Most professionals are bound by principles of confidentiality in respect of their clients. You will know that there are limits to the information that you can and should share with others about your client, so you must expect that other professionals from whom you are seeking information will also be bound by the same restrictions of confidentiality regarding your client. Information can be protected under a range of different legislation, as shown below.

Type of information	Relevant legislation
Medical information/hospital records	Access to Medical Records Act
Information relating to children and young people	Children Act
Information relating to people with mental health problems	Mental Health Act
Information relating to people with a disability	Disabled Persons Act
Any information which is stored on a computer database	Data Protection Act

All these Acts work on the basic principle that personal information which is given or received, in what is understood to be a confidential situation and for one particular purpose, may not be used for a different purpose. They also contain the proviso that information may not be passed to anyone else without the agreement of the person who provided the information. **The Access to Medical Records Act** ensures the individual has access to their own records but that these are not available to anyone else unless the individual gives express permission. This applies even after death where an individual has expressly forbidden any information to be passed to anyone else or to a specific individual.

The Data Protection Act relates specifically to information which is stored by computer. This also meets the broad proviso about the purpose which information has been supplied and also contains the requirement that information may not be passed on to others without the express consent of the person to whom it relates.

You should always take great care that you are not contravening any laws when you are accessing information from other agencies in respect of your client.

Family and friends

Family and friends are an invaluable source of information about a client and the needs they have. However, you must be sure before you discuss anything with family or friends that this is being done with the express consent of the client. It is easy to make assumptions that because someone is a relative or close friend that the client will have no objections to them being involved in talking to you and giving information. Always confirm with the client that they have no objection to you discussing their case with family or friends.

How to organise recorded information for easy access

When you have gathered information that you need about your client, it is important that it is readily accessible for all those who are going to be involved in the planning and delivering of the services. Your agency is likely to have a specific form that you need to complete. This will describe your client's needs and will also contain your assessment of the best way in which those needs can be met.

The way in which this information is recorded is important if you are to provide an effective service for your client. It must be recorded in a way which those who need can easily access it. Those who may need to access the information will vary depending on your client and their circumstances. They could be:

Those who may need to access recorded information about clients

The information that you obtain during this initial stage will be vital in its contribution to the next stage of the process, which is planning the service provision for your client, which you will have a vital role in contributing to.

Keys to good practice

1 Ensure that your client understands your role and the role and limitations of what your agency can provide.

2 Make sure that you keep your client informed at all times so that they can make informed choices about the service they need.

3 Use all sources of information that you are able to locate but ensure that you have the client's agreement to do so.

4 Organise and record the information in a way which is clear and easily accessible for all others who may need to make use of it.

Active knowledge

Try preparing a record sheet which you will use for all clients about whom you have to gather information. This should include the basic factual information which is required by your agency, however make sure you add to it information which you have obtained through your own observation or through your understanding of the client's values, beliefs and culture. You could organise this as a checklist so that you can use it whenever you work with clients in obtaining information. Check your list against any forms which are already provided by your agency and see how many additional aspects you have included. This should give you some indication of the importance of obtaining information on all aspects of your client, not just the basic factual information which is often all that is required on agency forms.

Element SC8.2 Contribute to planning how clients' needs can best be met

WHAT YOU NEED TO LEARN

- Your role in planning for service provision.
- How to involve the client in planning the provision.
- How to record the decisions about meeting a client's needs.

Your role in planning for service provision

You may be involved in a care planning meeting. This may be because your agency is the main provider or commissioner of services for the particular client and you have been involved in collecting information and making the initial assessment of the client's needs. Or you may be involved because you are one of the other service providers and you need to plan and agree the services which your agency will provide. If you are responsible for carrying out the initial information gathering and assessment of needs, you must make sure that you provide all the information to the participants in the meeting as early as possible. People need time to read and consider background information before coming to a meeting. This way they are most likely to be able to make firm decisions about the services which should be provided. If they only receive information when they arrive at the meeting it may not be possible for a decision to be made on the spot. This can result in delays, causing frustration and disappointment for your client, and may, depending on their circumstances, increase risk.

The responsibility for organising the meeting may lie with you or it may be someone else in your agency or in another agency. You must ensure that you contact whoever is responsible for the meetings and provide all your information as soon as possible so that the meeting may proceed smoothly.

Health and care workers may need to meet to plan the services a client needs

The following table provides a list of care workers and what their responsibilities are.

Worker	Responsible for
Social worker	Managing and coordinating the delivery of service provision for an individual client
Domiciliary services organiser	Managing and delivering domiciliary support services, such as home help, and for assessing service level requirements
Voluntary coordinator	Coordinating and organising volunteers who provide a wide range of support services to clients in the community
Support worker	Providing direct support to a wide range of clients in their own homes or in hostel accommodation. This support enables people with a range of different types of needs to maintain an independent or supported living situation
Health visitor	Works with GP practice and provides help with monitoring review and promotion within the community
Occupational therapist	Assesses needs for aids and adaptations to enable independent or supported living

How to involve the client in planning the provision

Meetings held between health care professionals can be very intimidating for clients and they may feel that they do not have the confidence to participate. It is important that you work to encourage the client, and their family and any friends they wish to be involved in the process, to feel able to make an active and effective contribution to the meeting. The meeting is about the client and they are the most important person. It is easy to lose sight of this and to allow the client to feel that their role is purely a passive one. There are a range of actions that you can take prior to the meeting to help the client feel they have a useful and important contribution to make to the meeting. You should:

1 Go through the procedure of the meeting with them so that they know exactly who will be there, what will happen, in what order matters will be discussed and the type of contributions that all of those present at the meeting will make.

2 Help them to decide what they want to say and to work out the best way to present it. This could be in a written form or they could prepare some notes in advance to ensure that they cover all the points they want to make.

3 Make sure they know the different results which could come from the meeting so that they will not be surprised by any of the decisions which could be made. Explain to them that there could be a range of options for the meeting to consider.

4 Where necessary make practical arrangements for them to attend. This could include ensuring the client's accessibility to the meeting, providing transport where necessary, or providing linguistic translation or other communication assistance.

Putting the client's views

Your client may feel confident and well able to put across their own point of view. If so your role is simply to support and encourage them in doing so. However, if your client does not feel able to put their own views across adequately, or if they have done so and there is either a misunderstanding or a difference of opinion within the care planning meeting as to how this client's needs are best met, then your role is to ensure that the client's views are clearly represented and understood. This is particularly important when the client cannot communicate for themselves, because the client is a young child or because they have learning or communication difficulties or because they suffer from dementia or some other condition which may inhibit communication.

Active knowledge

Try to remember a situation where you have felt you were not in control and that other people held the power. This may have been a medical situation, for example where you were a patient and felt that you were unable to ask all the questions that you wanted to because the doctor simply did not seem to have time to answer them. It may have been one which involved lawyers or other professionals, or it could have involved your child's teacher or head teacher who had made you feel you were lacking in the skill and ability to put across what you really wanted to say. Remember how you felt in those situations, and choose one of them to act as your 'trigger' to recall those feelings whenever you are in a care planning meeting, or any other situation, with a client. This should remind you to encourage your client to put across their views if they are having difficulty doing so. Think how much easier it might have been if somebody had been acting as a support for you.

It is important not only for the accuracy of the views, but also to make sure the client knows that it is their views which are being represented and not the carer's own views, and that they are the person who is actually in control of what is happening to them

There is a fine balance between representing the client's point of view and putting across your own views about what you think may be best for them. You will need to be careful that it is the client's viewpoint that you represent and not your own, even if you think their views are not the most appropriate. When you are making contributions at a meeting you should always ensure that you begin with, 'Mr X has told me that', or 'Mrs Y has explained to me that she would prefer', rather than, 'I think that' or 'In my opinion the best course of action would be.' It is important not only for the accuracy of the views, but also to make sure the client knows that it is their views which are being represented and not your own, and that they are the person who is in control of what is happening to them.

Difficult situations

You can find yourself in a difficult position when your client's views and expectations of the service that they need are different from the views of the other professionals at the care planning meeting, or from the client's own relatives or carers, and particularly if they differ from the views of your own agency. Your role is to represent the views of your client. However you should not get drawn into the role of attempting to manipulate the meeting to ensure that your client achieves their desired outcome. Neither should you get involved in arguments with other professionals, you should simply ensure that the client's views are clearly expressed. You may also wish to add your own views as a professional and these will be based on your client's needs and wishes, however it is not necessary for you to act beyond the limits of this role. Your own agency may have a particular view on the type of service which can be provided, and this may be based on resource limitations or agency policy and guidelines. For example, you may have a client who wants a regular home help but refuses to accept a home help of a particular race or gender and wishes to specify the race or the gender of the home help. If your agency has an equal opportunities policy in respect of its employees it may not be prepared to comply with that request. In these circumstances you would simply have to make the views of your client known. However, you would be bound in your professional actions by the equal opportunities policy under which you work with your agency.

You will also need to be aware of the potential for the stereotyping or labelling of your client at the care planning meeting, and be ready to counteract any such attitudes towards your client. Be aware that assumptions may be made about the abilities of your client. For example, in the case of clients with learning difficulties, it is not uncommon for assumptions to be made which underestimate their abilities based on a generalisation of what can be achieved by those who have learning difficulties. There is also a very commonly held belief that people with Alzheimer's disease need round-the-clock protection. However, this is not always the case and many people who suffer from Alzheimer's are capable of achieving a great deal of independence, provided the environment in which they live is suitably adapted. You need to be aware of the assumptions being made about clients and you should refer back to Unit CL1 for details of the ways in which stereotyping and labelling can affect individuals.

Case study

G is a 30-year-old man with Down's syndrome. His mother had just died and his father had died two years previously. G had always lived at home and attended a local day care facility. He also enjoyed socialising at a club which was organised by Mencap on two evenings each week. G often complained that he was restricted by the very protective attitude of his parents and wanted to have a more independent existence and to be able to participate in a wide range of sporting and social activities. His parents had always felt he would be placing himself at risk if they agreed to his plans to join in this sort of activity. G has an older brother and two older sisters who had always been supportive of his parents during G's upbringing, but none were able to accommodate him full time within their own families. Following the death of their mother they were heavily involved in discussions with the social services department and voluntary agencies about the most appropriate solution to meet the long-term needs of G.

G was most insistent to the key worker that he wished to live completely independently and to remain in his own home. He felt that he was extremely capable of living in this way and that he intended to now take up some of the activities, such as hang-gliding and parachute jumping, which his mother had never allowed him to become involved in. He believed that he was capable of meeting all of his own needs and was unwilling to listen to the concerns of his brother and sisters. His family felt that G needed to be in residential care. They had found a residential facility with a vacancy which was only a few miles from their home town and would enable G to continue attending his regular day centre and his twice-weekly social club. They felt this was the only way in which they could ensure that G would be properly cared for and that his safety would be ensured. The family fully intended to continue their regular contact with G and were enthusiastic at the prospect of him moving into the residential facility. The family were supported in their view by the GP and the staff from the day care facility, which was linked to the residential accommodation. However, the staff from the social club were supportive of G's wishes to extend his independence.

The key worker proposed that G accompany her to look at a supported living situation where six people with a certain degree of learning difficulty shared a house and were responsible between them for shopping, cooking and meeting their own needs. However, they had daily access to a support worker and received a visit each day to provide an agreed level of assistance. This living situation would, within reason, allow G to increase his level of independence and to introduce more risk and challenge into his life. G and the family (although they had reservations) accepted this as a useful way forward, so G moved and settled in happily. He was finally dissuaded from hang-gliding and parachute jumping but did become involved in sand yachting, at which he was highly competitive and quite successful, and he also frequently assisted as navigator for one of the drivers in the local car rally club.

1   Why do you believe the family felt as they did about G?

2   What may have been the basis for the GP's views in this situation?

3   Examine your own feelings about a young man with learning difficulties living in the way G wished to. What is your initial response? What is your response after consideration and reflection on the issues?

4   What was the potential if either solution, that proposed by the family or that proposed by G himself, had been followed?

5   Whose views were of paramount consideration in this situation?

6   Which of the professionals involved is likely to have the best knowledge of G?

7   What other factors may influence the views of both professionals?

8   Do you consider this situation was resolved satisfactorily?

9   If so, identify the needs of all of the parties involved and how they were met by this solution.

10   If not, what alternative solution would you propose?

Case study

Mr J is 72 years old. His wife has recently died and although he has children they do not live locally. He is insisting that he wishes to go into residential care. Mr J is not confused, nor is he physically frail. He is a fit and healthy 72-year-old, but he is very lonely following the death of his wife and he finds it impossible to carry out domestic tasks. He never did any domestic tasks within the house as his wife did everything, and he has no idea how to cook, clean or shop. However, he is still able to maintain his garden, which he has always done, and is happy to carry out physical tasks around the house. The key worker has suggested that services be provided for Mr J in his own home and that it would be possible for him to have support to learn how to cook simple meals and how to maintain the cleanliness of his house. However, Mr J has refused these offers of help, saying that he does not believe that it is a man's role to carry out these tasks and that he needs to be in residential care so that he can have women who will look after him.

1   Identify Mr J's needs.

2   Do you consider that his needs will be met by residential care?

3   What are the alternatives which could be considered?

4   Do you think that Mr J's demands mask other needs?

5   There are three suggested outcomes to this situation. Select which one you consider to be most appropriate or develop one of your own.

Outcome 1

Mr J's request for residential care is agreed to and he is admitted into full-time care. All of his physical needs are met, he has his own room and appears to be very content with the way in which care is provided for him. He spends his days reading the newspapers and watching TV. He is gradually becoming more and more confused but appears happy in the residential setting.

Outcome 2

The key worker has another client a few streets away whose husband died about nine months ago. She is very lonely and is finding that the physical upkeep of her house is increasingly difficult for her to manage. She has little idea how to maintain the garden and has never undertaken jobs around the house. She also misses having meals to cook and a man to look after. The key worker introduces the two and they develop a friendship and share the tasks of daily living between them. Mr J maintains the gardens and houses, and she cooks, shops and does the washing and cleaning for both of them. Both appear to be very happy with the arrangement.

Outcome 3

Mr J's request for residential care is refused. However, the key worker introduces him to a cookery course at his local college which also includes the basics of home management, shopping and cleaning. He attends very reluctantly but realises that he has little choice. As a result of his attending college he finds out about other courses which are available, he has bought himself a computer and discovered the Internet. He has also joined his local over-50s swimming club, which he found out about whilst at college, and goes there three mornings a week, as well as attending college two other days each week. He spends his time at home surfing the Internet and 'chatting' to a wide range of people from all over the world.

6 List the advantages and disadvantages of each of these solutions. If you are curious, outcome 2 was what actually happened in this particular situation.

How to record the decisions about meeting a client's needs

The outcomes of any meeting to discuss care and meeting a client's needs must be recorded. The needs which clients are likely to have could include:

- **Educational**. For example, selection of appropriate school or college provision, access to information about services or systems or access to information relating to their current circumstances.

- **Recreational**. This could include identifying activities and opportunities to pursue interests.

- **Financial**. This could include identifying needs for budgeting or obtaining additional income.

- **Legal or advocacy**. This would involve identifying or enabling access to advice and support services or to solicitors or barristers via the legal aid system if necessary.

- **Emotional**. The need for love and close relationships.

- **Social**. Access to company and friends.

- **Physical**. This can be a wide range depending on the client's circumstances, but they need to be met in order for clients to survive.

Recording the outcomes of meetings is essential in order to avoid the possibility of confusion and misunderstanding. It is likely that your agency will have a specific format for recording decisions. If not, then very careful minutes must be taken of the meeting and all of the conclusions reached must be recorded. It is important that the discussions which were undertaken at the meeting are briefly recorded. This enables the people who have taken part in the meeting to check that their contribution and views have been noted, but the key is to have a clear record of all final decisions. The form which your agency has, or any documents which you subsequently develop, may look something like this:

Record of care planning decisions
Client name
Date of meeting
Those present at meeting
Main points of discussion
Decisions (Please show each decision with a separate number, e.g. 1,2,3, a,b,c, etc.)

It will be important to make sure, either through you directly or through whoever organises it within your agency, that the information recorded from the care planning meeting is circulated to all those who were present. There may be also be those who were not present at the meeting but who would still have an interest in knowing the outcome. The most important person who must receive a copy of this information is the client, regardless of whether or not they were present at the meeting. The information about decisions should also go to any carers or relatives whom the client wishes to be involved, and to the relevant health or other care professionals who are involved with the client. You must ensure that your client is aware of the fact that this information will be circulated and you must take their views into account if there are particular people who they do not wish to receive this information.

Element SC8.3　Agree services to be provided to meet clients' needs

WHAT YOU NEED TO LEARN

- How to communicate the care options to the client.
- How to ensure your client's agreement.
- How to keep all parties informed.
- How to record decisions.

How to communicate the care options to the client

If a care planning meeting has gone well and there is sufficient information on which to base the plans, then you should be able to present the client with a proposal that they are able to consider, and hopefully one which has met their original needs and expectations. You may find that you need to explain in detail the options which are available. Even if your client and their family and friends have been present at the care planning meeting, you may find that you need to go over again the information that was discussed and the decisions which were reached. It is extremely important that you provide the client with a written or other form of accessible record of the decisions taken at the planning meeting so that there is no misunderstanding about the options which they have for service provision.

It is also important that you do not present a *fait accompli* to your client and that you do not, by your behaviour, discourage them from commenting on the proposals. It is sometimes easy to give a client the impression that everything is organised and agreed and that they do not have the option to disagree or possibly even reject the proposals which are made. You can often do this unwittingly, so you should check against your own method of communicating information to ensure that you are giving your client the opportunity to comment on any proposals. For example, you should always check that:

- you are not suggesting these are the only options and that if the client did not agree to them the service could not be provided at all
- you are not 'selling' the proposal by making it sound so ideal that the client feels that they will disappoint you if they reject it
- you are not making the client feel guilty if they are dissatisfied with the proposals by implying that there are a great many others who would be grateful for the level of service which is being suggested for them.

Being aware of how you come across to your client is an important part of working in a reflective way, as is being aware always of the effect which your actions are having on others. You can never afford to make assumptions that your client will agree with your perspective or that of your agency.

How to ensure your client's agreement

Any proposals which have resulted from the planning meeting must receive the agreement of your client. It is important that you seek out confirmation of this agreement even if your client has been present at the planning meeting. This is important for two reasons:

1 They have had time to reflect and think things over since the planning meeting and their views may have changed.

2 They might not have felt confident enough to express any reservations that they may have had during the meeting.

You will need to make sure you give them the opportunity to express any doubts or concerns they have at this stage. It is always more helpful to establish concerns before service provision has begun than to have to adapt and change the service during its provision. With the client's agreement you should also ensure that those who are involved with their care, such as friends and family, are also given the opportunity to comment on the proposals and the extent to which they consider the service will meet the client's needs and the needs of those who are involved in providing informal care. There may be disagreements between a client and members of their family or close friends about the way in which services should be provided. It may be useful to provide your client and any of their friends or family who are involved with a list of the decisions which were taken with space for them to make notes about whether they agree or disagree with the proposals and make any comments that they have. If they can have this in advance of you seeing them, it will give them a chance to discuss and consider in their own time whether or not they feel that the proposed services are appropriate.

Dealing with a client whose choice is limited

There are some circumstances in which proposals for service provision can be imposed upon a client. These do happen but are rare. This could be as a result of the client being:

- the subject of an order made by the court
- the subject of a compulsory admission to hospital under the Mental Health Act
- the subject of a compulsory admission to hospital or residential care under the National Assistance Act
- the subject of a guardianship order under the Mental Health Act
- the subject of an order made under the Children Act.

When service provision is imposed on a client, it is considerably more difficult to work with that client and to assist them to feel that they do have a contribution to make to the planning process. Obviously, because of the compulsory nature of the service provision, there are some aspects over which they have no choice. However, where this is the case you should encourage your client to exercise choice in the areas where it is possible for them to do so. Simply because they are living in a particular setting or in receipt of a particular service as a result of compulsion, does not remove their rights to exercise choice within the limitations of the setting in which they find themselves. You should ensure that where possible clients are able to exercise choice, however limited those options may be.

How to keep all parties informed

One of your key roles in this process is to provide information to your client and those who are involved in the process with them about precisely the services which are proposed. You cannot expect your client to agree to a service, for example that 'day care will be provided', unless they have all the information needed to make a choice. This will include information about:

- the exact nature of the day care proposed
- the location of the day care
- the type of care offered
- the general atmosphere and ethos of the facility
- the number of people who attend
- what the transport arrangements will be.

These are just a few of the questions which a client or their family may have about services which will be provided. Informed choice must be made with full information. It is not sufficient to simply tell your client that the proposal is for day care. If necessary you should offer to assist your client or to make arrangements for your client and those who are supporting them to visit any establishments which are part of the proposal for care services.

We all have the right to make informed choices about all aspects of our lives. For example, you would not purchase a house simply because the estate agent said 'Oh, I have got a nice house for you.' You would want a great deal of information about the house, you would want to visit the house for yourself and to carry out extensive planning and questioning before you finally made that decision. Similarly, you would not buy a holiday or a car simply because somebody said to you, 'I have got a nice holiday here that I am sure would suit you.' You would want to ask questions about where, when, how much, what type of accommodation, and so on. If you always ask yourself the question, 'Does the client have sufficient information to make this decision?', then you should never fall into the trap of failing to provide them with everything they need to make an informed choice.

The key word in the whole process is agreement. What has been proposed at the care planning meeting as a result of your initial information gathering is simply a proposal and it requires the client's agreement in most circumstances.

How to record decisions

Once you have obtained the agreement of the client to the proposals, and any changes have been discussed with all the relevant people involved, then you should ensure that those decisions are recorded in a way that all of those involved with the process can access them readily. You may want to consider using a similar form to that used for recording the outcomes of the planning meeting (see page 213) and to simply add to it any subsequent changes made and agreed with the client.

Keys to good practice

1 Communicate all information to your client clearly and in a way they can understand.

2 Make sure their views are clearly represented to any forum where decisions are being taken or proposals being formulated.

3 Support the client to put forward their own views wherever possible.

4 Clearly record information and planning proposals and ensure that all the relevant people involved receive them.

5 Make sure your client and those involved with them receive the planning proposals in a form they can access and understand.

6 Ensure the client and those involved with them have the opportunity to comment in their own time on the proposals and in an atmosphere where they feel able to make adverse comments if necessary.

7 Ensure that all final proposals for care provision have the agreement of your client and those who are involved with them.

8 Always provide your clients with the information they need to make informed choices, even if those are restricted by their circumstances.

9 Ensure that all of those involved with the process are kept informed of any changes and updates made to the proposals.

Active knowledge

Think about a client you are currently working with. Consider all your actions in respect of the client and whether or not the client was given a choice in the services provided for them. If you believe they were given every possible choice then list the ways in which you ensured that was the case. If you believe their choice was restricted in some way, identify the reasons why this happened and the steps you can take to ensure it is not repeated.

Element SC8.4 Contribute to reviewing the effectiveness of care programmes

WHAT YOU NEED TO LEARN

- How to monitor provision.
- How to identify changes in needs and services.
- How to implement changes in provision
- How to record the review process.

How to monitor provision

Once an agreed programme of care has been put into place for your client, you should not assume that this will now continue indefinitely. All situations change on a regular basis and the change can be brought about by a wide range of factors. Therefore it is important to monitor the service which a client receives on an ongoing basis and to periodically review the service to see if any changes are needed.

Active knowledge

Look at yourself and your circumstances over the last 10 years and make a list of the ways in which your circumstances have changed. For example, you may have more children than you had 10 years ago, or you may have some children who have left home and moved away. Members of your family may have died or been born in the last 10 years, you could be living in a larger house or a smaller house, you could have more money or less money, you could be doing the same job or a different job. All these are major changes which have taken place in your life in just the short period of 10 years. Listing the changes will help you see the sorts of situations which change and affect people's lives.

Then take a much shorter period, for example the last year, and look at much smaller changes which may have happened to you during that time. They could be changes in your finances and your job role, you could now be undertaking a qualification, you may be driving a different car, you may have acquired digital television – any number of small changes which have affected the way you are living your life. Again, make a list of these changes and consider the impact each of them has had. Although the

✓

second list may have had a smaller impact than some of the big changes you listed in your first reflection, they will nonetheless have combined together to illustrate some quite large changes in your lifestyle. Consider the results of this exercise when you are thinking about how you will monitor the care programmes which are in place for your clients.

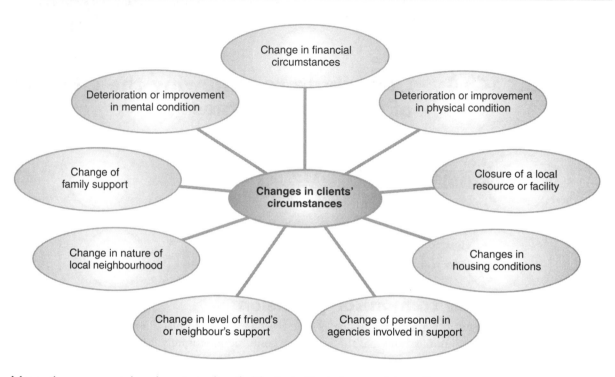

Many changes can take place in a client's life that affect the provision of care

Monitoring a care programme

At the start of the service delivery of a care programme, you should establish with your client a process for **monitoring** the care programme. This can be done on an ongoing basis and you should encourage your client to keep a record, especially about problems or difficulties or about the service no longer meeting their changed needs. You should plan regular contact with your client in order to participate in the monitoring process. Ideally this should involve visiting the client so that you can observe for yourself any conditions which may be changing. At the very least there should be contact by letter or telephone or other suitable means, so that you can provide your client with the opportunity to inform you of any changes. It will also allow you to review the adequacy of the service that has been provided and whether or not it is meeting the client's needs in the way that was anticipated at the planning stage.

Methods of monitoring

There are two main aspects of the care programme which need to be monitored. The first is the client's situation and any changes which could alter their needs, and the other is the service provision itself and any changes which may be required in the nature of the provision or the way in which it is delivered. You will need to ensure that your monitoring process enables you to keep a regular check on both aspects of the care programme. You can do this through either:

- devising a checklist which you would go through with your client on a regular basis

or

- providing the client and the service provider with a form or checklist that enables them to record any changes they have noticed that need to be made in the provision of the service.

How to identify changes in needs and services

You will have a key role in being the contact between the client and the agency providing the service. It will be your role to ensure the client is aware of any changes in agency policy or in the resources that may alter the way in which their service is provided, and you will need to ensure that the agency providing the service is aware of any changes in your client's circumstances. If you have provided your client with, or if you use a regular checklist, this will be a useful way of keeping a record of the information so that you can pass it on as appropriate.

Client checklist		
Changes in circumstances	YES	NO
Are my living circumstances the same	☐	☐
Do I still have the same support from family/friends/neighbours	☐	☐
Are my finances the same	☐	☐
Has my physical condition changed	☐	☐
Has my medical condition changed	☐	☐

Agency/organisation checklist		
	YES	NO
Is the level of service provided still appropriate	☐	☐
Is it still possible to provide this service within current resources	☐	☐
Have agency policies changed in respect of the provision of this service	☐	☐

Examples of checklists to identify changes in clients' needs and care provision

How to implement changes in provision

There is little point in monitoring the service to a client unless there is a procedure in place to then review that service and to make any changes which are necessary. This could take the form of recalling the original planning meeting, although in many agencies the process of review is undertaken on a much smaller scale, given that it is unlikely that all the people who attended the original meeting would be free or available to attend review meetings on a regular basis.

The most likely composition of a review meeting will consist of the key worker, the client, any supportive members of the family or friends, and the main agency who is providing the service. This group should be able to review on a regular basis the effectiveness of the service currently being provided and should be able to put forward ideas and proposals for any changes needed. It is important that the client is involved directly in the process of monitoring and review and that any of the changes proposed are agreed by the client and clearly understood.

This is likely to be an easier process if changes occur as a result of requests from the client. However, there may be occasions when service provisions have to be changed because of changes within the agency or because of a reduction in the availability of resources. This will have to be explained to the client and plans made for alternative services or other support which can be used to make up for the short-fall in service provision. This can be difficult for clients to accept and understand, and they may feel that they have been let down by a service on which they have relied. This can be a difficult situation to manage. You will need to use good communication skills to ensure the client has the opportunity to express their feelings about any changes in their service. They should also be made to feel they can question and make suggestions as to how you can move things forward in a positive way to maintain and support them within their present circumstances.

Case study

Miss P is aged 73. She lives alone and is a retired millinery buyer from a local large department store. She has had support from the home help and mobile meals service since her mobility deteriorated with the increasing severity of her arthritis over the last five years. She was a fiercely independent lady who had always refused to accept any benefits or support in addition to her state pension. After finally getting her agreement to review her finances her key worker had identified that she had some additional benefits due to her from her company pension scheme. This had increased Miss P's monthly income considerably and had eased her financial situation. However, this change in circumstances had also put her income above the payment threshold for home-help service and she now had to pay for the service that she had previously received at no charge. Miss P is angry at this and is considering cancelling the home-help service, although she would find it extremely difficult to manage without it.

1 How would you explain this situation to Miss P?

2 What are the skills you would need in order to successfully encourage Miss P to continue using support services?

3 How do you think Miss P is likely to feel?

4 Should this potential problem have been foreseen by the key worker in pursuing additional finances?

5 Should it have been discussed with Miss P in advance of obtaining her agreement to review her finances?

How to record the review process

As with all parts of the care programme planning process, it is essential that any changes agreed at a review are recorded and copies of this are provided to all of those who are involved with the client. This should include any of the agencies involved in providing any part of the client's programme of care, as well as the client and whoever else is involved in their support. This will reduce the possibility of confusion or misunderstanding about the way in which the service should be delivered.

If there is disagreement at a care review meeting this is usually resolved by consensus following discussion. It is rare that such decisions are taken on a vote, but it has occurred in exceptional circumstances. Normally, changes to a care programme are agreed by all parties concerned even if the discussion has been lengthy and lively. Even those parties present or involved in the review who have not supported the changes will comply with the review decisions. It is the responsibility of the key worker for the client to record review decisions and to briefly record the discussions which took place. This will need to be kept as part of the client's record and circulated to all those concerned.

The records can be fairly short, however they need to include full details of any changes and who is responsible for the implementation of them. The record forms can vary depending on the agency, however each one is likely to contain information which will identify what decisions were made and who is responsible for ensuring that they are carried out.

Keys to good practice

As a key worker in the planning and delivery of care programmes there are basic principles which you can follow which are likely to provide your client with the best possible service and the best possible care programme in order to meet their needs.

1   Always ensure that you have information about all of the client's circumstances, using observation as well as direct questioning.

2   Make sure you have the client's agreement to use any of the information you have acquired.

3   Ensure that all those who are involved in planning the care provision have access to all the relevant information about the client and their circumstances.

4   Support the client in making a direct contribution to the process of planning their own care programme.

5   Make sure that proposals made by professional agencies meet with the agreement of the client before starting any programme of care.

6   Make arrangements to regularly monitor provision of the service.

7   Set up regular arrangements for reviewing the service and make sure that the client is involved throughout the process.

8   Keep all the relevant agencies and individuals who are involved in the programme of care informed about any changes which are made.

Unit test

1. What factors do you need to take into account when dealing with a client whose programme of care is being provided with their consent?

2. What factors do you need to take into account when dealing with a client whose programme of care is being provided without their consent?

3. Why is it important to provide information at each stage of the process to the client and to their family and friends who may be involved in supporting them?

4. What is the value of involving all agencies and professionals who may be involved with a client in a care planning meeting?

5. What is the purpose of regularly monitoring and reviewing a programme of care?

6. What are the potential changes to a client's circumstances which could alter their care provision. How could the level of care provision be altered by changes in circumstances at the providing agency?

7. What factors must the key worker take into account when balancing issues such as risk and challenge against protection and safety for a client?

8. To what extent can information about a client be shared with other agencies?

9. Why is it important that clients agree to the programme of care which is being provided for them?

10. What is the main skill needed by a key worker when informing clients of changes in their care programme?

Unit X12 Support clients during clinical activities

This unit is about working alongside professionals to provide support for your clients during treatments, investigations or any other clinical activities. These could be taking place in either a hospital, residential or nursing home setting, or in the client's own home in the community. Your role will be slightly different depending on the setting, however the underlying key principles will remain the same. This unit links to CU1, CU2, X13 and X19. You should refer to these units throughout your work for this unit.

Element X12.1 Prepare clients for treatments, investigations and procedures

WHAT YOU NEED TO LEARN

- The ways of ensuring clients are aware of all relevant information.
- The records and information which need to be checked.

Ways of ensuring clients are aware of all relevant information

Depending upon your role and the setting in which you work, you may find that being asked to support clients during a wide range of clinical activities, as well as assisting the professional carrying out the treatment or investigation, is a regular part of your working day. These activities could include:

- X-rays
- minor surgery under local anaesthetic
- enderscopic investigations
- blood tests
- scans
- chemotherapy
- radiotherapy
- dressing changes
- blood transfusions
- enemas
- suture removals
- catheterisation.

These are just a selection of the wide range of clinical procedures which your clients may need to undertake. Your role will vary depending on the procedure, its location, and the needs of both the client and the professional involved. For example, if your client is having an X-ray investigation then your role is unlikely to extend beyond assisting them to get ready for the X-ray and to wear the appropriate clothing, ensuring they have all the information they need and that their questions have been answered in so far as you are able to. You may then assist them to get changed and to return to their home setting. For safety reasons you will not be able to be present during the X-ray itself, and it is unlikely that the radiographer would require help and support, unless you had been specifically trained to provide assistance. However, if a client was being given an enema by a district nurse then your role is likely to be far more extensive. You are likely to be present throughout the procedure, provided this is what your client wishes, and you are likely to be involved in dealing with the subsequent effects of the treatment!

Before the start of any clinical procedure you should consult with the professional who is to carry out the activity to discuss exactly what your role, if any, will be in the procedure itself, and to establish if they will need your support or assistance. This information will assist you plan the way you will work with your client and deal with any other demands on your skills.

A carer's role is limited in the case of minor clinical procedures such as X-rays

Clients' concerns

Most clinical procedures, treatments or investigations are likely to raise concerns with clients. This will differ according to the clients themselves, the nature of the clinical procedure, and the extent to which they are familiar with it. If the procedure is something they have experienced several times before they are likely to respond very differently to someone who is experiencing a procedure for the first time, or is having a familiar procedure performed by somebody different, or is having it done in a different location. The purpose of the procedure will also have an affect on the client's response to it. A procedure which is familiar and carried out regularly is likely to raise far fewer worries and concerns than one which is investigating a potentially serious condition, about which the client has worries and fears but as yet no confirmation.

Case study

T is 32 years old and is the mother of four young children under the age of 7. She is a single parent and you have been involved in supporting her in bringing up her children for the last three years. T has no immediate family or close friends who are able to support her and she has come to rely on your support. She has recently experienced rectal bleeding on passing faeces and her GP has arranged for her to have an endoscopic examination. T has asked you to accompany her to the hospital.

J is 87 years old and lives with her daughter and son-in-law. She has extremely poor mobility and can walk a few steps with the aid of a walking frame. She has an ulcer on her leg for which she has been seeing the district nurse on a regular basis for several months. The district nurse visits on a regular basis in order to change the dressings. You provide support for her and her family each morning and are usually there when the district nurse changes the dressings.

1 How do you think each client will be feeling in these two very different scenarios?

2 Note down as many differences as you can between the two circumstances.

3 How different would your role be in each of the two situations?

Although the examples above are at opposite extremes, they serve to illustrate that you will need to consider how a client is likely to be feeling, given the main key factors you should always bear in mind. These are:

- Purpose of the procedure.
- The client's familiarity with the procedure.
- The likely outcome of the procedure.
- The possible consequences for the client.
- The nature and format of the procedure.

Finding out about the procedure

Wherever possible you should familiarise yourself with the procedure which your client is to undergo. Find out as much as you can by checking with the professional concerned as to exactly when, how and by whom the procedure will be carried out, and how the client needs to be prepared for the procedure. Also try to find out how long it will last, if it is likely to be uncomfortable, if there are likely to be any after-effects and how long in general it takes to recover. Your client is likely to have been told this in advance, possibly verbally, but more likely in a written form. However, if you are familiar to them and they trust you, they are likely to ask you to clarify matters for them, and may well want to discuss the information they were given. It is important that you are familiar with the information and are sure you have obtained it from a reliable source. Do not accept information based on hearsay from other clients or from anyone who has undergone the procedure or knows someone who has done so. The information about any clinical activities in which you will need to support a client must be obtained directly from the professional concerned or from the setting where the procedure is to be carried out.

Appropriate communication with the client

For obvious reasons, you should limit your responses to clients' questions to the areas outlined above. Do not attempt to answer questions relating to the clinical component of the procedure or any potential medical consequences. Do not discuss the likely implications of any symptoms or any possible results from any tests or investigations. This is not your role. Also, any incorrect information or information which is incorrectly explained or misunderstood could be dangerous, distressing and have potentially serious consequences. It is, however, very valuable for you to be fully familiar with the process and details of any procedure or investigation and the preparation and recovery from it, so that you are able to provide your client with sufficient information to reassure them and to deal with any worries or concerns that they may have.

If you know your client well, it will be easier to ensure that the information you give to them is the right level and amount they wish to receive. In the case of a client you are meeting for the first time it is harder to be sure that the information you are giving them and your responses to their questions or concerns are at the level they need. However, using your communication and listening skills you should be able to determine from the client's verbal and non-verbal responses whether you are responding in an appropriate way.

You may find there are occasions when you need to intervene on the client's behalf with the professional carrying out the procedure. You should only intervene if it is clear that the professional is providing responses to client questions or concerns at an inappropriate level, where the client is not able to benefit from the information they are receiving, either because it is too technical or too detailed, or the professional is using inappropriate means of communication for that client. For example, they may be speaking too quietly for a client who is hard of hearing. If this is the case it is important that you intervene by saying something like, 'I am sorry sister, but could you speak up. Mrs S is a little hard of hearing.' Your intervention could ensure that clients do not feel confused or worried after a clinical procedure. Any intervention you need to make should only be in respect of issues such as communication or access. It is not your role to intervene or comment on the procedure itself or any clinical or medical judgements, conclusions or information which is given to the client.

A carer should intervene if the client has a problem receiving the information they need

Wherever possible you should ask for information to be written down so that it is readily available for future reference and to avoid any confusion. If you are aware that clients have been provided with information in advance of their treatment or investigation, then it is important that you check with them when they arrive that they understand it, they remember it and they do not have any further questions. It can be useful to anticipate the sorts of questions which people may want to ask but do not feel are appropriate. These may be questions about why people are dressed in the way that they are, why the treatment room is set out in the way that it is, what the instruments will be used for, and so on. Be sure you have the information to answer the clients' questions and that they are answered honestly and clearly. If there are any questions about an area beyond your competence, such as the clinical or medical nature of the process, or information about which you are not completely sure, then do not guess. Always refer the client to the professional involved or to another member of the care team who may have the answers. Either get the client to ask the questions for themselves or find out the answer for them.

Records and information which need to be checked

One of the first things which must be checked before any treatment or investigation is carried out is that the client has given their consent. Consent is extremely important and is a key concept in the provision of health care. Consent has been dealt with in detail in Unit X13, however a review of the general principles here may be useful. The legal principle which applies to medical treatment is that a patient/client has the right under common law to give or withhold consent to medical examination or treatment. This is one of the basic principles of health care. Patients/clients are entitled to receive sufficient information in a way they can understand about the proposed treatments, the possible alternatives and any substantial risks of the treatment so they can make a balanced judgement. The legal ruling is that anyone who is mentally competent has an absolute right to refuse consent to medical treatment for any reason, whether that reason is rational or irrational, or for no reason at all, even where the decision may lead to his or her own death.

Did you know?

In general, medical treatment can be undertaken in an emergency even if, because of unconsciousness or inability, no consent has been given, provided that the treatment is necessary and does no more than is reasonably required in the best interests of the patient. However, treatment cannot be given if the patient has previously refused the treatment and this refusal was given when the patient was competent and is clearly applicable to the present circumstances.

In some cases, depending on the treatment or investigation, written consent will need to be obtained. Consent is usually obtained by a doctor, however it is essential that a check is made with the doctor that the consent has been obtained. For some minor treatments consent can be given verbally and quite informally. Remember, the key principle with consent is that it must be informed consent, that is the client was aware of all of the relevant factors about their proposed treatment before they agreed to it. You should never allow anyone to undertake treatment on a client until you are satisfied that their consent has been obtained. You should not ever be party to treating or carrying out a clinical procedure on somebody against their will, unless this is being done through an order of the court or because of the legal status of the individual.

Identity

If the client is not someone with whom you are familiar, then it is essential that their identity is checked. All hospital in-patients will wear an identity band from the time of their admission until their discharge. This band will contain the patient's name and unit number. These must be checked against the patient's notes, which will accompany them to the treatment, and must be checked again against any documentation in relation to the treatment or investigation which is being carried out. Also, where patients are attending a hospital or health centre for treatment as an outpatient, then it is essential that their name and details are checked with them

- on arrival
- at the hospital/health centre
- before treatment or investigation commences.

Their identity should be checked and confirmed with the professional who is to carry out the treatment or investigation. Correct identification of every individual before they undergo any sort of clinical procedure is absolutely essential. There are well recorded incidents of surgery being performed on the wrong people, the wrong operation being performed and new-born babies being mixed up. Fortunately these incidents are extremely rare, however the fact they happen should alert all health and care workers. After checking and confirming the identity of the patient/client you should again check the documentation for the procedure that the correct procedure or investigation is the one which is about to be undertaken and that this is also the patients' understanding of what is about to take place. This is a further reassurance that the right person is about to undergo the right procedure.

A carer needs to make sure of the identity of the client

WHAT YOU NEED TO LEARN

- How to reassure clients.
- How to maintain safe practice.

How to reassure clients

If you are present during a clinical procedure you may find that the patient or client requires reassurance or has questions still to ask while the procedure is taking place. You may be able to answer them from your own knowledge of the processes and arrangement surrounding the treatment or investigation, or you may need to refer them to the professional involved. If a patient's concerns are questions to do with the treatment or investigation, such as 'Why is she doing that?', then these are questions which need to be referred to the professional who is carrying out the procedure. If, on the other hand, they are more general questions, such as 'Will I be able to go home straight afterwards?', then you may be able to answer these questions, either because of your own knowledge and experience or because this is information which you have established before the start of the clinical activity.

Clients often just need a few words of support

Whatever the nature of the questions being asked it is important that you respond to them yourself or obtain a response for the client. In some cases the client may simply be seeking general reassurance and to know that you are there to support them. In such a case it may be sufficient to provide a hand to hold or to stroke someone's arm and to offer encouragement in fairly straightforward terms, such as 'That's it', 'Well done', 'Nearly there now', 'Almost over', and so on.

Monitoring the client

Another key support role is monitoring the client for any signs of distress or adverse reaction to the procedure. Depending on the nature of the procedure, the client may be monitored clinically to ensure that their physical condition is maintaining its normal state. In the absence of clinical monitoring you should constantly observe the patient or client and note if there are any signs of distress or an adverse physical reaction, such as: rapid change in colour, becoming pale or very flushed, sweating or trembling, shivering, or signs of extreme pain or discomfort. Any of these signs can indicate that the client is responding poorly to the clinical activity and that it should be suspended or undertaken in a different way. It is essential that you report any such observations immediately to the professional who is carrying out the process. Depending on the nature of the treatment or investigation being carried out, the professional who is doing it may not be in a position to readily observe the patient or client for these signs. You should ensure that you are familiar with the client's medical history in so far as it may affect the present procedure. Keeping in mind the constraints of confidentiality and the patient's information being available on a need-to-know basis, you will only need to be told or to make yourself familiar with any information which could have a direct bearing on the treatment or investigation. For example, if a client has a history of a heart condition or of epilepsy or of fainting or if they are diabetic, then it is important you are aware of any such medical condition which could affect their response to the procedure, so that you can rapidly identify any response which indicates an adverse reaction or a deterioration in their condition and report it immediately.

How to maintain safe practice

The requirements of sterilisation, disinfection and cleaning of instruments, materials and equipment are dealt with in Units CU1 and CU2. It is important that the principles set out in those units are followed, whether you are responsible for preparing the environment for clinical activity or whether your role is as a support for the client and possibly for the professional involved. If you are required to assist those carrying out the procedures and investigations by preparing and passing materials or instruments, then you will need to follow universal precautions to ensure that both yourself and the client are protected from the risk of infection and cross-infection.

There may be occasions when you are required to use a sterile procedure in order to ensure that instruments or materials are not contaminated. If sterile practice is required then the process must be followed strictly and absolutely, otherwise contamination will be a risk. The process of working in a sterile way is given in detail in Unit X13, and this applies regardless of the setting or the circumstances. The requirements for sterile procedures do not alter, but not all procedures are required to be carried out in a sterile way.

In order to ensure that safety is maintained throughout the procedure, you will need to check with the client that they have complied with any pre-procedure instructions they have been given. Depending on the procedure to be carried out, there could be significant consequences if the procedures have not been followed. This could result in either a significant risk to the patient or client or the invalidation of any tests or investigations, or it could meant that the treatment being carried out is ineffective. An example is someone who is having a **barium enema** investigation, for which it is necessary to starve for 24 hours before the procedure and to empty the bowel completely by taking a laxative. If this is not complied with it will not be possible to carry out the barium enema and to obtain any useful or meaningful results. If by asking questions you establish that the patient/client has not complied with the instructions they have been given about preparing for this procedure, then you must report this immediately to the person responsible for that procedure. You should never take a decision yourself about what may or may not be acceptable in terms of missing out some or all of the preparations.

Safe disposal of waste

If part of your support role is to dispose of any waste or spillage following treatment, then you must ensure that you follow all of the correct procedures for disposal of **hazardous** and **non-hazardous waste** and that you are able to correctly identify the difference between the two types of waste. This is covered in detail in Units CU1 and CU2. It is essential that you ensure you are familiar with these disposal processes. Correct waste disposal is a requirement for all settings where any clinical procedures take place. Any failure to comply with the requirements for the correct and safe disposal of potentially infected waste could place the community at large at risk of severe outbreaks of infection.

Element X12.3 | Assist clients to recover from treatments, investigations and procedures

WHAT YOU NEED TO LEARN

- The key features of the recovery period.
- The practical steps to assist and support clients.

The key features of the recovery period

Recovery from clinical procedures varies depending on the procedure undertaken. For a painless, non-invasive investigation such as an X-ray there is no recovery period required from a medical or clinical perspective. However, this is not to underestimate the emotional support which the client may require if the reason for their X-ray has raised concerns and anxieties for them, particularly if they face a period of waiting before being informed of the results of the investigation. Recovery can be more than a gradual returning to physical normality; it can also involve returning to emotional normality, and clients may need support to do this. During this period it might be important that you can answer questions which they may have, or refer them to other sources for the answers to their worries, questions and concerns. They should also be able to discuss their anxieties and concerns at the pace they want and in a setting where they are comfortable.

Types of recovery periods

Some procedures will produce very specific physical effects which need to be observed during a recovery period. Following surgery there is a period of recovery during which a patient remains in a recovery room close to the operating theatre where they can be regularly observed and measured for physical recovery. This is to ensure that recovery from surgery and anaesthetic is taking place normally and that the patient's body systems and functions are gradually returning to normal. In these situations recovery is observed by medically qualified staff following laid-down procedures and protocols. Other types of recovery periods are involved following more minor procedures. For example, minor surgery in a health centre to remove a small cyst will require the patient to rest for a short while before leaving, so that checks can be made for adverse reactions, that the patient has not suffered from shock and that no excessive bleeding occurs. The recovery period can also be more extensive, in which case the procedure is not completed until sutures are removed and the wound completely healed.

Supporting recovery

The recovery period after a medical intervention or procedure can be a time when people feel particularly vulnerable and in need of support. They may have undergone a procedure which has been uncomfortable, painful, embarrassing or undignified, and they may need to recover not only physically but emotionally from the experience. Many people choose to talk about their clinical experiences as a way of coming to terms with them and reducing to them to the level of normality so that they no longer appear frightening, worrying or out of the ordinary. Discussing operations, tests, scars and tubes is a favourite pastime amongst many of the clients who are supported by workers in health and social care!

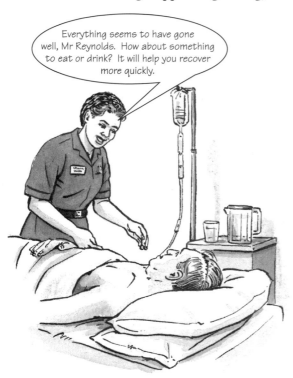

Eating and drinking are important for recovery

Some procedures simply require people to take a short rest, with perhaps some refreshment. This is especially important if they have had to refrain from eating or drinking prior to the procedure. If this is the case it is important to encourage the individual to have a drink in order to avoid becoming dehydrated. The resumption of eating and drinking is part of recovery and should be encouraged. However, the opposite may be the case for those who have had an ultrasound scan. For them disposing of liquid is more desirable then adding to it!

In general, the recovery period is a time of a gradual return to normality, physically and emotionally. Your role is to support the recovery process. This means you have to be fully aware of any clinical requirements of your role, as in taking measurements of pulse or blood pressure. You will also need to be aware of the normal progress of recovery following the particular procedure undertaken. You should ensure that you are aware of the pace and the nature of the different stages of the recovery process, so that if a patient you are monitoring does not respond within the normal range you are able to report this immediately and to obtain urgent assistance.

You should also consider any emotional recovery period which your client may need, and plan, if possible, for time to allow them to discuss any concerns they may have over the procedure which has been undertaken. If it is not your role to continue working with the clients you support through the procedures, then you should ensure that any need for ongoing support which you identified is recorded, and that those who are responsible for, or who are able to provide ongoing support, are made aware of this.

Practical steps to assist and support clients

After procedures are completed you may need to support clients in getting dressed or returning to their usual setting. Some clinical procedures require the wearing of suitable gowns or other clothing, and in such cases you should offer assistance to remove the gown and get dressed in their own clothing. It may also be necessary to collect a client's medications which have been prescribed or to return any materials or equipment which have been loaned to a client. You should offer assistance if it is required for any of these practical tasks.

Transport to and from hospitals or health centres or clinics can often be difficult for those who do not possess their own transport or do not have family or friends who are able to bring them. Not all clinical settings are well served by public transport and many clients are unable to use public transport. Where this is the case they will need to be transported to where their treatments or investigations are to take place. This is normally arranged through the ambulance service for most National Health Service facilities. Local health centres or other clinics may have their own means of transport or may use a local taxi service. You should make yourself familiar with the transport arrangements of your work setting and ensure that it is arranged where necessary. It is most likely you will need to arrange an ambulance to provide the transport. This will be a non-emergency transport ambulance and will need to be booked in advance if possible, and may involve a considerable wait. You must be sure the patient or client is aware of the time when their transport can be expected and you should try to keep them updated and informed of any likely delays or changes to the arrangements you have made.

Unit test

1 What types of information are clients likely to have concerns about?

2 What are the general legal principles of consent?

3 How is consent confirmed?

4 What is your role in checking consent?

5 When should you intervene on behalf of a client during a clinical procedure?

6 What is the importance of identification?

7 What is the difference between clean, disinfected and sterilised?

8 Why are they important in relation to clinical procedures?

9 What are key features of safe disposal of hazardous clinical waste?

10 What are the two main aspects of recovery?

11 How would you offer support for both recovery aspects?

Unit X13

Undertake agreed clinical activities with clients whose health is stable in non-acute care settings

This unit will provide you with information about working with clients who require clinical support but whose general health condition is stable. You are most likely to be able to provide evidence for this unit if you work in a nursing home, residential setting or care for people in their own homes. The unit covers a wide range of clinical and associated activities, from obtaining client consent and making appropriate preparations through to taking measurements and specimens. Depending on the procedures in your workplace, you may also be involved in supporting a qualified clinical practitioner in administering medication. Developing skills and understanding of clinical activities will often mean that procedures which are simple and straightforward can be carried out in the client's own environment rather than having to attend a hospital or have another practitioner visit.

Candidates who are undertaking Unit X19 will find that much of the information in that unit is a duplicate of the information available in this unit, as many of the activities and procedures are relevant to both acute and non-acute settings.

Element X13.1 — Prepare clients for clinical activities

WHAT YOU NEED TO LEARN

- How to prepare for a clinical activity.
- What protective clothing is needed for a clinical activity.

How to prepare for a clinical activity

This element is about ensuring that the client understands and has given their agreement to the **clinical activity** which is about to be undertaken and that all the necessary preparations have been made, including documentation, equipment and the correct environment. Clinical activities cover a wide range of procedures which are undertaken in order to improve or maintain a client's health.

These can include:

- dressing wounds
- taking specimens
- taking measurements
- providing clients with medication.

All these activities require adequate preparation. It is important you take all the required steps in advance of beginning the clinical activity rather than having to break off because you forgot an important item of equipment, or you do not have the necessary chart or documents to hand.

Records, charts and documents

Throughout this unit you will recognise the importance of charts, tables and record sheets for monitoring and recording a client's state of health. They are also important for recording the requirement for and the outcome of any investigations which need to be carried out for the client's benefit. The following table lists the most likely documentation that you will need and the purposes for which you are likely to need them.

Document	Purpose
Case notes/case file	This records all information about the client and holds copies of any relevant documentation. This is the major source of information about the client's previous and current state of health and is the source of information regarding their social circumstances and any specific needs or other aspects which need to be taken into account.
Measurement charts	These can be charts recording the client's temperature, blood pressure, respiration rate, fluid balance, etc., or they can be used to record height and weight.
Care plan	This can record vital details of the way in which a client is to be cared for and records essential information for anyone who is providing any type of care for the client.
Requests for investigations	Each organisation is likely to have its own forms which are used for requesting any investigations which need to be carried out on collected specimens
Reports of investigations	These report back on the outcome of investigations carried out and they are usually recorded and maintained in the case file or case notes.
Consent forms	Where a major activity is being undertaken, such as surgery or other invasive procedure, then clients will be asked to sign written consent forms, copies of which will be maintained in the case notes.

Consent

As a broad principle, client **consent** should be obtained before carrying out any kind of activity. Even something as simple as moving somebody or plumping their pillows should always be preceded by a question such as, 'Would you like me to plump your pillows?' However, in a clinical setting client consent has a very specific meaning and assumes a great deal of importance. There have been several well-publicised legal cases where clients have maintained that clinical procedures were carried out on them without them giving prior consent. It is essential that clients not only consent, but wherever possible understand what it is they are consenting to and the implications of this. This type of consent is referred to as **informed consent**. Informed consent means that the person who is about to carry out the procedure has given the client full information about what they are going to do, why they are going to do it and the possible effects of the procedure, both positive and negative. All the risks should have been explained to the client so that they are in a position to make a judgement about whether or not they wish to

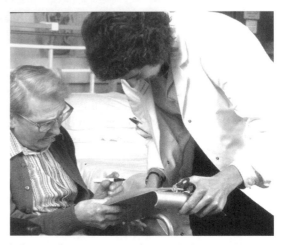

Informed consent can be verbal or written depending on the nature of the procedure to be carried out

go ahead with the procedure. Informed consent can be written, as in the case of somebody undergoing surgery, or it can be a verbal consent, for example if somebody is having blood taken, then the procedure, the purpose of the blood test and what will be discovered could be explained to them before they agreed to it.

> I'm just going to give you your medication now, John. Is that OK?

The carer usually obtains the client's consent to a procedure being carried out

Implied consent

This is a common principle in all clinical settings. It is reasonable to assume that someone implies their consent to you taking their blood pressure if they present their arm when they see you arriving and taking out the blood pressure cuff. If somebody opens their mouth when you appear with a thermometer, it is reasonable for you to assume that they are implying consent to you taking their temperature. For these relatively minor and non-invasive procedures implied consent is perfectly acceptable. It would be a bureaucratic nightmare if client consent to these type of activities had to be recorded on every occasion.

Written consent

Each setting will have its own form for written consent. However, these forms are broadly similar in their content as they all require clients, or their relatives in the case of an emergency, to sign their agreement for the named clinical procedure to be undertaken. Generally, written consent is likely to also be informed consent as on most occasions the procedures will have been explained carefully to the client before they sign. However, sometimes in the case of emergency procedures the consent may not be informed consent as there may not have been time to explain the procedure.

Verbal consent

By requesting medication a patient is giving verbal consent to being given that medication

Verbal consent is normally understood to exist when a client requests that a clinical procedure be undertaken. For example, a client asking for pain relief who has been told, 'yes, we will give you an injection for pain but it will make you sleepy', and has responded, 'OK, I understand but give it to me anyway', is taken to have given verbal consent for the procedure. This consent must be recorded in the case notes. This could also apply to, for example, a client who is severally constipated and has asked for an enema, or to somebody who has requested that they are moved from the bed to the chair using lifting equipment.

Why consent is important

It is a vital part of modern-day clinical care that client consent is always obtained. This is not only to protect clinicians and care workers against legal challenge, it is also because of the growth in recognition and understanding of the rights of the individual and the importance of recognising and valuing the rights of clients to determine what happens to them. Historically, clinical practice has always 'acted in the best interests' of clients, and there are still many older people who believe that 'Doctor or nurse knows best', and would not presume to question any medical suggestions about the way their treatment should proceed. As the traditional view of medical practitioners has changed it has become more common to question and challenge the opinions of doctors, nurses and other health workers. People have become more comfortable with the idea of being asked their views and being asked for their consent. Consent is taken very seriously. In the past consent may have been obtained where required in written format, however very often full information was not given and nor was client consent sought for more minor or non-invasive procedures.

If you are in the position where you are asked to obtain client consent for an activity you must take great care that:

- you answer any questions honestly and as fully as you can
- you never attempt to answer a question that you are not sure of and that you always refer the question on to somebody who has the knowledge to give the client a full answer
- you immediately report any refusal of consent or any reservations expressed by the client to your supervisor or to the clinical practitioner responsible for the procedure.

Make sure wherever possible you direct your information to the client. Even if the client has a relative or friend with them be careful that your information is directed to the client. In most cases it is the client's consent you must obtain, not that of their friend or relative. Where your client is a young child, or a person with learning difficulties, or someone who is extremely confused and is unable to understand the information which you are giving to them, then you should explain the procedure carefully to the person who is acting as their advocate. This could be a relative, friend or possibly a social worker or representative of the court if the person is subject to guardianship or a court order.

If, however, the client is capable of understanding but has difficulty with communications, then you must use the communication skills you have learned in completing Unit CL2 to provide the client with the information they need in order to make their decision. Clients who have hearing, seeing or speaking difficulties should not be prevented from making their own decisions and asking their own questions by the limitations of either your time or communication skills. If there are language difficulties then an interpreter should be used as appropriate. You should always consider the nature of the consent being sought before a decision is made about whether or not to use a member of the client's family. It may be that because of the need for confidentiality or because of the nature of the procedure being discussed it may not be appropriate, so the use of an interpreter may be preferable to the client.

Preparing the client

Preparing the client for any clinical activity is about more than simply obtaining their consent. It is also important to reassure the client and to explain to them exactly what is to happen. It also reduces the anxiety for clients. This may involve you in explaining exactly what equipment will be used, how people will be dressed, for example in masks and gowns, and why, and to explain where the procedure will take place, if it is not in an environment familiar to the client.

You also need to check with your client for any known allergies or reactions that they may have to the procedure you are about to carry out. If the procedure involves a medical practitioner administering medication then it will be essential to check with the client if they have any known allergic reactions to particular medications. Bear in mind that people have allergies which you may not immediately consider relevant, however all of them should be reported.

Observing the client

Throughout any clinical activity you will need to regularly observe your client to ensure that they are not reacting to the activity in a way which could indicate the deterioration or a change in their condition. Although the health of the clients with whom you are working may be stable it may also be quite poor, so it is still important that you regularly check that they are not suffering any ill-effects from any clinical activity. Checking this out will include what you can observe and asking the client if they are feeling alright. You will need to be sure that you do not ask so many times as to make them more anxious and start to wonder if they ought to be feeling some adverse effect! You should ask just enough to give them the opportunity to say if things are not feeling right.

You should check for signs of an adverse reaction such as:

- a sudden change in temperature
- becoming cold and clammy
- starting to sweat
- a change in breathing rate

- a change in colour, either becoming very flushed or very pale
- any complaint of pain or dizziness
- any indication of faintness.

You should also ask your questions:

- at the outset of the activity
- part way through the activity
- at any point at which you change what you do.

For example, in changing from removing a dressing to cleaning a wound area, a simple 'Everything alright Mrs ...?' is quite sufficient. It will give the client the opportunity to let you know if there are any difficulties.

Regardless of the setting in which you work, if you notice any change or your client complains of feeling unwell you must immediately stop the activity and report to your supervisor or the clinical practitioner responsible for the activity.

Did you know?

Many anaesthetics are based on egg. People have become seriously ill as a result of having an egg allergy which has not been reported prior to the commencement of surgery. There are other types of anaesthetics not based on egg which can be substituted for people who have an egg allergy.

A relatively common allergy is to latex (rubber). Where this is the case the consequences can be extremely serious for clients, who can go into **anaphylactic shock**, which is potentially fatal. Clients going into anaphylactic shock become cold, clammy, show a rapid pulse and breathing, and quickly become unconscious. Any signs of such symptoms should be reported immediately and medical assistance obtained. Allergies to latex means that alternatives must be used for the usual rubber gloves with which clients are touched. It can also be a problem for clients who have catheters, as the catheter tubing is normally made from latex. Where such allergies are known alternatives can be used.

Throughout the preparation time you should remember to:

- collect all equipment together
- collect any paperwork and documentation needed
- continually observe your client and note any changes in their behaviour or condition
- reassure the client and provide as much information as within your knowledge
- ensure that additional information is provided where a client's questions are outside your own knowledge and responsibility
- reassure the client and make them as comfortable as possible.

What protective clothing is needed for a clinical activity

You are likely to need to wear some form of protective clothing for most clinical procedures. This can vary depending on the nature of the procedure and regardless of the type or extent of protective clothing. You should always explain the purpose of it to your client. Broadly, the following items of protective clothing are the most commonly used in clinical procedures in both acute and non-acute care settings:

- **Gloves** – these are usually latex gloves (with the exceptions for clients with allergies, see above) and they should be worn during procedures or in situations where you may be exposed to body fluids, excretions, blood or any exudates from wounds.

- **Gown or apron** – these should be worn in similar situations to those for gloves.

- **Mask** – this should be worn during procedures that produce droplets of body fluids or blood or where you have a client who is coughing extensively.

If you have any open cuts, sores or dermatitis on your hands gloves must also be worn whenever you have contact with a client.

The use of such protective clothing is linked to a set of procedures called **standard precautions** or **universal precautions**. These precautions are designed to reduce the risk of spreading infection and to reduce your risk of exposure to disease-causing micro-organisms. Universal precautions are designed to protect both you and the client and they assist in reducing the risk of infections, particularly blood-borne viruses, and those which clients can acquire in a hospital or other medical environment. These infections are called **nosocomial** infections, the most well known of which is **MRSA (Methicillin-Resistant Staphylococcus aureus)**. These infections are extremely resistant to treatment and are very hard to improve once a client has acquired them. Therefore the use of precautions is important, particularly because clients who already have poor health are much more vulnerable to infection and the spread of disease. Universal precautions also protect you and the client from blood-borne viruses such as Hepatitis, AIDS and HIV. The following table may help when checking on the requirements for precautions.

Standard precautions required for selected procedures					
Procedure	**Hand washing**	**Gloves**	**Gown**	**Mask**	**Eye-wear**
Talking to patient					
Obtaining patient's blood pressure	✔				
Performing any procedure in which hands can become soiled with blood/body fluids	✔	✔			
Examining patient without touching blood/body fluids or mucous membranes	✔	✔			
Touching blood/body fluids, mucous membranes, broken skin, lesions or contaminated equipment	✔	✔			
Obtaining blood sample	✔	✔			
Between patient contact	✔				
Handling soiled waste, linen and other materials	✔	✔	Note: Use gown if waste or linen is saturated and may soil your clothing		
Participating in surgical or other procedures that produce splattering or spraying of blood/body fluids	✔	✔	✔	✔	✔

Putting on gloves

1 Wash hands.

2 Check to make sure the gloves are sterile by checking that the package is sealed and that there are no openings or any dampness anywhere. Make sure that the gloves are the right size.

3 Place the package on a clean, dry, flat surface. Open the wrapper handling only the outside. If either glove tears or becomes contaminated as you open the wrapper and put the gloves on, you should remove them both and start again.

4 Use your opposite hand to pick up a glove, touch only the inside of the folded cuff, do not touch the outside of the glove.

5 Put the glove on still holding only the inside of the folded cuff.

6 Use your gloved hand to pick up the remaining glove, place the finger of your gloved hand under the cuff of the remaining glove, pull it away from the wrapper and onto your hand, continue to pull the glove up the wrist. Be sure that no part of your gloves touch your skin or clothing.

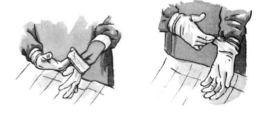

7 Now use your gloved hand to roll back the cuff of the first glove.

8 Adjust the fingers of the gloves to fit comfortably.

Removing gloves

1 With the gloved fingers of one hand grasp the glove of the other hand at the wrist.

2 Turn the glove inside out as you pull it off your hand.

3 Place your fingers of your un-gloved hand inside the cuff of the remaining glove.

4 Pull the cuff downwards and pull it inside out as you remove your hand whilst continuing to hold the other empty glove in your hand so that both gloves are folded together inside out before disposal.

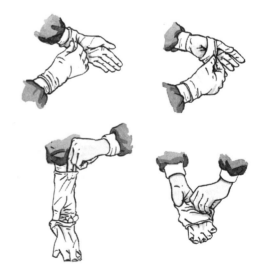

Putting on a gown

1 Wash your hands. If your uniform or working clothes have long sleeves roll your sleeves up until they are above your elbows.

2 Unfold the gown so that the opening is facing you.

3 Put your arms into the sleeves of the gown.

4 Make sure all parts of your uniform, including the neck, are covered.

5 Tie the back of the neck of the gown in a bow or use the velcro fastening strips.

6 Overlap the edges of the gown at the back, covering your uniform completely.

7 Tie the waist ties in a bow or fasten with the velcro fastening strips.

Removing a gown

1 Untie the waist bow or undo the strings at the back of the neck but do be careful not to touch your neck with your gloved hands; it may be safer if someone else helped you.

2 Take the sleeves off by pulling from the shoulders, turn the sleeves inside out as you take your arms out.

3 Hold the gown away from you by the inside of the shoulder seams, fold it inside out.

4 Roll the gown up inside out and place it in the soiled linen container.

5 Remove gloves as shown previously.

6 If you have worn a mask remove it by touching only the strings of the mask, and dispose of it.

7 Wash your hands.

Hand washing

Hand washing is an important procedure which you should do at the start and the end of every clinical activity you undertake. You should also wash your hands before and after placing gloves on your hands. In order to wash your hands properly you should follow this procedure:

1 You will need soap, paper towels, running water, and a place to dispose of your paper towels.

2 Wet your hands and wrists under running water. You should always keep your hands lower than your elbows whilst washing.

3 Apply soap and work up a good lather, spread the soap and lather over your hands and wrists and under your nails. Use the fingers of each hand to work between the fingers of the other hand, make sure you wash the back of your hands.

4 Clean under your nails by rubbing your nails across the palm of your hand.

5 Wash by using a rotating frictional motion, rubbing one hand against the other and interlacing your fingers. You should wash all skin surfaces on your hands between your fingers and two inches above your wrists.

6 Rub the tips of your fingers against your palms so that you clean around the nail beds.

7 Rinse well in running water from two inches above your wrists to your finger tips, hold your hands and finger tips downwards under the water.

8 Dry thoroughly with paper towels and dispose of them without touching the waste paper receptacle, which should have a lid which can be operated by a foot pedal.

9 Do not touch either the taps or the sink with your hands after you have washed them. The tap should either have levers which you can turn off using your forearms above the area you have washed or if not you should turn it off by holding a paper towel in your hands and then dispose of the paper towel by using the foot pedal to open the lid of the receptacle.

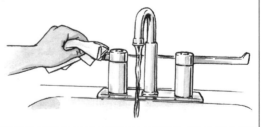

Active knowledge

Check the guidance in your workplace about the use of universal precautions. Consider the times when you should take precautions before carrying out procedures. Make a note of the number of times you should take precautions but do not do so either because of lack of time, lack of appropriate equipment or the generally accepted practice in your workplace. If you find that you are not taking the necessary precautions on every occasion, resolve to improve your practice!

Element X13.2 Undertake clinical procedures, treatments and dressings

WHAT YOU NEED TO LEARN

- How to use a sterile technique.
- How to use a clean technique.
- Procedures, treatments and dressings.

In this element you will need to learn about the range of procedures you could be asked to undertake in your workplace. There are likely to be variations between workplaces as to the type of activities that you are asked to undertake. In some settings a qualified medical practitioner, such as a nurse, midwife or doctor, may be required to carry out some of the procedures, whereas in other settings you may be asked to undertake the activity. The procedures outlined for this element are generally those which are considered appropriate. However, you should always check with your supervisor about the procedures which are required in your own particular work setting.

The procedures covered in this section are:

- changing dressings
- stoma care
- catheter care
- care of eyes, ears and mouth.

How to use a sterile technique

Regardless of the work setting in which you operate you will need to understand the nature of a **sterile field**. For many of the clinical procedures that you carry out, particularly those which are **invasive**, that is those that involve entry into parts of the client's body system or dealing with an exposed part of the client's body, you will need to know how to work in a sterile way. This minimises the risk of your client acquiring an infection during the process.

When you are undertaking a sterile procedure, such as applying a dressing to an open wound or dealing with procedures which can introduce infection into a client, such as stoma care or catheter care, then you must operate from a sterile field. This is the description given to an area which you create which is sterile and safe for your client. There are specific processes which you must undertake in order to first of all establish and then maintain a sterile field. The simplest way to create a sterile field is

A medical trolley can be used as a sterile field

to use the sterile wrap from a dressing package to create the field, or you could use sterile towels which are supplied as part of a sterile kit.

Once you have established a sterile field only sterile items can be in it. If anything which has not been through the sterilisation process is placed in the field, the whole field becomes un-sterile. You must then discard it and start again.

If one of the items in your sterile field is touched by something which is not sterile, then that item becomes un-sterile and as a result so does your whole field. So it must be discarded and you have to start again.

You will have established your sterile field on the top of a table or trolley. Only the top of the table or trolley is then considered sterile. If anything hangs over the edge of the sterile field it has become un-sterile. You should also note that the final inch of the sterile field at the edges are considered un-sterile, so be careful you do not place any of your sterile items at the edges or touch this area with any of your sterile items.

Unless you are wearing a sterile gown and gloves you must not stretch over your sterile field. If you do it is possible that micro-organisms from your arms or hands could make the field un-sterile.

You should always observe your sterile field. If you turn your back on it you do not know what is happening to it and so have no way of knowing that it has remained sterile and uncontaminated. You need to think carefully about where you place your sterile field so that you can keep it in sight at the same time as carrying out your activity

It goes without saying that you must never touch anything on your sterile field unless you are wearing sterile gloves.

Your hands should always be kept above your waist and in front of you where you can see them all the time you are working in a sterile field. If you touch an un-sterile item you must remove and discard your gloves using the procedure shown previously (page 241) and replace them with new sterile gloves.

Sterile items may be added to your sterile field but if they touch anything un-sterile or go within one inch of the edge of the field they become contaminated and must be discarded.

One of the key factors in containing a sterile field is that the field remains dry. If it absorbs moisture from any un-sterile item then the field becomes un-sterile. For example, if on the trolley on which you set out your sterile field there was dampness which was absorbed by one of the towels, then your whole field would be contaminated.

You must become very aware of the importance of sterile technique and maintaining sterile conditions. Although this may seen extremely complicated, with practice it will become second nature. You are responsible for maintaining the sterile field in the interests of your client. There will not necessarily be anybody else who will be aware of what you are doing, so you must be aware if you contaminate your own sterile field in any way. If you do contaminate it, you must start the procedure again.

How to use a clean technique

Some procedures may be carried out using a clean rather than a sterile technique. Clean techniques may be used, for example, to change a dressing over a healed wound or to add to an existing dressing. To do this you should use gloves and supplies which are clean, though not necessarily sterile. In reality, the gloves and supplies you use are likely to be sterile, although you do not have to create a sterile field in which to use them. However, it is important that you maintain a clean area in order to carry out the procedure and that you avoid contamination of your clean supplies. If you were, for example, to drop your gloves on the floor they would become dirty and contaminated and could not be used to continue any procedure using a clean technique. Similarly, if you were to touch a dirty item, for example an item which was already known to be contaminated, such as a container of bodily fluids, then the gloves would become dirty and could no longer be used.

If you are applying a sterile dressing or are using sterile instruments in a sterile field, then you must ensure that you open sterile packages in a way that does not contaminate them. If you follow this procedure and remember not to contaminate your sterile field, then you should be able to carry it out in a sterile way which will minimise the risk to your client:

1   Wash your hands.

2   Make sure you have all the equipment and supplies that you need. In this case it is likely to be sterile gloves and a sterile package containing the dressing or equipment you are going to use.

3   Check the packages have not been contaminated, they are not open, have no tears in them and are not damp.

4   Place the package on a dry, flat, clean surface. Position the package so that the first edge to be unfolded will be pulled away from you. (This is important because if you open the package away from you this will be the only time that you will have to reach across your sterile field.) The outer wrapping of the package will provide you with a sterile field to work on.

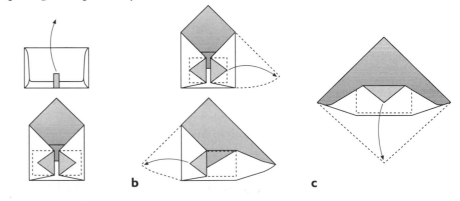

a   b   c

5   Pull the corners at the left and right of the package, which will expose the inside of the package, and carefully pull back the corner which points towards you.

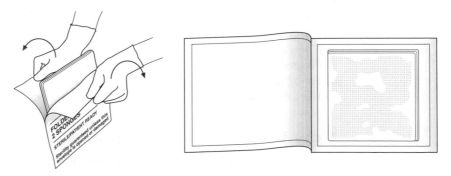

6 You have now opened your sterile package, which will provide you with a sterile field and you can add further sterile items to that field.

7 Do not forget that the outside one inch and anything hanging over the edge of the trolley or table is not sterile.

Procedures, treatments and dressings

How to change a dressing

Dressings are used to cover wounds in order to speed up healing and to keep the wound clean and free from infection. Clean dressings are used when a wound is almost healed or there is a minimal risk of infection. For open wounds or situations where there is a risk of infection, a sterile dressing would be used. This is what you must do when changing a dressing.

1 Prepare all the equipment you will need.

2 Explain to your client what you are intending to do and what the procedure will involve. Make sure they are in agreement with you changing their dressing. Follow the procedures to make sure that you are working in either a clean or a sterile environment.

3 Make sure the client is comfortable and they have privacy as far as possible.

4 Remove and inspect the old dressing. You may need to keep the dressing for a medical practitioner to examine if you have been asked to do so. Make sure you keep it in an appropriate clean or sterile container. If there is no need to keep the dressing you should inspect it to ensure there is no obvious sign of infection or deterioration of the wound, and then discard it in the appropriate waste container for contaminated waste.

5 Remove the gloves you have used to take off the old dressing and put on a new pair.

6 Re-dress the wound using a clean or sterile dressing.

Applying a clean dressing gauze wrap (two people are needed for this procedure)

7 Make sure you have discarded all waste appropriately, including your gloves, and wash your hands. Check that the client is comfortable.

8 Record in the care plan or case notes the fact that you have changed the dressing and any observations that you made of the wound and the site.

Stoma care

Stoma care is the care of clients who have had surgery to provide an additional means of eliminating waste from their bodies, either faeces or urine. The most usual stoma care is given to clients who have a colostomy. This is the result of providing an additional surgical opening for clients who are unable, either on a temporary or permanent basis, to use their bowel in the normal way. This can be the result of colon cancer, ulcerative colitis or a series of other diseases. Following a colostomy faeces are collected in a special stoma bag which needs to be changed regularly. Many clients are able to do this for themselves, but it may be necessary to provide stoma care for them in the early days after the colostomy has been performed or because the client is ill or becoming frail.

It is likely you would only be asked to provide stoma care for a client who has an established colostomy and therefore likely to be familiar with the procedure. However, you should still check that they are happy for you to change their appliance and that they understand the procedure you are about to undertake. This is what you must do to carry out the procedure:

1 Wash hands.

2 Ensure the client understands the procedure and that you have provided for privacy.

3 Expose the appliance, the stoma bag. Place a towel over the client's abdomen and a protector on the client's bed to keep the bed clean.

4 Make sure you have all the necessary equipment and put on gloves.

5 Gently remove the old pouch and the wafer, which is the thin layer that provides the seal between the pouch or bag and the client.

6 Measure the contents of the bag, note any changes from normal to the contents and then dispose of it in accordance with the policy of your work setting.

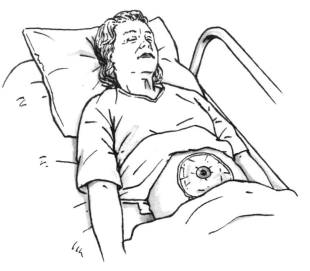

7 Wipe the skin around the stoma using a warm cloth to ensure that any faeces are removed. Dry the area with a towel.

8 Prepare the new wafer by cutting it to fit over the stoma. There should not be any visible skin between the stoma and the wafer.

9 Apply the new wafer to the skin, make sure there are no air pockets under the wafer, and hold it in place for 30 seconds to help the adhesive to work.

10 Apply the stoma pouch or bag to the flange on the wafer, and make sure that the bag is sealed.

11 Remove the protectors and clean the area.

12 Wash your hands.

13 Record the procedure in the client's care plan or case notes.

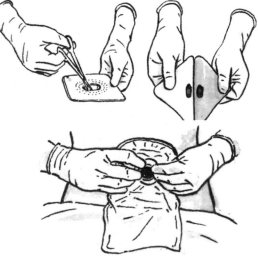

Catheter care

Clients who have an indwelling catheter, which is likely to be a Foley's catheter, may need support in ensuring that the risk of infection is reduced as far as possible. Clients with catheters are prone to infections, and hygiene and sterile techniques must be observed to minimise the risk. In order to maintain hygiene the site at which the catheter enters the client's body should be cleaned regularly. You should follow procedures laid down for your workplace, which may vary slightly but are generally likely to be:

1 Wash hands.

2 Take universal precautions.

3 Ensure that the client understands the procedure and that you have provided for privacy.

4 Using a sterile technique, prepare a tray with either saline or savlon or any other medium identified in your workplace procedures.

5 Using swabs, dip one swab into the solution and wipe in one direction around one side of the entry site.

6 In a female client you should ensure that you wipe away from the rectal opening in one direction only.

7 Discard the swab after one wipe and take a fresh swab to wipe the other side of the entry site.

8 Discard that swab.

9 Continue using fresh swabs for each wipe until the area is clean.

10 Do not wipe the area excessively as this can lead to irritation and introduce infection. It should be sufficient for one wipe each side of the entry site.

11 Dispose of the used swabs and tray in accordance with the procedures for your workplace for disposal of contaminated waste.

12 Remove your gloves.

13 Wash your hands.

14 Record the procedure in the client's care plan or case notes.

You are unlikely to be involved in the insertion or removal of catheters as this is undertaken by a qualified clinical practitioner, although you may be asked to assist under direction on occasions.

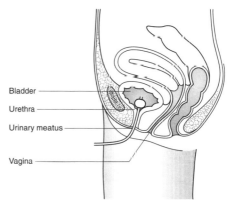

Indwelling urinary catheter in place in female body

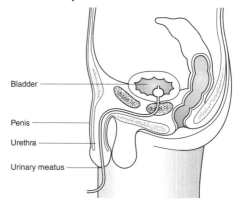

Indwelling urinary catheter in place in male body

Extended personal care
Mouth care

Mouth care can be done either with a small, soft toothbrush or, more usually, with swabs which are used to clean around the teeth, gums, palate and inside the cheeks.

Use the swabs to remove any food particles and clean all the surfaces of the mouth. You can obtain liquid toothpaste, which is probably the easiest sort to use. A diluted solution of sodium bicarbonate (one teaspoon in 500 ml of warm water) is commonly used for mouth care, particularly where the mouth is dry and crusted, but it can leave a very unpleasant after taste and is better followed by swabbing out with a more pleasant-tasting mouthwash. After you have finished cleaning and moistening the person's mouth, protect his or her lips with lip salve or Vaseline. Remember that all the equipment you use should be maintained for that individual only and should be clearly labelled and kept together.

Eye care

Before you begin cleaning a client's eyes, make sure you have cotton wool swabs and a suitable bag in which to dispose of them, a bowl of clean water or saline, a paper towel, and eye drops, if the client uses them.

To bathe clients' eyes you will need to:

1 Make the client comfortable and explain what you are going to do.

2 Ensure that the client is in agreement and wants you to carry this out.

3 Ideally, the client should lie flat, with you behind their head. However, this may not be possible and you may need to work with the client's head leaning slightly backwards with the shoulders supported.

4 Wash your hands to ensure that they are clean, and take universal precautions.

5 Arrange the paper towel under the client's face, usually tucked into the clothing just below the chin.

6 Dip a swab into the water or saline, squeeze it gently and swab the eye once, working from the nose to the outside. This should be done in a single movement.

7 Throw the swab away.

8 Repeat the procedure on both eyes until the eyes are clean and clear of any crusting or infection. Dry the skin around the eyes with clean dry swabs.

9 Remember to use each swab once only, as it is easy to cross-infect from one eye to the other or to introduce infections into the eye.

Active knowledge

Check your workplace practices for the response that you are required to make if a client has an adverse reaction to a clinical procedure. If you imagine the situation where a client suddenly begins to become cold and clammy, their speech becomes slurred and they complain of feeling faint, ask yourself the following questions:

1 What would I do?

2 Who would I contact?

3 What steps would I take while waiting for help to arrive?

You should ensure that you are able to establish the answers to these three questions by checking through the procedures or talking to your supervisor in your own workplace.

WHAT YOU NEED TO LEARN

How to obtain specimens of:

- Urine
- Faeces
- Exudates
- Blood
- Sputum.

In this element you will learn about how to obtain specimens of a range of bodily fluids, each of which can provide medical practitioners with significant information about the state of health of the client. There are specific methods for obtaining correct uncontaminated specimens and for storing them in appropriate containers and in appropriate ways to ensure they are in the right condition to provide the best possible information when they are tested.

Specimen containers are *never* prelabelled. You should only label a container with your client's name after you have collected the specimen. This reduces the risk of a container being picked up by someone else and mistakenly used to put their client's specimen in.

Containers are generally sterile regardless of the type of specimen which is being collected. This is important so that the laboratories carrying out the tests are not dealing with specimens which are contaminated by any micro-organisms from a source other than the client. You should make sure you always use the correct container for the type of specimen you are collecting.

Urine

It is easiest to take a sterile urine specimen from a client who has a catheter and to obtain it from the catheter line. To collect this you should:

1 Wash your hands.

2 Explain to the client what you are going to do and answer any questions they may have.

3 Make sure you have collected all the equipment you need and put on your gloves.

4 Clamp the catheter line below the port by folding the tubing in half and apply the clamp.

5 Wait for a small amount of urine to collect in the tubing above the port.

6 Insert a sterile syringe gently into the port. Make sure you do not pierce the tubing itself.

7 Withdraw approximately 10cc of urine into the syringe.

A catheter line

8 Empty the syringe into the sterile specimen container.

9 Make sure you do not contaminate the insides or the lid of the container.

10 Unclamp the catheter tubing and make sure the urine is freely flowing.

11 Label the container and complete the documentation for your workplace and send it to the laboratory following the procedures for your own work setting.

12 Record in the case notes or care plan the fact you have taken the specimen.

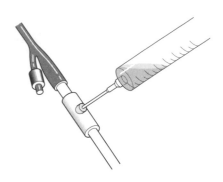

Withdrawing a urine specimen

Clients who do not have a catheter should be supplied with the appropriate equipment to provide a **mid-stream sample of urine** (**MSSU**). The equipment consists of a funnel and a sterile urine container. The funnel and container should come in a sterile pack and the client should be asked to pass urine into the funnel and fill the pot.

Testing urine

The condition of a client's urine can provide a great deal of information about their state of health. There are simple tests which can be carried out on urine and you may be asked to undertake some of these. However, it is important before carrying out any tests that you follow some basic observations which will provide you with an initial indication of any problems.

Equipment for obtaining mid-stream sample of urine

Healthy urine should be clear, pale yellow and not have an offensive smell. If urine smells offensive, is cloudy, has particles in it, has blood in it, is a bright orange colour, or any other colour apart from clear pale yellow, then these are the first signs of concern. You should also check with your client whether they have experienced any pain or burning when they pass urine as either of these could be indicators of more serious underlying conditions. These simple observations are indicators of further problems but are insufficient on their own to establish that there really are problems. It is necessary to carry out further tests on the client's urine in order to find out more detailed information about their state of health.

Urine Tests

There are two methods of testing urine. It can be sent to a laboratory, which would normally be a specialist **uro-genital bacteriology** section, where extensive testing and the growing of cultures can be carried out. However, if an initial indication of any possible underlying problems is required the most normal method is to use **urine-analysis sticks**. These are short flexible sticks a few inches long containing sensitive material which changes colour depending on the substances they come into contact with in the urine. It is possible to test for a range of factors in urine by using urine-analysis sticks. The following table shows some examples.

Test for	Indications
1 Leucocytes, ((white blood cells), an indicator of infection)	Change of colour – sticks range from white through to dark purple
2 Protein (another indicator of infection)	Colour changes from light green through to dark green
3 Blood	Colour changes from white to dark blue
4 Glucose (high blood sugar)	Colour changes from light blue to yellow

Urinc storage

If you need to store urine prior to testing, it is important that it should be in a tightly sealed sterile containcr. It should be kept in a separate specimen fridge, *never* in a fridge which is used for storing ordinary food stuff. It must also be clearly labelled with the:

- client's name
- type of specimen
- date the specimen was collected.

Faeces

To collect a specimen of faeces for testing first collect the faeces from your client in a bedpan or commode. Thcn take the specimen from this into a sterile universal container. A sterile container for faeces contains an implement attached to the inside of the lid of the container which allows you to collect a small amount of the faeces and place them inside the container.

A faecal collection container

Testing faeces

All testing of stool samples will be carried out in a laboratory, so you should ensure that you clearly label the container with the:

- client's name
- type of sample
- date the sample was collected.

It should then be sent to the laboratory with the required documentation for your workplace. If a specimen has to be stored you must ensure that it is stored in a separate specimen fridge and not in an ordinary fridge with any food stuff.

Many clients may be embarrassed about providing a sample of faeces, so you will need to obtain the sample at a time when the client has a normal bowel movement, rather than expecting them to provide a sample at a time which is convenient for you. You should explain the reason for needing the sample and explain why it is necessary for them to provide a sample into a bedpan or other suitable receptacle rather than use the toilet in the normal way.

Sputum

Sputum specimens are important indicators of possible respiratory infections or respiratory diseases such as tuberculosis, pneumonia or bronchitis. Sputum specimens are often better collected in the morning as clients often have more secretions in their lungs and bronchial tubes after lying down sleeping during the night. In order to obtain a specimen you must first explain to your client what you need the specimen for and what you want them to do, and then take the following steps:

1 Wash hands and put on gloves.

2 Make sure you have the correct supplies, which will be a sterile sputum container, similar to a normal sterile container except that it will have an inverted funnel in the top to assist the collection of the sputum.

3 You should explain to the client that you wish them to cough up sputum from their lungs and then spit it out into the container. This is called 'to expectorate'.

4 After the client has expectorated their sample, make sure you give them tissues to wipe their mouth and a drink if they need one.

5 Note that if your client has recently eaten then you should get them to rinse their mouth before providing a sample, to lessen the risk of contamination.

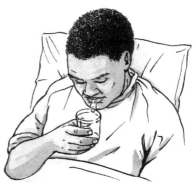

Patient giving sputum specimen

6 Cover the specimen and seal the container, ensuring that you do not touch the inside of the container.

7 Label the specimen correctly with the:
   • client's name
   • type of specimen
   • date collected.

8 Record in the care plan or case notes that this specimen has been obtained and whether it has been stored or sent to the laboratory.

Exudates

You may occasionally be asked to obtain a sample of an exudates from a wound or other lesion. This requires a sterile technique. You should do the following:

1 Wash hands.

2 Ensure that you have all the materials and equipment you will need.

3 Apply gloves and take universal precautions.

4 Take the swab and wipe on the surface of the wound or lesion once, ensuring that you collect some of the exudates onto the swab.

5 Unscrew the top of the specimen tube.

6 Insert the swab into the tube and screw the end firmly.

7 The swab should reach into the medium contained in the tube.

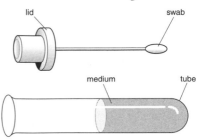

Equipment for taking exudate specimens

8 Label the specimen clearly.

9 Clear away and dispose of all of the equipment and materials in accordance with disposal procedures for contaminated waste.

10 Remove gloves.

11 Wash hands.

12 Record the activity in the client's case notes or care plan.

Blood

There are two ways of obtaining blood samples. One is through a finger prick using a small lancet blade and the other is through **venipuncture**, which involves using a needle and syringe to take blood from a client's vein.

Blood which is obtained from a finger prick is obtained from capillary vessels, which are the tiny blood vessels near the surface of the skin. The blood from there is squeezed onto the testing apparatus. The most commonly used method is using testing strips for testing blood sugar levels, or the **phenylketonuria (PKU) test**, which is done by pricking the heels of babies during the first few days of life. Where larger amounts of

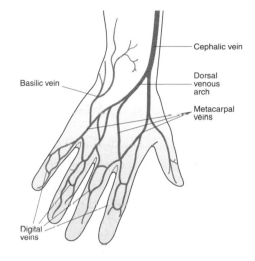

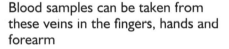

Blood samples can be taken from these veins in the fingers, hands and forearm

blood are required for more extensive tests, then it is necessary to understand where to find the relevant veins in the arm and hand.

You need to be specially trained to take blood from a client. There are courses that provide this training. The information in this unit will give you some guidance and assistance, however it will not enable you to have the skill to undertake the procedure on clients. You should never attempt to carry out this procedure without the specific agreement and under the instructions of a medical practitioner or your supervisor, unless you have been trained by your workplace to carry out these procedures.

Obtaining blood samples by finger prick

Blood sugar levels are tested on a regular basis (often daily) for clients who are diabetic. The most usual method is to prick the side of the finger using a small lancet and then read the results with a blood glucose meter. There are many different types of meters so you should make sure you are familiar with the one which is used in your work setting. In order to test a client's blood sugar level, you should do the following:

1 Wash your hands.

2 Explain to the client if necessary what the process involves. However, if the client has been a diabetic for some time they are likely to be very familiar with the procedure and many carry it out for themselves. If you do need to undertake the procedure for them you should ensure that you have their consent.

3 Assemble the equipment that you will need, which is:
- gloves
- meter
- test strips
- lancet.

4 Check that the test strips are the appropriate ones for the meter, remove a test strip from the container, then close the container. Do not touch the white area on the strip.

5 Place the end of the lancet firmly on the side of the client's finger, press the button on the top of the lancet in order to pierce the skin.

6 Squeeze the finger gently to obtain a large drop of blood.

7 Apply the blood sample to the test strip.

8 Wait the indicated amount of time for the result to appear on the meter.

9 Clean the meter and dispose of the strips in accordance with procedures in your workplace.

10 Document and record and results in the client's care plan or case notes.

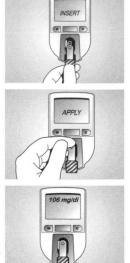

Obtaining blood sample by finger prick

Testing blood for sugar

Blood probably can tell more about the health and well-being of a client than any other bodily fluid. Most blood tests are carried out in laboratories.

However, you may be asked to carry out a blood sugar analysis. This is a test used regularly for clients who are diabetic and who need to ensure that their medication or diet regime is maintaining their blood sugar at an appropriate level.

Diabetes is the disorder caused by the body's inability to use insulin properly or to provide sufficient insulin to convert sugar into energy, which is the normal role of insulin. When this happens the levels of sugar within the client's blood becomes abnormally high or low and results in potentially dangerous symptoms.

Hyperglycemia is an excessively high level of blood sugar and **hypoglycemia** is an abnormally low level of blood sugar. The symptoms of hyperglycemia are heavy and laboured breathing, nausea, vomiting, increased thirst, increased urination, loss of appetite and sweet-smelling breath. The symptoms of hypoglycemia are excessive sweating, hunger, feeling of faintness, trembling, blurred vision and headaches.

You should observe your client carefully for any of these signs or symptoms and immediately obtain medical assistance if any of them are present, or if your client reports any of them to you.

Element X13.4 Measure and monitor the physical characteristics and condition of clients

WHAT YOU NEED TO LEARN

Measuring and monitoring:

- Temperature
- Respiration
- Height, weight and girth
- Fluid balance

- Pulse
- Blood pressure
- Peak flow.

Taking measurements gives you physiological information, and tells you much about your client and their state of health. Simply observing your client will also indicate to you whether there are any changes, a deterioration or an improvement in your client's condition, and these should be immediately reported.

Even though taking measurements such as temperature, pulse and blood pressure are routine exercises, you should still not assume that either your client's consent is given or that they understand the process. You should always check this first. It may be something as simple as, 'I am just going to take your temperature, OK?', or you can get implied consent from your client if they hold their hand up when you say, 'Can I just take your pulse?' Check that they know what you are doing and why. If you begin to carry out these simple routine measurements without either explaining or obtaining the client's consent it may develop into a familiar pattern and could lead to you ignoring the client and their wishes when carrying out more extensive or invasive procedures. If the client has any questions, then you should answer them to the best of your ability. If their questions go beyond your knowledge then you must refer the query to your supervisor or to a medical practitioner.

Temperature

Temperature is a useful indicator of health or illness. Temperature rises when a client has an infection, or possibly following injury or trauma, whereas a low temperature indicates a serious condition such as hypothermia. Temperature can be taken with a traditional thermometer containing mercury. The mercury rises up the glass tube of the thermometer and indicates the client's temperature on the gauge printed on the tube. This type of thermometer has increasingly been replaced by a thermometer which operates with a battery and has a liquid crystal display which shows the client's body temperature. Many health and care settings now use a disposable thermometer which records the client's temperature on a series of dots which will change colour to indicate temperature.

The normal temperature of the human body is 37° Centigrade, 98.4° Fahrenheit. Any significant variation from this must be reported immediately. Temperature should be recorded on a temperature chart (see Unit CU5 in *NVQ Level 2 Care*).

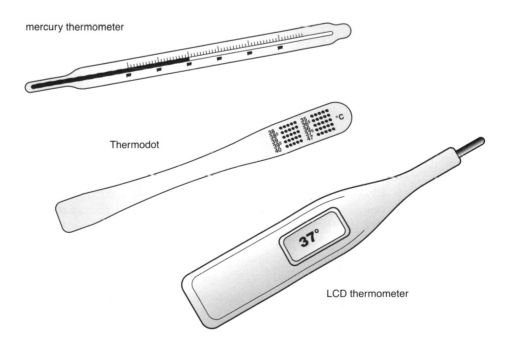

mercury thermometer

Thermodot

LCD thermometer

Pulse

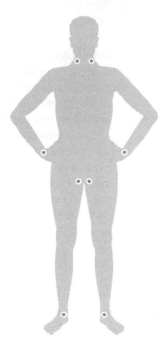

The pulse points in the human body – neck, wrists, groin, ankles

Taking a pulse is a way of establishing a client's heart rate by measuring the beats of the heart through a main artery, usually in the wrist. It is possible to take a client's pulse at various other points in the body.

To take a pulse manually, place your first two fingers lightly on the client's wrist directly below the heel of the thumb.

Through your fingers you will then feel the client's pulse in their brachial artery. You will need to use your first two fingers to feel the pulse. You cannot feel somebody else's pulse through your thumb because you have a pulse in your own thumb. When you can feel a pulse you should then count the number of beats you can feel for a period of 30 seconds. You will need to look at your watch whilst you count the pulse. You then multiply the number of beats by two, which will give you a pulse rate of beats per minute.

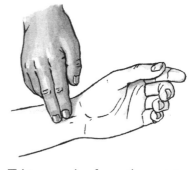

Taking a pulse from the wrist

Pulse can also be taken by a **pulseoximeter** which fits onto the client's finger and records the pulse electronically. If you take any exercise in a gym or use an exercise bike you may well have seen a pulseoximeter.

Pulse can also be taken as part of a combined reading with blood pressure on an instrument called a **dynomap**. Normal pulse rate is around 70 beats per minute, although this can be raised by illness, anxiety or exercise. People who are extremely fit will have a lower pulse rate; some athletes have pulse rates as low as 50. You will need to know if your client takes regular exercise as this could explain a low pulse rate.

Respiration

A client's respiration is measured in breaths per minute. You will need to observe the number of times that the chest rises and falls per minute. A rise and fall constitutes one respiration. You will need to time your observations for 30 seconds and then multiple by 2 to obtain the number of respirations per minute. A sudden increase or decrease in a client's respiration rate can indicate a deterioration or change in condition and should immediately be reported to a qualified clinical practitioner as giving cause for concern.

Blood pressure

Blood pressure indicates the pressure at which blood is being pumped around the body from the heart. It is important that blood pressure remains within a defined area of measurement. Excessively high or low blood pressure can indicate illness or disease and can directly cause a health problem. Blood pressure is measured with a sphygmomanometer and a stethoscope. The process is as follows:

1   Attach the blood pressure cuff to the client's arm.

2   Put a stethoscope on the pulse in the arm at the inner elbow.

3 Ensure that you can hear the client's pulse.

4 Pump up the cuff until the mercury in the sphygmomanometer reaches approximately 180.

5 Keep on listening to the pulse in the arm until the point at which the sound disappears.

6 When you are no longer able to hear the pulse, note the level on the sphygmomanometer.

7 This will provide you with your **systolic** (top reading). This is normally around 120.

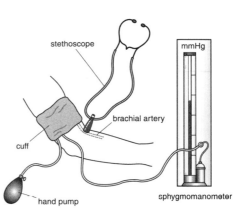

Taking blood pressure

8 Then decrease the air in the cuff slowly, letting it out using the valve on the sphygmomanometer, until you hear the pulse in the arm again.

9 This will give you your **diastolic** (lower reading), which should be around 80.

There can be many reasons for blood pressure being higher or lower than 120/80 and there is a fairly wide acceptable range, which can alter with age. However, you should ensure that all measurements of blood pressure are recorded and any significant variations are reported.

Height and weight

A person's weight in relation to their height can indicate the extent to which their

Weight and health

Underweight The health of clients who are severely underweight could be adversely affected. This could be as a result of illness or as a result of deliberate over-dieting, which is also dangerous to health. Excessive dieting can lead to eating disorders, such as anorexia nervosa or bulimia, caused by clients not getting sufficient nutrients to remain healthy. However, most clients who are underweight are likely to be suffering from some illness.

Overweight, very overweight and obese. The risk to health associated with being overweight or obese grows with the increase in weight. Excess weight can increase the risk of cardiovascular disease, diabetes, arthritis and other weight associated complications.

Note: There is quite a wide range of accepted weights for height which will not represent any threat to the client's health.

health is being put at risk by them being excessively underweight or overweight.

There are ideal weights for heights which have been calculated to present the least risk to health. This can be identified in a height/weight chart.

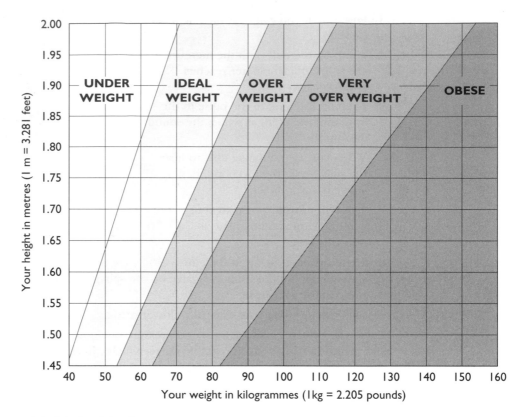

A height/weight chart

Measuring weight

Where possible clients should be able to stand on a set of scales for the measurement to be taken. Heavy items of clothing such as shoes and outdoor coats should be removed. Clients should stand on the scales and the weight adjusted until the scales balance. A client's weight should be read in kilograms and recorded in their case notes or care plan.

Where clients are unable to stand safely on a set of weighing scales then a scale which provides a seat should be used and the weight recorded in the same way.

Measuring height

Height should be measured using a fixed height ruler which should be attached to the wall of an examination room, or a portable fixed height rule should be used. The client should be asked to stand against the wall with their heels back against the door and stand as straight as they can. The height-measuring bar should be lowered until it rests gently on the top of their head. The resulting height should then be read from the upright ruler. The height, which is likely to be in metres and centimetres, should be recorded in the client's case notes or care plan.

Measuring girth

This should be done around the middle of the client's torso in approximately the waist area. A tape measure should be placed around the waist area and read at the point where both ends meet comfortably without over tightening. The measurement in centimetres should be recorded in the client's case notes or care plan.

Body mass index

Another way to measure a person's weight is to measure and calculate their **body mass index** (**BMI**):

$$BMI = \frac{Weight\ (kg)}{Height\ (m^2)}$$

The result obtained from this calculation indicates whether a person is underweight, at normal weight, overweight or obese:

BMI < 20 kg   underweight
BMI 20–25 kg   normal
BMI 25–30 kg   overweight
BMI > 30 kg   obese
BMI > 40 kg   severely obese

How to calculate BMI

A person weighs 16 stone and is 5 ft 6 ins tall. What is their BMI?

- For the top line (weight):
  Convert 16 stones to kilograms
  There are 2.2 lbs to 1 kg.
  Convert 16 stones to pounds
  16 stone is $16 \times 14 lb = 224$ lbs
  224 lbs divided by 2.2 = 102 kg

- For the bottom line (height squared – m^2 means the height is squared, i.e. multiplied by itself):
  Convert 5 ft 6 inches to metres
  There are 39.5 inches to 1 metre. Convert 5 feet to inches
  $5 ft = 5 \times 12 ins = 60 + 6 ins = 66.ins$
  Then convert inches to metres
  66 divided by 39.5 = 1.67 m
  The height squared is $1.67 \times 1.67 = 2.79$ m
  So,

$$BMI = \frac{102\,kg}{2.79\,m} = 36.6$$

(If you are able to measure weight in kilograms and measure height in metres this will save doing any conversions).
This value indicates that the person's health is at risk and that they would benefit from losing weight. We should all aim to be in the 20–25 kg range as this represents least risk to health.

Did you know?

That up to 56 per cent of men and 45 per cent women in the United Kingdom are classified as being overweight (this is identified as having a BMI of more than 25).

The table shows the percentage of males and females who have excess weight at certain ages.

	Age (years)					
	16–24	25–34	35–44	45–54	55–64	All ages
Males Total with excess weights (%)	31	50	62	68	69	56
Females Total with excess weights (%)	28	38	45	44	64	45

Peak flow

Peak flow measures lung capacity. This is a useful indicator of illness or lung damage. A reduced peak flow is evident in people who are asthmatic or have any chronic respiratory disease. A peak flow meter, a hollow plastic tube about eight inches long, is used to measure peak flow. It has a small gauge on the top and a disposable cardboard blow pipe is inserted into one end. The client should be asked to blow a short, sharp breath into the tube and this will then register on the gauge. The normal rate of lung capacity should be around about 500. In asthmatics or people with chronic lung disease, such as emphysema, a peak flow can be as low as 150 or 200.

A peak flow meter

Fluid balance

The **fluid balance** is the amount of fluid is taken in and excreted out from the body. It is a very important indicator of health. If more fluid is excreted than is taken in then a client can become dehydrated. Conversely if they retain too much fluid in their body this can result in swelling, oedema and ultimately heart failure.

Intake and output is measured by keeping a record of the volume of fluids in and out. This is recorded on a fluid balance chart.

Input

In order to keep an accurate record of input and output of fluid, all fluid which the client takes into their body, either through the mouth or through an intravenous drip. must be measured. If drinks are left for the clients to pour for themselves, you should measure the drinks in the jug and constantly check how much has been used. Explain to the client that they should not take any drinks from anywhere unless they are recorded on the chart.

FLUID CHART
(ADULT)

PLEASE SEE REVERSE SIDE FOR
NOTES ON USE OF THIS CHART

ORAL INTAKE				INTRAVENOUS THERAPY						OUTPUT						
				* Before starting this section remember to enter TIME and name of I.V. fluid already in progress and amount brought forward from previous chart												
TIME	FLUID	ml	ORAL TOTAL SO FAR ml	STARTED		ENDED		* BROUGHT FORWARD ml		TIME	URINE ml	URINE TOTAL SO FAR ml	ASPIRATE OR VOMIT ml	ASP/VOM TOTAL SO FAR ml	DRAIN ml	DRAIN ml	COMMENTS
				TIME	FLUID	TIME	ml	COMMENTS									

TIME	TOTAL – ORAL	ml	TOTAL – I.V.	ml	CARRIED FORWARD	ml	TOTALS	URINE ml	ASPIRATE/VOMIT ml	DRAIN ml	DRAIN ml

SURNAME	OTHER NAME/S	UNIT NUMBER	WARD	DATE / /

A fluid balance chart

Output

All fluid output should be measured. The urine in a catheter bag or in a bedpan or commode should be measured before disposal. All vomit should also be measured and its volume recorded.

Maintaining a fluid balance chart

Maintaining a fluid balance chart is not difficult provided you carry out the basic sums correctly! You will need to be sure you have done the addition and subtraction so that the balance of fluid for your client is clearly recorded. Each individual is different as to the amount of fluid they take in and excrete from their bodies but, broadly speaking, everyone should have a positive fluid balance, that is they should put out slightly more fluid than they take in.

Active knowledge

1 Take your own height and weight and then using the calculations in this element work out your own body mass index. Try to do this for two or three other friends or family members until you are confident with the calculations.

2 Work out the fluid balance for the following figures and calculate whether or not this client is maintaining a positive fluid balance.

Intake
0800: IV Therapy – Hartman's 1000 ml
1200: Hartman's discontinued
1300: T 250 ml
1400 : Juice 250 ml
1630 : T 250 ml
Output
1230: 300 ml urine
1600: 500 ml urine; 100 ml vomit
1830: 600 ml urine

Assist in the administration of clients' medication

WHAT YOU NEED TO LEARN

*   How to administer medication to a client.
*   How to store medication and record its use.

If you are working in a nursing home or other long-term residential setting, or if you are supporting clients in their own home, then you may be involved in assisting them to take their medication, which may have been prescribed by a doctor or purchased over the counter.

The range of medication that you may need to help administer is:

*   oral medicines
*   inhaled medicines
*   eye, nose and ear drops
*   vaginal and rectal preparations
*   topical preparations – applied to the skin.

How to administer medication to a client

You may have to obtain medication for a client which had been prescribed by their doctor. Your workplace may have a system of obtaining batches of medication from a local chemist. If a client asks you to purchase a particular medicine for them, then you should check with their care plan and their medical practitioner that the medication they have requested is not going to interfere with any prescribed medicines they are taking.

Administering medication should be carried out using a clean technique. You should always wash your hands before providing any medication, whether this is in tablet, cream, lotion, drops or pessary form.

Check the label

When medications are prescribed for a client it is essential you check each time that the medication you are administering is the correct medication for that client. There should be a label on the medication itself, clearly marked with the name of the drug and the name of the client. You must check:

*   the client's name
*   the name of the drug
*   the dosage
*   the frequency of the dosage.

Before you administer any medication make sure that all these details are correct.

In many workplaces drugs are only administered by a qualified medical practitioner (usually a qualified nurse). You may need to assist in the administration of this. If class A drugs – diamorphine, opiates, barbiturates – are being administered, only a qualified practitioner will have the keys to the locked cupboard containing these drugs.

As good practice you should learn about any medication you are administering to a client. This is part of the rules and regulations which govern qualified medical practitioners such as nurses and midwives, who are required to understand the nature and potential side-effects of any drug they administer. It is potentially dangerous to administer medications that you do not understand and with potential side-effects you are not aware of. The danger is that you could fail to recognise the importance of symptoms reported by a client who has suffered an adverse reaction to a particular medication.

You must also carefully read the instructions on your client's medication before administering it. This is particularly important if you are using creams, eye or ear drops, vaginal or anal pessaries. You must ensure that you follow the administration instructions as supplied with the drug and report any difficulties in using the drug or administering it.

Refusal or inability to take medication

If a client is unable to take the medication prescribed, perhaps because they have difficulty in swallowing or because they are feeling ill, or are just unwilling to take it, then you must immediately report this to your supervisor or line manager or to the clinical practitioner responsible for prescribing or administering the medicine. You should never allow a situation to continue in the hope that they may feel like taking medication later. Even if one dose is refused or a client is not able to take it, it is essential that this is reported immediately.

Individual medication

All medication is prescribed for a specific individual. When any drug is prescribed there are a wide range of factors taken into account. These include:

- other conditions which the client may have
- their age
- their size
- their social circumstances
- their likely ability to be able to take it
- any potential side-effects, and their ability to deal with them.

The range of considerations which are essential in prescribing mean that under no circumstances can medication prescribed for one individual be used for another without the express agreement of a qualified medical practitioner. If you are faced with a situation of clients sharing medication, then you should explain very carefully the reasons why medication may have been selected for them as an individual and why it may be inappropriate for another individual. You should also explain to them that the possible consequences may be:

- an adverse reaction
- the drug will be ineffective
- the drug may react with other medication that is being taken
- it may be at the wrong dosage or concentration
- it may not be in the most appropriate form for that individual to take.

Problems or queries

If a client has questions, you should answer them within the limits of your knowledge. If they ask a question about their medication which is beyond your knowledge, then you must refer the question to a qualified practitioner or to your supervisor. If you have a client who refuses to take prescribed medication, this must be immediately reported to your supervisor and recorded in the case notes or care plan.

How to store medication and record its use

All medicines should be stored in a locked cupboard or cabinet. They must be clearly labelled and should be regularly checked for their expiry date. Medicines which are out of date can either become ineffective or they can increase in their toxicity levels, and so cause serious problems.

Your workplace will have a system for recording the administration and use of drugs and medications. You should ensure that you complete the necessary documentation and record the administration of any drugs or medicines in the client's case notes or care plan.

Active knowledge

Check out the procedures for administering medication in your own work setting. You should also find out what the procedures are when a client refuses medication or if there is evidence that medication is being shared. You should be able to identify from the drug procedures in your workplace those clinical practitioners who are registered and qualified to prescribe and administer different types of drugs.

Unit X19

Prepare and undertake agreed clinical activities with clients in acute care settings

This unit is designed to provide you with information about the knowledge and skills you will need to carry out the clinical activities with clients in your work setting.

Throughout the unit you will find that many of the clinical activities are described in an identical way to those in Unit X13. Although the skills and knowledge required for the two units are similar there are some significant differences in the way in which you will need to carry out your activities because of the nature of the setting in which you work.

This unit is aimed at people who work in acute care settings where people's health is likely to be unstable, and where therefore your skills in observing and recognising changes in condition will be very significant. It is also likely that within your setting you will have access to a wide range of clinical expertise amongst your colleagues and the work which you are able to carry out may be less extensive than the range of activities carried out for clients whose health is more stable.

The final element in Unit X13, on assisting in the administration of clients' medication, is not included in this unit. This is not something which will fall within your work role if you are working with clients who have unstable health. In an acute setting this role will be undertaken by qualified clinical practitioners.

Element X19.1   Prepare clients for clinical activities

WHAT YOU NEED TO LEARN

- How to prepare for a clinical activity.
- What protective clothing is needed for a clinical activity.

How to prepare for a clinical activity

This element is about ensuring that the client understands and has given their agreement to the **clinical activity** which is about to be undertaken, and that all the necessary preparations have been made, including documentation, equipment and the correct environment. Clinical activities cover a wide range of procedures which are undertaken to improve or maintain a client's health. This can include:

- dressing wounds
- taking specimens
- taking measurements
- providing clients with medication.

All these activities require adequate preparation. It is important you take all the required steps in advance of beginning the clinical activity rather than having to break off because you forgot an important item of equipment, or you do not have the necessary chart or documents to hand.

Records, charts and documents

Throughout this unit you will recognise the importance of charts, tables and record sheets for monitoring and recording a client's state of health. They are also important for recording the requirement for and the outcome of any investigations which need to be carried out for the client's benefit. The following table lists the most likely documentation that you will need and the purposes for which you are likely to need them.

Document	Purpose
Case notes/case file	This records all information about the client and holds copies of any relevant documentation. This is the major source of information about the client's previous and current state of health and is the source of information regarding their social circumstances and any specific needs or other aspects which need to be taken into account.
Measurement charts	These can be charts recording the client's temperature, blood pressure, respiration rate, fluid balance, etc., or they can be used to record height and weight.
Care plan	This can record vital details of the way in which a client is to be cared for and records essential information for anyone who is providing any type of care for the client.
Requests for investigations	Each organisation is likely to have its own forms which are used for requesting any investigations which need to be carried out on collected specimens.
Reports of investigations	These report back on the outcome of investigations carried out and they are usually recorded and maintained in the case file or case notes.
Consent forms	Where a major activity is being undertaken, such as surgery or other invasive procedure, then clients will be asked to sign written consent forms, copies of which will be maintained in the case notes.

Consent

As a broad principle, client **consent** should be obtained before carrying out any kind of activity. Even something as simple as moving somebody or plumping their pillows should always be preceded by a question such as, 'Would you like me to plump your pillows?' However, in a clinical setting client consent has a very specific meaning and assumes a great deal of importance. There have been several well-publicised legal cases where clients have maintained that clinical procedures were carried out on them without them giving prior consent. It is essential that clients not only consent, but wherever possible understand what it is they are consenting to and the implications of this. This type of consent is referred to as **informed consent**. Informed consent means that the person who is about to carry out the procedure has given the client full information about what they are going to do, why they are going to do it and the possible effects of the procedure,

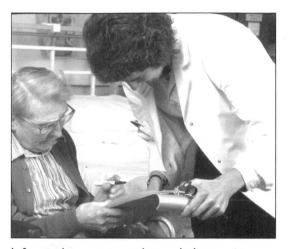

Informed consent can be verbal or written depending on the nature of the procedure to be carried out

both positive and negative. All the risks should have been explained to the client so that they are in a position to make a judgement about whether or not they wish to go ahead with the procedure. Informed consent can be written, as in the case of somebody undergoing surgery, or it can be a verbal consent, for example if somebody is having blood taken, then the procedure, the purpose of the blood test and what will be discovered would be explained to them before they agreed to it.

I'm just going to give you your medication now, John. Is that OK?

The carer usually obtains the client's consent to a procedure being carried out

Implied consent

This is a common principle in all clinical settings. It is reasonable to assume that someone implies their consent to you taking their blood pressure if they present their arm when they see you arriving and taking out the blood pressure cuff. If somebody opens their mouth when you appear with a thermometer, it is reasonable for you to assume that they are implying consent to you taking their temperature.

For these relatively minor and non-invasive procedures implied consent is perfectly acceptable. It would be a bureaucratic nightmare if client consent to these type of activities had to be recorded on every occasion.

Written consent

Each setting will have its own form for written consent. However, these forms are broadly similar in their content as they all require clients, or their relatives in the case of an emergency, to sign their agreement for the named clinical procedure to be undertaken. Generally, written consent is likely to also be informed consent as on most occasions the procedures will have been explained carefully to the client before they sign. However, sometimes in the case of emergency procedures the consent may not be informed consent as there may not have been time to explain the procedure.

Verbal consent

I've got a really bad headache, can you give me somthing for it, nurse?

By requesting medication a patient is giving verbal consent to being given that medication

Verbal consent is normally understood to exist when a client requests that a clinical procedure be undertaken. For example, a client asking for pain relief who has been told, 'OK, I understand, but, we will give you an injection for pain but it will make you sleepy', and has responded, 'Yes give it to me anyway', is taken to have given verbal consent for the procedure. This consent must be recorded in the case notes. This could also apply to, for example, a client who is severally constipated and has asked for an enema, or to somebody who has requested that they are moved from the bed to the chair using lifting equipment.

Why consent is important

It is a vital part of modern-day clinical care that client consent is always obtained. This is not only to protect clinicians and care workers against legal challenge, it is also because of the growth in recognition and understanding of the rights of the individual and the importance of recognising and valuing the rights of clients to determine what happens to them. Historically, clinical practice has always 'acted in the best interests' of clients, and there are still many older people who believe that 'Doctor or nurse knows best', and would not presume to question any medical suggestions about the way their treatment should proceed. As the traditional view of medical practitioners has changed it has become more common to question and challenge the opinions of doctors, nurses and other health workers. People have become more comfortable with the idea of being asked their views and being asked for their consent. Consent is taken very seriously. In the past consent may have been obtained where required in written format, however very often full information was not given and nor was client consent sought for more minor or non-invasive procedures.

If you are in the position where you are asked to obtain client consent for an activity you must take great care that:

- you answer any questions honestly and as fully as you can
- you never attempt to answer a question that you are not sure of and that you always refer the question on to somebody who has the knowledge to give the client a full answer

- you immediately report any refusal of consent or any reservations expressed by the client to your supervisor or to the clinical practitioner responsible for the procedure.

Make sure wherever possible you direct your information to the client. Even if the client has a relative or friend with them be careful that your information is directed to the client. In most cases it is the client's consent you must obtain, not that of their friend or relative. Where your client is a young child, or a person with learning difficulties, or someone who is extremely confused and is unable to understand the information which you are giving to them, then you should explain the procedure carefully to the person who is acting as their advocate. This could be a relative, friend or possibly a social worker or representative of the court if the person is subject to guardianship or a court order.

If, however, the client is capable of understanding but has difficulty with communications, then you must use the communication skills you have learned in completing Unit CL2 to provide the client with the information they need in order to make their decision. Clients who have hearing, seeing or speaking difficulties should not be prevented from making their own decisions and asking their own questions by the limitations of either your time or communication skills. If there are language difficulties then an interpreter should be used as appropriate. You should always consider the nature of the consent being sought before a decision is made about whether or not to use a member of the client's family. It may be that because of the need for confidentiality or because of the nature of the procedure being discussed it may not be appropriate, so the use of an interpreter may be preferable to the client.

Preparing the client

Preparing the client for any clinical activity is about more than simply obtaining their consent. It is also important to reassure the client and to explain to them exactly what is to happen. It also reduces anxiety for clients. This may involve you in explaining exactly what equipment will be used, how people will be dressed, for example in masks and gowns, and why, and to explain where the procedure will take place, if it is not in an environment familiar to the client.

You also need to check with your client for any known allergies or reactions that they may have to the procedure you are about to carry out. If the procedure involves a medical practitioner administering medication then it will be essential to check with the client if they have any known allergic reactions to particular medications. Bear in mind that people have allergies which you may not immediately consider relevant, however, all of them should be reported.

Observing the client

Throughout the activity it is important that you continue to observe your client. This is particularly the case if you are working in a hospital or other acute care setting where the client's health may not be stable and their condition can be prone to change. You will need to check your client regularly for any obvious signs of a deterioration or a change in their condition. The signs could be:

- becoming cold and clammy
- a sudden rise or fall in temperature
- a sudden rise or fall in breathing rate
- becoming flushed or very pale
- complaining of pain, discomfort or dizziness
- appearing to be unconscious.

All these conditions and any other changes that you observe must be immediately reported to the clinical practitioner responsible for the activity. If you are the person undertaking the clinical procedure then you must immediately stop the activity and get assistance.

Did you know?

Many anaesthetics are based on egg. People have become seriously ill as a result of having an egg allergy which has not been reported prior to the commencement of surgery. There are other types of anaesthetics not based on egg which can be substituted for people who have an egg allergy.

A relatively common allergy is to latex (rubber). Where this is the case the consequences can be extremely serious for clients, who can go into **anaphylactic shock**, which is potentially fatal. Clients going into anaphylactic shock become cold, clammy, show a rapid pulse and breathing, and quickly become unconscious. Any signs of such symptoms should be reported immediately and medical assistance obtained. Allergies to latex means that alternatives must be used for the usual rubber gloves with which clients are touched. It can also be a problem for clients who have catheters, as the catheter tubing is normally made from latex. Where such allergies are known alternatives can be used.

Throughout the preparation time you should remember to:

- collect all equipment together
- collect any paperwork and documentation needed
- continually observe your client and note any changes in their behaviour or condition
- reassure the client and provide as much information as within your knowledge
- ensure that additional information is provided where a client's questions are outside your own knowledge and responsibility
- reassure the client and make them as comfortable as possible.

What protective clothing is needed for a clinical activity

You are likely to need to wear some form of protective clothing for most clinical procedures. This can vary depending on the nature of the procedure and regardless of the type or extent of protective clothing. You should always explain the purpose of it to your client. Broadly, the following items of protective clothing are the most commonly used in clinical procedures in both acute and non-acute care settings:

- **Gloves** – these are usually latex gloves (with the exceptions for clients with allergies, see above) and they should be worn during procedures or in situations where you may be exposed to body fluids, excretions, blood or any exudates from wounds.
- **Gown or apron** – these should be worn in similar situations to those for gloves.
- **Mask** – this should be worn during procedures that produce droplets of body fluids or blood or where you have a client who is coughing extensively.

If you have any open cuts, sores or dermatitis on your hands gloves must also be worn whenever you have contact with a client.

The use of such protective clothing is linked to a set of procedures called **universal precautions** or **standard precautions**. These precautions are designed to reduce the risk of spreading infection and to reduce your risk of exposure to disease-causing micro-organisms. Universal precautions are designed to protect both you and the client and they assist in reducing the risk of infections, particularly blood-borne viruses and those which clients can acquire in a hospital or other medical environment. These infections are called **nosocomial** infections, the most well known of which is **MRSA (Methicillin-Resistant Staphylococcus aurea)**. These infections are extremely resistant to treatment and are very hard to improve once a client has acquired them. Therefore the use of standard precautions is important, particularly because clients who already have poor health are much more vulnerable to infection and the spread of disease. Universal precautions also protect you and the client from blood-borne viruses such as hepatitis, AIDS and HIV. The following table may help when checking on the requirements for precautions.

Standard precautions required for selected procedures					
Procedure	**Hand washing**	**Gloves**	**Gown**	**Mask**	**Eye-wear**
Talking to patient					
Obtaining patient's blood pressure	✔				
Performing any procedure in which hands can become soiled with blood/ body fluids	✔	✔			
Examining patient without touching blood/body fluids or mucous membranes	✔	✔			
Touching blood/body fluids, mucous membranes, broken skin, lesions or contaminated equipment	✔	✔			
Obtaining blood sample	✔	✔			
Between patient contact	✔				
Handling soiled waste, linen and other materials	✔	✔	Note: Use gown if waste or linen is saturated and may soil your clothing		
Participating in surgical or other procedures that produce splattering or spraying of blood/body fluids	✔	✔	✔	✔	✔

Procedures to follow

Putting on and taking off protective clothing
For the procedures to follow for putting on gloves, removing gloves, putting on a gown, and taking off a gown, see Unit X13, pages 241-243.

Hand washing
Hand washing is an important procedure which you should practice at the start and the end of every clinical activity you undertake. You should also wash your hands before and after placing gloves on your hands. In order to wash your hands properly you should follow the procedure described in Unit X13, page 243.

Active knowledge

Check the guidance in your workplace about the use of universal precautions. Consider the times when you should take precautions before carrying out procedures. Make a note of the number of times you should take precautions but do not do so either because of lack of time, lack of appropriate equipment or the generally accepted practice in your workplace. If you find that you are not taking the necessary precautions on every occasion, resolve to improve your practice!

Element X19.2 | **Undertake clinical procedures, treatments and dressings**

WHAT YOU NEED TO LEARN

- How to use a sterile technique.
- How to use a clean technique.
- Procedures, treatments and dressings.

In this element you will need to learn about the range of procedures you could be asked to undertake in your workplace. There are likely to be variations between workplaces as to the type of activities that you are asked to undertake. In some settings a qualified medical practitioner, such as a nurse, midwife or doctor, may be required to carry out some of the procedures, whereas in other settings you may be asked to undertake the activity. The procedures outlined for this element are generally those which are considered appropriate. However, you should always check with your supervisor about the procedures which are required in your own particular work setting.

The procedures covered in this section are:

- changing dressings
- stoma care
- catheter care
- care of eyes, ears and mouth.

How to use a sterile technique

Regardless of the work setting in which you operate you will need to understand the nature of a **sterile field**. For many of the clinical procedures that you carry out, particularly those which are **invasive**, that is those that involve entry into parts of the client's body system or dealing with an exposed part of the client's body, you will need to know how to work in a sterile way. This minimises the risk of your client acquiring an infection during the process.

When you are undertaking a sterile procedure, such as applying a dressing to an open wound or dealing with procedures which can introduce infection into a client, such as stoma care or catheter care, then you must operate from a sterile field. This is the description given to an area which you create which is sterile and safe for your client. There are specific processes which you must undertake in order to first of all establish and then maintain a sterile field. The simplest way to create a sterile field is

A medical trolley can be used as a sterile field

to use the sterile wrap from a dressing package to create the field, or you could use sterile towels which are supplied as part of a sterile kit.

Once you have established a sterile field only sterile items can be in it. If anything which has not been through the sterilisation process is placed in the field, the whole field becomes un-sterile. You must then discard it and start again.

If one of the items in your sterile field is touched by something which is not sterile, then that item becomes un-sterile and as a result so does your whole field. So it must be discarded and you have to start again.

You will have established your sterile field on the top of a table or trolley. Only the top of the table or trolley is then considered sterile. If anything hangs over the edge of the sterile field it has become un-sterile. You should also note that the final inch of the sterile field at the edges are considered un-sterile, so be careful you do not place any of your sterile items at the edges or touch this area with any of your sterile items.

Unless you are wearing a sterile gown and gloves you must not stretch over your sterile field. If you do it is possible that micro-organisms from your arms or hands could make the field un-sterile.

You should always observe your sterile field. If you turn your back on it you do not know what is happening to it and so have no way of knowing that it has remained sterile and uncontaminated. You need to think carefully about where you place your sterile field so that you can keep it in sight at the same time as carrying out your activity.

It goes without saying that you must never touch anything on your sterile field unless you are wearing sterile gloves.

Your hands should always be kept above your waist and in front of you where you can see them all the time you are working in a sterile field. If you touch an un-sterile item you must remove and discard your gloves using the procedure shown previously (Unit X13, pages 241) and replace them with new sterile gloves.

Sterile items may be added to your sterile field but if they touch anything un-sterile or go within one inch of the edge of the field they become contaminated and must be discarded.

One of the key factors in containing a sterile field is that the field remains dry. If it absorbs moisture from any un-sterile item then the field becomes un-sterile. For example, if on the trolley on which you set out your sterile field there was dampness which was absorbed by one of the towels, then your whole field would be contaminated.

You must become very aware of the importance of sterile technique and maintaining sterile conditions. Although this may seen extremely complicated, with practice it will become second nature. You are responsible for maintaining the sterile field in the interests of your client. There will not necessarily be anybody else who will be aware of what you are doing, so you must be aware if you contaminate your own sterile field in any way. If you do contaminate it, you must start the procedure again.

How to use a clean technique

Some procedures may be carried out using a clean rather than a sterile technique. Clean techniques may be used, for example, to change a dressing over a healed wound or to add to an existing dressing. To do this you should use gloves and supplies which are clean, though not necessarily sterile. In reality, the gloves and supplies you use are likely to be sterile, although you do not have to create a sterile field in which to use them. However, it is important that you maintain a clean area in order to carry out the procedure and that you avoid contamination of your clean supplies. If you were, for example, to drop your gloves on the floor they would become dirty and contaminated and could not be used to continue any procedure using a clean technique. Similarly, if you were to touch a dirty item, for example an item which was already known to be contaminated, such as a container of bodily fluids, then the gloves would become dirty and could no longer be used.

If you are applying a sterile dressing or are using sterile instruments in a sterile field, then you must ensure that you open sterile packages in a way that does not contaminate them. If you follow the procedure in unit X13, page 246, and remember not to contaminate your sterile field, then you should be able to carry out this procedure in a sterile way which will minimise the risk to your client.

Procedures, treatments and dressings

How to change a dressing
Dressings are used to cover wounds in order to speed up healing and to keep the wound clean and free from infection. Clean dressings are used when a wound is almost healed or there is a minimal risk of infection. For open wounds or situations where there is a risk of infection, a sterile dressing would be used. See Unit X13, page 247, for what you must do when changing a dressing.

Stoma Care
Stoma care is the care of clients who have had surgery to provide an additional means of eliminating waste from their bodies, either faeces or urine. The most usual stoma care is given to clients who have a colostomy. This is the result of providing an additional surgical opening for clients who are unable, either on a temporary or permanent basis, to use their bowel in the normal way. This can be the result of colon cancer, ulcerative colitis or a series of other diseases. Following a colostomy faeces are collected in a special stoma bag which needs to be changed regularly. Many clients are able to do this for themselves, but it may be necessary to provide stoma care for them in the early days after the colostomy has been performed or because the client is ill or becoming frail.

It is likely that you would only be asked to provide stoma care for a client who has an established colostomy and therefore likely to be familiar with the procedure. However, you should still check that they are happy for you to change their appliance and that they understand the procedure you are about to undertake.

See Unit X13, page 248, for what you must do to carry out this procedure.

Catheter care
Clients who have an indwelling catheter, which is likely to be a Foley's catheter, may need support in ensuring that the risk of infection is reduced as far as possible. Clients with catheters are prone to infections, and hygiene and sterile techniques must be observed to minimise the risk. In order to maintain hygiene the site at which the catheter enters the client's body should be cleaned regularly. You should

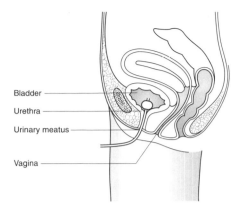

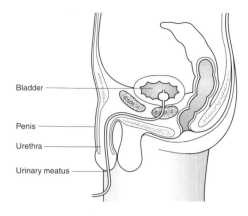

Indwelling urinary catheter in place in female body

Indwelling urinary catheter in place in male body

follow procedures laid down for your workplace, which may vary slightly. See Unit X13, page 249 for the procedures.

You are unlikely to be involved in the insertion or removal of catheters as this is undertaken by a qualified clinical practitioner, although you may be asked to assist under direction on occasions.

Extended personal care

Mouth care

Mouth care can be done either with a small, soft toothbrush or, more usually, with swabs which are used to clean around the teeth, gums, palate and inside the cheeks. Use the swabs to remove any food particles and clean all the surfaces of the mouth. You can obtain liquid toothpaste, which is probably the easiest sort to use. A diluted solution of sodium bicarbonate (one teaspoon in 500 ml of warm water) is commonly used for mouth care, particularly where the mouth is dry and crusted, but it can leave a very unpleasant after taste and is better followed by swabbing out with a more pleasant-tasting mouthwash. After you have finished cleaning and moistening the person's mouth, protect his or her lips with lip salve or Vaseline. Remember that all the equipment you use should be maintained for that individual only and should be clearly labelled and kept together.

Eye care

Before you begin cleaning a client's eyes, make sure you have cotton wool swabs and a suitable bag in which to dispose of them, a bowl of clean water or saline, a paper towel, and eye drops, if the client uses them. For the procedure to follow in bathing a client's eyes, see Unit X13, page 250.

Checking and cleaning naso-gastric feeding tubes

Clients who have a naso-gastric tube in place for either feeding purposes or possibly obtaining specimens will need to have the tube checked and cleaned. The tube is inserted by a qualified clinical practitioner through the nose down the oesophagus.

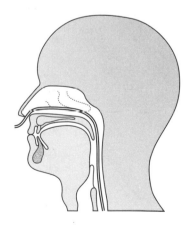

The position of a naso-gastric tube

Naso-gastric tubes can often be uncomfortable for the client, particularly elderly people or those with sensitive skin, which can be irritated by the pressure of the tube on their nostrils, and some may find it uncomfortable as it passes down their throat and oesophagus. You should attempt to reassure the client that any checking and cleaning of the tube will not cause them any additional discomfort. Any indication from a client of

Using a naso-gastric tube to take a specimen

additional or serious pain or discomfort from their naso-gastric tube should immediately be reported to the clinical practitioner responsible.

Clients who have naso-gastric tubes in place must remain with the head of the bed elevated to 45 degrees. This is in order to prevent gastric secretions being aspirated into the lungs. It is essential that this positioning is maintained. Your work setting will have protocols in place and you will be given full instructions as to how to maintain this position for such clients.

If you are asked to clean a naso-gastric feeding tube when changing a feeding solution bag you should:

1 Wash hands.

2 Disconnect empty bag from end of tube.

3 Clean connector with alcohol wipe or other cleaning material as identified in your own workplace protocols.

4 Connect new feeding bag.

5 Re-hang on drip stand.

6 Wash hands.

Throughout the process you should reassure the client that changing the bag will not in any way add to their discomfort.

Active knowledge

Check your workplace practices for the response that you are required to make if a client has an adverse reaction to a clinical procedure. If you imagine the situation where a client suddenly begins to become cold and clammy, their speech becomes slurred and they complain of feeling faint, ask yourself the following questions:

1 What would I do?

2 Who would I contact?

3 What steps would I take while waiting for help to arrive?

You should ensure that you are able to establish the answers to these three questions by checking through the procedures or talking to your supervisor in your own workplace.

WHAT YOU NEED TO LEARN

How to obtain specimens of:

• Urine

• Faeces

• Exudates

• Blood

• Sputum.

In this element you will learn about how to obtain specimens of a range of bodily fluids, each of which can provide medical practitioners with significant information about the state of health of the client. There are specific methods for obtaining correct uncontaminated specimens and for storing them in appropriate containers and in appropriate ways to ensure that they are in the right condition to provide the best possible information when they are tested.

Specimen containers are *never* prelabelled. You should only label a container with your client's name after you have collected the specimen. This reduces the risk of a container being picked up by someone else and mistakenly used to put their client's specimen in.

Containers are generally sterile regardless of the type of specimen which is being collected. This is important so that the laboratories carrying out the tests are not dealing with specimens which are contaminated by any micro-organisms from a source other than the client. You should make sure you always use the correct container for the type of specimen you are collecting.

Urine

It is easiest to take a sterile urine specimen from a client who has a catheter and to obtain it from the catheter line. To collect this you should follow the procedure in Unit X13, pages 251–252.

Clients who do not have a catheter should be supplied with the appropriate equipment to provide a **mid-stream sample of urine** (**MSSU**). The equipment consists of a funnel and a sterile urine container. The funnel and container should come in a sterile pack and the client should be asked to pass urine into the funnel and fill the pot.

Equipment for obtaining mid-stream sample of urine

Testing urine

The condition of a client's urine can provide a great deal of information about their state of health. There are simple tests which can be carried out on urine and you may be asked to undertake some of these. However, it is important before carrying out any tests that you follow some basic observations which will provide you with an initial indication of any problems.

Healthy urine should be clear, pale yellow and not have an offensive smell. If urine smells offensive, is cloudy, has particles in it, has blood in it, is a bright orange colour, or any other colour apart from clear pale yellow, then these are the first signs of concern. You should also check with your client whether they have experienced any pain or burning when they pass urine as either of these could be indicators of more serious underlying conditions. These simple observations are indicators of further problems but are insufficient on their own to establish that there really are problems. It is necessary to carry out further tests on the client's urine in order to find out more detailed information about their state of health.

Urine tests

There are two methods of testing urine. It can be sent to a laboratory, which would normally be a specialist **uro-genital bacteriology** section, where extensive testing and the growing of cultures can be carried out. However, if an initial indication of any possible underlying problems is required the most normal method is to use **urine-analysis sticks**. These are short flexible sticks a few inches long containing sensitive material which changes colour depending on the substances they come into contact with in the urine. It is possible to test for a range of factors in urine by using urine-analysis sticks. The following table shows some examples.

Test for	Indications
1 Leucocytes, ((white blood cells), an indicator of infection)	Change of colour – sticks range from white through to dark purple
2 Protein (another indicator of infection)	Colour changes from light green through to dark green
3 Blood	Colour changes from white to dark blue
4 Glucose (high blood sugar)	Colour changes from light blue to yellow

Urine storage

If you need to store urine prior to testing, it is important that it should be in a tightly sealed sterile container. It should be kept in a separate specimen fridge, *never* in a fridge which is used for storing ordinary food stuff. It must also be clearly labelled with the:

- client's name
- type of specimen
- date the specimen was collected.

Faeces

To collect a specimen of faeces for testing first collect the faeces from your client in a bedpan or commode. Then take the specimen from this into a sterile universal container. A sterile container for faeces contains an implement attached to the inside of the lid of the container which allows you to collect a small amount of the faeces and place them inside the container.

A faecal collection container

Testing faeces

All testing of stool samples will be carried out in a laboratory, so you should ensure that you clearly label the container with the:

- client's name
- type of sample
- date the sample was collected.

It should then be sent to the laboratory with the required documentation for your workplace. If a specimen has to be stored you must ensure that it is stored in a separate specimen fridge and not in an ordinary fridge with any food stuff.

Many clients may be embarrassed about providing a sample of faeces, so you will need to obtain the sample at a time when the client has a normal bowel movement, rather than expecting them to provide a sample at a time which is convenient for you. You should explain the reason for needing the sample and explain why it is necessary for them to provide a sample into a bedpan or other suitable receptacle rather than use the toilet in the normal way.

Sputum

Sputum specimens are important indicators of possible respiratory infections or respiratory diseases such as tuberculosis, pneumonia or bronchitis. Sputum specimens are often better collected in the morning as clients often have more secretions in their lungs and bronchial tubes after lying down sleeping during the night. In order to obtain a specimen you must first explain to your client what you need the specimen for and what you want them to do, and then take the following steps set out in Unit X13, page 254.

Exudates

You may occasionally be asked to obtain a sample of an exudates from a wound or other lesion. This requires a sterile technique. Follow the procedure set out in Unit X13, page 254–255.

Blood

There are two ways of obtaining blood samples. One is through a finger prick using a small lancet blade and the other is through **venipuncture**, which involves using a needle and syringe to take blood from a client's vein.

Blood which is obtained from a finger prick is obtained from capillary vessels, which are the tiny blood vessels near the surface of the skin. The blood from there is squeezed onto the testing apparatus. The most commonly used method is that using testing strips for testing blood sugar levels, or the **phenylketonuria (PKU) test**, which is done by pricking the heels of babies during the first few days of life. Where larger amounts of

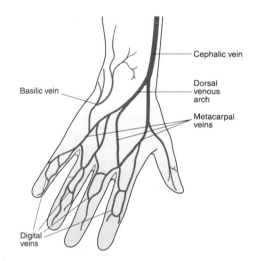

Blood samples can be taken from these veins in the fingers, hands and forearm

blood are required for more extensive tests, then it is necessary to understand where to find the relevant veins in the arm and hand.

You need to be specially trained to take blood from a client. There are courses that provide this training. The information in this unit will give you some guidance and assistance, however it will not enable you to have the skill to undertake the procedure on clients. You should never attempt to carry out this procedure without the specific agreement and under the instructions of a medical practitioner or your supervisor, unless you have been trained by your workplace to carry out these procedures.

Obtaining blood samples by venipuncture

You should only take blood from a vein which you can palpate (this means a vein which you can feel and see). The easiest place to find a vein is in the arm or client on the inside of the elbow. You may need to apply a tourniquet just above the elbow in order to make the veins more prominent so you can see them. If you are unable to see or feel any veins then you should not attempt the venipuncture, instead you should refer the situation to your supervisor or a medical practitioner. The most suitable veins are likely to be the **cephalic vein** or the **basilic vein**. They are the major veins in the arm and they run from the fingers right up to the shoulders, as illustrated in the figure on page 281.

Another basic rule of venipuncture is that you should never attempt to draw blood from a client more than twice. If you are unable to take a sample after the second attempt you should get assistance.

Most blood samples are obtained using a vacutainer, into which the blood is drawn, directly into the container. It is then sent to the laboratory for testing. In some workplaces blood may still be obtained by using a syringe, and then placed into tubes which are then sent to the laboratory for testing. The procedures are similar regardless of the method used.

1   Wash hands.

2   Ensure that you have all the equipment that you need. This consists of:
    - vacutainer with tubes and needles or appropriate syringes
    - tourniquet
    - clean gloves
    - alcohol swabs
    - sterile gauze
    - sterile adhesive plaster.

3   Explain the procedure to the client and the importance of holding their arm as still as possible whilst the sample is obtained. You should reassure the client if they are anxious about the procedure and explain to them that it may hurt a little but that this will not be excessive or prolonged.

4   Put on gloves.

5   Ensure that you have the correct tubes for the blood samples.

6   Apply tourniquet three to four inches above the elbow. You must never leave a tourniquet on a client for longer than two minutes.

7   Select a suitable vein. Remember you should never attempt venipuncture if you are unable to feel and see a vein.

8   Clean your chosen site with an alcohol swab and allow it to dry. Do not touch the site again after you have cleaned it.

9   Remove the needle cover.

10 Using your free hand, secure and stretch the skin below the site. This helps to stabilise the vein.

11 Carefully insert the needle through the skin.

12 If you are using a vacutainer secure the holder with one hand and push the tube into the holder with the thumb of the other hand. The tube will fill automatically, and when it is full withdraw it and add the next tube into the holder. Repeat this process until all the samples required have been obtained. If you are withdrawing blood samples with a syringe, pull back on the syringe until you have obtained the required amount of blood.

13 Release the tourniquet.

14 Place the sterile gauze over the venipuncture site and withdraw the needle from the skin.

15 Apply pressure to the site for two to three minutes. This can be normally done by the client. If the client is already on anti-coagulation therapy, more time may be needed.

16 Discard the needle and/or syringe in a sharps container.

17 If necessary apply a sterile adhesive plaster to the site.

18 Clean the area you have worked in and dispose of the waste in line with your organisation's policy.

19 Label the tubes with the client's name and the date the sample was taken.

20 Ensure that the necessary documentation is completed and prepare the samples to be sent to the appropriate testing laboratory.

21 Record in the case notes or care plan the fact that this blood sample has been collected and the tests which have been requested.

Testing blood

Blood probably can tell more about the health and well-being of a client than any other bodily fluid. Most blood tests are carried out in laboratories. However, you may be asked to carry out a blood sugar analysis. This is a test used regularly for clients who are diabetic and who need to ensure that their medication or diet regime is maintaining their blood sugar at an appropriate level.

Diabetes is the disorder caused by the body's inability to use insulin properly or to provide sufficient insulin to convert sugar into energy, which is the normal role of insulin. When this happens the levels of sugar within the client's blood becomes abnormally high or low and results in potentially dangerous symptoms.

Hyperglycemia is an excessively high level of blood sugar and **hypoglycemia** is an abnormally low level of blood sugar. The symptoms of hyperglycemia are heavy and laboured breathing, nausea, vomiting, increased thirst, increased urination, loss of appetite and sweet-smelling breath. The symptoms of hypoglycemia are excessive sweating, hunger, feeling of faintness, trembling, blurred vision and headaches.

You should observe your client carefully for any of these signs or symptoms and immediately obtain medical assistance if any of them are present, or if your client reports any of them to you.

Obtaining blood samples by finger prick

Blood sugar levels are tested on a regular basis (often daily) for clients who are a diabetic. The most usual method is to prick the side of the finger using a small lancet and to then read the results with a blood glucose meter. There are many different types of meters and you should ensure that you are familiar with the one which is used in your work setting. In order to test a clients blood sugar level, you should follow the procedure described in Unit X13, pages 255–256.

Element X19.4   Measure and monitor the physical characteristics and condition of clients

WHAT YOU NEED TO LEARN

Measuring and monitoring:

- Temperature
- Pulse
- Respiration
- Blood pressure
- Height, weight and girth
- Peak flow
- Fluid balance.

Taking measurements gives you physiological information, and tells you much about your client and their state of health. Simply observing your client will also indicate to you whether there are any changes, a deterioration or an improvement in your client's condition, and these should be immediately reported.

Even though taking measurements such as temperature, pulse and blood pressure are routine exercises, you should still not assume that either your client's consent is given or that they understand the process. You should always check this first. It may be something as simple as, 'I am just going to take your temperature, OK?', or you can get implied consent from your client if they hold their hand up when you say, 'Can I just take your pulse?' Check that they know what you are doing and why. If you begin to carry these simple routine measurements without either explaining or obtaining the client's consent it may develop into a familiar pattern and could lead to you ignoring the client and their wishes when carrying out more extensive or invasive procedures. If the client has any questions, then you should answer them to the best of your ability. If their questions go beyond your knowledge then you must refer the query to your supervisor or to a medical practitioner.

Temperature

Temperature is a useful indicator of health or illness. Temperature rises when a client has an infection, or possibly following injury or trauma, whereas a low temperature indicates a serious condition such as hypothermia. Temperature can be taken with a traditional thermometer containing mercury. The mercury rises up the glass tube of the thermometer and indicates the client's temperature on the gauge printed on the tube. This type of thermometer has increasingly been replaced by a thermometer which operates with a battery and has a liquid crystal display

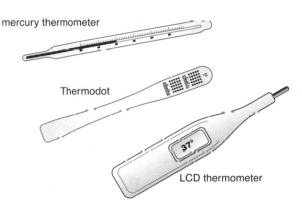

mercury thermometer

Thermodot

LCD thermometer

which shows the client's body temperature. Many health and care settings now use a disposable thermometer which records the client's temperature on a series of dots which will change colour to indicate temperature.

The normal temperature of the human body is 37° Centigrade, 98.4° Fahrenheit. Any significant variation from this must be reported immediately. Temperature should be recorded on a temperature chart (see Unit CU5 in *NVQ Level 2 Care*).

Pulse

Taking a pulse is a way of establishing a client's heart rate by measuring the beats of the heart through a main artery, usually in the wrist. It is possible to take a client's pulse at various other points in the body.

To take a pulse manually, place your first two fingers lightly on the client's wrist directly below the heel of the thumb.

Through your fingers you will then feel the client's pulse in their brachial artery. You will need to use your first two fingers to feel the pulse. You cannot feel somebody else's pulse through your thumb because you have a pulse in your own thumb. When

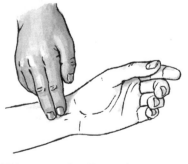

Taking a pulse from the wrist

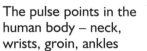

The pulse points in the human body – neck, wrists, groin, ankles

you can feel a pulse you should then count the number of beats you can feel for a period of 30 seconds. You will need to look at your watch whilst you count the pulse. You then multiply the number of beats by two, which will give you a pulse rate of beats per minute.

Pulse can also be taken by a **pulseoximeter**, which fits onto the client's finger and records the pulse electronically. If you take any exercise in a gym or use an exercise bike you may well have seen a pulseoximeter.

Pulse can also be taken as part of a combined reading with blood pressure on an instrument called a **dynomap**. Normal pulse rate is around 70 beats per minute, although this can be raised by illness, anxiety or exercise. Extremely fit people will have a lower pulse rate; some athletes have pulse rates as low as 60. You will need to know if your client takes regular exercise as this could explain a low pulse rate.

Respiration

A client's respiration is measured in breaths per minute. You will need to observe the number of times that the chest rises and falls per minute. A rise and fall constitutes one respiration. You will need to time your observations for 30 seconds and then multiply by 2 to obtain the number of respirations per minute. A sudden increase or decrease in a client's respiration rate can indicate a deterioration or change in condition and should immediately be reported to a qualified clinical practitioner as giving cause for concern.

Blood pressure

Blood pressure indicates the pressure at which blood is being pumped around the body from the heart. It is important that blood pressure remains within a defined area of measurement. Excessively high or low blood pressure can indicate illness or disease and can directly cause a health problem. Blood pressure is measured with a **sphygmomanometer** and a stethoscope. For how to take blood pressure see the procedure in Unit X13, page 258-259.

There can be many reasons for blood pressure being higher or lower than the normal 120/80 and there is a fairly wide acceptable range, which can alter with age. However, you should ensure that all measurements of blood pressure are recorded and any significant variations are reported.

Height and weight

A person's weight in relation to their height can indicate the extent to which their health is being put at risk by them being excessively underweight or overweight.

Measuring weight

Where possible clients should be able to stand on a set of scales for the measurement to be taken. Heavy items of clothing such as shoes and outdoor coats should be removed. Clients should stand on the scales and the weight adjusted until the scales balance. A client's weight should be read more usually in kilograms and recorded in their case notes or care plan.

Where clients are unable to stand safely on a set of weighing scales then a scale which provides a seat should be used and the weight recorded in the same way.

There are ideal weights for heights which have been calculated to present the least risk to health. This can be identified in a height/weight chart.

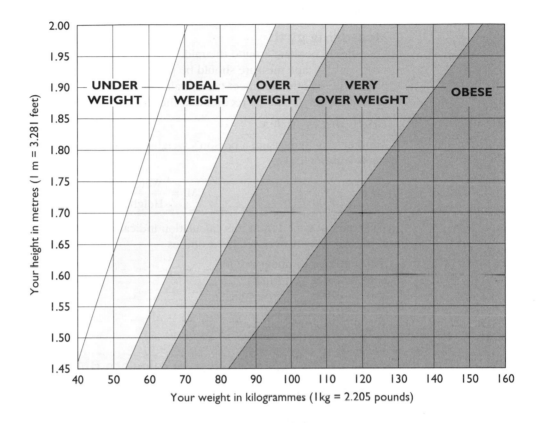

Weight and health

Underweight The health of clients who are severely underweight could be adversely affected. This could be as a result of illness or as a result of deliberate over-dieting, which is also dangerous to health. Excessive dieting can lead to eating disorders, such as anorexia nervosa or bulimia, caused by clients not getting sufficient nutrients to remain healthy. However, most clients who are underweight are likely to be suffering from some illness.

Overweight, very overweight and obese. The risk to health associated with being overweight or obese grows with the increase in weight. Excess weight can increase the risk of cardiovascular disease, diabetes, arthritis and other weight associated complications.

Note: There is quite a wide range of accepted weights for height which will not represent any threat to the client's health.

Measuring height

Height should be measured using a fixed height ruler which should be attached to the wall of an examination room, or a portable fixed height rule should be used. The client should be asked to stand against the wall with their heels back against the door and stand as straight as they can. The height-measuring bar should be lowered until it rests gently on the top of their head. The resulting height should then be read from the upright ruler. The height, which is likely to be in metres and centimetres, should be recorded in the client's case notes or care plan.

Measuring girth

This should be done around the middle of the client's torso in approximately the waist area. A tape measure should be placed around the waist area and read at the point where both ends meet comfortably without over tightening. The measurement in centimetres should be recorded in the client's case notes or care plan.

Body mass index

Another way to measure a person's weight is to measure and calculate their **body mass index** (**BMI**):

$$\text{BMI} = \frac{\text{Weight (kg)}}{\text{Height (m}^2)}$$

The result obtained from this calculation indicates whether a person is underweight, at normal weight, overweight or obese:

BMI < 20 kg	underweight
BMI 20–25 kg	normal
BMI 25–30 kg	overweight
BMI > 30 kg	obese
BMI > 40 kg	severely obese

How to calculate BMI

A person weighs 16 stone and is 5 ft 6 ins tall. What is their BMI?
- For the top line (weight):
  Convert 16 stones to kilograms
  There are 2.2 lbs to 1 kg.
  Convert 16 stones to pounds
  16 stone is $16 \times 14\,\text{lb} = 224\,\text{lbs}$
  224 lbs divided by 2.2 = 102 kg

- For the bottom line (height squared – m² means the height is squared, i.e. multiplied by itself):
  Convert 5 ft 6 inches to metres
  There are 39.5 inches to 1 metre. Convert 5 feet to inches
  $5\,\text{ft} = 5 \times 12\,\text{ins} = 60 + 6\,\text{ins} = 66\,\text{ins}$
  Then convert inches to metres
  66 divided by 39.5 = 1.67 m
  The height squared is $1.67 \times 1.67 = 2.79\,\text{m}$
  So,

$$\text{BMI} = \frac{102\,\text{kg}}{2.79\,\text{m}} = 36.6$$

(If you are able to measure weight in kilograms and measure height in metres this will save doing any conversions).
This value indicates that the person's health is at risk and that they would benefit from losing weight. We should all aim to be in the 20–25 kg range as this represents least risk to health.

Did you know?

That up to 56 per cent of men and 45 per cent women in the United Kingdom are classified as being overweight (this is identified as having a BMI of more than 25).

The table shows the percentage of males and females who have excess weight at certain ages.

	Age (years)					
	16–24	25–34	35–44	45–54	55–64	All ages
Males Total with excess weights (%)	31	50	62	68	69	56
Females Total with excess weights (%)	28	38	45	44	64	45

Peak flow

Peak flow measures lung capacity. This is a useful indicator of illness or lung damage. A reduced peak flow is evident in people who are asthmatic or have any chronic respiratory disease. A peak flow meter, a hollow plastic tube about eight inches long, is used to measure peak flow. It has a small gauge on the top and a disposable cardboard blow pipe is inserted into one end. The client should be asked to blow a short, sharp breath into the tube and this will then register on the gauge. The normal rate of lung capacity should be around about 500. In asthmatics or people with chronic lung disease, such as emphysema, a peak flow can be as low as 150 or 200.

A peak flow meter

Fluid balance

The **fluid balance** is the amount of fluid is taken in and excreted out from the body. It is a very important indicator of health. If more fluid is excreted than is taken in then a client can become dehydrated. Conversely if they retain too much fluid in their body this can result in swelling, oedema and ultimately heart failure.

Intake and output is measured by keeping a record of the volume of fluids in and out. This is recorded on a fluid balance chart.

Input

In order to keep an accurate record of input and output of fluid, all fluid which the client takes into their body, either through the mouth or through an intravenous drip, must be measured. If drinks are left for the clients to pour for themselves, you should measure the drinks in the jug and constantly check how much has been used. Explain to the client that they should not take any drinks from anywhere unless they are recorded on the chart.

FLUID CHART (ADULT)

PLEASE SEE REVERSE SIDE FOR NOTES ON USE OF THIS CHART

ORAL INTAKE			INTRAVENOUS THERAPY *Before starting this section remember to enter TIME and name of I.V. fluid already in progress and amount brought forward from previous chart					OUTPUT							
			STARTED		ENDED		*BROUGHT FORWARD ml								
TIME	FLUID	ORAL TOTAL SO FAR ml	ml	TIME	FLUID	TIME	ml	COMMENTS	TIME	URINE ml	URINE TOTAL SO FAR ml	ASPIRATE OR VOMIT ml	ASP/VOM TOTAL SO FAR ml	DRAIN ml	DRAIN ml	COMMENTS

TIME	TOTAL – ORAL [ ] ml	TOTAL – I.V. [ ] ml	CARRIED FORWARD [ ] ml	TOTALS	URINE [ ] ml	ASPIRATE/VOMIT [ ] ml	DRAIN [ ] ml	DRAIN [ ] ml

SURNAME	OTHER NAME/S	UNIT NUMBER	WARD	DATE / /

A fluid balance chart

Output

All fluid output should be measured. The urine in a catheter bag or in a bedpan or commode should be measured before disposal. All vomit should also be measured and its volume recorded.

Maintaining a fluid balance chart

Maintaining a fluid balance chart is not difficult provided you carry out the basic sums correctly! You will need to be sure you have done the addition and subtraction so that the balance of fluid for your client is clearly recorded. Each individual is different as to the amount of fluid they take in and excrete from their bodies but, broadly speaking, everyone should have a positive fluid balance, that is they should put out slightly more fluid than they take in.

Active knowledge

1. Take your own height and weight and then using the calculations in this element work out your own body mass index. Try to do this for two or three other friends or family members until you are confident with the calculations.

2. Work out the fluid balance for the following figures and calculate whether or not this client is maintaining a positive fluid balance.

   Intake
   0800: IV Therapy – Hartman's 1000 ml
   1200: Hartman's discontinued
   1300: T 250 ml
   1400 : Juice 250 ml
   1630 : T 250 ml
   Output
   1230: 300 ml urine
   1600: 500 ml urine; 100 ml vomit
   1830: 600 ml urine

Unit Y2

Enable individuals to find out about and use services and facilities

In this unit you will have the opportunity to think about how you pass information to your clients and how you help them to gain access to the most useful services and facilities. Regardless of your role and area of work, you will at some point need to provide information to those you care for or to their relatives or friends. It is important that you understand how to access and update that information and how you can assist people, not only to consider services but to use them where they need support.

Enable individuals to find out about services and facilities

WHAT YOU NEED TO LEARN

- How to establish the services clients need.
- How to obtain accurate information.
- How to provide information.

How to establish the services clients need

The key word in the heading for this section is 'clients'. You need to be sure that you establish what your client needs and wants in the way of services and facilities.

This is not about what you think would be best for your client, tempting as it may be to try persuade your client to use a facility you think would benefit them. This is not your role – even if they would benefit enormously! Your role is to find out what your clients want and need and to give them the information to help them reach their own conclusions.

Do not assume your clients will necessarily be in a position to directly ask for the information they need. This is not as odd as it sounds. To be able to ask for what you need, you have to know the right questions to ask and you have to know that something exists. To establish the services that a client needs you may have to ask quite a few questions. You will not be able to rely on them being able to identify what it is they want. For example, how could an elderly client ask about attending a luncheon club unless they know that such a thing exists? How could a carer looking after an elderly patient with Alzheimers ask about a local carers' support group unless they were aware of its existence?

Finding out clients' wants and needs

You will need to use your listening skills to pick up what it is that clients are looking for. It can also help if you ask some prompting questions. This may help point clients in the general direction of a service or facility they would like to use. The sort of questions are those that begin, 'Would you like…?', 'Would it help if …?', 'Would you enjoy…?' To allow your client the maximum possible independence in reaching their decisions, it may be better to phrase your questions generally, so 'Would you enjoy some company for lunch once or twice a week?' may be better than 'Would you like to go to the luncheon club at the community centre once or twice a week?' Posing a question in this way allows your client to gradually get used to the idea and to think about their preferences. It also allows people to stop at the point where they feel they have made sufficient commitment for the present. To continue with our elderly client and the luncheon club, it may be sufficient in a first conversation for them to establish they would like some company. It may take a little more time for them to decide they would like to join a group of other people rather than arrange for somebody to come and join them once or twice a week. The general question has allowed them, first of all, to make a decision about the idea of company. Later questions and discussion can establish exactly the form and the setting in which they would welcome the company. If you had begun the discussion by providing the full

What sort of things would you like to do to keep you active Mr Thorpe?

I don't know. I just don't know what's available for me to do.

Clients need to know what is available before deciding what they would like to do

details of the luncheon club and the community centre, you may have received a negative response from the client, who actually would welcome company, but may not be totally convinced about meeting a lot of strangers or going to a strange building with which they were unfamiliar. However, with time and thought and full information, decisions can be taken at a pace which suits the client.

Of course, you may not always be in the position of gradually widening the options for your client. There may be circumstances where you are faced with the opposite. For example, you may have a young enthusiastic client with learning difficulties, or a disability, who wants to know a range of information about a wide choice of opportunities and facilities with which they can become involved. In such a case you may have to carefully help them to take a realistic view of how many things they are able to undertake at any one time. The golden rule is to make sure that you are going at the client's pace, whatever that may be, and that you are providing the information they require about the services they consider to be important. Be careful not to limit the information you provide or the ways in which you provide it because you believe that particular facility or service is unsuitable for your client. It is for them to decide once they have the information whether or not a particular service meets their needs or not.

If you have worked with a client for a period of time and have got to know them, it will be much easier for you to know their interests and the sorts of services and facilities they are likely to need and make use of. It is then much easier to regularly talk to them and raise questions about any new facilities or services they may wish to try.

You also need to take care you do not provide clients with unrealistic expectations about any services and facilities available to them in the local area. When you are asking questions about services and facilities they would like to use, take care you only provide positive and definite information about those of which you are certain. If you have any doubts whether a service or facility is provided in your local area or is unavailable or restricted due to lack of resources, then you should advise your client that you will find out more information for them and let them know if such a service is possible, rather than indicating that the service is definitely available.

It may be useful to have a regular list which you check in respect of all of your clients about the sorts of services and facilities which may interest them and be of value to them. Facilities vary greatly from area to area and from setting to setting. However, the following table gives a general picture of the sorts of services and facilities which clients may find useful and which you should be able to provide information about. It may help if you think of it as the 'What, Who, and Where list'.

Services and facilities checklist

What	Who	Where
Meals	Social services or voluntary organisation	Social services department
Home-help	Social services or independent provider	Social services department
Family support	Social services or independent sector	Social services department
Shopping	Local voluntary organisations	Library, Citizens Advice Bureau, social services department, local church
Lunch or social clubs	Social services or local voluntary organisations	Social services department, library, Citizens Advice Bureau, local church
Holidays	Specialist travel companies, e.g. Saga, Winged Fellowship, etc. social services, specialist voluntary organisations, e.g. Royal National Institute for the Blind, Mencap, Scope, Age Concern, etc.	Social services department, library, Citizens Advice Bureau, Internet, travel agent
Pensions/Benefits	Benefits Agency, social services, Welfare Rights Centres	Welfare Rights Centre, Claimant's Union, Benefits Agency, Citizens Advice Bureau

What	Who	Where
Sports and leisure facilities	Leisure services department, National Organisation for Sport for the Disabled, International Paraolympic Committee, Riding for the Disabled, etc.	Town hall, Citizens Advice Bureau, library, Internet
Mobile library	Libraries/leisure department	Town hall
Cinema, theatre and entertainment	Leisure services department, theatres and cinemas	Town hall, library, Internet, What's on Guide

Case study

J was a young man in his mid-twenties who used a wheelchair following a spinal injury. J was provided with 24-hour care and had a team of support workers. Recently J had appeared to be very fed up and somewhat unhappy. He said that he was bored and wanted something more exciting to do. His support worker suggested a range of options, including visiting the cinema, the theatre, going to a social club or visiting an art gallery – all of which were interests of J's. However, every suggestion was rejected without J giving any clear reason why.

A few days later a different support worker decided to approach matters in a different way and, through questioning, established that J would very much like to take up any of the suggestions made earlier, but had made the assumption that to do any of them he needed to take a taxi to get to them and this was something he felt unable to afford. J had not liked to say he could not afford the taxi and so had simply refused any of the suggestions.

The second support worker was able to explain to J that the local authority operated a dial-a-ride service with a small bus specially adapted for wheelchairs and that J could book this service and use it for a nominal charge. J was delighted and began to make plans for a range of visits and activities.

What may have happened if the second support worker had not spoken to J?

How to obtain accurate information

No one expects you to have your head full of information that you can pass on to your clients! However, you do need to know where to find information and what are the best and most effective ways of doing it. You also need to know how to keep that information so that you have easy access to it whenever you need to use it and update it. We now live in an information society. Masses of information is available, on more subjects then you ever knew existed. The trouble is that it is easy to become confused and end up with information which is irrelevant and will not serve a useful purpose for your clients.

Local sources of information

One of the most useful sources of information is the 'one stop shop' approach of organisations such as the Citizens Advice Bureau. You may also find in your area that your local council's voluntary services or your local authority may have an information point. These are often located in libraries, town halls, civic centres, or other easily accessible places. At these points you can usually obtain leaflets and information and there are staff available to find out more for you and to offer advice on specific areas of need. Most advice centres will find information for you, if they do not already have it to hand. You may be looking for specific information in response to a client's request or you may be generally updating your own information so that you are ready to deal promptly with any information requests from your clients. Whatever your information needs, any of these facilities is a very good starting point.

Special interest groups

Other excellent sources of information are specific issue interest groups, such as Age Concern, the Alzheimers Society, Mencap, Scope, etc. These provide information about facilities and services specifically related to those with a particular condition. The contact addresses and telephone numbers for these organisations will be found at your starting point advice centre, whether it be a Citizens Advice Centre or your local library or your council's voluntary services.

The Internet

One of the best sources of information is the Internet, if you have access to it. To use this you will need access to a computer which is connected to the Internet. You will also need instructions in how to use the various search engines in order to locate sites of the organisations you are interested in. The information you can obtain from the Internet is almost unlimited and covers every possible subject you could imagine. However, you must be aware that information on the Internet is not subject to verification or control, and therefore its accuracy is not always possible to confirm. If you are finding information from the Internet to pass on to clients you would be advised to obtain it primarily from official web sites of relevant organisations, either for the particular area of interest or the particular area reflecting your clients' needs. Other useful web sites are official government sites and those of universities and research establishments. Using the World Wide Web via the Internet can be a very quick and easy way of getting very accurate and up-to-date information, often before it has appeared in print or is readily accessible in other ways.

Providing the opportunity for clients to access information for themselves through the Internet can be useful and can motivate them to go on looking for more information and to explore the huge potential of using the Internet. There are an increasing number of opportunities for people without computers to access the Internet. Cyber cafés and many libraries, local town halls, colleges and universities have facilities for public access to the Internet, usually for a small fee. You might encourage your clients to do this where appropriate and it may lead to clients taking an interest in the Internet and pursuing information through it. As always the best approach to take, if possible, is to support your client to be self-managing and to find out information for themselves rather than rely on you. Once you have obtained information for your client or to update your knowledge, you need to be sure that you can store this information in an accessible way.

Cyber cafés provide people without a computer the opportunity to access the Internet

Storing information

You may remember that you can locate information in the Citizens Advice Bureau or Welfare Rights Centre, and what information is available there, but you will not be able to recall the individual addresses, telephone numbers or detailed information about the services provided. So it is a good idea to create an information store for yourself, where you can keep leaflets, notes, telephone numbers, cuttings from newspapers or magazine advertisements, all of which relate to areas you believe may be of interest either to your current clients or to others in the future. A simple filing system, organised alphabetically or by subject and stored in a concertina file or in a filing drawer, is probably the easiest way to do this. A small library of information is very useful provided it is maintained and kept up to date. It is important to regularly go through it, perhaps every three months, and discard outdated information and replace it with the most current. You could store information electronically on a computer. It could be stored where you record the website and e-mail addresses of relevant services. It is also useful to keep important websites in the 'favourites' menu so they are easily accessible.

Active knowledge

Collect information and prepare an information store for yourself either in hard copy or on a computer. File the information under clearly distinguishable headings or alphabetically, and make sure you can find any information you require easily and accurately. Make plans to revisit your sources of information or the relevant websites at least once every three months and update any information, discarding anything which has become outdated. Make a note of how many times you refer to your information store during the first three months of use.

How to provide information

Once you establish what your client's needs are and referred to your own store of information or made other enquiries to find out further details or established new facts, then you have to provide information to your client in a way which they are going to find useful. Providing people with information isn't just a matter of telling them what it is. You need to give careful thought to:

- The needs of the person receiving the information.
- The nature of that information.

The needs of the client

You need to give information in a way which can be understood by your client. Your client may need to be communicated with in specific ways. For example, they may require the information in a particular form, such as in large print or in braille, or to be written or provided in sign language. There are many other considerations. You will also need to consider the circumstances of giving somebody information on a particular service or facility. For example, you would not communicate information about social clubs and outings to a man whose wife had just died. He is unlikely to be interested or ready to receive such information at this time, but would be in a few weeks or months. Though this an extreme example, the point it makes can be applied in other less extreme circumstances. You also need to take into account the client's state of health and any planned or current medical treatment they may be undertaking.

There is also a right way and a right time for giving information. From work on communication skills, you will remember that in communicating effectively it is important that you do not rush or hurry what you say and that clients are more receptive if they are comfortable and at ease. Do not pass on something to a client as you are rushing out of the door. A client may not remember your hurried 'Oh Betty, I did check and there is a painting class on Tuesday afternoons at 2.30, or Thursday mornings at 10.30, and you can go along to either of them if you just phone the library first.'

Carers need to take the time to impart information to their clients

The nature of the information

For many clients it can be beneficial to write down information or to give them an information leaflet relevant to their needs. This may be sufficient for many clients, who may undertake the next stages of information search for themselves. Many others, however, may want you to do further research for them. For most people it is important to have information in a form they can refer to again while they consider it or commit it to memory.

Before meeting a client always prepare the information in the form, written or recorded, that is appropriate for passing on to that client.

WHAT YOU NEED TO LEARN

- How to encourage clients to use services.
- Potential barriers to accessing services and how to overcome them.
- How to support clients in using services.

How to encourage clients to use services

The range of services your clients may want to use is large and varied. By no means all the services and facilities which clients will want to take advantage of are those provided by the health and care services. Many other services and facilities provided by the world of commerce, industry, entertainment and retail will also be services that clients may wish to access and enjoy.

Home services

Depending on clients' individual circumstances, they may wish to take advantage of services which can be supplied to them in their own home setting rather than having to travel to the service. If you have a client who is unable or unwilling to travel to a service then you will need to find out and establish whether or not it is possible for them to receive the service in their own home. There are many services with facilities to provide an off-site service. Examples are mobile shops, mobile libraries, many firms of solicitors and all of the services provided by a social services department. Using the Internet service, many banks and building societies provide services on-line, as do many large and small retail shopping facilities. Home delivery take-away food is readily available in most areas, as is access to films via rented videos or through satellite or cable television.

There are many services provided to people in their home

Travelling to services

Clients will have to travel if they want to participate in many forms of entertainment and culture, such as the theatre, concerts, art galleries, or sporting events. They will also have to travel to make essential appointments, such as an appearance in court or a visit to the hospital. When you are encouraging clients to make maximum use of services you may need to discuss with them arrangements to access these services if they need to travel to reach them.

Providing information on services

Many clients may need to be encouraged to use services by you providing information so they can make an informed choice or reassuring them about particular services or facilities. However, you must be careful not to cross the boundary between encouraging them and pressurising them into using a particular facility or service. Everyone has a right to choose or not to choose to take up services and facilities available to them. You are unlikely to pressurise somebody into reading a particular book or seeing a particular film, simply because you thought that it was good, even if you really felt they would enjoy it. You are unlikely to go beyond simply telling them how enjoyable you found the book or film and strongly recommending that they read it or go see it.

However, it is easy to step over the boundary when you believe the client needs to be encouraged to use a service in their interests. For example, receiving additional support services, attending a physiotherapy session or making a claim for additional benefit. All these are services you may genuinely feel would be of great benefit to your client. However, your role is limited to providing the information they need to make an informed choice. You should avoid exercising undue pressure on them to take a particular course of action. Similarly, you should not attempt to prevent a client from following a particular course of action simply because you believe it is risky or unsuitable for them. This can create major problems for carers whose clients insist in acting in ways which may expose them to undue risk of injury or other dangers. There is a fine line between neglect and restriction and it is one which is easy to overstep. Most of those working in health and care are likely to err on the side of overcaution. Although this concern for the safety of clients is well-intentioned, it results in restricting the rights of the clients to fully enjoy facilities and services available to them.

Case study

E has lived in a residential facility for people with learning difficulties since she was 5 years old. She is now 25 and although perfectly able to live in supported group accommodation in the community, she has chosen to remain in the same residential facility in which she has grown up. Because of her unique circumstances of having been there since she was a young child, a decision has been taken that E can remain in the residential facility even though all the present residents require a much higher degree of care than E does. All the former residents who functioned in the way that E does have long since moved on into group homes out in the community.

E helps a great deal at the residential home and carries out simple tasks to support members of staff. She also still requires a considerable degree of protection herself as she has an extremely naïve understanding of the world and has no understanding of any risk to her personal safety.

E is extremely sociable and has recently decided that she wishes to make regular visits to a local nightclub. This arose after she became friendly with some local young people and started to visit the local pub with them, and then decided she would like to take up their invitations to join them on nights out further afield. Staff at the residential home are concerned that E will be at risk in an unsupervised social environment because she has little or no understanding of the personal safety or sexual risks to which she could be exposed. They are therefore considering whether or not they are able to, or ought to, restrict or refuse permission for E to go on these outings to nightclubs.

1 Do the staff have any legal right to stop E going to a nightclub?

2 Do the staff have any moral right to stop E going to a nightclub?

3 How do you think this situation should be handled?

4 To what extent should E be allowed to make her own choices?

5 Would the circumstances and your views be any different if E were living in group accommodation in the community rather than in a residential setting?

6 Was the decision to allow E to remain in the residential setting the right one?

Checklist of how to encourage (or discourage) clients to use services

- Make sure that clients have a full range of information.

- Try to answer as many questions as possible.

- If you do not have information or cannot answer questions then tell the client you will find out, and make sure you do.

- Give any information you have on the consequences of using the service or facility, including information about others who may have benefited. Remember, if you are using information from other people you should not identify them, in order to maintain their confidentiality.

- Provide the client with all the information they may need to know about what they will have to do in order to access the service, such as whether the service is one which they can use at home or have to travel to, and if so what will the travel arrangements need to be.

- Offer to assist and support the client in any way you can, such as offering to introduce (by previous agreement) them to others who may be using the service or facility. Remember, if you do this do not forget to respect the confidentiality of both clients and never offer to undertake this without the express agreement of both parties involved.

Potential barriers to accessing services and how to overcome them

There are many barriers which can restrict or prevent people from accessing facilities or services. These tend to fall into three categories: environmental, communication, psychological. These are general indicators only, so the circumstances of a particular client may mean they will experience particular barriers.

Environmental barriers

These are the most common barriers, and include:

* lack of wheelchair access
* lack of disabled toilet facilities
* no ramps
* no lifts
* narrow doorways
* high risk or threatening location, e.g. A Well Woman Centre situated across the road from a busy pub or parade of shops which is a known hang-out for gangs of young men
* lack of transport or lack of access by transport.

Communication barriers

These barriers can be:

* lack of information in an appropriate language or format
* lack of loop system
* poor quality communication skills from staff at the facility, e.g. The unhelpful and obstructive receptionist
* lack of translators or interpreters
* lack of information or publicity about the service or facility.

Psychological barriers

These barriers are:

* fear of anxiety
* unfamiliarity
* unwillingness to accept help
* concern at loss of independence
* lack of confidence.

How to overcome the barriers

Your role is encouraging your client to make maximum use of services and facilities available to them is likely to involve you in making plans to overcome whatever barriers are standing in the way of them doing this. For example, you may need to search out alternative facilities if the ones you originally intended to use do not have wheelchair access, as in the case of a local theatre which does not have wheelchair access, forcing you to make arrangements for your client to travel to one which does. Of course, you would raise the issue with the local theatre and encourage them to improve their access for people with disabilities. If there are problems getting suitable transport then it may be necessary to provide transport facilities by accessing local transport with provision for your particular client group or by using taxi or public transport facilities which have the necessary adaptations. Most train companies, for instance, have support services for people with disabilities by way of providing ramps and a porter service to enable people to get on and off the trains. However, many trains that do provide portage and ramps do not have readily accessible toilets for the disabled. You may need to arrange or to assist the client to arrange for translators or interpreters.

Before you agree any particular arrangements with a facility to provide access for a client, you must ensure that you have agreed this with the client. If a client has to make an important visit to a particular location which cannot be changed or substituted and there is no wheelchair access through the main entrance, it may be suggested that the client use a back entrance or goods entrance and the goods lift to reach the appropriate facility. You should always check with a client before agreeing to this type of arrangement, as your client may not be prepared to access a building through a rear or goods entrance. In such a case, you may need to arrange for the visit to take place at a different location. It is essential you never compromise the right of a client to choose their own means of access and to set their own boundaries as to what is acceptable to them in terms of their own personal space and dignity.

Active knowledge

Choose three different types of facility which clients may wish to access in your locality. They should each be located in a different part of your area. For each, list the potential barriers to access and the ways in which you would begin to tackle the barriers for each one.

How to support clients in using services

The level of support which you need to provide to a client will vary depending on their circumstances. Your support can range from handing them an information leaflet to making all the arrangements for them to use a service and accompanying them to use it. Between these extremes there is a wide range of alternatives. Some clients may simply need you to make the initial contact for them. Others may need you to accompany them on a first visit to a new support facility or to meet a new group of people, and then to gradually withdraw your support as they grow in confidence in using the service. On other occasions your role may be to enlist the support of other people who are either better qualified or more experienced or who have the resources, time or experience, to provide a better or more consistent level of service for the client.

It is important you encourage clients to dispense with your support as soon as they feel able to manage independently. You should do this when you notice them becoming more confident in using the facility or the service, and you should do it by gradually and appropriately reducing the level of support. You may have accompanied a client on their first visit to a Welfare Rights Advice Centre. They needed you with them because they were unfamiliar with the service and they did not understand the benefit system to be able to clearly explain what their problem was. However, as the visits continue and the work of the Welfare Rights Advice Centre is underway you may be able to withdraw from accompanying the client as they become more familiar with the workers in the Advice Centre. Your involvement perhaps may be then limited to driving the client to the centre, or maybe holding a support session when the client returns from their visit.

It may take clients longer to adjust with confidence to new social situations. For instance, if a client has been supported by you accompanying them to a new day centre or social club, it may take a few visits before they are confident enough to go on their own, in the certainty they will find enough friendly and familiar faces there. As always your role is to do the minimum and to allow clients the maximum opportunities to make their own lives and to be as independent as possible.

Unit test

1 What are the main sources of information about services and facilities for clients?

2 How would you go about collecting and storing a general information bank?

3 What are the key factors to take into account when providing clients with information?

4 What are the potential pitfalls in the way that information is provided?

5 What are the effective ways of encouraging clients to use services?

6 Name six potential barriers to accessing services and facilities.

7 How could these barriers be overcome?

8 What are the different ways in which you could offer support to clients using services?

Unit Y3 Enable individuals to administer their financial affairs

In this unit you will learn about ways of supporting a range of clients in managing their finances in the most independent way possible. This unit is most likely to be of importance to those working in the community supporting clients in their own homes, however many supported living environments and some types of residential setting provide for clients to have a significant degree of financial independence. Even within a residential setting it is important that you are aware of some of the financial regulations in case you are asked questions by clients or their relatives.

Element Y3.1   Enable individuals to make payments

WHAT YOU NEED TO LEARN

- Ways of establishing payments clients need to make.
- Methods of making payments.
- Ways of recording payments made.
- Ways of dealing with potential conflicts.

Ways of establishing payments clients need to make

Much of what you need to do to establish the payments which are due will depend upon your client. You could be carrying out this sort of task for a wide range of clients, each with varying levels of ability to manage their own financial affairs. The first thing that you should do in any situation where a client has requested financial management assistance is to make sure exactly what level of assistance they need and how much information they feel comfortable with you having about their financial affairs. For example, some clients may be happy for you to collect their pension or to pay their TV licence or gas bill, but would not consider showing you their bank statement. This is the kind of level of involvement that you must establish and must ensure is agreed with the client.

It is important that you establish the difference between a client who needs support to manage their own financial affairs and one who is not capable of managing their financial affairs. It is one thing to agree a level of support you will provide for a client and quite another to take over the administration of their affairs completely, because they are incapable. Administering totally the entire financial affairs of

When a client cannot deal with their financial affairs you may need to help

another person is not part of your role and if you feel that you are working with a client who is not capable of understanding their financial affairs then this must be reported to your supervisor at once. The appropriate legal steps to protect the client can then be taken. There are a range of legal provisions in place to ensure that those who are unable to make financial decisions for themselves are protected from the possibility of being exploited. This process is likely to involve either a member of the family or a solicitor assuming the **power of attorney** in respect of the client's financial affairs. In some cases, depending on the circumstances, the law provides for the social services department to assume responsibility under guardianship arrangements. You could find in working with a client for several years, perhaps helping them in managing their finances, that as they deteriorate you are doing more and more. It is important that from time to time, particularly where you have a client with a degenerative condition such as Alzheimer's disease, that you check their level of understanding of what is happening to their finances and that you report any concerns as soon as possible.

Establishing the level of help and support

One of the best ways to work out with your client the level of support they require is to look at the reasons why they need assistance to make their payments. Is it because:

- they are specifically unable to make payments
- they are confused and forget to make payments
- they are unsure what payments they have to make
- they are unlikely to be able to motivate or organise themselves to make payments on time
- they do not recognise the importance of making payments.

Once you have established the reasons why they need support and help, it is then much easier to agree a level with them. For example, if your assistance is required simply because somebody is physically unable to write a cheque or to walk to the post office or the bank, then it may be quite sufficient for you to write cheques for them or take things to the post office. There may be no need for you to assist with the process of identifying payments which are due or becoming involved in any financial planning.

If your client is unable to make payments because they are confused or unable to recognise the importance of making payments of bills when they become due, for a wide range of reasons, then they may be happy for you to become involved at a more detailed level in their financial budgeting and planning.

Encouraging clients to be self-managing

One of the keys to working effectively with clients, whatever your role, is that you should always encourage clients to take as much active responsibility for their own lives and actions as is possible. Never assume that they will always require assistance at the level you currently provide. You should always review progress and wherever possible, either because their condition has improved or because they have learned from working with you, the client should resume or take on as much responsibility as possible for their financial planning, budgeting and payments.

Keys to good practice

- Always begin by asking the client to do as much as possible of the preparation for planning their finances.

- Find out what the client can do first, then support where necessary.

- Always check back with the client on everything which you are doing and ask 'What do you think?'

- Always make a regular review time for any financial support plan for a client. This could be three or six months, depending on their circumstances. At this stage you should review your level of support to see if the client's needs have changed.

- If you notice changes in between reviews, for example bills which have not been paid which the client used to deal with themselves, then you should follow this up and make changes if necessary.

- If your client is beginning to take more of an interest in thier finances and making suggestions, check if they would like to take more responsibility themselves and reduce your involvement.

Range of payments

We all have our own range of payments to make, either regularly or as one-offs. Whilst everyone has different financial demands made on their income there are some types of payments which are more likely to occur for most of the clients you work with. When you are looking at the payments which need to be made by any particular client, you should first ask them to identify, if they are able, which payments they need to make. It can be helpful to have a written checklist which you can use to try to make sure no payments have been forgotten. The following list is a suggestion only and it will obviously vary for each individual.

insurance

telephone

mortgage

council tax

heating and lighting

TV licence

water rates

credit cards

A client may have trouble remembering all the things they have to do

Checklist of payments

Regular payments (which could be weekly/monthly/annually):

- Rent
- Council tax
- Water
- Repair or maintenance charges
- TV licence
- Catalogue payments
- Hire purchase or loan payments

- Mortgage
- Heating and lighting
- Insurance
- Telephone
- TV/video/satellite rental
- Credit card payments

Occasional payments:

- Food
- Furniture

- Clothes
- Holidays

Such a checklist can be used for any client with whom you are working. Additional items may need to be added to meet the circumstances of any given individual. Once you have identified all of the payments which your client needs to make, then you should discuss with them which payments they wish you to undertake and which payments they will continue to undertake themselves. At this stage it is also useful to discuss methods of payment with your client and to look at the advantages and disadvantages of the range of payment methods available.

Methods of making payments

The following table lists the different methods of payment for goods and services and the advantages and disadvantages of these.

Method	Advantages	Disadvantages
Cash	• Easy for those who receive wages or benefits in cash. • Easily understood. • Allows people to see exactly their financial position.	• Safety – keeping cash represents a serious burglary risk. • Loss – cash is easy to lose, particularly if a client is confused or forgetful. • Inconvenience – cash cannot be sent in the post, so cash payments have to be made direct or through a bank, and this can mean having to make arrangements to visit the offices or the bank of the payee.
Cheque	• Convenient – can be sent by post. • More secure than cash. • Generally accepted (with a cheque guarantee card).	• Requires bank account. • Can incur considerable bank charges. • Becoming less used with the advent of electronic bank cards. • Cheque book can be lost or stolen. • Cheques can be misused.
Electronic bank card, e.g. Switch or Delta	• Convenient, generally accepted. • Easy to carry and convenient. • Easy to stop if stolen.	• Requires bank account. • May confuse some clients. • Can be stolen and misused.
Standing order – set up by client	• Regular payments made by bank. • No action needed by client. • Makes payments direct.	• Requires bank account. • Client needs to remember to alter if payments change. • Incurs bank charges.
Direct debit – set up by payee	• Regular payments made by bank. • No action needed by client. • Makes payments direct.	• Requires bank account. • Can incur bank charges.
Credit card	• Makes payments even if temporarily short of money. • Convenient.	• Can accumulate large amounts of debt. • Has higher interest charges. • Is easily stolen and misused. • Not accepted for all types of payment.
Armchair/On-line banking	• Can be used by clients who have bank accounts with access via telephone/Internet/satellite TV. • Can be used without leaving the house. • Does not require any permanent set up arrangement. • Is safe and secure.	• Only available to those with the necessary hardware and level of technological understanding to use the equipment.

Active knowledge

If you are not currently working with a client that involves assisting with finances, you could carry out this exercise on your own personal finances. Make a list, as above, of all of the payments that you make and look at the range of methods you use to pay. Check which items you pay using which methods. If you include grocery and general household shopping, you may find that the balance of methods you use alters. Similarly, if you look at methods of payments for large items you may also find that this alters the balance of the different types of payments you use. Review the payment methods that you currently use and see how you could benefit by changing any of them in order to either save on charges, interest rates or to improve the convenience or safety.

Case study

P has suffered from severe depression since the birth of her third child, now one year old. Her other children are aged two and four. Her husband left six months ago as he felt unable to cope with her depressed state. P has been receiving medication from her GP for her depression which helps to some extent, but she finds it very difficult to cope on a day-to-day basis. She was referred for support by her health visitor who was concerned about her motivation and her seeming lack of ability to organise the basic requirements of living for herself and her three children. P had neglected to pay the mortgage on their house, not because of a lack of income but because she had not been motivated to make the required arrangements to transfer the payments after her husband left. She was now being threatened with repossession of the house, and as she had not paid recent utility bills and there were various threatening letters from the companies.

A support worker began to work with P and her family, and following agreement with her made arrangements for all of her utility bills and mortgage payments to be made via direct debit. The support worker negotiated with the building society to extend the mortgage period by the missing six months and negotiated with the utility companies to allow P to pay off the excess amounts over a period of time.

1 What could have been the consequences for P and her family had the support worker not begun to work with them?

2 What alternative ways could have been used to resolve P's problems?

3 What other effects might you reasonably expect to see from the improvement in P's financial situation?

4 What skills would the support worker need to have used in order to improve P's circumstances?

Budgeting

Where you are working with a client who has found managing their financial affairs difficult and who is experiencing financial difficulty, either because of problems with management and organisation or because of **low income**, then doing some budget planning with them could be extremely valuable. This can only be done with the agreement of the client. If your client agrees you should be careful not to impose your own values and beliefs on them. For example, if you have always been brought up to believe that you should never owe money and that you should always 'pay your way' and pay all bills as they fall due, then you may find it difficult to accept the philosophy of a client who never pays bills until the bailiffs arrive at the doorstep, or who is happy to allow debts to mount and bills to go unpaid. However, if a client wants to work to resolve financial difficulties or simply wants to organise their finances better and is happy to plan a budget with your assistance, there are various ways in which you can do this, however the following approach is simple, easy to understand and works in most circumstances.

An 'income and expenditure budget' chart

These are the steps you can take in filling in the income and expenditure budget chart that follows on page 311.

Step 1 List the income that your client has from whatever source. The headings clearly cover the individual circumstances of a wide range of clients, so you should simply select the sources of income which are appropriate for the client with whom you are working.

Step 2 List expenditure. Similarly, the expenditure is designed to cover the circumstances of a wide range of clients and you should simply list those which relate to your client. There are advantages in completing the weekly, monthly and yearly columns. This means that you are less likely to miss any payments which occur less frequently and it also allows an overview of the client's complete financial position.

Step 3 This allows you to see the financial position by looking at the total of the yearly income and taking away the total yearly expenditure. It will show you whether the client is able to live within the income they currently receive. If they are not and the expenditure is greater than their income, then you need to look at ways of either increasing their income or reducing their expenditure. This may be through claiming additional benefits or, if they are working, they may wish to consider whether it is possible to work additional hours or to explore the possibility of finding additional sources of income. For those on a low income, make sure they are receiving all the government support to which they are entitled. If your client is dependent upon income from pensions and savings they may wish to consider whether to move savings into an account which will provide a higher rate of interest. If this is a step to be considered then you must strongly advise the client to consult a financial adviser before making such a decision. You should not, under any circumstances, offer financial advice of this nature unless you are qualified to do so.

The other alternative for any client whose expenditure exceeds their income is to review expenditure and to examine where reductions can be made.

Dealing with debt

If you are supporting a client who is in debt then you should encourage them to enlist the support of an experienced debt counsellor. These are available through the **Citizens Advice Bureau**, **Welfare Rights Advice Centres** and local **Money Advice Centres**. However, it is useful if you understand the steps that a debt counsellor will take in order to resolve the client's problems.

Citizens Advice Bureaux can provide the support of an experienced debt counsellor

The first thing that the debt councillor will do is establish the nature of the debts which the client has. Debts are

Income and expenditure budget chart			
Step 1 – Income	**Weekly**	**Monthly**	**Yearly**
Salary/wage			
Other income			
Pension			
Jobseekers allowance			
Income support			
Housing benefit			
Other benefits			
Interest on savings			
Total			
Step 2 – Expenditure			
Mortgage or rent			
Second mortgage/secured loan			
Council tax			
Water rates			
Ground rent			
Repairs & maintenance charges			
Buildings insurance			
Contents insurance			
Gas			
Electricity			
Telephone			
Food			
Clothing			
TV rental and licence			
Prescriptions			
Health insurance			
Car tax and insurance			
Petrol/diesel			
Car repairs and servicing			
Public transport			
School fees, uniform, etc.			
Holidays			
Credit cards and loans			
Maintenance payments			
Contribution to pension			
Reserve for emergencies			
Regular savings			
Total			
Step 3 – Financial position			
Total income			
Total expenditure			
Financial position			

defined **as priority debts** and **non-priority debts**.

Priority debits include:
- mortgage or rent
- council tax
- water charges
- gas
- electricity
- payments ordered by courts
- maintenance payments also ordered by courts or the Child Support Agency.

Non-priority debts include:
- hire purchase debts.

The difference between the two kinds of debts is that failure to pay priority debts could mean the loss of a client's home or having to live without heat or light if services are disconnected. The consequences of failure to meet non-priority debts, whilst unpleasant are not as serious. The repossession of goods by a hire purchase company may make life awkward but does not make it impossible. If a television or satellite system is repossessed the family may be bored, whereas the failure to purchase a TV licence could result in a large fine and an even higher amount of debt to be repaid.

Once the debt counsellor has established the level of income, and they may work it out on both a weekly and a monthly basis, they will then look at basic expense levels – those required for the basics of living, such as food and essential clothing. They will then identify priority debts. They will look at the amount of debt that there is and what that represents in terms of repayments over a period of time. They will concentrate on ensuring that the priority debts are met in the first instance.

Once a debt counsellor has this information they will then negotiate with all of the creditors involved and agree a schedule of repayments. Creditors are usually happy to agree deferred payments of outstanding debts as this is preferable to not receiving

> OK, so we couldn't pay the licence and we haven't got a TV anymore. But at least we've still got the house.

It could be worse

any payment at all from the debt. Debt counsellors are trained and experienced in this type of debt management and you should encourage your client to make use of their services if necessary. However, if they are unwilling to do so and wish you to carry out the negotiations or to do it themselves, then you may wish to consult your local Citizens Advice Bureau or a Money Advice Centre for any further information or guidance before you begin negotiation with creditors.

It is important that you encourage your client to abide by any arrangements which have been made for the repayment of their debt. It frequently happens that once arrangements have been negotiated for repayment the client believes that the problem has somehow 'gone away' and they no longer need to concern themselves with it.

Budget repayment plan for those in debt

Here is an example of how to budget the repayment of debt.

Income/expenses	Weekly	Monthly
List income per week/month		
List basic expense per week/month		
Deduct basic expenses from income		
Total money for debt repayment plan		
List priority debts		
Deduct priority debts from repayment plan		
Total money for other debt repayment		

Did you know?

The reason that many clients and families are in debt is because they receive such a low income. In the UK today 25 per cent of the population, one person in four, lives in poverty. Poverty is officially defined as 50 per cent or less of average national income after housing costs. One in three, or 34 per cent, of children live in poverty.

Being aware of the benefits

When identifying and supporting clients in making payments you should also ensure you are aware of any benefits or concessions they can receive on those payments. For example, from November 2000 people aged 75 and over will qualify for a free TV licence. From 1 April 2000 people who are registered blind received a 50 per cent reduction in the cost of their television licence. If you are working with a client who lives in sheltered housing or other supported living, you should check whether it is a scheme which qualifies for a concessionry licence. Many older people, people with disabilities and people on low incomes are entitled to concessions for travel, use of local leisure facilities and libraries. There are also reductions in council tax for people who live alone and for people who have severe disabilities. It is important that you are aware of these concessions and reductions and that you encourage your clients to take full advantage of them. You should keep your knowledge updated through regular contact with local advice centres and Citizens Advice Bureaux.

Ways of recording payments made

All payments made for any goods or services require a receipt. It is important that you encourage your clients to always obtain and keep receipts for any payments they make. By doing this it will always be possible to resolve any disputes about the time and amount of payments which have been made and it avoids confusion over which bills have and have not been paid.

If you are making payments on behalf of a client then it is essential you obtain a receipt and keep a copy in the client's case notes or receipts file. This protects you and the client if any question about the payment is ever raised. Receipts can come in a range of formats. Payments made via a bank will be recorded on a bank statement, so an individual receipt will not be needed. However, payments made by cheque,

Clients may need to be advised how to organise their financial affairs for easy access

debit card or credit card need a receipt of individual transactions, which are kept until the transactions appear on either the bank statement or credit card statement. This makes it easy to identify any unexpected or unauthorised payments which appear on the statement. Also a transaction receipt helps to easily resolve any dispute over the transaction.

Receipts should be maintained in a system where they are easily accessible – the sideboard draw does not qualify as easily accessible! A simple filing system where receipts are identified as utility bills, food, TV licence, clothing, holidays, etc. may be the easiest way of locating them when they are needed. Receipts should not be kept indefinitely and the system will have to be maintained. Receipts for any item under guarantee should be kept at least for the life of the guarantee. Other payment receipts should be kept until the payment itself shows on an overall statement of that particular account. Many clients do not see the importance of keeping receipts or may forget where they have put them or may lose them. You should try to obtain the client's agreement to set up a system which they can use or if that is beyond what they feel able to undertake initially, then to hand over their receipts to you until they become more familiar with the system. This is likely to prove the most effective way of recording your client's financial transactions.

Ways of dealing with potential conflicts

You may be faced with a dilemma if clients ask you to make payments in certain situations or tell you they intend not to make certain payments. This could involve:

- making payments for illegal items
- making payments for items of which you personally disapprove
- a client telling you they intend to avoid making payments which are due.

Illegal payments

If a client asks you to make a payment which you know to be illegal, for example to pay for stolen goods or any other illegal items, then you should explain that it will not be possible for you to assist them and that it is inappropriate for them to ask you to undertake this. If you become aware that your client is involved in criminal activity then you must report this to your line manager and follow your agency's policies and procedures.

Payments of which you disapprove

A client may ask you to assist them with making payments for an activity which is in conflict with your own beliefs and values. An example would be a client asking you, who are strongly opposed to gambling, to place a

You cannot allow your beliefs and values to affect the service you provide to clients

bet with a bookmaker on their behalf. In such a case you must be sure that you do not allow your own beliefs and values to influence the level of service which you provide for your client.

The intention not to make payments

If your client advises you that they are not going to make payments for goods or services or to meet their legal requirements, then you can find yourself in a difficult position. For example, a client advises you during the budgeting process not to include an allowance for a TV licence as they do not intend to purchase one. In this situation you should advise the client of the consequences of their actions and of the levels of fines which are imposed on those who fail to purchase a TV licence. You are not, however, in a position to insist on a certain action or to override your client's wishes. You are only able to advise them and ensure that any decisions they make about failing to maintain or make payments are based on an informed choice. You should record this information and advise your line manager accordingly. You must explain to your client that you are doing this. You should never actively condone or encourage clients to avoid making payments which they are required to make. Be careful that you do not give the appearance of encouragement by failing to comment. You do have a responsibility to ensure that a client is informed of the potential consequences of any actions.

Active knowledge

Make a two-column list, one with all the payments which your client has to make, the other with the consequences in each case of failure to pay. This should enable you to clearly see which payments need to take priority because of the consequences for the client.

Element Y3.2 — Enable individuals to claim benefits and allowances

WHAT YOU NEED TO LEARN

- How to find out about benefits and allowances for your client.
- How to help clients apply for benefits and allowances.

How to find out about benefits and allowances

As always your initial step is to establish with the client the level of help they are going to need. It is always preferable to encourage and enable clients to find out as much information for themselves as possible. You should only directly intervene in the provision of information when the client is unable to do so and it is not possible for you to empower them. Sources of information about benefits and allowances are extremely varied throughout the country and whether or not you are working in a rural or urban area. The most comprehensive advice and information is available at centres such as the local Citizens Advice Bureau, at a Welfare Rights Centre or a money advice centre. Citizens Advice Bureau is a national organisation with branches in most towns and cities throughout the UK. It also has a comprehensive website and telephone advice lines. The welfare rights centres and Money Advice Centres are often run by local authorities, so your local council should be able to tell you the nearest location of these. The local library is always a good source of information about the location of advice centres and they will also be able to advise on the nearest Citizens Advice Bureau. The Benefits Agency provides a benefits helpline where information about specific allowances and benefits can be obtained. However, this only relates to state benefits. Any broader or more general advice will

Welfare Rights Centres are a source of comprehensive advice on benefits and allowances

need to be obtained from a Citizens Advice Bureau or a Money Advice Centre.

There is a wide range of reasons why a client may need assistance and support to find out about benefits and allowances, and in many circumstances you will find that offering some additional support may be all that is required to allow a client to assess their own information. Below is a list of why people need help and ways of finding out what can be done.

Possible difficulty	Assistance which could be offered
Mobility	Arrange transport, check in advance of access to information centre, library, etc.
Lack of confidence	Offer to accompany client to find out information.
Unable to use telephone	Explore use of telephone adaptations if appropriate.
No access to Internet	Arrange support to visit library, cyber café, and computer centre to access the website information.

Client's entitlements

Depending on their circumstances your client may be eligible for a number of state benefits or allowances. However, state benefits are not the only source of income that you may need to assist your client with. If your client has been in employment they may have access to a company or private pension scheme or they may be eligible for financial support from a charity or benevolent fund specifically for retired or former members of particular occupations. The *Charity Digest*, a copy of which should be available in your local library, gives information about every charity in the country and explains the help provided by each charitable organisation.

Clients may be entitled to other sorts of help in addition to any particular benefits. Some of these may be 'passported' because the clients are eligible for a particular allowance (e.g. income support). Or they may be entitled because of age or level of disability. These benefits can make a significant difference to a client's financial situation, so it is important that you ensure that clients obtain information about their entitlements. You don't have to have full knowledge of welfare rights and all the allowances available for your clients. However, it is an advantage for you know in general terms what a client may be eligible to receive, and more importantly that you can advise them where to obtain further information.

General information on benefits

Pensions

Women over 60 and men over 65 are entitled to the state retirement pension. This basic pension is paid to people who have reached pensionable age and who have sufficient National Insurance contributions. People who do not have sufficient National Insurance contributions made or credited throughout their working life may get a reduced pension or possibly no pension at all. Married women, if they do not have sufficient contributions of their own, can claim a pension based on their husband's contributions. In 2000 the full basic pension is £67.50 for an individual. The reduced rate for married women whose claims are based on their husband's contributions is £40.40.

Help with residential or nursing home fees

People wishing to enter residential or nursing home care will have their care needs assessed by their local authority. Assistance with nursing home fees will be provided on a sliding scale after a financial assessment or means test is carried out. Any potential resident who has more than £16,000 in savings will have to pay the full cost of their residential or nursing home care. This is a broad guideline which applies throughout the UK.

Prescription charges

People over 60 are entitled to free prescription charges and free sight tests regardless of their level of savings or their income.

Transport

Most local authorities offer free or reduced bus/train fares to local older people. These vary so you should ask your local council what the provisions are. Many rail companies give reductions on national rail fares to people aged 60 or over, and some of the national bus companies provide similar discounts.

Attendance allowance

This allowance is designed for people who need assistance with washing, dressing, mobility or feeding, or who need supervision so they are not a risk to themselves. In 2000 this is paid at two different rates: one is a weekly rate of £35.80 for clients who need help during the day or night and the other, higher rate, is currently £53.55 for help needed round the clock. Clients are eligible to claim for attendance allowance regardless of their living circumstances. They can claim even if they live alone. The requirement is that the client needs help. They do not actually have to be getting help in order to qualify for the allowance. As a general rule clients must meet the conditions for the allowance for a period of at least six months before it is payable. However, special rules apply for clients who are terminally ill.

Child benefit

Child benefit – called Family Allowance until 1977 – is payable as a universal benefit, regardless of income or savings, to the mothers of all children who are in full-time education. It is interesting to see how since its introduction in 1946 child benefit has risen from 5 shillings (25p) a week for each child after the first one to £1 a week in 1977, when it began to be paid for the first child as well as others, to the present rate of £14.40 for the first child and £9.60 for the second and subsequent children.

Rates of benefit from 1946 to date

Family allowanceDate Rate

06/08/46	5s a week for each child other than the first child
02/09/52	8s a week for each child other than the first child
02/10/56	10s a week for the third and each subsequent child
24/10/67	15s a week for the fourth and each subsequent child
09/04/68	15s a week for the second child, 17s a week for the third and each subsequent child
08/10/68	18s a week for the second child, £1.00 a week for the third and each subsequent child
08/04/75	£1.50 a week for the second and each subsequent child

Child benefit/One parent benefit

Date	Eldest child	Other children	OPB
05/04/77	£1.00	£1.00	0.50
24/11/80	£4.75	£4.75	£3.00
25/11/85	£7.00	£7.00	£4.55
09/04/90	£7.25	£7.25	£5.60
10/04/95	£10.40	£8.45	£6.30
12/04/99	£14.40	£9.60	N/A

Benefits for those on low incomes

All the benefits designed to support people with low incomes are based on a means test which includes savings and income. These benefits are related to the amount of National Insurance contributions.

People on low incomes are eligible for certain benefits

Income support (also called minimum income guarantee)

This benefit is widely claimed by older people but is available to those who are both under 60 and are ill or who are carers and are not registered as unemployed.

Did you know?

That 70 per cent of pensioner households depend on state benefits for at least 50 per cent of their income. That 13 per cent of pensioner households receive all their income from state benefits and over 1.7 million people aged 60 or over are receiving income support because of their low income. Income support is available for people who have no more than £8,000 in savings. It has been announced that this level will increase to £12,000 in 2001 for people aged 60. The level of income support is set by Parliament. Income and savings are taken into account along with allowances for items such as housing costs, and these are then deducted from the amounts which Parliament has set down as being the minimum amount required to live on. Full details of the current income support rates can be obtained from the Benefits Agency or any of the advice centres.

Housing benefit and council tax benefit

Housing benefit provides assistance towards the rent of those on a low income, and council tax benefit provides support for the payment of council tax. Both these benefits are only available to claimants with less than £16,000 in savings. A broad guide is that if a client is eligible for income support they are also likely to be entitled to housing benefit and council tax benefit. As in the case of income support, the circumstances of an individual are taken into account, including income, savings, how many in the family, level of disability and so on. There are also schemes which provide a reduction in council tax for people who live alone and for those who live with another person who has a low income. Those in receipt of income support will automatically be sent the appropriate forms to complete for housing and council tax benefit. Otherwise the forms will be available from the local authority.

Health costs

People in receipt of income support will receive free prescriptions, free dental treatment, help with travel costs for hospital visits, free sight tests and help towards the purchase of glasses. Those who do not receive income support, and do not have more than £8,000 worth of savings, can still get some help towards these costs by completing a form which is available from their dentist, optician or the hospital.

Social fund

The social fund can provide lump sum cash payments to cover extra expenses which cannot be met from normal weekly incomes. For example, the purchase of large furniture items such as beds and cookers, or to cover funeral costs. The social fund can also make loans in a crisis or an emergency but it is important to take into account that these loans must be repaid.

Working families tax credit

This is a tax credit to ensure that low-income families who are working will receive an income which meets the minimum income guarantee regardless. Further information on this benefit, which is dependent upon levels of wages, allowances for housing and other costs, and the number of dependant children, can be obtained from the Benefits Agency.

Benefits for people with disabilities and for carers

There are a range of benefits that disabled people can claim

Disability living allowance

This is a benefit for those who are disabled and require the same sort of care and assistance that qualifies people for the attendance allowance. It provides benefit for those unable to walk or have great difficulty walking outdoors, and have a mobility element included. The rates at which it is paid are complex. Information should be obtained from the Benefits Agency or a local advice centre.

Invalid care allowance

This is paid to carers who are unable to work full time because of the care they are giving to someone else. Carers are eligible to claim this allowance if the person they are caring for qualifies for an attendance allowance or disability living allowance. To qualify carers must be under 65 when they first apply for the allowance and must not be earning more than £50 a week. Carers who are getting other benefits may not be able to get invalid care allowance.

Incapacity benefit (previously called invalidity benefit)

This is paid to people who cannot work because they are sick or disabled. It is based on the National Insurance contributions paid. The rates at which it is paid depends on the length of time that a person is unable to work. Incapacity benefit stops when a person reaches pensionable age.

Severe disablement allowance

This is benefit is paid to severely disabled people who cannot work but do not have sufficient contributions to get incapacity benefit. It is only applicable to disabled people aged under 65. A medical examination by the Benefits Agency is also required and there are strict guidelines as to the definition of severely disabled. The rate is the same as income support but it is not means tested, and so is applicable to people with a severe disability regardless of income or savings they have.

Independent living fund

This helps severely disabled people who need to pay for care or support in order to remain living at home. Local authorities can also make payments as an alternative to providing community care services, thus enabling a disabled individual to make their own arrangements for care and support. Payments are not age restricted and are available to anyone aged over 16 who is severely disabled.

Disabled person's tax credit

This benefit is designed for people with disabilities who are in work but earn a low income. Through the **tax credit** they are able to ensure that their income does not fall below the minimum income guarantee level.

All this information is intended only to provide you with a guide as to the range of benefits which may be available for any individual client you are working with. It is not an exhaustive list, so it is vitally important for your client's benefit that you obtain information from expert sources, either at advice centres or direct from the Benefits Agency, about any benefits to which your client may be entitled.

How to help clients apply for benefits and allowances

A client may choose not to claim benefits to which they are entitled. This can be extremely frustrating if you are trying to support them in surviving on a limited income. And it can often be difficult to encourage people to claim their entitlements. Many people, particularly older people, may feel that claiming benefit is a form of charity and something they are not prepared to contemplate. Others may feel it is an admission of failure or defeat that they are unable to provide their own income through working. Some find it hard to acknowledge that a change in their circumstances or the development of a disability means they are no longer able to earn a living independently. For many in these circumstances the claiming of a benefit seems like the final admission and acknowledgement of their disability or illness. You should also be aware that a client may have literacy difficulties if there appears to be no logical explanation as to why they are refusing to claim a benefit. If you suspect this is the case, and that the client is too embarrassed to discuss the problem with you, then you need to try to overcome the difficulty. You could offer to complete the relevant application form for the client, perhaps on the grounds that the forms are lengthy to complete, or you could advise them that there is a telephone application line for people who do not wish to complete a written form. If you find that the client responds positively to such suggestions, you should consider that your client may have literacy problems. If you establish this, then you could find a way of finding out if they want support and help to improve their literacy.

Did you know?

The Benefits Agency estimates that between 27 per cent and 37 per cent of pensioners entitled to income support, and up to 12 per cent of those entitled to housing benefit and somewhere between 20 per cent and 30 per cent of those entitled to council tax benefit do not claim it.

Despite the frustrations that it may cause you as a worker attempting to support a client who does not want to claim benefits, you must be prepared to support them in their decision. This does not mean you should not try to encourage them to claim the benefit and to ensure they have all the necessary information, however you should recognise the point at which encouragement becomes harassment or bullying and allow your client to make their informed decision. Once the decision has been made then you must support them to manage their finances on the level of income they have. This does not mean decisions cannot be periodically reviewed and revisited and this is something you should encourage your client to do from time to time in the hope they may have changed their views. If they do change their views on claiming a particular benefit you should offer an appropriate level of support in assisting them to make the claim.

Case study

Mrs F had lived alone since her husband died 25 years ago. She kept her small house neat and clean and had always been very independent doing all her own shopping, gardening and cleaning. She has a son in another part of the country who she sees about twice a year, she is friendly with her neighbours and attends her local church where she has a wide circle of friends. Mrs F has been finding it increasingly difficult to manage on her single state pension. Until she was admitted to hospital for investigations for a bowel condition she had no idea that she may have been entitled to additional support. Despite having a wide circle of friends and contacts in the local church she never considered discussing her personal financial circumstances with anyone outside her family, and on the rare occasions when she saw her son even then she did not want to burden him with discussions of her financial circumstances. It was a passing comment she made to one of the support workers at the hospital about the quality of hospital food being a considerable improvement on what she could afford at home that prompted a few further questions to Mrs F, and to the discovery of the amount of pension she was receiving.

Mrs F who advised about what she could claim and was supported to make a claim for income support. As a result she received additional income, bringing her weekly income to the guaranteed minimum level. This made a huge difference to Mrs F, who was now able to run her home and do her shopping without the sort of worry and anxiety that she had endured for so many years.

1 What steps could have been taken to have provided Mrs F with this information much earlier?

2 How would you organise an information campaign for people like Mrs F?

3 What sources would you have targeted for information to help people such as Mrs F?

Completing the paperwork

Benefit claim forms are usually very long. However, great improvements have been made in the way they have been structured to make them much simpler to understand and easier to know what information is required. Nevertheless, it is often the length of these forms that inhibit people from filling them in. For example, the claim form for income support is 20 pages long. Actually completing the forms is not as arduous as it appears, as for the vast majority of people large parts of the forms will not require filling in. These are the sections asking about savings, property owned and other sources of income. Even so, the mere appearance of the form makes some people feel that they are unable to complete it.

Filling in a form may not be as bad as it looks

The Benefits Agency has a system of filling them in over the telephone and sending them to clients for checking and completing. This is a valuable service for many people and ensures the information is filled in correctly and in the correct places on the form. However, for clients who do not want to do this by telephone you may be asked to support and assist them in completing application forms. This does not mean you would take over the filling in of the forms, however the client may ask you to check that the form they have completed has been filled in correctly. It is important to make sure that a client with no income or no savings writes 'none' in the appropriate boxes.

You may need to make sure that a client making a claim fills in the form legibly. This is important as any difficulty in marking out the filled in details may cause a delay in processing the claim. Also the information could be interpreted wrongly and the wrong decisions made in respect of the benefit. If a client's writing legibility is a problem, you will need to handle this with tact and care. A client may be offended if you imply they cannot complete a form legibly. If a client has literacy problems then you could either offer to assist them or complete the form on their behalf. Another course is to encourage them to use the telephone application line.

You may have to deal with a client who refuses to complete the whole form because they feel it is too long and complex or because they are not willing to provide all the information the form asks for, such as information about their finances. You can only explain to them what the consequences will be of not providing that information. For example, if the client is claiming a means tested benefit then the claim will not be considered unless the financial information is provided. The client must be aware of the consequences of their actions in order to make an informed decision about whether or not they wish to pursue the claim for a particular benefit and to provide all of the necessary information.

Potential difficulties

If you are aware that a client is attempting to make a deliberately fraudulent claim for a benefit or is making a deliberate attempt to mislead an agency providing a benefit about their circumstances then you must:

- explain that you cannot support them in this action and that you will be unable to assist them in making the claim
- make it clear that if they persist in making a fraudulent or misleading claim then you will have to record the matter and report it to your agency
- report the matter to your line manager who will advise you as to your agency's policy.

Section 2
Your claim for *Incapacity Benefit*

Please read through **Section 1** of this form. Your employer has filled in **Section 1** to tell you why you cannot get Statutory Sick Pay (SSP).

Statutory Sick Pay (SSP) is money paid by employers to employees who are away from work for 4 days or more in a row because they are sick. If you disagree with the decision, ask your employer to explain it to you. If you still disagree with the decision, ask the Inland Revenue (NI contributions) office for advice. You may be able to ask for an Inland Revenue officer's decision. You can contact them by phone, their phone number and address are in the phone book under **Inland Revenue.** Leaflet **NI244** *Statutory Sick Pay – check your rights* tells you more about this. You can get this leaflet from any social security office.

Please fill in the rest of this form if you want to claim Incapacity Benefit.
If you need help filling in this form, get in touch with your social security office. If you cannot fill in this form yourself, you can ask someone else to fill it in for you.

▍Part 1 **About you**

Benefit you can get because of this claim can be paid more quickly if you
- answer all the questions on this form that apply to you and your partner, if you have one
- send us all the documents we ask for.

If you cannot do this, get in touch with us, but benefit you can get because of this claim may be delayed.

Surname or family name	Mr/Mrs/Miss/Ms
All other names – in full	
All other surnames or family names you have been known by or are using now. Please include maiden name, all former married names and all changes of family name.	
Address	
	Postcode
Daytime phone number	Code Number
Date of birth	/ /

National Insurance (NI) number
You can find the number on your NI numbercard, letters from social security or payslips.

Letters   Numbers   Letter
☐☐ ☐☐ ☐☐ ☐☐ ☐

If you do not know your NI number, have you ever had one or used one at any time?
No ☐
Yes ☐

Marital status
married ☐   widow or widower ☐   separated ☐
single ☐   divorced ☐

Please tell us about any other personal details you think we should know about in **Part 18** Other information. For example, other names or recent previous addresses.

Copyright Department of Social Security 2000
Page from the application form for Statutory Sick Pay and Incapacity Benefit

Active knowledge

Obtain a copy of a benefits claim form (e.g. income support). Check it through to familiarise yourself with its style.

Enable individuals to collect benefits and allowances

WHAT YOU NEED TO LEARN

- Methods of collecting benefits and allowances.
- Ways of ensuring clients keep their money safe.

Methods of collecting benefits and allowances

Payment into bank account

You really must trust a bank to look after your money for you. It will be safer there.

There are safer places to keep money

You will need to discuss and agree with your client the best way you can support them in collecting any benefits or allowances to which they are entitled. State benefits and many other payments from private pensions or employer pensions are now paid directly into clients' bank accounts. If your client does not have a bank account then it may be helpful if you can explain to them the value of having one, and give them information on how their benefit could be paid directly into it and how relatively easy it is to access it.

Payment by giro cheque

The Benefits Agency pays some state benefits direct by a regular giro cheque, which can be cashed at the local post office. This requires the client to attend the post office in person and to produce some identity. Where people are ill or unable to attend the post office it is possible for a cheque to be cashed on their behalf provided that appropriate identity and authority is produced.

Payment by order book

Many regular payments, such as income support, child benefit and the state retirement pension, are paid through a regular order book. In these cases the client collects their benefit each week (or month) from the post office where the appropriate counterfoil is stamped and removed from their book and the cash is paid to them. Cash is welcomed by a many people on low incomes. It gives them immediate access to their money, so there is no need to go to the bank to access it. Also, this avoids the additional expense of bank charges for writing cheques or making payments with a debit card. However, it means that people on a low income who are totally dependent on receiving cash each week have no emergency funds and often experience severe difficulties after they have spent all their money and have to wait for the next cash payment.

When you don't have much money you need to make it last

Help may be needed

If clients are physically unable to visit a post office to collect their benefit or allowance because of temporary illness or disability, then you can arrange to collect their benefits for them by them signing the appropriate sections on the back of the payment counterfoil in their order book. If you do collect a client's payments in this way it is essential for your protection and theirs that they sign for the receipt of the money as soon as you hand it over to them. You could use a simple form for this. All you need is a record of the amount of money which you have given to them, the date on which it was handed over and a record of the client's signature.

Record of Monies Collected	
Date	*25 May 2000*
Received from	*A N Other*
The sum of	*£67.50*
Pension collected by	*Mary P - Home help*
Signature	

It is also important you record in the client's case notes or records that you have collected and handed over any benefits to them. If the client is collecting their own benefits you should encourage them to check that the amount they are given is correct and if there are any problems they should immediately report them. Where payments are being made directly into a client's bank account, you should encourage them to check their bank statements regularly to make sure that all the necessary payments are being recorded in their account.

If you are dealing with money for clients in residential care your work setting will have its own form of recording what money is received on behalf of each resident and how much is spent. This will have to be recorded, as well as any payments which are made into any bank accounts which are held in the client's name.

Ways of ensuring clients keep their money safe

In settings where you are working with vulnerable clients, whether they are residential or in the client's own home, it is necessary to discuss with your client the subject of the safety and security of any money they have. Many vulnerable people who continue to live in their own homes, particularly those who are elderly or with disabilities, are at high risk of being robbed if they keep cash in the house. Elderly people are more likely to keep large amounts of cash in the house and you should discourage this wherever possible. They and their money will be much safer if they can be persuaded to put the money into a bank, building society or post office savings account.

Older people who keep large sums of money in the home risk being robbed

In a residential setting there will be arrangements for the safe keeping of clients' valuables and money. They should be encouraged to use this facility rather than keep money in their room or handbag or wallet. If a client refuses to use the safe-keeping facility provided by the residential establishment, then it is likely they will be asked to sign a disclaimer form to acknowledge they have been offered the facility but have chosen to take care of their valuables themselves. You will explore this in more detail when you do Unit CU1.

If you are aware of any cash being lost or stolen from your client you must immediately report the loss – to your line manager if you are in a residential setting or to the police if you are working with clients in their own homes. Clients are likely to be distressed by the loss of valuables, so you will need to offer them a lot of support during this time.

Managing finances is an important part of the lives of all adults. People will need your support to a greater or lesser degree in order to be able to manage their finances effectively. You will need to have a broad and general understanding of how finances work and the sort of support and benefits to which your clients may be entitled. Above all you will need to know where to obtain advice and guidance for clients on all financial matters.

Active knowledge

Check out the system for recording clients' finances in your workplace. Think about how it could be improved, in terms of ease of use and its suitability. If you feel improvements could be made to update, simplify or extend it, then have a go at designing a new system of recording. When you have done this you may want to discuss it with your line manager. You never know, it might be brought into use in your work setting!

Unit test

1   Where can information be obtained about benefits and allowances? Name at least three sources.

2   List the different ways in which payments can be made.

3   List the different ways in which benefits and allowances can be received.

4   Identify four reasons why people may refuse to claim benefits to which they are entitled.

5   What would be the general areas of benefit that you would advise people over 60 to consider?

6   What would be the general areas of benefit that you would advise families on a low income to consider?

7   What would be the general areas of benefit that you would advise people with a disability to consider?

8   What are the ways in which the benefit system can contribute to the independence of individuals?

9   Think about the ways in which you feel the benefit system could be improved.

10 What other sources of income could you explore other than state benefits and allowances?

Unit Y4: Support individuals in undertaking health care

Being able to provide support, advice and guidance to those who are undertaking their own health care or to carers who are providing health care for friends or relatives is an important and key role for workers in health and social care. There are many situations in which the ability to deliver health care in the community contributes to the key factors in enabling clients to remain in their own homes. The additional support provided by a health or care worker to a client or their carer can ensure that a plan of care can be developed and undertaken successfully to provide the maximum possible benefit for the client.

Element Y4.1 — Support individuals in undertaking procedures, treatments and dressings

WHAT YOU NEED TO LEARN

- Ways to ensure clients have all they need for their health care.
- The range of procedures clients may need to undertake.

Ways to ensure clients have all they need for their health care

You need to establish with clients the level of support they are happy for you to provide. This may involve you in directly supporting a carer rather than the client, so you may need to discuss with them the level of support they need. The support you could be asked to provide includes:

- assisting in the ordering or collection of the supplies and equipment needed
- providing explanations and guidance on carrying out the health care procedures
- demonstrating the correct techniques and procedures to be followed
- observing and offering advice
- being present in order to offer emotional support and reassurance
- providing advice, information or assistance in the disposal of waste.

Level of support

You need to discuss carefully with your client and their carers, if any, the level of support they need you to provide, taking into account the degree of independence your clients wants in managing their own health care. If you have been working with a client for some time, you will be aware of the degree of independence they want and level of support needed. However, if you have a new client or a job in which your role involves short periods of support to clients, then you need to discuss with your client or clients the type and level of support they require. You need to remember that your client may not be aware of the types of help available to them and the supplies and equipment which could be provided to improve and extend their level of independence. So, you must take a proactive role in providing this information and making sure that your client has the maximum possible information about what is available, so they can make an informed decision about how much they feel able to undertake for themselves.

Equipment and supplies

Once you have decided with the client the level of support you will provide, the next stage is to make sure they have all of the equipment and supplies which they need to carry out their treatments. The client may have a list of the supplies they need. This may have been given to them by their GP, district nurse, hospital doctor or nurse, or by a specialist health care professional. If they do not have a list of supplies, then check with the care team responsible for the health care of the client exactly what supplies will be needed and check the quantities needed at any one time to ensure that storage recommendations are complied with.

The supplies are likely to be obtained through a pharmacy or possibly from the health centre or specialist hospital clinic, depending on the treatments to be undertaken. However, it is unlikely that large quantities would be supplied from a hospital, as NHS prescribing is usually only available for in-patients receiving care or treatment. All prescribing, including supplies, is undertaken by the GP in the community and supplied through a local pharmacy. It can be useful to check the following list to make sure your client has all of the necessary equipment and supplies:

1 **Source of supply**. This needs to be checked with the local GP for any medications or supplies subject to a prescription. You need to check or get the client to check that there is a facility for a regular repeat prescription when needed. If the supplies do not require a prescription, you should ensure that the local pharmacy always has an adequate supply and work out with your client how often the supplies will need to be renewed.

2 **Storage facilities**. Many items needed for health care require special storage. All items need to be stored in a place not subject to extreme temperatures. Damp or excessively hot or cold places can contaminate or spoil medical supplies, equipment and medication. All medications and sterilised items will have an expiry date. Clients should be encouraged to set up a regular system of reviewing their supplies and returning any which are outdated to the pharmacy for proper disposal. Never use outdated medications or medical supplies. If special storage requirements are needed, for example insulin has to be kept in a refrigerator, then it is essential to follow the instructions. Failing to do this could result in medication becoming ineffective or even dangerous.

3 **Ability to understand and comply with instruction**. You must stress to your clients the need to store medications correctly and you must satisfy yourself they have understood this. If you are concerned a client has not understood or is not able or willing to comply with storage requirements for medical supplies or medication, then you should refer the matter immediately to the care team and your line manager. Alternative arrangements for administering medication will need to be considered.

Medical equipment and supplies should be stored correctly and kept up to date.

The range of procedures clients may need to undertake

Many clients can undertake their own health care in their home setting. Some may require the support of their carer, if they have one, to carry out health care procedures at home. Whether you are supporting a client or a carer or a combination of both, you could be involved in making sure they are able to undertake any health procedures, including dealing with dressings for lesions such as ulcers or pressure sores or other wounds which have been stitched.

Dressing a wound or lesion

If a client is doing this in their home setting, they will need supplies of sterile dressing packs, which contain gauze packs, cotton wool and sterile cotton wool balls, tweezers and a dish. They will also need small packs of saline solution (Normasol). The type of dressing used will vary depending on the individual client and their particular condition. This could be a standard gauze dressing, an artificial skin (Tagaderm) or other specialist dressing which may be impregnated with particular substances. The length of time between changing dressings will vary, depending on the nature of the wound or lesion. For example, in some surgical wounds which have been sutured the dressing will not be changed until the sutures are removed. It has been found that a lower incident of post-operative wound infection occurs if dressings are left untouched in most cases.

Following a clean procedure

Dressing and cleaning an area will need to follow a clean procedure. You need to make sure your client understands the importance of thoroughly washing their hands before dealing with any dressing. Although the risk of cross-infection is obviously less if the individual concerned is carrying out their own personal health care, it is still essential they wash their hands before and after completing the procedure. The steps they should take are:

1 Wash hands.

2 Open dressing pack.

3 Remove old dressing and place in a bag for disposal.

4 Use cotton wool balls held with tweezers and dipped in saline solution to clean the affected area.

5 Apply any medication required.

6 Pick up new dressing with tweezers, place on the affected area and hold in place with adhesive tape (Micropore).

This is a general guide only and specific procedures may need to be followed for a particular individual. It is essential that you and/or the client check with the district nurse or the hospital the exact procedure which will be necessary. You should refer to Unit Z7 for details of how to deal with lesions caused by pressure sores.

Catheters and stoma care

Clients are likely to manage catheters and stoma care in their own home setting. Detailed instructions for changing a catheter and stoma appliances are in Unit X13, pages 247–249. The processes for changing stoma appliances are the same whether they are being changed by a carer or by the individual client. The same level of hygienic practice carried out by a health care worker must be observed by the individual client. Many people who need stoma care prefer to do it themselves if possible, as they find it embarrassing having someone else do it.

Diabetes

Clients and carers could undertake treatments and health care at home for other conditions, such as the control of diabetes. This depends on the type of diabetes. The treatment may consist of insulin injections which the client needs to take on a regular, prescribed basis. Insulin needs to be stored in a refrigerator and a supply of insulin syringes must be kept. It is essential to regularly check the supply to ensure the client does not run short. Diabetics have close contact with a specialist diabetic nurse at the local hospital and most diabetics are well-informed of the care they must provide to control their illness, and of the consequences of failure to do this. If you become aware that a client with diabetes is failing to follow the prescribed treatment, then you must contact an appropriate member of the care team, as the consequences can be extremely serious. Not all diabetes is controlled by the injection of insulin. Type II diabetes, which has its onset later in life, is controlled through diet rather than through medication. This will be indicated in the plan of care for the particular client.

Drainage or feeding tubes

Clients having ongoing treatment for a chronic condition may have drainage or feeding tubes or shunts in place. The sites of these will need to be maintained. Any client with an implanted appliance receives a comprehensive set of instructions about how to maintain it. This needs to be included in the care plan for the individual client and you must ensure that care is undertaken as identified in the instructions. If there is anything about which you are unclear, then you must refer to the appropriate specialist member of the care team.

Monitoring the clients

One of your key roles is to be aware of the potential for adverse reactions to particular treatments or procedures and to report these without delay to the appropriate care team member. Where lesions, sores or wounds are being dressed check for any signs of potential infection such as reddening, swelling or excessive heat in the area. You also need to report any pain, discomfort, nausea or clamminess, sweating or fever experienced by clients who are undertaking any health care procedures at home.

Safe disposal of waste

Most health care procedures leave some element of waste. This could be used dressings or empty syringes or emptied catheter bags. All waste of this nature must be disposed of appropriately. Waste should not simply be placed in a dustbin, it should be carefully bagged and ideally incinerated. If incineration is not possible then it must be placed in a sealed bag before disposal. Used syringes or other glass containers must never be placed in a dustbin. They should be put into a special sharps box, which you can get from your health centre, pharmacy or hospital. The sharps box is a rigid container which ensures that syringes do not put anyone at risk of a needle stick injury. Sharps boxes can be collected from the individual or arranged for collection through the local health centre.

Active knowledge

Identify a client for whom you provide support in undertaking health care. If you do not currently work in this way, use a relative or friend as your example.

Make a detailed list of:

- the medical/pharmaceutical supplies needed
- where they can be obtained
- where they would be stored
- how any waste will need to be disposed of.

Element Y4.2 | Support individuals in obtaining specimens and taking physical measurements

WHAT YOU NEED TO LEARN

- How to ensure that clients understand how to obtain specimens.
- How to identify the level of support clients need.

How to ensure that clients understand how to obtain specimens

Individuals managing their own medical conditions while remaining at home may need to take a variety of different measurements and to obtain specimens on a regular basis to monitor their current state of health.

Measurements of health can be:

- Blood pressure.
- Samples of urine.
- Blood samples.
- Peak flow readings.
- Height/weight ratio readings.

Some of these will be obtained by taking physical measurements and others through the analysis of specimens. Where specimens are required, for example, blood or urine samples, you should refer to Unit X13 (pages 252-257) for detailed instructions on how to obtain these.

Taking specimens

Any client who needs to take specimens as part of a monitoring process will also receive very specific instructions by the appropriate member of the care team about how the specimen should be obtained and how, if appropriate, it should be analysed. The commonest condition requiring an analysis of specimens at home is diabetes. However, there are many other conditions where clients may need to test their urine on a regular basis to ensure that their body systems are functioning correctly. Unit X13 (pages 252-254 and 255-257) contains detailed information on how to analyse both blood and urine.

Taking physical measurements

Physical measurements, such as blood pressure and peak flow, may be an important part of ongoing health care for a great many clients. High or low blood pressure is symptomatic of many medical conditions and can give an early warning about a client's health. Similarly, regular peak flow readings enable people with respiratory diseases, such as asthma, bronchitis or emphysema, to monitor lung function and identify any cause for concern about their health. It can also be useful in identifying any potential change or adaptation in the use of medication. Detailed information on the taking of physical measurements and the normal range of expected results from these is in Unit X13 (pages 256-263). It is essential you are aware of the normal range of measurements expected from your client and their condition. This information should be included in the plan of care and you will need to become familiar with it so that you can report any changes to the appropriate member of the care team.

How to identify the level of support clients need

Many clients become familiar and comfortable with routines involved in monitoring a long-term health condition. They often know in detail about their own condition and the factors likely to cause improvement or deterioration, and they can identify very quickly alterations in measurements and the steps which need to be taken. In such cases your role will be restricted to offering any support they feel will be useful to them. On the other hand, a client who is concerned or anxious about their condition, possibly because it is newly diagnosed or a new development for them, may not feel confident enough to recognise the implications of the measurements they are taking. So, you may need to have a more proactive role in monitoring the results of measurements and specimens in order to identify early indications of potential problems.

Through discussion and agreement with your client you need to establish the level of intervention and activity you should undertake and precisely the nature of your role. All the key principles concerning your level of involvement are the same if the health care procedures are being undertaken for the client by a carer. In this case you would take into account when deciding on your role the carer's level of familiarity with the procedures and their confidence in undertaking them. Many people who spend a long time caring for someone with a chronic medical condition develop a high level of expertise in obtaining the necessary specimens and measurements and interpreting them accurately. This should be recognised and acknowledged and your role limited to those areas the carer has identified as requiring support.

However many carers may feel concerned or have little confidence in their ability to maintain an extensive monitoring regime. Or they may be under extreme stress and find the level of care too much. In this case more extensive support may be welcomed and it may be appropriate for you to extend your role to provide some relief for the carer.

Active knowledge

Use an example of a client where you provide support for obtaining specimens, or use a friend or relative. Imagine you were leaving detailed instructions for a colleague who was to carry out your role. Make sure you have given enough information on the specimen/measurement to be obtained to enable them to undertake the task effectively.

Element Y4.3   Support individuals to administer the client's own medication

WHAT YOU NEED TO LEARN

- The regulations and procedures for administering medicines.
- The correct methods of administering medicines.
- How to ensure safe practice.

Regulations and procedures for administering medicines

The handling and use of medicines, drugs and poisons is governed by a series of Acts and Regulations of Parliament. The main ones are:

- The Medicines Act 1968 – which regulates the manufacture, distribution, import, export, sale and supply of medicinal products and medications.
- The Misuse of Drugs Act 1971 – which controls the availability of drugs which could be misused.
- The Misuse of Drugs Regulations 1985 – which enables specified health care professionals to possess, supply, prescribe and/or administer controlled drugs in their practice.

Misuse of Drugs Act

The Misuse of Drugs Act is designed to check and reduce the unlawful use of the kinds of drugs which could produce dependence, if they are misused. These drugs are referred to as **controlled drugs** and they include cocaine, diamorphine (heroin), methadone, levorphanol, morphine, opium, pethidine, amphetamine, dexamphetamine, dihydrocodeine injection, mephentermine, methylphenidate.

Controlled drugs may be prescribed by medical practitioners and registered dentists.

A prescription must clearly show:
- patient's name and address.
- date.
- signature of the prescriber.
- total quantity to be supplied in words or figures.

Every GP or dentist is required to keep a record of all the controlled drugs which are issued. Hospital pharmacies also have controls over the supply of controlled drugs and they are administered under strict control in a hospital setting. The regulations which govern the administration of controlled drugs are:

- A special cupboard must be used for storing controlled drugs and it should be clearly marked 'Controlled Drugs Cupboard'.
- The cupboard is locked and the key must be held by a state registered nurse or midwife who is in charge of the setting in which the drugs cupboard is kept.
- The supplies of controlled drugs can only be obtained on the signature of a medical practitioner and the drugs can only be administered to patients if there are written instructions from a medical practitioner.
- Each dose of controlled drugs administered must be entered into the special register with the date, the patient's name and the time the dose was given.
- The practitioner who gives the drugs and who checks the drugs must sign the entry.
- In most hospitals the doses must be checked by two people, one of whom should be a state registered nurse or midwife.
- The person checking should see the bottle from which the drug is taken and check the dose with the written prescription.
- All bottles or packages containing controlled drugs must be clearly labelled.
- The nurse or midwife in charge of the ward needs to check the controlled drugs and the accompanying records every seven days.

Medicines Act 1968

The Medicines Act covers all substances used as medical products or ingredients in medicinal products. This Act divides medicines into three categories:

1 **Prescription only medicine (POM)**. This includes controlled drugs, although they are subject to the additional regulations discussed above. These may be prescribed for a patient and subsequently supplied by a pharmacist.
2 **Pharmacy medicine (P)**. This is supplied by a pharmacist but can be dispensed without a prescription.
3 **General sale list (GSL)**. This need not be obtained through a pharmacist.

The prescription only medicines are those which can only be obtained from a GP or a dentist. They include the majority of medicines which are used to control or relieve the symptoms of a wide range of diseases. They may or may not include controlled drugs, but where they do they are subject to the regulations.

The pharmacy medicines will include items such as very strong painkillers, some forms of cold or flu remedies and a wide range of specialist preparations which are designed to alleviate the symptoms of common illnesses.

The general sale list includes mild painkillers and preparations designed to cause temporary alleviation of symptoms of some mild common illnesses, such as throat lozenges and those designed to clear congestion.

In hospital or nursing home settings all drugs are kept in lockable cupboards, freezers or fridges; and even portable drugs trolleys need to be lockable. Normally, in a home setting drugs are not required to be kept in locked containers or cupboards, however they should wherever possible be kept in a secure cupboard and must be kept out of the reach of children.

Doctors and dentists may administer or supply prescription only medicines directly to the patient. Nurses and other health care workers can only supply medicines under the direction of the doctor, however midwives may administer specified controlled drugs under certain conditions. When prescription drugs are supplied by a pharmacist they must be labelled and the name and the label must show the name of the patient, the date of the prescription, the name of the drug, the quantity in the container, the dosage to be taken, any specific instructions about how to take the medication, and the name of the pharmacist supplying the medication. If the drugs are supplied for someone who is in hospital the label is also likely to show their unit number, their date of birth and the name of their consultant.

The correct methods of administering medicines

Medicines on prescription will be accompanied by instructions for how they are to be taken. This could be a short instruction on the label or there may be more detailed instructions contained within the packaging of the medication. Instructions should be carefully read and followed. The label on the medication will also show the dosage. It is absolutely essential that the correct dose of a medicine is always taken. If a client is unwilling to take the required dose or wishes to stop taking the medicine prescribed because they feel it is having unwanted side-effects, then you should refer them to the appropriate member of the care team. They should be discouraged from stopping the medication until they have discussed the problems they are experiencing with their medical practitioner. It is likely that an alternative medication or a different dosage can be prescribed.

It is useful to keep a check on the levels of medication remaining in bottles or packages, particularly where clients are vulnerable or maintain their medication without support of a carer. If you have reason to suspect that a client has exceeded the prescribed dose you must take immediate action to seek medical assistance.

Dosage instruction will be on the label of the medication. Instructions are written now in English although some doctors and other health care professionals still write in the abbreviations, taken from instructions in Latin. The abbreviations you may occasionally see and should be aware of are:

Abbreviation	Latin	English
a.c.	Ante cibum	Before food
Ad lib.	Ad libitum	To the desired amount
b.d. or b.i.d.	Bis in die	Twice a day
c.	Cum	With
o.m.	Omni mane	Every morning
o.n.	Omni nocte	Every night
p.c.	Post cibum	After food
p.r.n.	Pro re nata	Whenever necessary
q.d.	Quaque die	Every day

Abbreviation	Latin	English
q.d.s.	Quarter die sumemdum	Four times daily
q.i.d.	Quarter in die	Four times a day
q.q.h.	Quarter quaque hora	Every four hours
R	Recipe	Take
s.o.s.	Si opus sit	If necessary
Stat.	Statim	At once
t.d.s.	Ter die sumendum	Three times a day
t.i.d.	Ter in die	Three times a day

Types of medication

All medications have specific ways of being taken or administered. These will be detailed in instructions with the medication but they are likely to follow a general pattern.

Oral medicines

Tablets or capsules are one of the commonest ways of taking medicines. Not only is the content of the tablet or capsule important, very often the structure and the materials used for the tablet or capsule will react only in certain environments. This often means that the coating on a capsule will dissolve or react in a particular way at a particular point in the digestive system, depending on the environment in that particular part of the system. This is why instructions are often given to take before food, take after food, or take with a hot or cold drink. These instructions are important to ensure that medicines are absorbed into the metabolism in the correct way.

Failure to follow instructions and take medicine in the way in which it has been prescribed can result in it being less effective or having different effects from those intended. If there are no specific instructions about taking tablets or capsules, then they should be taken at specific times each day to comply with the dosage requirements and are usually better swallowed with liquid, such as water, which is unlikely to have any effect. For clients who are managing their medication without the support of a carer, the pharmacist can supply boxes designed for keeping the required doses of medication, with each compartment within the box labelled with a specific day and number of doses. In this way it is easier for a client who may be likely to forget to keep track of which dose of their medication they have taken, and it reduces the risk of an accidental overdose. Most pharmacists will supply these boxes ready filled with the client's medication in the correct compartments at the correct times of each day.

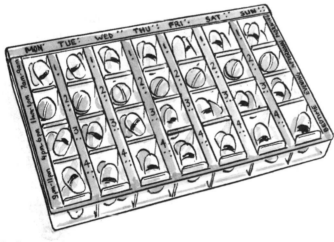

Medication box

Medication spoon and cup

Liquid is the other common form of oral medication. Many of these are in suspension and will need to be shaken before being taken. All oral liquid medicines come supplied with a 5ml plastic spoon, or with a small medicine cup which is marked at different dose levels, usually 2.5ml, 5ml and 10ml. Having the correct dose of medicine is important and the correct spoon must be used for administering medicines. A teaspoon from the kitchen drawer is not adequate as they differ in size and can result in either too small a quantity of medicine being ingested or an accidental overdose. You should encourage your client to wash the spoon after each dose of medicine so that it is ready to be used for the next dose.

Inhaled medicines

Those who have chronic respiratory conditions, such as asthma and chronic bronchitis, are likely to be prescribed inhalant medicines. These are usually in the form of an aerosol puff inhaler, though they can be in the form of a 'spinhaler', which works on the inhalation of breath. The principles of all of these inhaled medications is the same. The client needs to breathe out and then insert the inhaler in the mouth, take a puff and breathe inwards deeply for the required dosage. The dosage for all inhaled medicines is measured in the number of puffs.

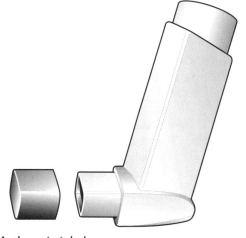

Asthmatic inhaler

There is a range of inhaled medicines available which serve different purposes. A client may be prescribed several different inhalers, some of which will be used to relieve symptoms and some of which will be for long-term daily use for preventive medication. It is important that the client understands that inhalers serve different purposes and that they must comply with the instructions for the number of times they need to be used.

Clients with severe respiratory conditions may also require a nebuliser. This is a machine which pumps air through a chamber containing the drug. A fine must of the drug then passes into the face mask worn by the client, who inhales the drug. This needs to be used when symptoms are severe.

Eye preparations

Clients are most likely to be prescribed eye drops or eye ointment at some time. The method of administration is largely the same. The lower eyelid should be pulled downwards and the correct number of drops inserted in the 'pocket'. Some clients find it easier to tip the head back slightly to achieve this, however it should not be necessary to tip the head right back, as it is almost impossible to self-administer eye drops if the head is tipped too far backwards. Eye ointment should be applied in a

Administering eye preparations

similar way. As with the administration of all medications, you should encourage the client to wash their hands both before and after administering eye drops or ointment.

Nasal preparations

Nasal medication is likely to be prescribed in one or two forms, either as drops or as spray. Nasal sprays should be applied by placing the spray bottle into the end of one nostril while holding the other nostril closed. The client should be encouraged to breath deeply through their nose while spraying. This process should then be repeated for the other nostril.

Nasal drops, in order to be effective, should be taken with the head tipped as far forward as possible. Ideally, the client should kneel on the floor and bend over until they are resting the top of their head on the floor and then apply the nasal drops. This way the drops have the most effect on the nasal passages. Alternatively, the same angle can be achieved by lying on a bed or across a stool with the head hanging over the edge. Unless otherwise advised, nasal drops should not be applied by tipping the head backwards. In this position the drops will run down the back of the client's throat and so will be less effective in the nasal area where they are intended. If a client is unable to achieve the optimum position for applying nasal drops because

Administering nasal preparations

of lack of flexibility or mobility, you may need to discuss this with the prescribing doctor. They may reconsider the type of preparation they have prescribed.

Administering ear drops

Ear drops

Ear drops are likely to be supplied in an applicator bottle, so there is no requirement to use a separate applicator for them. The required number of drops should be dropped into the ear, being careful not to insert the applicator inside the ear and risk causing damage. It may be helpful to keep the head tipped over slightly while inserting the drops and for a few seconds afterwards to ensure they have run inside the ear as intended. Unless directed otherwise by the prescribing doctor, it is not generally necessary or advisable to insert cotton wool into the ear after administering eardrops.

Vaginal and rectal preparations

Clients may wish to administer these themselves and it will depend on their degree of mobility and flexibility whether they are able to achieve this. If vaginal and rectal preparations are being self-administered by somebody who has the required level of fitness and mobility, then the simplest administration involves placing one foot on a chair or low stool and inserting the preparation. This is likely to be in pessary form or it may be a cream or vaginal spray. A similar procedure is likely to be effective for the application of pessaries or ointment into the rectal passage. It is more likely that vaginal and rectal preparations will be administered by a carer, in which case the optimum positions for achieving this are likely to be:

- For vaginal preparations, the client should lie on a bed with their legs bent at the knees and slightly apart to allow easy access to the vagina. Clients should be encouraged to relax whilst the preparation is inserted.

Administering vaginal preparations

- For rectal preparations, the client should lie on one side with their knees drawn up towards their chest. This allows the most straightforward access for inserting preparations into the rectal passage.

Administering rectal preparations

It is essential that proper hand washing is undertaken by the client or the carer administering these preparations both before and after administration. If these are being administered by a carer then gloves should be worn. Surgical gloves for carers use at home can be obtained from the pharmacy.

Topical preparations

Where clients have been prescribed specific ointments or creams for particular areas, these should be applied in the dosage and with the frequency prescribed. They should be applied with clean hands washed prior to application and gently spread over the affected area. They should not be rubbed in

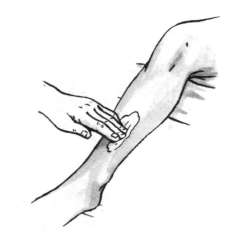

Applying topical preparations

unless specifically instructed. Most ointments or creams are designed to be gradually absorbed and rubbing may cause damage or infection in the affected area.

How to ensure safe practice

Adverse reactions and side-effects

Many drugs have side-effects, so the prescribing doctor should explain the possibility of the effects on a client taking the medication. Also, a leaflet identifying the potential side-effects is likely to accompany the medication. The client may find the side-effects acceptable if they are counterbalanced by the benefits of taking the medication, and they may tolerate some of the milder side-effects that medication can cause, for example dry mouth, drowsiness, etc. However, if side-effects cause serious disruption to a client's daily life or make the client feel worse than not taking the medication, then they must contact the prescribing doctor and discuss the difficulties they are having. They should be discouraged from simply stopping the medication.

It is important to recognise the difference between side-effects and adverse reactions. Side-effects are relatively minor and do not interfere seriously with a client's general state of health. An adverse reaction to a medication can indicate an allergy or other serious side-effect. This could take the form of swelling of the hands or face, blotchiness of the skin, reddening of the skin in any part of the body, sweating or clamminess, shivering or becoming faint. If any of these conditions occur you must immediately summon medical assistance as adverse or allergic reactions to medication can be extremely rapid and extremely serious, even fatal in some cases. One other thing you should consider when you observe a client showing serious symptoms is that they could be reacting to medication equipment, particularly that which includes latex or rubber, for example gloves and some clinical tubing. The effects of an allergic reaction to latex can be extremely serious and require immediate medical attention.

Your role

Your support can be a key factor in ensuring that clients are able to manage their medical conditions safely and effectively in the community. It may also make it possible for carers to feel more confident and able to continue caring for their friend or relative knowing that support and advice is readily available to them. A central part of your role will be to ensure that there is regular liaison and contact with other members of the care team, particularly those responsible for prescribing and those who are responsible for maintaining health services to clients in the community, such as district nurses and other members of the primary care team.

Active knowledge

Check the procedures in your workplace for the administration of medication.

Make sure that you know:

- who are the people who have access to controlled drugs
- who is allowed to check drugs
- how many people have to check controlled drugs
- where drugs are kept.

Unit test

1   What are the main Acts which govern drug administration?

2   What essential preparations must be made before administering any drugs or medication?

3   Why is it important to follow the instructions on how drugs should be taken?

4   What are the essentials of safe and effective drug storage in the home?

5   How does this differ from drugs storage in a hospital or nursing home?

6   How should blood samples be obtained?

7   How should urine samples be obtained?

8   What are the likely testing methods which clients at home would use?

9   Why is it important to regularly check the levels of medication remaining in bottles or packaging?

10 Who are the key members of the care team in respect of maintaining a drug regime for clients at home?

Unit Z7

Contribute to the movement and handling of individuals to maximise their physical comfort

This unit is primarily concerned with those individuals with whom you work who are most dependent upon your assistance. The level of assistance they need can vary from needing help to get out of a chair to being completely dependent on others to move them, to turn them over and to alter their position in any way, for example if they are unconscious or paralysed. When individuals require this degree of care it is essential that they are moved and handled in the most sensitive and safe way. This is also vital for you as a worker – the commonest causes of people being unable to continue to work in health or care are that they suffer injuries, usually back injuries, from lifting and moving individuals. It is possible to minimise the risk to both you and the individuals for whom you provide care by following the correct procedures and using the right equipment.

The first element is about preparing individuals for being moved. In the second element you will need to learn about how to carry out the move and to ensure that you know the way to carry it out correctly and safely, and offer all the support which is needed to the individual. The final element deals with pressure sores, which are painful, debilitating and a serious potential risk of infection for an individual. Understanding the causes of pressure sores and methods of avoiding them is very important – they take so long to heal that steps should be taken to prevent them, as far as possible.

Element Z7.1 Prepare individuals and environments for moving and handling

WHAT YOU NEED TO LEARN

* How to assess risks.
* How to encourage independence.

How to assess risks

As you may remember from Unit CU1 your employer has a responsibility under health and safety legislation to examine and assess all procedures which take place in your working environment involving risk. All risks must be noted, assessed and steps taken to minimise them as far as possible. Your employer is required to provide adequate equipment for such tasks as moving and handling individuals who require assistance.

The risk assessments your employer carries out are, however, general risks for your work environment. Each time *you* move or lift any individual, you too must make an assessment of the risks involved in carrying out that particular manoeuvre. Even if you have moved this individual every day for the past six months, you should still assess the risks on each occasion before you put anything into practice. No two lifts are ever the same – there are always some factors that are different. These factors could be to do with the individual and his or her mood or health on that particular day, they could be about the environment, or they could be about you and your current physical condition.

You should run through the same checklist each time before you carry out any activity which involves you in physically moving a person from one place to another. A suggested checklist is shown below. You may need to adapt it to fit your own place of work and the circumstances in which you work.

Checklist

1	Is individual weight-bearing?	Yes	☐
		No	☐
2	Is individual unsteady?	Yes	☐
		No	☐
3	What is the general level of mobility?	Good	☐
		Poor	☐
4 (a)	What is the individual's weight?	_____	
(b)	What is the individual's height?	_____	
(c)	How many people does this lift require?	_____	
	(Work this out on the scale devised by your workplace.)		
7	What lifting equipment is required?	Hoist	☐
		Sling	☐
		Trapeze	☐
		Transfer board	☐
8	Is equipment available?	Yes	☐
		No	☐
9	If not, is there a safe alternative?	Yes	☐
		No	☐
10	Are the required number of people available?	Yes	☐
		No	☐
11	What is the purpose of the move?	_____	
12	Can this be achieved?	Yes	☐
		No	☐

A checklist for assessing risks before moving an individual

You also need to consider carefully the environment when you are assessing risk. You should take into account all of the following factors:

- Is the floor surface safe? Are there wet or slippery patches?
- Are you wearing appropriate clothing – low-heeled shoes, tunic or dress which has enough room to stretch and reach?
- Is the immediate area clear of items that may cause a trip or a fall, or items which could cause injury following a fall?
- Is all the equipment, both to carry out the lift and the place to which the individual is to be moved, ready?
- Does the individual have privacy and can his or her dignity be maintained during the move?
- Is there anyone you could ask for help, for example a porter or member of the ambulance service?

Working with the individual to be moved

The individual who is going to be moved is the key person to be actively involved, as far as possible, in decisions about the best way to carry out the move. Unless the person concerned is unconscious or semi-conscious or so confused as to be unable to contribute to any discussion about the best way to proceed, then it is important that you discuss with the person the way that he or she would feel most comfortable with. Many people who have a long-standing disability will be very experienced in how to deal with it. They are the best people to ask for advice as they know the most effective ways for them to be lifted, avoiding pain and discomfort as far as possible.

Tell me how you prefer to be lifted Mr Jackson.

Active knowledge

Your workplace probably uses an assessment form similar to the one on the next page. Find the one your workplace uses and make sure you know how to fill it in. It may be similar to the checklist on page 346.

ASSESSMENT FORM FOR PATIENTS WHO REQUIRE
MANUAL HANDLING

Name: _Mr K_   Weight: _8 stone 8 lbs_

                                            Height: _5.3_

Any relevant physical disabilities: _Congenital foot deformity_

Patient's mental ability and comprehension: _Sometimes aggressive_

History of falls?   Yes   No   _when being dealt with_

	Yes	No
		✓

Any equipment used by patient

The hoist must be used at all times when moving and handling due to his inability to bear weight.

Handling constraints

Skin   _Dry_

Pain   _occasionally on movement._

Infusions   –

Catheters, etc.   –

Other   –

Abilities in following situations

Walking   _Unable – needs wheelchair to mobilise_

Standing   _Unable to bear weight – needs hoist_

Toiletting   _Use toiletting sling and hoist_

Transferring in/out of bed   _Use of hoist and quick fit deluxe sling_

Transferring in/out bath   _Use of ambulift bathchair_

TO BE COMPLETED WITHIN 24 HOURS OF ADMISSION AND THE RELEVANT
INFORMATION WRITTEN INTO THE CARE PLAN. UPDATE THE ASSESSMENT
FORM AND CARE PLAN AS NECESSARY.

Assessor's signature _____

Grade _Officer in charge_

Date _1.5.98_

A risk assessment form for manual handling

Remember

Your first port of call for advice on how to carry out a lift, after you have checked out the safety aspect and the risk factors, should be the individual himself or herself.

Once you have carried out all of the necessary assessments, you should explain carefully to the individual exactly what you intend to do and what his or her role is in contributing to the effectiveness and safety of the move. This will vary according to the person's ability, but nonetheless most individuals will be able to participate to some extent. Even where individuals are unconscious or appear to have no understanding of what is going on, you should still explain exactly what you are doing and why you are doing it and what the effects will be. We have a limited understanding of what a state of unconsciousness means to the person experiencing it. *Every* individual has the same right to be treated with dignity and respect and to have procedures explained rather than simply having things done to him or her by care workers who believe that 'they know best'. Each stage of the proposed move should be explained in detail before it is carried out, and it is essential to obtain the individual's consent before you move or handle him or her in any way. If you move an individual without his or her consent this could be construed as an assault. So you should always be sure that you are carrying out the individual's wishes before you commence any move.

Keys to good practice

- Assess risks to the individual and to yourself before starting any lift or move.
- Ask the individual about the best way of moving, or assisting, him or her.
- Explain the procedure at each stage, even where it may not be obvious that you are understood.
- Explain how the equipment operates.
- Check that you have the agreement of the person you are moving.
- Stop immediately if the individual does not wish you to continue – you may not move a person without his or her consent.

Your clothing

The type of clothing you wear when you are moving individuals is very important. It can make the difference between carrying out a procedure safely and doing it with difficulty and possible risk of injury. Footwear should be supportive and flat, with soles that grip firmly.

Recent recommendations in respect of uniforms are that dresses should have a pleat in the skirt and a similar pleat in the sleeves. These are to allow you to move so that you do not find that your own movements are restricted by your clothing, possibly forcing you to lift in an awkward way. It may be necessary, for example, to place one knee on a bed in certain types of manoevres. This is impossible if you are wearing a dress with a straight skirt. Even if not totally impossible, it can be very difficult to manage at the same time as maintaining dignity – yours, not the client's!

If you are in a situation where you do a great deal of lifting and handling, it is a good idea to wear trousers with a tunic top, which also has plenty of room in the sleeves and shoulders to allow free movement. Your employer should have carried out a risk assessment and ensured that the clothing that is provided for you to wear is appropriate and complies with current best practice and requirements in terms of lifting and handling.

Equipment

In your work you may use many different types of equipment, including several types of lifting and moving equipment. It is important that you check every time you use a piece of equipment that it is safe and that it is fit for use for that particular individual.

If you do find equipment has become worn, damaged or appears to be unsafe in any way, you should immediately stop using it, take it out of service and report it to your supervisor. You must do this even if it means having to change your handling assessment for the individual you were about to move. Under no circumstances is it acceptable to take a risk with equipment which may be faulty. It is better that the

Work clothing should allow for free movement when handling individuals.

individual waits a little longer for a move or is moved in an alternative way rather than being exposed to risks from potentially unsafe equipment.

Make sure that you have read the instruction manual for each piece of equipment you use. It should give you a safety checklist – make sure you follow it.

Active knowledge

Find out the procedure in your workplace for reporting faulty equipment. Check whether there is a file or a book where you need to record the fault. You may only need to make a verbal report, or you may have to enter the details of the fault into a computer. Make sure that you know what the correct procedure is.

How to encourage independence

There are many ways in which an individual can assist and co-operate with care workers who are lifting or moving him or her. It is important that this is encouraged and that individuals are not made to feel as though they are simply being transported from place to place like 'a piece of meat'. Co-operation from the individual is invaluable, both for maintaining his or her own independence and for assisting those who have to carry out the lift. For example, you may be transferring an individual from a bed to a wheelchair. The first part of the process – getting to the edge of the bed and sitting on it – may well be possible for the individual to accomplish if he or she follows a correct set of instructions, rather than having to be moved by carers.

Any independence which can be achieved is vitally important in terms of the individual's self-esteem and sense of well-being. A person may be able to transfer himself or herself from a wheelchair to a chair, to a car seat or into bed, either by the use of transfer boards or by simply being able to use sufficient upper body strength to slide across from chair to wheelchair, and vice versa, once the arm is removed.

You may wish to employ techniques such as bridging when you need to give an individual a bed pan. Rather than having to lift the person manually, he or she can be encouraged, with some simple instructions, to bend the knees and raise the bottom to allow the bed pan to be slid underneath him or her (see pages 356–357).

Techniques like this involve the active co-operation of the individual. Obviously they are not suitable for use where individuals are unable to co-operate, either because of their state of consciousness or because they have almost total paralysis. Some individuals may not be able to co-operate for emotional reasons – they may lack the confidence to make any moves for themselves because of fear of falling or fear of pain or discomfort. Where the plan of care has identified that the individual is capable of co-operation in moving and handling, this should be gently encouraged and the reasons for his or her reluctance to co-operate should be explored with the individual.

Good preparation is the key to a successful lift or transfer. Where the individual and the worker are working together, there is likely to be the maximum safety and minimum risk, pain and discomfort.

ement Z7.2 Assist individuals to move from one position to another

WHAT YOU NEED TO LEARN

- Equipment for moving and handling.
- Methods for manual moving and handling.
- Recording and passing on information.

Equipment for moving and handling

There is a wide range of equipment available and technological advances are being made continuously in the field of medical equipment. Regardless of the individual products and improvements which may be made to them, lifting and handling equipment broadly falls into the following categories:

- hoists, slings and other equipment, which move the full weight of an individual
- equipment designed to assist in a move and to take some of the weight of individual, such as transfer boards
- equipment designed to assist the individual to help himself or herself, such as lifting handles positioned above a bed to allow individuals to pull themselves up. This category also includes grab handles, raised toilet seats, and lifting seat chairs.

Depending on the setting in which you work, you may have to use some or all of the equipment shown below. If you work with individuals in their own homes, your access to equipment may be more limited, although there is now an extensive range of equipment that can be used very effectively within an individual's own home, often removing the need for residential care.

Using equipment

Each piece of equipment will have an instruction manual. You must read this and be sure that you follow the instructions for its use. There are some general points about how to use particular types of equipment, but you must know how to use the particular type of equipment in your workplace.

Hoists

- Make sure that you use the correct sling for the hoist and for the weight of the client.
- Most slings are colour-coded. Check that you have the right one for the weight of the client.
- Ensure that the seams on the hoist are facing outwards, as they can be rough and can easily damage the skin.
- Only attempt to manoeuvre a hoist using the steering handles – do not try to move it with the jib, as it can overbalance.
- Place the sling around or under the client. Lower the bed to its lowest position. *Then* lift the client. It is only necessary to have a small clearance from the bed or chair – there is no need to raise the client a great distance.

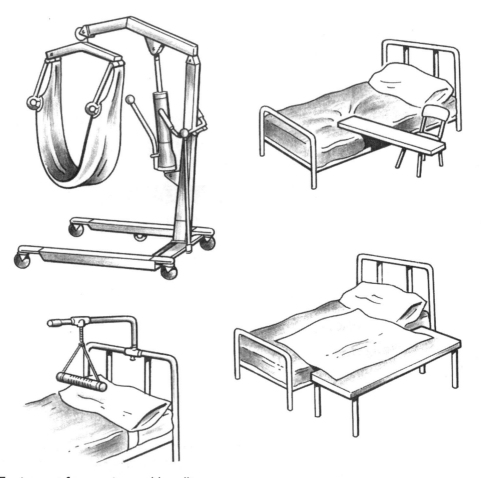

Equipment for moving and handling

You cannot learn to use a hoist safely by reading a book – you must familiarise yourself with the hoists in your workplace and ask to be shown how to operate them.

Transfer boards/sheets

These require at least two people standing on opposite sides of the bed. They allow people to be moved from bed to trolley and vice versa. They can be used regardless of the level of consciousness of the individual.

They all work on the same principles. They are made of friction-free material which is placed half under the person and half under the sheet he or she is lying on. One worker then pulls and the other pushes. The sheet, complete with person, then slides easily from one to the other. There are several types available: 'Pat-slide', 'Easy-glide' and 'Easy-slide' are amongst the most common.

Slideboards

The slideboard is a small board placed between a bed and a chair or wheelchair. It is designed for use by clients who are able to be quite active in the transfer and only require assistance. The board allows the client to slide from bed to chair, and vice versa, with some assistance in steadying and some encouragement.

Monkey pole or lifting handle

This is a handle which is fixed above a bed, and swings from a metal frame. It is designed to allow people to assist themselves. They have to pull on the bar to lift the upper part of the body off the bed. This can enable people to help themselves to sit up, turn over and change position without having to call for assistance.

When you are assessing how to assist a person to move and which equipment to use, you need to consider:

* the potential risks
* what the person can do to help himself or herself to move, and what he or she cannot do – remember that it is important to encourage as much independence as possible
* what the person knows from experience to be the best method, or the method he or she prefers.

If the person's preference conflicts with safe practice, you should tactfully explain this, pointing out the potential risks and suggesting the best method. Reassure the person, if necessary. If there is still a problem, you will need to tell your supervisor immediately.

Remember

You should never move anyone without his or her agreement.

Active knowledge

Investigate the equipment available in your workplace for moving and handling. Make sure you know where different items are kept and how they work. Make notes to refer to when necessary.

Methods for manual moving and handling

There are very few situations in which manual lifting should be carried out. Unless it is an emergency or a life-threatening situation, there should be no need to move anyone without the correct equipment. Manual handling should only be carried out in situations which do not involve lifting all, or most, of a person's weight.

This means that even shoulder lifts are no longer considered to be safe. There is no safe weight limit for lifting, so the only workplaces where lifting should now take place are units caring for babies and small children. Even there, it is important to ensure that risk assessments are carried out to avoid the likelihood of injury.

If you need to move someone manually in order to change his or her position or to provide assistance, you should follow the principles of effective manual moving and handling:

- The procedures should be well-planned and assessed in advance. Technique rather than strength is what is important.
- The procedure should be comfortable and safe for the individual – creating confidence that being moved is not something to be anxious about and that he or she can relax and co-operate with the procedure.
- The procedure should be safe for the workers carrying it out. A worker who is injured during a badly planned or executed transfer or move is likely in turn to injure the individual he or she is attempting to move. Similarly, an individual who is injured during a move is likely to cause an injury to those who are moving him or her.

Remember
The interests and safety of the individual and the workers are so closely linked that you must consider them both together.

Active knowledge
Find out what the rules for manual handling are in your workplace. Make a note of them for your portfolio.

Team work
Most moving procedures, whether manual or assisted, are carried out by more than one person. If you are to work successfully as part of a team, you need to follow some simple rules:

- Decide who is going to 'shout'.
- That person will check that everyone is ready.
- He or she will say '1-2-3 lift' or '1-2-3 move' or (depending on familiarity with American TV) 'on my count 1-2-3'.
- Everyone must follow the count of the person who shouts.

Transfer
If you are assisting an individual to transfer from a bed or chair to a wheelchair, this can be done with one person providing assistance to steady the person as he or she uses the transfer board, providing that there are no complicating factors such as an individual who is particularly heavy or tall or who has serious disabilities. In that case, they should be moved using a hoist or a turntable.

Rolling or turning
If you need to roll or turn someone who is unable to assist, either because of paralysis, unconsciousness, seriously illness or confusion, you should:

- always carry this out with at least two workers

- roll the person using a transfer sheet or board, or use the bottom sheet to roll the person onto his or her side
- support the person with pillows or packing.

When the person needs to be turned again, remove the pillows, lower him or her onto the back and repeat the other way.

Overcoming 'pyjama-induced paralysis'

One of the key factors in a safe handling policy is to encourage people to help themselves. There is a great temptation for people to believe that they can do far less than they are capable of. This is often encouraged by staff who find it quicker and easier to do things rather than wait for people to help themselves.

If you encourage individuals to make their own way out of bed, for example, then they would need to follow the simple set of instructions shown in the diagram below.

Instructions for getting out of bed

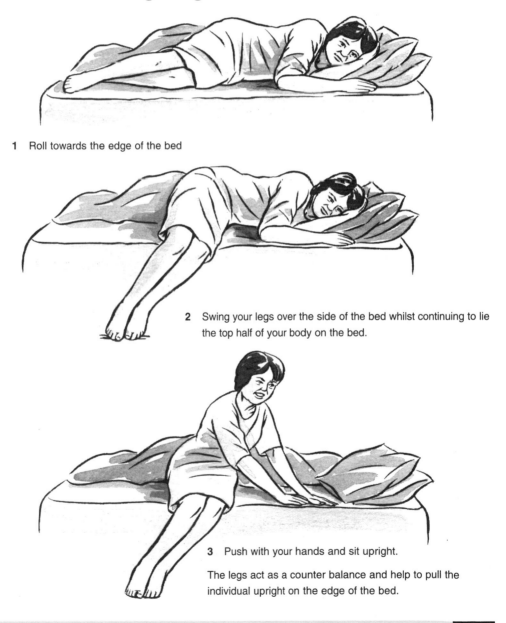

1 Roll towards the edge of the bed

2 Swing your legs over the side of the bed whilst continuing to lie the top half of your body on the bed.

3 Push with your hands and sit upright.

The legs act as a counter balance and help to pull the individual upright on the edge of the bed.

You may wish to encourage an individual to roll over in the bed, rather than having to be manually rolled by a care worker. This could be necessary to allow changing of bedding, a bed bath or to change clothes. The instructions for achieving this are quite simple, and can be carried out by all but the most severely ill or disabled individuals, as shown in the diagram below.

Instructions for rolling over in bed

1 Turn to face the direction in which you are rolling

2 Bend the leg of the other side and keep your foot flat on the bed

3 Reach across your body with the opposite arm. This uses the counter weight of moving the arm across the upper body to assist with the movement of achieving a roll.

If you need to get someone to raise his or her bottom from the bed in order to give a bedpan, or to prepare for rolling or turning (known as bridging), then you should ask the person to follow the instructions below.

Instructions for bridging

1 Bend both knees

2 Keep your feet flat on the bed and push up on your feet and hands, so that your bottom is raised.

Even in community settings, where previously it was unusual for carers to be using equipment, it is now much more common to see domiciliary services carrying out risk assessments for their carers and support workers, and insisting that unless equipment like hoists are made available it is not possible to continue to provide a service without putting the care workers at risk of injury.

Recording and passing on information

Information about the most effective ways of moving someone, or techniques which have proved effective in encouraging a person to assist himself or herself, should be recorded in the plan of care.

The plan of care should contain information on the moving needs of each individual, and it is important that these are followed. However, you may notice a change in behaviour or response. This could be:

- a person finding movement more painful
- a loss of confidence in a particular technique
- an improvement in how much assistance a person can give
- a changed reaction following being moved.

Any of these changes, or anything else you notice, are significant and must be reported to your supervisor. Any changes may be indications of overall changes in the person's condition and should never be ignored.

The information you record should be:

- clear
- easily understood
- a good description of the person's needs.

NURSING CARE PLAN

Date	No.	PATIENT'S NURSING NEEDS/PROBLEMS AND CAUSES OF PROBLEMS (N.B. Physiological, Psychological, Social and Family Problems)	Objectives	Nursing Instructions	Review On/By	Date Resolved
1.5.98	8	Mobility:			8.5.98	
					15.5.98	
		Due to suffering from	To prevent	a) Encourage Mr. K to be as	22.5.98	
		a congenital foot	complications of	independent as possible.	29.5.98	
		deformity, Mr. K	immobility and	b) Always give clear, concise	5.6.98	
		is unable to bear weight	maintain Mr. K's	instructions when moving and	12.6.98	
		and needs the hoist	safety as far	handling to gain client's full	19.6.98	
		to be used when	as is reasonably	co-operation.	26.6.98	
		moving and handling	practicable.	c) The hoist must be used at all	3.7.98	
				times with either the Quickfit	10.7.98	
				deluxe sling or the toiletting sling –	17.7.98	
				depending upon circumstances.	24.7.98	
				d) Ensure safe practice maintained	31.7.98	
				when moving and handling client.	7.8.98	
				e) Observe for any problems and		
				reassess appropriately.		
				f) Review problem weekly.		

An example of notes on an individual's mobility in his plan of care

Case study

Shireen is the carer for Mrs G, who is 80. Shireen needs to move Mrs G from a bed into a chair. Mrs G is only able to assist a little as she has very painful joints and is unable to bear weight. She weighs 16 stones (101.6 kg).

1 What would you expect to see in Mrs G's care plan in respect of moving procedure? Give reasons.
2 What factors should Shireen take into account before starting to move Mrs G?
3 What should Shireen say to her?

When you are carrying out a moving procedure, it may be necessary to move items of furniture so that you can work safely. Whether you are working in a care setting or in an individual's own home, it is important that furniture is returned to its original position afterwards, so the individual can easily locate personal items in their usual places and feel reassured by the familiar surroundings.

Element Z7.3 — Assist individuals to prevent and minimise the adverse effects of pressure

WHAT YOU NEED TO LEARN

- How pressure sores can happen.
- How to prevent pressure sores.
- How to treat pressure sores.

How pressure sores can happen

Pressure sores are the result of an interruption to the blood supply, which causes the tissue in that particular area to break down. The interruption to the blood supply is caused by various types of pressure, exerted in different ways, but the effect is the same – it causes the tissue in the affected area to die and to degenerate into a sore. Every one of us would get pressure sores if we were not able to move regularly each night whilst we were asleep. For individuals who are unable to change their own position regularly, whether that is lying down or sitting in a wheelchair, the pressure can result in a sore. There are some areas which are particularly vulnerable:

- back of the head
- shoulders
- sacrum (the bottom of the back)
- buttocks
- backs of legs and calves
- heels.

The diagram on page 359 shows the most common sites of pressure sores.

Compression

There are several ways in which pressure sores are caused, but one of the commonest is compression, where the weight of a part of the skeleton presses through the flesh and skin against a relatively hard surface, such as a bed or a chair.

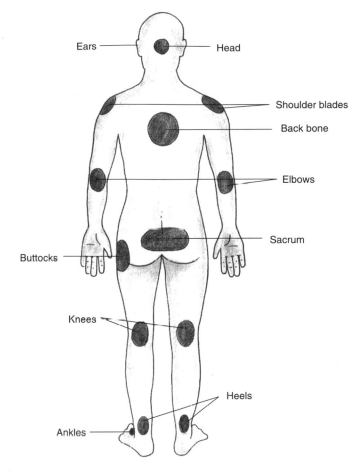

Common sites of pressure sores

This compression causes the blood supply to be cut off to that area of tissue, which then dies and degenerates into a sore. This is commonly seen in people who are confined to a chair or a wheelchair. These sores develop on the buttocks because of the weight of their skeleton on their buttocks and against the chair. It also happens where people are confined to bed and are not able to move their position regularly and here other pressure points, such as shoulder blades, elbows, the back of the head and the heels, are all likely to suffer sores as a result of compression.

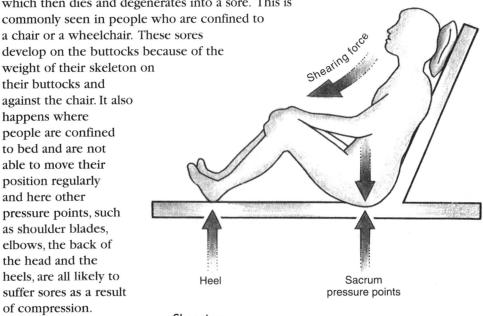

Shearing

Shearing

Another way in which pressure sores can be caused is called shearing. This is when an individual is left in a half lying, propped up position in bed and the downward pressure, which gradually slides him or her down in bed, drags the skin across the surface of the bed and grazes it, damaging the small blood vessels (see the diagram on page 359). These pressure sores are commonly seen on the sacrum (bottom of the back) and the heels.

Friction

Pressure sores can also be caused by friction when two areas rub against each other. This can often be seen with rumpled nightclothes or when crumbs or other debris are left in the bed, or when there is a wet area around the buttocks and sacrum caused by incontinence.

Assessing risk of pressure sores

There has been considerable research into the care of pressure areas and several different assessment scales have been developed to judge the people who are most likely to be at risk from pressure sores and for whom preventive action can be taken at an early stage. The commonest assessment score is called the Norton Score (shown below). The lower the score a person has, the greater the chance of developing sores.

The Norton Score for pressure sore risk assessment

Physical condition		Mental state		Activity		Mobility		Incontinence	
Good	4	Alert	4	Ambulant	4	Full	4	Not	4
Fair	3	Apathetic	3	Walks with help	3	Slightly limited	3	Occasionally	3
Poor	2	Confused	2	Chair-bound	2	Very limited	2	Usually urine	2
Very bad	1	Stuporous	1	Bedfast	1	Immobile	1	Double	1

How to prevent pressure sores

It is always better to work on preventing pressure sores, rather than having to treat them once they have already developed. The best way to ensure that pressure sores do not develop is to keep people as active as possible, so that they are less likely to remain in one position. It is also important for individuals who are confined to bed or a chair to have a special mattress or cushion (such as a Roho cushion), which is designed to distribute weight more evenly so that the downward pressure from the skeleton is evenly spread and does not concentrate pressure in one area.

You should also ensure that individuals eat a good balanced diet with a significant protein content, as protein is required for cell renewal – this is a significant way of reducing the risk of tissue breakdown and the development of pressure sores.

It is vital to ensure that clients who are incontinent are never left sitting in wet clothes or incontinence pads which have become soaked. The effect of wet, urine-soaked clothing on skin is to render it very likely to develop sores in the pressure areas.

Sheepskin or artificial sheepskin is another useful way of preventing the development of pressure sores. This tends to be used particularly on heels where sheepskin booties are used. It has the effect of relieving the pressure and spreading the weight of the joint more easily. Some individuals are comfortable with an artificial sheepskin under their shoulders or their buttocks or to sit on one in their wheelchair. Increasingly, these are now being replaced by the more technologically advanced forms of mattresses and cushions which use a combination of specially devised air pockets or, in some cases, water to spread the pressure more evenly across areas of the body.

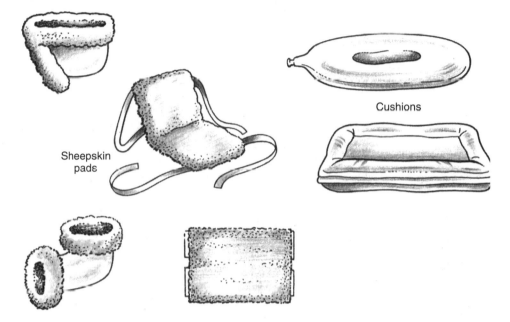

Sheepskin pads

Cushions

Aids to prevent pressure sores

Reporting and recording

Just as the plans for moving and handling should be in a person's care plan, so should information on any pressure area care. There should be notes about any sore places which may be developing, and any changes in the skin, such as reddening or grazes, must be reported at once. Skin becomes very fragile as people get older, and it can be easily injured. It is these apparently minor skin injuries which often develop into sores that can take months to heal.

Keys to good practice
- Move people regularly.
- Turn an unconscious or paralysed person every two hours.
- Use aids such as a Roho cushion, a special mattress or fleece pads.
- Check that the person's diet contains adequate protein.
- Change wet clothes and bedclothes immediately.
- Report any changes you notice in a person's skin.

Active knowledge

Try to sit in a propped up position without moving for as long as possible without altering your position. You will find that before very long you will begin to feel uncomfortable, and after a fairly short period of time it is painful to remain without moving. Imagine how that feels for somebody who is totally unable to move.

How to treat pressure sores

Pressure sore treatments are constantly being developed and improved, so you should seek advice from a qualified medical or nursing practitioner about the latest developments. Current practice is to use dressings which will allow moist healing of the sore. At one time it was believed that pressure sores should be dried and were best allowed to heal in their dry state. There is now little argument that all wounds including pressure sores heal far better in a warm, moist environment.

There are various dressings available which adhere very closely to the skin and will allow oxygen through but no moisture, enabling the wound to retain any moisture to assist healing. As long as a wound is not infected, these types of dressings, such as Op-site, appear to achieve quite good results.

Did you know?

The benefits of moist wound healing were first demonstrated almost 30 years ago However, in a recent study carried out in a large hospital, less than 50 per cent of the people questioned knew about the procedure.

An individual's care plan will identify the treatment regime which needs to be used for his or her particular pressure sores, and the treatment will be supervised by a qualified practitioner. Treatments today will not include practices such as massaging the area or washing with soap and water, which were common some years ago. There is no evidence to support the theory that massaging the area will play any part in healing the sore and, in fact, it is likely to aggravate the situation.

The key to effective treatment of pressure sores is to attempt, where possible, to increase the general health of the individual – people who are malnourished or debilitated because of an illness or long periods of neglect are unlikely to heal pressure sores effectively until their general state of health has been considerably improved. The care plan should include arrangements for the individual to receive, if possible, a high protein, high carbohydrate diet.

Pressure sores are extremely unpleasant, but they are avoidable. Good practice and good levels of care can prevent pressure sores from occurring and can speed the healing of any which existed before the individual received care.

Did you know?

When the Egyptian pyramids were investigated, evidence was found that some of the people mummified within the tombs had suffered with pressure sores. This makes it very clear that the problem of pressure sores has always existed.

Unit test

1 Name three factors you would take into account when assessing the risk of carrying out a lift.

2 In what sort of circumstances would you consider asking an individual to move him or herself across the bed?

3 What type of clothing is most suitable for carrying out lifting?

4 What steps should you take if you have concerns about the safety of equipment?

5 What are the three categories of lifting and handling equipment?

6 Describe how the following are used:

   a a hoist
   b a transfer board or sheet
   c a slideboard
   d a monkey pole.

7 What are the three principles of effective manual handling?

8 Describe the procedures for:

   a bridging
   b rolling or turning
   c transfer.

9 Why should information and changes regarding mobility be recorded and passed on?

10 Which areas are most likely to suffer from pressure sores?

11 Name two ways of relieving pressure sores.

12 What are the best ways of preventing an individual from developing pressure sores?

13 Which individuals are likely to be the most vulnerable to pressure sores?

Unit Z8 Support individuals when they are distressed

Most people get distressed at some point in their life. It can be brought on by a range of circumstances, such as major traumas and disasters or minor incidents. People can become distressed by being in a difficult or stressful situation for a long period of time or by being in an environment where they find it difficult to cope or adjust. As a worker in health or care services you may find yourself supporting clients, carers or your colleagues in situations where they are stressed for a wide variety of reasons. Whatever the reasons or the effects of their distress, it is important you are able to offer support and comfort and to reduce and alleviate the distress wherever possible.

Element Z8.1 Contribute to the prevention of individuals' distress

WHAT YOU NEED TO LEARN

- The reasons why people become distressed.
- How to identify when someone is becoming distressed.
- What you can do to prevent distress.

Reasons why people become distressed

The causes of distress are varied and differ from individual to individual. What distresses one person will not distress another. A situation which reduces one person to a fit of sobbing is shrugged off by another. Be careful you do not confuse the causes of distress with the reasons for distress. The causes can be a range of external factors, however the reasons are a much deeper, psychological influence which affects the way different people respond in different circumstances. All of us have a broadly similar process of emotional development, but as each of us is an individual who has grown and developed in different circumstances, then it is inevitable that the overall effects will be different for each of us. However, psychologists have established that there are some basic forms of behaviour which can be broadly applied to explain the reasons why people behave in the way they do.

Inborn or environment?

There has always been much debate in the psychological world about whether our emotional responses are inborn or learnt from our environment. The most likely and feasible explanation is that they are a mixture of the two. Most psychologists agree that there is an inborn response. The evidence for this comes from the study of very young babies in respect of their responses to pain and loss of support. However as we grow and develop we learn to respond to other different stimuli, in different ways. It is important you recognise that although these may be the basic stimuli which humans respond to, what you have to deal with when working in care is what humans respond with. In other words, what people do in response to an emotion expressing distress.

Psychologists have identified the crying response in young babies as the earliest human response. This response is extremely useful for babies because it alerts a mother to her baby's needs. It is the means by which the baby attracts its mother's attention to have its needs met. Thus crying provides an effective appeal for help – and it is a response many people continue into adulthood.

Crying alerts a mother to her baby's needs

Babies appear to demonstrate three different emotional responses: fear, rage and love. These are recognised as the basic building blocks on which the range of complex human emotions are subsequently built. These emotional responses are part of basic human behaviour, and are found in the emotions of older children, adolescents and adults. As people gain more experience of life and are exposed to a wider range of influences, the emotions become complex and more difficult to deal with.

Your role is not that of a psychologist or a psychiatrist, however it is important that you are aware of the way in which human beings develop emotionally and that you have a broad understanding of how the complex emotions that you are likely to deal with in your work setting has come about.

Did you know?

That psychologists and psychiatrists dealing with people suffering from mental health problems or disturbed emotional behaviour are able to identify the three basic emotional responses of rage, fear and love, plus a fourth category of depression which has never been identified in babies. There is a view which connects the emotional responses with the 'direction' of the behaviour. Much of human behaviour can be said to have a clear direction towards, away from, against or inwards. This is identified as rage directed against the cause of the frustration, fear causes people to move away from the object of their fear, love draws people towards the object of their affection and depression turns all behaviour inwards against oneself.

Physical effects of strong emotions

There are definite and measurable **physical effects** caused by strong and powerful emotional responses. It is useful to be aware of these psychical effects of emotion as they can often be an early indicator of a potentially highly charged or dangerous situation. The physical effects of strong emotion can be:

- Pupils dilate, the eyelids open wider than usual, and the eyes protrude.
- Speed and strength of the heart beat is increased.
- Blood pressure is increased and blood is forced outwards towards the surface of the body. This is clearly noticeable in flushing of the face and neck.
- The hair can stand up causing goose pimples.
- Breathing patterns will change, this can be either faster or slower.
- The lung function alters to allow up to 25 per cent more oxygen to be absorbed.
- More sweat is produced – this can be often identified as a 'cold sweat'.
- The salivary glands are inhibited – the dry mouth feeling.
- Digestive system is affected – the gastric fluids are reduced and blood is withdrawn from the digestive organs.
- Increase in adrenaline – reinforces all effects and increases blood clotting.

How people respond to strong emotions

This reaction of psychical responses to strong emotions is said to prepare humans for 'fight or flight'. This is thought to be a basic human response to being under threat, in which the body physically prepares us to fight or run away. There are other very noticeable effects in people in a highly emotional state. They will often have what appears to be increased energy. For example, they don't speak, they shout, they don't sit or stand still, they run or walk about, they will slam doors and possibly throw furniture or articles around. In these cases the additional energy and strength which results from powerful emotions can be extremely valuable and essential in preserving life. There are many stories about people performing heroic feats of strength when in the most severe emotional situations, as in the case of a house fire or an accident or some other life-threatening situation, where amazing feats of strength or endurance are often reported. Another apparent effect of strong emotional responses is a temporary lessening of the awareness of pain. This often occurs when people act regardless of severe injury, as on the battlefield or in an accident or other emergency, and it is only when the immediate threat has passed that they become aware of their injuries.

We can accept children having tantrums in public, but not adults

How people control strong emotions

In growing and developing most of us learn to control these powerful emotions. While the sight of a two-year-old lying on the floor in a supermarket kicking and screaming is not uncommon, it is one which is accepted as normal behaviour for a child of that age. On the other hand, it is not normal for an adult to do the same thing, however much we may want to on occasions! We don't behave in this way in public because we have been **socialised** into behaving in a way which is seen as acceptable and the **norm** within society. However, some people do find it beneficial and therapeutic to have a two-year-old tantrum in the privacy of their homes, to get relief from the rage they feel.

Active knowledge

Think about how you deal with strong and powerful emotions. Think of the occasions when: a) you have felt strong and powerful emotions but managed to keep them under control and not show your distress publicly and when you have experienced strong and powerful emotions which you have shown publicly.

Try to identify the difference in circumstances and the factors which caused the two different responses.

Becoming distressed

Most people most of the time behave within the accepted norms of society. However, on occasions the emotions may become too powerful or the normal control which people exercise over their emotional feelings may relax, resulting in a display of emotion which is recognised as distress. People can become distressed because of a wide range of causes and these can be the trigger for the underlying emotional response. It is impossible to list the number of causes of distress. They are as varied as the number of individuals, however there are some common causes of distress which can be identified and it is helpful for you to be aware of situations and circumstances which can act as triggers. People commonly become distressed when:

- They are informed of the death or serious illness of someone close to them.
- They receive bad or worrying news.
- There are problems with a relationship which is important to them.
- They become stressed through an overload of work or family pressures.
- They have serious issues which worry them, such as money, problems at work, problems with the family.

Everyone has a breaking point

- They are reacting to the behaviour of others towards them.
- They are responding to something that they have heard, seen or read in the media.
- They are in an environment which they find frustrating or restricting.
- They are in an environment which they find intensely irritating, e.g. it is noisy or they are unable to find any personal space.
- They are deprived of information and are fearful.
- They have full information about a situation and they remain fearful of it.
- They are anxious about a forthcoming event.
- They are unable to achieve the objectives which they have set themselves.

These are some of the more common triggers for distress. Clearly there are many others which you may come across depending on the setting in which you work.

Active knowledge

Identify six potential triggers for distress which relate to your own work setting.

How to identify when someone is becoming distressed

When you have a close working knowledge of a client's behaviour over a period of time it becomes easy to identify when they are becoming distressed. You will find that you have become well 'tuned-in' to their behaviour and can recognise the small signs that indicate a change in mood. However, you will not always know your clients so well. Also you may not only be dealing with distress in your client, you may also have to deal with it in a carer or a work colleague. There are some general indications that an individual is becoming distressed which you can use in order to take immediate action. You are most likely to notice:

- Changes in voice – it may be raised or at a higher pitch than usual.
- Changes in facial expression – this could be scowling, crying, snarling.
- Changes in eyes – pupils could be dilated and eyes open wider.
- Body language would demonstrate agitation and people may adopt an aggressive stance leaning forward with fists clenched.
- The face and neck are likely to be reddened.
- There may be excessive sweating.
- People's breathing patterns may change and they may breathe faster than normal.

You are likely to notice a significant change in normal behaviour when someone is becoming distressed. For example, someone who is normally talkative becomes quiet and someone who is normally quiet starts to shout and talk very quickly. Other examples are somebody who is normally lively and moves about changes to sitting still, rigid and unmoving, whereas somebody who is normally relaxed and still may start to walk around waving their arms. You need to be aware of changes in normal behaviour even if they are far less extreme than the examples given. Sometimes a subtle change in behaviour can indicate someone is becoming distressed, and you are far more likely to notice subtle changes in clients, colleagues or carers who you know well and have worked with over a period of time.

Case study

L is an elderly lady who has been in a residential home for the past three years. Like most of the residents she has her own chair and she likes to sit in a corner of the main lounge. L is normally bright and chatty and talks happily with the staff and other residents. As with many residential settings there is a regular introduction of new residents who usually managed to adapt into the setting extremely well. However, the previous week a new resident was admitted, who, like L, was very talkative and friendly, however she would continue to talk at great length and quite loudly for long periods of time. For the first couple of days L appeared to join in and respond to the new lady's conversation, but staff noticed she gradually responded less and less and appeared to be becoming more unhappy. One morning a staff member went into the lounge where the new lady was talking as usual and noticed that L was sitting in her usual corner with her head down but sitting bolt upright in her chair with her arms bent and fists clenched, and breathing faster than usual. When the staff member crouched down to talk to L she noticed she had bright red cheeks.

1 What conclusions would you reach about L's state of mind from looking at the physical indications?

2 What would be the next step you would take?

3 What are the potential responses from L?

4 What would be a satisfactory outcome?

What you can do to prevent distress

If somebody becomes distressed as the result of an outside event, such as the death of a close friend or relative or because they have received some other bad news, there is probably little you can do to prevent it. However, the way you handle the situation can often reduce the distress. If distress is being caused by factors in the immediate environment, then you may be able to act to prevent extreme distress and the reaction to it. It may not be immediately obvious what the cause is and you may need to encourage the individual to talk about what is upsetting, worrying or concerning them. You must be careful not to pressurise individuals to discuss more than want to. At first it is probably better to confine any discussion to the nature and cause of the distress. For example, you might wish to try the approach of, 'You seem angry/upset, do you want to talk … ?' Or 'Do you feel able to tell me…?' You must always give people the choice as to whether or not they wish to discuss their distress with you. You might even offer them a choice of talking to another member of staff or a relative or friend, if they appear to be unwilling to discuss their worries with you.

Jane, do you want to talk about why you're feeling so upset

Carers need to give clients the chance to decide whether they want them to help

Your acknowledgement and recognition of their distress may be sufficient for some people, in that they may be able to resolve their distress themselves if they know that they can obtain additional support from you if they need it.

Stress

Much of the distress people suffer comes from being stressed by many of the pressures in their lives. People are said to be suffering from stress when worries and pressures of everyday living reach a point where they cannot continue to function normally. What makes people stressed depends on the individual. There are some widely recognised 'stressful situations' such as:

There are various situations that can cause people to become stressed

But there are many other factors people respond to as individuals. Some people cope with huge workloads and demands on their time that most of us couldn't cope with. They still appear to manage and in many cases to thrive very happily with what is an extremely stressful situation. While the responses to stress are individual, so are, to a large extent, the effects. Again there are effects of stress which are likely to be commonly experienced by most people. These are likely to include:

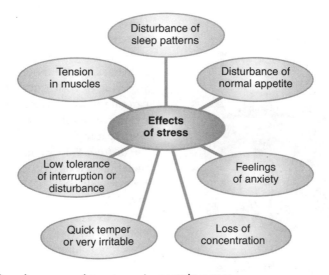

People respond to stress in certain ways

If people are under stress or suffering from any of the symptoms associated with stress, then they are likely to be distressed and to need support. Stress is dealt with in range of ways. Depending on the underlying forces, it can be dealt with by physical means, that is, an immediate removal from the cause of the stress, such as taking a break from work or from caring for a difficult, very ill or demanding relative. Or it can be dealt with by medical means, such as the prescribing of drugs which will reduce the physical effects of stress on the body and can alter mood and responses to the stressful factors. Another way would be to undertake a programme of relaxation exercises in order to physically relax the body.

Therapeutic means of dealing with stress

The therapeutic way of dealing with stress involves supporting sufferers to talk about it and discuss their stress in order to identify for themselves coping strategies for how they will continue their lives at the same time as managing the stress.

In many cases stress is addressed by a combination of all three approaches. Individuals may be shown how to carry out relaxation exercises, they may be recommended to take a few weeks away from work, they may be prescribed some mild mood-altering drugs and attend a course of counselling sessions. This combination approach is likely to be the most effective in terms of reducing serious and incapacitating stress.

Not all stress however is so serious and incapacitating as to prevent people from undertaking their normal day-to-day activities. However it is something which affects most people at some point in their lives and there are some simple guidelines which can help to relieve stress which has not reached a seriously incapacitating stage.

Relaxation

A simple way of encouraging the mind and body to relax is to practice abdominal breathing. It is generally accepted that people who are anxious and under stress breathe in a shallow way from their chest, rather than more slowly and deeply from their abdomen as in the case of those who are more relaxed. Practising abdominal breathing is an excellent way of relieving stress and anxiety and encouraging calmness and relaxation. It is a simple technique to learn and to practise and is useful to offer as advice to someone who is feeling distressed, anxious or stressed.

Relaxation breathing exercise

1 Place one hand on your abdomen just beneath your rib cage.

2 Inhale slowly and deeply through your nose feeling the air going as deep as possible into your lungs. You will know if you are breathing from your abdomen as your hand will rise. The chest will only move slightly. If your chest moves or rises while your abdomen falls or does not move, then you have not done it correctly and should try again. It is important your abdomen rises as you breath in.

3 Pause when you have breathed in. Then exhale slowly through your nose or mouth. Exhale fully and allow your whole body to relax and become loose and limp.

whole body to relax and become loose and limp.

4 Repeat.

In order to feel calm and relaxed you should try 10 slow full abdominal breaths. Keep your breathing smooth and regular.

For maximum benefit do 5 minutes of continuous abdominal breathing every

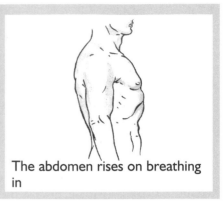

The abdomen rises on breathing in

This is also a useful exercise to undertake at any time when you feel the onset of distress, stress or anxiety.

Another simple but useful way of encouraging people to relax in order to minimise their distress is to use a very simple technique of progressive muscle relaxation. This is very useful for people who become very tense as a result of stress or anxiety, which can result in muscle tightness in the shoulders and neck or tension headaches, backaches and tightness around the jaw and eyes. Before commencing progressive muscle relaxation it is important to create the conditions for getting the most out of this.

Progressive muscle relaxation exercises

1 Choose a quiet setting where you will be undisturbed.

2 Play soothing gentle music in the background if you wish.

3 Practise on an empty stomach before meals.

4 Loosen any tight clothing and take off shoes, contact lens, watches, glasses, etc.

5 Assume a comfortable position. Your entire body should be supported, lying down on a sofa or bed, provided you don't fall asleep, or sitting in a reclining chair.

6 Once sitting or lying comfortably in a quiet and relaxing atmosphere you should:

- Start by taking 3 abdominal breaths, exhaling slowly each time.

- Clench your fists. Hold tightly for 7 to 10 seconds, then release for 15 to 20 seconds.

- Tighten your biceps by drawing your forearms up towards your shoulders. Hold as before for 7 to 10 seconds, then release for 15 to 20 seconds.

- Tighten your triceps (the muscles on the undersides of your upper arms) by extending your arms out straight and locking your elbows. Hold as before and then relax.

- Tense the muscles around your eyes by clenching your eyelids tightly shut. Hold and then relax.

- Tense your jaw muscles by opening your mouth widely to stretch the muscles around the hinges of your jaw. Hold and then relax.

- Tighten the muscles in the back of your neck by pulling your head back as if you were going to touch your head on your back. Hold and then relax.

- Tighten your shoulders by raising them towards your ears. Hold and then relax.

- Tense the muscles around your shoulder blades by pushing your shoulder blades back as if you were going to touch them together. Hold and then relax.

- Tighten the muscles of your chest by taking deep inner breaths. Hold for 10 seconds and then release slowly.

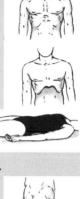

- Tense your stomach muscles by sucking your stomach in. Hold and then release.

- Tighten your lower back by arching it up. Hold and then relax.

- Tighten your buttocks by pulling them together. Hold and then relax.

- Squeeze the muscles in your thighs down to your knees. Hold and then relax.

- Tighten your calf muscles by pulling your toes towards you. Hold and then relax.

- Tighten your feet by curling your toes downwards. Hold and them relax.

- Scan your body to see if you can find any particular area which remains tense. If there is a tense area simply repeat the tense–relax cycles for that group of muscles.

You then need to imagine a wave of relaxation spreading throughout your body, starting at your head and penetrating every muscle group all the way to your toes. The entire muscle relaxation sequence is likely to take you between 20 and 30 minutes. You should enjoy the relaxing process and making that time for yourself.

For maximum benefit the exercises should be done on a daily basis, however they can be used in response to having been in a particularly tense or stressful situation.

The effects of your interactions

You need to be aware of the ways in which you are using your own communication skills to interact with somebody who is distressed. While you are taking into account their body language and the clues of non-verbal communication, you will need to be conscious of the messages your own non-verbal communication is providing to them. You need to demonstrate openness with an open welcoming position: standing or sitting where you are, not encroaching on an individual's personal space as this often heightens distress and tension, and making eye contact in a way which demonstrates you are willing to listen.

It is important you approach any individual who is distressed and displaying anger or great excitement in a calm and non-threatening way. This is likely to minimise the risks to the client, to any other people in the immediate area and to yourself. If at any point you identify the development of risk to your personal safety then you should immediately leave the immediate setting and summon help at once. No one is able to deal with every situation with which they are faced, and you may feel that a particular situation is beyond your capability. This is nothing to be ashamed of. The ability to know your own limitations is of far greater value and demonstrates a higher degree of maturity and self-awareness than a foolhardy person who takes risks beyond their skill and ability. You can contact other members of your team or other professionals with the experience to deal with the situation. You should never hesitate to summon help or assistance when you feel unsure in dealing with a client in distress.

A distressed client can become aggressive in some circumstances. If you observe a client becoming aggressive and potentially violent, as in the case of someone changing from crying or expressing anger to shouting or throwing things, then you should immediately summon help. As referred to earlier in this unit, anger is not always directed at others; it can be turned inwards to be directed against the individual themselves. You may be faced with a distressed, hurt and angry individual who makes it clear that they intend to harm themselves. In this case you have a responsibility to take immediate action in order to protect the individual. You must also advise the individual that you will have to take steps to protect them and attempt to stop them from harming themselves. Never agree to help somebody harm themselves or to allow them to knowingly harm themselves.

Element Z8.2   Support individuals in times of distress

WHAT YOU NEED TO LEARN

- How to identify the support individuals need.
- How to offer support.
- How others' distress can affect you.

How to identify the support individuals need

When dealing with somebody who is distressed, one of the first things to do is decide the support and assistance which you will offer. People in distress can benefit from a wide range of different forms of support.

Deciding the level of support

Sometimes all someone needs is having their hand held to enable them to go on coping with their distress themselves. You should therefore always establish with the individual themselves the extent of help they need and what you can usefully provide. Too much support can sometimes be as damaging and as unhelpful as too little or none at all. The risks of providing too much support are:

- People will feel that they are disempowered and are no longer able to help or support themselves. This is not good for people's self-esteem or self-confidence.
- People may feel you have interfered and they have been forced to reveal more about themselves and their personal life than they would have wished to.
- People may become over-dependent on you for help and support and it may reduce their own ability to manage for themselves.

Offering too little or no help can have the following effects:

- People feel they are isolated and there is nobody who cares for them or is interested in their problems.
- People feel they are unworthy and unlikeable individuals.
- People get very angry and frustrated at the apparent lack of care or interest from the rest of the world.

The level of help and support that you should offer is always best decided along with the individuals themselves. Wherever possible, this should be done through a process of discussion. Questions should be open-ended and clear, and designed to establish the level of support which is being sought, such as 'I can see that you are very upset, would it help to talk to me about it?' 'I can see that you are very upset, would you like me to find you someone to talk to?'

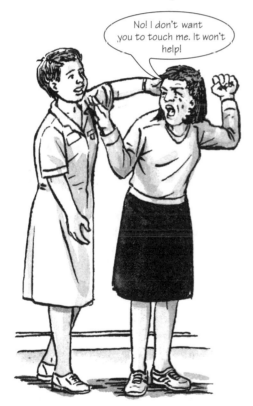

No! I don't want you to touch me. It won't help!

Trying to comfort someone in distress may not always be welcome

There may be circumstances in which it is not possible to discuss the level of intervention with an individual. This can be because they are extremely agitated or angry or are in an exceedingly distressed state and unable to hold a calm conversation, or it may be because they are threatening to harm themselves or others. In these circumstances you will need to judge how best to intervene. You could act in the same way as you would in dealing with a client who was calmer. For example, to put your arm around or your hand on the shoulder of somebody who is sobbing and clearly very upset is likely to result in them either shaking you off and walking away or turning around for a hug.

You may have to shout to get the attention of someone who is very angry and who is shouting themselves. This is likely to be most effective if it is also accompanied by gesticulation. As a general rule, most people's anger will subside in a relatively short period of time. Provided no one else is being threatened, it is probably most effective to allow somebody who is very angry to calm down before you attempt to talk to them. If, however, you feel that their anger represents a threat to themselves or others, then you may need to intervene by shouting and gesticulating in order to stop the tirade and shouting, and attempt to divert their anger into something more constructive. Short, clear commands are likely to be most effective, such as, 'STOP shouting Gary. Come with me into the other room and we will discuss it. Gary, come with me NOW.'

Where you have been able to identify that distress is caused through anxiety or fear or lack of knowledge, then the support which you can offer may be to provide necessary information or access to information. It is important that you can identify at an early stage what is causing someone's distress, so you are able to reassure them that you will be able to assist and to relieve the level of distress they are presently suffering.

Sometimes carers need to calm angry clients by shouting them down with constructive suggestions

Case study

P arrived for her regular weekly visit to F, an elderly lady who lives with her daughter and son-in-law. When P arrived she found F in tears. She asked what was the matter and F explained that she was due to be moved to a new day centre next week because the one which she had attended for the last five years was being temporarily closed due to shortage of funds. She said she was very afraid as she had never been there before and did not know what to expect. P's response was to say, 'Right, if that is all that's worrying you, get your coat, come and get in the car and I will take you down there right away so you can have a look round and meet people. That's a problem which is easily solved.' F looked at her and began to smile and said, 'Would you really take me, that would be wonderful.'

This case study serves to illustrate the importance of identifying and responding appropriately to whatever is causing someone's distress. In the case study above it was clear that F's distress was being caused by anxiety and worry about attending an unknown day centre. It would have been quite inappropriate for P to sit down and to start using a range of skills to ask F questions such as, 'Why do you think you are so concerned about going somewhere new?' 'Can you think of other situations like this you have been in before?', and so on. This was a situation in which an elderly lady was being caused a high degree of unnecessary distress and worry by a problem which could be easily solved by some practical action taken very quickly.

Broadly, the support you are likely to identify will probably fall into one of three categories.

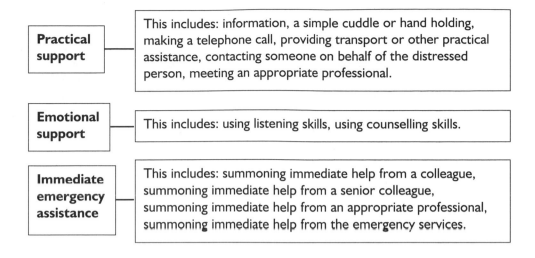

Practical support	This includes: information, a simple cuddle or hand holding, making a telephone call, providing transport or other practical assistance, contacting someone on behalf of the distressed person, meeting an appropriate professional.
Emotional support	This includes: using listening skills, using counselling skills.
Immediate emergency assistance	This includes: summoning immediate help from a colleague, summoning immediate help from a senior colleague, summoning immediate help from an appropriate professional, summoning immediate help from the emergency services.

How to offer support

The types of support you might need to give are identified in the table above. You will need to ensure that you have access to sources of information and appropriate support that can be offered in particular circumstances. There are specialist organisations which will offer particular support for those who are bereaved, for those who are experiencing relationship difficulties or for those who are feeling depressed and may harm themselves. You should be sure that you have access to all the relevant contact details and are fully aware of the range of organisations which can offer specialist support.

Active knowledge

Check the information stored in your workplace on sources of specialist support for people in distress. If there is an inadequate coverage of appropriate sources of support or if information is out of date, raise the issue with your line manager and offer to update and broaden the information available.

Using communication skills

When you identify the support most appropriate for you to talk to the individual about, you will need to use the communication skills you learned in Unit CL1, and may have learned in Unit CL2. If you have undertaken a training programme in counselling skills you will find this invaluable in improving the level of support you are able to offer to people in distress. A training course in counselling skills will not make you a counsellor, however it will provide you with the basic skills to use in your own work setting to assist people day to day. A therapeutic treatment programme could be offered through a qualified counsellor.

In a training programme for counselling skills you will learn how to develop further the communication skills you already have. You will learn how to begin and establish a supportive relationship by using skills such as setting boundaries, active listening, paraphrasing, mirroring and reflecting, challenging, facilitating, and ending a relationship. Such training can be extremely valuable for people working in any health or care setting. It will enable you to build on and develop the basic communication skills you already have and will enable you to offer a more comprehensive level of service to your clients.

Counselling should not be undertaken by anyone who has not been adequately trained and had the opportunity for supervised practise in the development of their counselling practice. However, this is not to underestimate the support you will be able to provide by effectively using good communication skills and a genuine empathy and care for your clients in order to encourage them to express how they feel about what is causing them worry, anxiety and distress.

If you feel the situation is going beyond the support you can usefully offer, then it is important you recognise this and make an appropriate referral to someone who has the necessary skills to offer that assistance.

You are likely to find there are many occasions when referral is not necessary. These situations can be resolved and the distress significantly reduced by the client talking constructively to someone who has good listening skills or simply by being offered clear, accurate practical advice and information. Or it can simply be a matter of knowing that somebody cares enough about them to sit and hold their hand for half and hour or to give them a big hug!

How distress can affect you

It can be very upsetting to deal with somebody who is displaying very strong and powerful emotions. People's stories or experiences can be so moving and distressing that you may feel very grateful, or perhaps even guilty, for your own happier circumstances. On the other hand, if you are having difficulties yourself, you could find these echoed or raised to the surface by dealing with a client in distress. If this occurs it is important to talk to your supervisor or line manager as soon as possible and arrange for someone else to continue to offer support to the client.

Feeling concerned, upset or even angry after a particularly emotional experience with a client is normal. You should not feel that such a response is in any way a reflection on the quality of your work or your ability as a care worker. After such an experience most people are likely to continue to think about it for some time. One of the best ways to deal with this is to discuss it with your line manager or supervisor or with a close friend or relative, always bearing in mind the principles of confidentiality, making sure you never compromise the right of a client to have information about them kept confidential. After a period of time you either succeed in putting the incident out of your mind or find it is interfering with your work, either with the client or with other clients. If this happens, there are plenty of sources of help available to you, both within and outside your workplace. Talk to your line manager or supervisor for advice on gaining access to any help you need.

The distress of others, whether in the form of anger or sadness or worry or anxiety, will always be distressing for the person who works with them. However, if you are able to develop your skills and knowledge so that you can identify distress, contribute towards reducing it and offer effective help and support to those who are experiencing it, then you are making a useful and meaningful contribution to the provision of quality care.

Unit test

1. What are the inborn emotions which psychologists have identified in work with young babies?

2. What are the physical indications of strong emotion?

3. What are the physical effects of strong emotions?

4. What are the key factors which would indicate that someone is becoming distressed?

5. What steps could you take that could reduce someone's distress?

6. What are the effects of muscle relaxation and abdominal breathing?

7. What are the major causes and effects of stress?

8. What types of help and support are you likely to be able to offer to someone in distress?

9. What action should be taken if someone threatens to harm themselves?

10. What action should be taken if someone becomes a threat to others?

Unit Z12 Contribute to the management of client continence

This unit is about supporting clients and assisting them to manage their own continence. This is an extremely important role for any care worker, as so many people suffer from incontinence, to varying degrees. The vast majority can be helped and their condition improved. This unit should enable you to identify the contribution you can make, regardless of your work role.

Element Z12.1 Encourage clients to maintain continence

WHAT YOU NEED TO LEARN

- What continence is.
- The most appropriate ways to assist clients to maintain continence.

What continence is

Continence is the ability to hold onto or retain the body's waste products, urine and faeces, until you are in a convenient and appropriate place to dispose of them. For many people, of all ages, this is a problem, that is, they suffer from incontinence, the inability to retain the body's waste products. It is often assumed that incontinence is a problem of old age. However, this is by no means the case, as significant numbers of younger people suffer from an inability to maintain continence, for a variety of reasons. Understanding the best ways of supporting people in maintaining continence is to understand how the process works and how the body functions in processing the waste products of eating and drinking.

How the bladder works

Surplus water and waste products in the body are filtered through the kidneys, which produce urine continuously. This passes down the ureters, the tubes which run from the kidneys to the bladder, and remains in the bladder until we are able to release the urine and empty the bladder. An average human being produces two to three pints of urine every day. This will vary depending on the amount eaten and drunk and how much the individual has perspired.

As the bladder fills with urine it gradually expands. It has an outlet valve known as a sphincter which holds the bladder closed and stops urine from leaking from the bladder during the process of filling. The pelvic floor has strong muscles and ligaments which support the bladder and keep it in position. The same muscles also support the rectum and bowels, holding them in the correct position, and in women

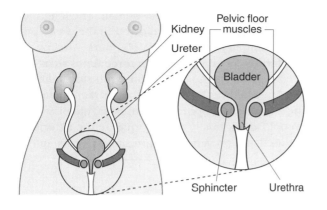

The bladder

they also support the womb. As the bladder begins to fill messages are sent to the brain indicating a need to empty it. Generally, these messages begin to be sent to the brain when the bladder is about half full, so there is plenty of time to find any appropriate opportunity to empty it. The capacity of an individual's bladder will vary, largely depending on how they have been 'trained'. Those who empty their bladders frequently tend to have bladders with less capacity. Those who need to empty their bladders less frequently tend to have bladders with a larger capacity and can allow them to fill to a greater extent before emptying them. On average, people need to empty their bladders between four and eight times each day. The process of emptying the bladder involves the relaxation of the sphincter muscles and the contraction of the muscles contained in the wall of the bladder. This then squeezes the urine out down the urethra and the bladder is then emptied. The muscles in the walls of the bladder relax to allow the bladder to expand and begin the process of refilling.

How the bowel works

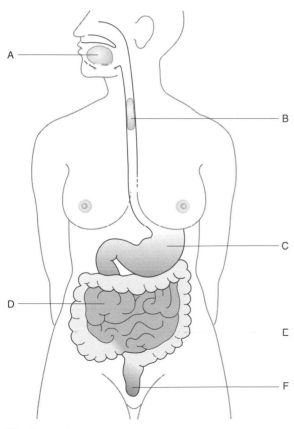

The bowel

A Food is chewed using the teeth and the tongue. At this point the first of the digestive enzymes are added to the food, as is saliva.

B Food is swallowed down to the oesophagus, the tube which transfers food from the mouth to the stomach. This tube constantly expands and contracts in waves of muscular activity known as peristalsis.

C Food arrives in the stomach, where the digestive process begins. Food is broken down through enzyme activity and the stomach's acids. Food remains for one to three hours in the stomach.

D By this stage food is completely liquidised and travels through the small intestine for two to six hours. Throughout this process nutrients are absorbed into the body.

E Food then moves into the large intestine where it remains for 12 to 48 hours. By this time most of the nutrients and water content have been absorbed and the remains solidify.

F The solidified waste products which are not required by the body are stored in the rectum as stools/faeces until they are expelled through the anus by the muscular contractions of the rectum.

How the digestive system operates varies from person to person. The length of time food takes to move through the system from being swallowed to the waste products being expelled as faeces can vary from 20 hours to over 100 hours. Also, people open their bowels at different intervals, anything between three times a day and three times a week is considered normal. As the rectum fills with stools the messages which are sent to the brain identify whether the contents of the rectum are solid, liquid (diarrhoea) or wind. The anus has two sphincter muscles which keep the anus closed and prevents leakage. People are normally able to squeeze the external sphincter to keep the rectum closed and prevent the expulsion of faeces until an appropriate time and place.

What can go wrong

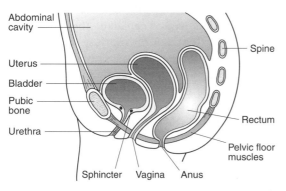

Female pelvic organs

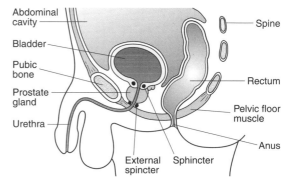

Male pelvic organs

Many things can go wrong with the system of expelling waste products. Any of these can cause incontinence. Somebody who is incontinent is unable to retain their urine or faeces until they are in an appropriate place, and may leak urine or faeces involuntarily. There are many different potential causes of urinary and faecal incontinence. Neither is a natural or normal part of the ageing process, so it is important, as a care worker, you do not subscribe to the view that incontinence is natural or normal for older clients. Most types of incontinence can be treated and possibly cured, certainly improved. However, before you can encourage clients to take steps to improve their condition, you need to understand what the possible causes are and their effects.

Causes of urinary incontinence

Urinary incontinence is the loss of control of the bladder in expelling urine. Some causes of urinary incontinence are temporary and can be managed with simple treatment. These are conditions such as:

- urinary tract infections
- vaginal infection
- constipation
- effects of medication – usually diuretics.

All these conditions are temporary and the incontinence should improve when the conditions have cleared up. A urinary tract infection means that the infection will cause irritation to the bladder and the urethra so that urine will be expelled more frequently than otherwise. It is important to seek medical advice and obtain antibiotic medication if necessary. Also it is important to maintain a large input of bland fluid, such as water and barley water, to allow the urinary system to 'flush' itself clear.

Constipation can cause urinary incontinence. This is because an overfull rectum causes pressure on the bladder which causes urine to be expelled. If a client is taking diuretic medication this can cause excessive amounts of urine to be processed through the body, which the bladder is unable to cope with. All these conditions should improve when the causes are removed.

Other causes of urinary incontinence which are more permanent in nature are:

- Damage or weakness of the pelvic floor muscles, which are important for maintaining the position of the bladder.
- Weakness of the sphincter muscles, which hold the neck of the bladder closed.
- Overactive or unstable bladder muscles, which cause the bladder to contract involuntarily and without warning.
- A blocked urethra (this is more normal in men and results from a large prostrate gland).
- Hormone imbalance (this is more usual in women).
- Neurological disorders such as multiple sclerosis or spinal cord injury.
- Lack of mobility.

Types of urinary incontinence

The conditions outlined above can cause different types of urinary incontinence. These affect people in different ways and cause different types of problems.

Urge incontinence

People with urge incontinence are unable to control urination long enough to reach the toilet in time. As soon as they have a strong desire to urinate they lose urine and are unable to 'hold on' until they reach a toilet.

Stress incontinence

This is the commonest type of incontinence among women. It is extremely common in women who have given birth because the muscles of the pelvic floor have been stretched during labour and the birth process. This can mean that the bladder is no longer held in its correct position by the muscles of the pelvic floor and that the sphincter muscles which control the neck and outlet of the bladder are no longer able to hold it shut because of its change in position. Stress incontinence means that urine is leaked when coughing, laughing, sneezing or undertaking any exercise or activity, sometimes even by walking and often by running or other physical exercise.

Mixed incontinence

This is when people suffer a mixture of both stress and urge incontinence. This is most commonly seen in older women.

Overflow incontinence

This results from retention of urine in the bladder when the bladder is not able to be completely emptied. This means the bladder is always full and leads to frequent or constant dribbling. It occurs most commonly in men and

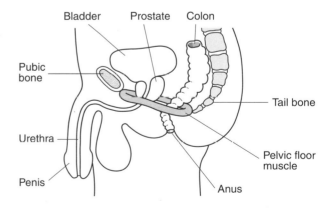

Overflow incontinence in men is commonly caused by an enlarged prostate gland

often because of an obstruction such as an enlarged prostrate gland. This can be treated by the removal of the obstruction, which is normally done by surgery. The prostrate gland in men is wrapped around the neck of the bladder like a collar. Its function is to squeeze fluid from the prostrate gland into semen when a man has an orgasm. The prostrate is small in boys and young men but it becomes larger as men age. It is a process which can cause problems for some men because it becomes so enlarged that it restricts the outlet from the bladder until it interrupts the flow of urine through the urethra. This can cause problems for men in urinating in that the flow of urine may be slow and the bladder may not empty completely as a result. It's also possible for the urethra to become blocked completely, and this will need emergency treatment.

Functional incontinence

This occurs when someone with normal bladder control is unable to reach toilet facilities in time because of poor mobility.

Tests for diagnosis of types and causes of urinary incontinence	
Test	**Purpose of test**
Cystoscopy	Explores possibility of abnormalities in bladder and urinary tract. A fibre optic tube is inserted into the bladder to enable an exploration.
PVR measurement (post void residual)	This measures how much urine is remaining in the bladder after it has been emptied. It can be done by placing a tube in the bladder or, more commonly these days, through an ultrasound scan.
Urinanalysis	This test examines the urine for signs of infection or any other abnormal content.
Urodynamic testing	This examines the function of the bladder and urethra. This may involve X-rays and the insertion of equipment to measure the strength of the sphincter and bladder muscles.
Blood tests	This examines the level of chemicals and hormones in the blood.
Stress tests	These examine how the bladder functions under stress when coughing, lifting or exercising.

These tests may be carried out at a specialist **urodynamics** department at a hospital, in the department of urogenitary medicine, and some of them may be carried out by the client's own general practitioner. It is important that tests are carried out in order to establish the causes of the incontinence and to ensure that it is not a symptom of a more serious underlying condition. The tests will help to identify the causes of the condition and this will indicate the treatments which are available in order to improve or cure it.

Causes of faecal incontinence

Faecal incontinence is the loss of bowel control. Like urinary incontinence, faecal incontinence has many different causes. It affects fewer people than urinary incontinence but is no less debilitating and embarrassing. Faecal incontinence can also be improved and cured by a range of treatments available for different types of incontinence. The most common causes of loss of bowel control are:

- Damage to the anal sphincter muscles around the back passage. This can be caused by childbirth where a significant tear across the perineum, which is the area of skin between the vagina and the anus, can cause damage to the sphincter muscles. Some types of surgery may result in damage to these muscles.

- An injury or a rectal prolapse where the pelvic floor muscles have been stretched or weakened to the extent that they no longer hold the rectum in the correct position, with the result that the anal sphincter muscles are unable to hold the rectum closed.

  If either or both of these muscles are weakened or injured, then they will be unable to tighten sufficiently to hold faeces in the rectum until a toilet can be reached. This means that a client may leak liquid or even solid faeces.

- Diarrhoea can be caused by infection or bowel disease or any other inflammation of the bowel. This means that the bowel experiences very high rates of contraction creating pressure waves, which can be so great that it is impossible to reach a toilet in time before the diarrhoea is expelled.

- Constipation can result from an immobility or illness. Some medications can cause constipation. Some types of neurological disease, such as Parkinson's disease, is also likely to cause constipation. This can cause incontinence even though the client may be constipated and unable to pass faeces. This happens if the bowel becomes very overloaded, so that small lumps of faeces break off and come away. The wall of the bowel can then be irritated by the hard and compacted constipated stools and produce additional fluid and mucus which leaks out through the anus.

- Nerve injury or disease. Bowel control involves the coordination of neurological and muscular functions, so any damage or disease of the nerve can affect the ability to control the evacuation of the bowels. This can affect people who have had a spinal injury or those with multiple sclerosis. Nerve damage is likely to mean that the brain does not receive the correct messages to say that the rectum is full and needs to be emptied, or it may be that the rectum will simply empty without any feeling.

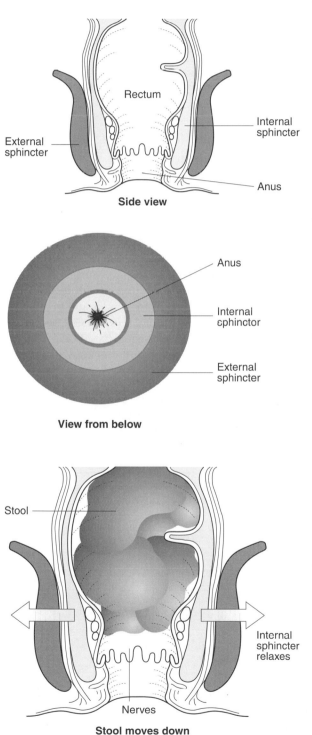

Side view

View from below

Stool moves down

The social and emotional effects of incontinence

The effect of people of their inability to get rid of body waste in the normal way can be devastating. People often avoid getting help or treatment for their incontinence because they are too embarrassed to discuss it, even with their own doctor. Incontinence can severely restrict people's social life and contact with others. Having had the embarrassing humiliating experience of an 'accident' in public, whether involving loss of control of bladder or the bowel, they live in constant fear of it happening again. Many people simply stop going out because of this fear. It is also one of the reasons why many come into residential forms of care, either because they or their carers are unable to cope with their incontinence.

How many suffer from incontinence?

Most people who suffer from incontinence are unaware of the very large numbers of fellow sufferers. In fact, as many as one in three adults have problems of bladder or bowel control at some point in their lives.

At least three million adults in this country have problems with urinary incontinence or bladder control. Only half this number suffer from diabetes, and yet they have no problem discussing their condition with others; neither do people who suffer from arthritis or other common conditions. However, the taboos around body waste are such that many of the three million suffer in silence and privacy.

About half a million people suffer from faecal incontinence or bowel control problems. Only a quarter of this number suffer with Parkinson's disease. However this disease is researched, publicised and commonly discussed, whereas the problem of bowel incontinence is seen as embarrassing and humiliating. A survey carried out in 1995 by the Royal College of Physicians established the numbers of those with urinary and faecal incontinence and categorised them by gender and by living circumstances – whether they were at home, in residential or nursing homes or long stay hospitals (see tables below). These results are estimates based on a wide range of studies and surveys but only record the numbers of sufferers known. There could be many more who suffer without seeking assistance.

Percentage of adults with urinary incontinence		Age	%
Women living at home		15–44 45–64 65+	5–7 8–15 10–20
Men living at home		15–44 45–64 65+	3 3 7–10
Men and women in	Residential homes		25
	Nursing homes		40
	Long stay hospitals		50–70
Percentage of adults with faecal incontinence		Age	%
Men and women living at home		15–44 45–64 65+	0.4 3–5 15
Men and women in	Residential homes		25
	Nursing homes		40
	Long stay hospitals		50–70

Incontinence is not simply a problem for the elderly. Large numbers of middle-aged women experience difficulties in bladder control as do significant numbers of young women following childbirth.

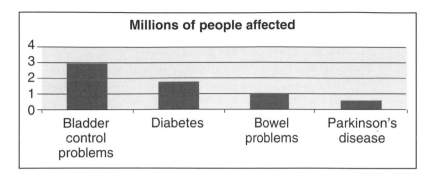

The most appropriate ways to assist clients to maintain continence

You have a vital role as a care worker with a client suffering from incontinence. You need to support them in establishing the cause of their incontinence and in identifying ways it can be improved. Always adopt the positive attitude that incontinence is not inevitable and that there are a great many options available for improving the condition. Ideally, preventing incontinence is always the preferable option, so you should do as much as possible to support clients to make it possible for them to remain continent despite any difficulties they may have.

Maintaining liquid and food intake

Clients afraid of becoming incontinent may be inclined to reduce their intake of liquids, and even food. This is one of the worst things they can do as it results in a concentration of urine which is more inclined to irritate the bladder and cause a greater sense of urgency, and possibly even an infection or inflammation. A reduction in the intake of liquids is also likely to contribute to constipation which can in itself cause problems of faecal incontinence and will certainly contribute to weakening the pelvic floor muscles if the client is straining to pass a constipated stool. Clients should be advised to drink at least six cups or glasses of fluid each day. This is a minimum amount and some clients may choose to drink more than this. Drinks which contain large amounts of caffeine, such as tea or coffee, should not be drunk in large quantities, neither should fizzy sweet drinks. These can irritate the bladder and actually make the problem worse. Plain water, fruit juice, fruit or herbal teas are all beneficial and will assist in maintaining the correct balance of fluid in the body.

Diet

A healthy diet should include foods which are high in fibre, as these will greatly assist any bowel problems. Fruit, vegetables, wholemeal bread and wholemeal pasta are all high in fibre. All clients should be encouraged to east fresh fruit and vegetables daily.

Exercise

Exercise is important for maintaining good digestive functions and will greatly assist people who suffer from constipation. Exercise is also good for improving general muscle tone and any form of exercise which improves the pelvic and anal muscles is likely to maintain continence. Exercise must be appropriate to the individual client, however for many people swimming is ideal and is something most people can do.

Regular toiletting

In Unit Z11 you will have learned about assisting people to use toilet facilities. It is important that you discuss with the client the kind of toilet facilities which they are able to manage and feel most comfortable with. It is important they are able to easily access the toilet facilities and that if they need assistance to reach them, this is readily available. No one should have to be incontinent because they are unable to obtain the assistance they need.

It will be helpful if you can discuss with your client their regular pattern of elimination of body waste. For example, how often they need to empty their bladder and bowels and at what times of the day. It is useful to know if they have a regular pattern because you can then arrange to make sure that everything they need is available at the times they need it. If you recap on the work you did for Unit Z11 you will recall that the provision of assistance to reach a toilet facility may be all that is needed, whereas for other clients you may need to make sure that commode facilities or a urine bottle are available close to them, so they can maintain their own continence.

After discussing and noting down a client's regular pattern of elimination you should always ensure that any changes in the pattern are noted and reported. More details on this will be found in Unit Z11. Any changes to the normal pattern of elimination can indicate potential problems or some underlying disease or infection. The volume frequency and condition of waste products are a useful indicator of overall health. In Units X13 and X19 you will find details of how to maintain a fluid balance chart which shows the intake and output of fluids each day for an individual client. This is important in keeping a regular check that a positive fluid balance is being maintained.

Active knowledge

Try to maintain a regular chart for your own pattern of elimination. If you keep it for a week you should have a fairly clear pattern of how often you empty your bladder and your bowels and at what times of the day. Out of interest you may want to keep a fluid balance chart for 24 hours just to check that you are maintaining a positive fluid balance.

Disposal of waste products

Many clients unable to use a toilet who but need to use alternative methods of maintaining continence, such as a commode or urine bottle, will want to be able, wherever possible, to dispose of their own waste. This may be difficult for those who have reduced mobility, but wherever possible they should be assisted to do this, or if this is not possible then you should ensure that correct hygiene procedures are followed when disposing of waste products. This means that you should:

* Wash your hands, wear gloves and an apron.
* If the waste is in a commode or bed pan or urine bottle and is for disposal, it should be covered and taken to the sluice or toilet where it should be flushed away in accordance with the procedures of your workplace. You should then remove your gloves and apron, dispose of them properly and wash your hands.
* If the waste is required for examination, then it should be covered and left in an appropriate place, such as the sluice, until the examination is carried out, and then it can be disposed of. You must ensure that disposal of any body waste complies with the procedures for your workplace and the requirements outlined in Unit CU1.

Support clients in the management of incontinence

WHAT YOU NEED TO LEARN

* Ways of managing incontinence and improving it.
* Equipment to support clients in managing their incontinence.

Ways of managing incontinence and improving it

Clients who suffer any kind of incontinence should be encouraged and supported in finding the best way of managing and improving their condition. The use of pads, sheaths and bags to absorb waste products resulting from incontinence should only be used after all other attempts at improving or curing the condition have been tried and found to be unsuccessful. You should always attempt to work alongside your client and encourage them to look for the positive ways of managing their incontinence which link in with methods of improving and lessening the severity of their condition. Simply providing the kind of atmosphere in which your client can talk freely and openly about their difficulties will be of enormous assistance. Dealing in a kind, open and unembarrassed way with the issues around incontinence make it far more likely that your client will be willing to discuss the options and explore alternative methods of treatment. If they feel embarrassed and humiliated by their condition they are less likely to be willing to consider treatment and the options which may be available to them.

Many GP surgeries and all hospitals provide specialist incontinence advisers. Many departments of genito-urinary medicine run special clinics, so you should encourage your clients to ask to be referred to such a clinic for evaluation as to how best to work to improve their condition. There are a range of ways in which incontinence can be improved, depending on its cause and its severity. Broadly, these fall into the following categories:

* Behavioural
* Devices
* Medication
* Surgery.

Urinary incontinence
Behavioural options

The major behavioural technique used to deal with urge incontinence is bladder training. This involves encouraging the client to gradually extend the period between visits to the toilet to empty their bladder. This is particularly useful for clients who suffer from urge incontinence, as over a period of time it gradually reduces the urgency for visiting the toilet.

The first stage of bladder training is to establish with the client the pattern of how often they need to empty their bladder. For example, if they empty their bladder every hour then the first aim should be to extend this period to an hour and five minutes. Every time they have the urge to rush to the toilet, they should attempt to 'hang on' for an extra five minutes. This may seem a very daunting prospect for someone who suffers from urge incontinence, however if they are also taught at the same time to use distraction techniques, such as counting backwards from 100 or counting backwards in groups of 3 from 100, in fact any activity which will distract them, they will be surprised to find that the urge which seemed so imperative before has reduced considerably. Another useful exercise is to sit on the edge of a hard chair or over the arm of a chair or on a rolled up towel. All these will support the pelvic floor muscles in holding the bladder sphincter muscles closed.

Bladder retraining is a long-term exercise and may take months before any benefit occurs, however there is a very high degree of success assisting people with urge incontinence through teaching them to retrain their bladder. The aim of bladder retraining should be to reach the normal times a day the bladder is emptied, that is, between four and eight, and to extend the period between emptying the bladder to three to four hours. This should also assist those who wake frequently in the night in order to urinate.

Hygiene

The rules of basic personal hygiene apply to anyone who suffers from incontinence. By following these they should avoid the soreness and skin irritations which can accompany urinary incontinence.

*   The area around the urethra needs to be kept clean and the skin should not be allowed to dry out. Incontinence cleansers are available for frequent cleansings without causing irritation. Most of them are simply applied by wiping with an impregnated cloth.

*   After a bath or shower, a moisturiser and a barrier cream should be applied. Moisturisers are very important as they stop the skin becoming dried out and prone to soreness and irritation. A barrier cream, such as zinc oxide or petroleum jelly or lanolin, protects the skin from the effects of the urine.

*   Deodorising tablets (Derisil or Nullo) can help to reduce the smell of urine. Apparently there are studies which have suggested that taking alfalfa several times a day reduces odour, and because it is a herbal preparation alfalfa does not react with any other medications the client may be taking.

Change in diet

Cranberry juice is known to help prevent urinary tract infections and is clearly of benefit to those who already suffer from incontinence. It is known that some foods and drinks are likely to increase levels of incontinence, such as coffee, tea and any other caffeinated beverages, fizzy drinks, alcoholic drinks, citrus juices, tomato-based juices and tomato-based foods, spicy foods, chocolate, sugar, honey, artificial sweeteners, milk and milk products. Some practitioners have suggested that eliminating one of the above items for a day over a period of time should help to establish whether there is any noticeable improvement in the incontinence.

The kind of foods that can increase incontinence

People who are incontinent during the night are recommended to stop drinking any beverages two to four hours before going to bed.

Constipation can make urinary incontinence worse so diets should be high in fibre, fruit and vegetables.

Prompted voiding

This is a form of bladder training widely practised in residential and nursing homes. Clients are reminded to urinate and assisted to do so at regular intervals, usually starting every hour. Once this regular emptying of the bladder results in dryness then the interval between emptying the bladder increases. This is used primarily for clients who may be unable to remember the timing for themselves and need a reminder to use the toilet.

Exercises

Stress incontinence is particularly common amongst women and results in many cases from pelvic floor muscles stretched and strained during childbirth. The techniques for improving stress incontinence largely concentrate on exercise rather than behavioural changes.

Pelvic floor exercises (Kegel exercises) were named after Dr Kegel, who developed them to assist women prepare for and deal with the after-effects of childbirth. They are extremely useful for both men and women to improve stress incontinence. They work by strengthening the pelvic floor muscles which hold the bladder sphincter firmly in place. The exercises can also be useful for people who suffer from urge incontinence.

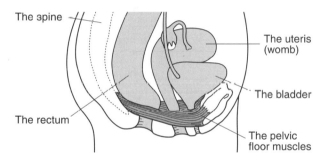

Female pelvic floor muscles

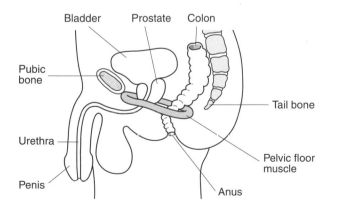

Male pelvic floor muscles

The pelvic floor is a large sling of muscles stretching across the floor of the pelvis. It reaches from the pubic bone at the front and attaches to the coccyx, which is the base of the spine behind. The openings from the bladder, bowels and vagina all pass through the pelvic floor. Its function is to support the pelvic organs and abdominal contents and hold them in place to prevent any leakage of waste products. It is possible to exercise the pelvic floor muscles and to strengthen them by carrying out the exercises on the next page.

Men also experience weakness of the muscles of the pelvic floor. This can lead to urinary incontinence, particularly following prostrate surgery when men often experience dribbling following urination. The male pelvic floor muscles are similar to those in women and stretch from the pubic bone to the coccyx (see exercises on page 394). The urethra and rectum also pass through the pelvic floor muscles and support the bladder and the bowel in the same way as in the female anatomy. In men the commonest reasons for weakness of the pelvic floor muscles are:

- Surgery for enlarged or diseased prostrates.
- Continual straining to pass stools following constipation.
- A chronic lung condition such as bronchitis, asthma or a smoker's cough.
- Being overweight.
- Neurological damage such as a stroke or spinal injury. However, people who suffer from this type of neurological damage would need specialist treatment for incontinence.

Crossing the legs exercise for women

This very simple but effective movement was shown to help 73 per cent of women with stress incontinence. It involves women crossing their legs whenever they feel a cough or sneeze coming on. It prevented urine leakage almost completely in the women it helped.

Pelvic floor exercises for women

Exercise 1

Tighten the pelvic floor muscles around the back passage, vagina and urethra and pull them up inside as if you were trying to stop the flow of urine in mid-stream. Hold the pelvic floor muscles tightly for up to ten seconds, then rest for four or five seconds, and then repeat. This should gradually build up to a period of ten contractions. The exercises should be done about six times a day working up to ten contractions each time.

Note: It is important to only use the pelvic floor muscles. You should tell your client not to:

- pull in their tummy
- squeeze their legs together
- tighten their buttocks
- hold their breath.

In this way most of the effort should work from the pelvic floor.

Exercise 2

This exercise helps the muscles of the pelvic floor respond quickly to sudden stresses from coughing, laughing or exercise.

Practise quick contractions which draw up the pelvic floor. Hold for one second before releasing the muscles. This should be done in a controlled and steady way with strong muscle tightening for each contraction.

Repeat up to ten times.

Add to the first one in the six times daily routine.

Note: Clients should see significant results within three to six months, however they should be prepared to continue with pelvic floor exercises almost indefinitely.

If a client has problems identifying the correct muscles they could practise trying to stop a flow or urine while sitting on the toilet. However, this should not be regularly practised once the client has learnt the correct muscles as it can cause further bladder problems.

It is important that the exercises are continued regularly as it is only by constant repetition that the condition will improve. If they are stopped the previous level of incontinence is likely to return. Exercises should not be undertaken more than five or six times a day; more than this can tire the muscles and cause more leakage than before. Generally, Kegel exercises have been very effective in improving stress incontinence. They may not cure incontinence, however up to 75 per cent of clients have reported significant improvement in their stress incontinence after using the exercises.

Biofeedback

Pelvic floor exercises are often more effective if used with biofeedback. This uses a vaginal or rectal probe to relay information to monitoring equipment which emits auditory or visual signals to show how strongly the client is contracting the pelvic floor. This is a useful guide for clients in showing them how well they are carrying out their exercises.

This technique can be used for men though there is no current evidence to show it is effective.

Vaginal weighted cones

These are small weights which can be placed inside the vagina to assist pelvic floor exercises. These are sometimes useful for women who have difficulty in identifying the correct pelvic floor muscles and doing the usual exercises. The idea is to place the weighted cones in the vagina for 15 to 20 minutes while walking around and moving as usual. The pelvic floor muscles are exercised by holding the cones in place. Cones usually come in sets of different weights or as one cone which unscrews so that different weights can be placed inside it. The exercises begin by using the lightest weight and gradually increasing the weight and the length of time. The cones are available from major chemists or ask at your GP surgery for a list of suppliers. One problem with the cones is that it can slip out of the vagina, another is that it simply lodges there without any muscle work required to keep it in place. A study carried out in 1999, and reported in the *British Medical Journal*, concluded that vagina cones did not add any benefit to pelvic floor exercises that were carried out correctly. However, some women have reported that the cones have been of assistance in identifying the correct muscles and helping them to carry out their exercises properly.

Electrical stimulation

Electrical stimulation is useful for stress incontinence and urge incontinence. However, it is normally a treatment carried out under medical supervision with a specialist continence practitioner. It uses a small battery powered unit to produce an electric current to the muscles around the bladder. This current is passed by a small vaginal or anal probe in close contact with the pelvic floor muscles or via surface electrodes. This produces an involuntary tightening of the pelvic floor muscles and is normally used for about 20 minutes to half an hour a day. This treatment produces a similar effect to pelvic floor exercises, but is not as convenient to carry out. However, it can be useful for people who find the exercises difficult.

This technique can be used with men, however, as in the case of biofeedback, there is no evidence so far that it is effective.

Pelvic floor exercises for men

1 Tighten the ring of muscles around the anus (back passage) as if trying to control diarrhoea or wind. Then relax. Repeat this tightening and relaxing several times until sure the correct muscles have been identified.

Note: Do not tighten the buttocks, thighs or tummy muscles at this stage.

To help identify the correct muscles imagine passing urine and trying to stop the flow in mid-stream. This can be tried out in the toilet. However, this should not be encouraged as a regular practice as it can interfere with normal bladder emptying. Having identified the correct muscles, tighten the pelvic floor. The base of the penis should move towards the abdomen and this should stop or slow down the flow of urine.

2 Tighten and draw in the muscles around the anus and urethra, lift them up inside. Hold this contraction strongly, count to five and release slowly.

Repeat squeeze and lift, then relax.

It is important to leave four or five seconds between each contraction. Build up the length of time the contractions are held until it is up to 10 seconds. Repeat this up to a maximum of eight to ten squeezes. Do five or ten short and fast (1-2 seconds) contractions.

Put the two parts of this routine together and carry out the whole routine four to six times every day.

Remember to advise your client that while doing the exercises they should not hold their breath and they should not tighten their tummy, buttocks or thighs.

As with women it takes some months to reach the maximum effect and the exercises should be continued in order to maintain any improvement.

Devices

Mild stress incontinence can sometimes be effectively managed using a tampon which compresses the urethra as it pushes on the vaginal wall. In one study 86 per cent of women with mild incontinence remained continent during exercise sessions when using tampons. This does not appear to be as effective with severe incontinence, as in the same study only 29 per cent remained dry.

Adhesive pads

Foam pads, under a variety of brand names, have an adhesive coating and are effective for women who have stress incontinence. They do not work for women with urge or other forms of incontinence and should not be used if there is a urinal tract or vaginal infection. The pad is placed over the opening of the urethra where it creates a seal to prevent leakage. It has to be removed before urinating and replaced afterwards. In one study, the average number of leaks dropped from 14 a week to 5, and women who were more severely incontinent saw a drop from an average of 34 leaks during a week to 10. When leakage occurred it was slight. The pad can be worn up to five hours a day and during the night.

Shields

This is a nipple-shaped shield that fits over the urethral opening. It is an effective way to manage stress incontinence. In one study, it reduced urine loss by 96 per cent within a week and 82 per cent of participants were completely dry. This is only available on prescription and there are side-effects, which can include irritation and urinary tract infections.

Reliance urinary control device

This is a small tube which is inserted into the urethra using a reusable syringe. The tip of the tube has a small balloon which is inflated against the urethra and blocks the expulsion of urine. In order to urinate, a string must be pulled to deflate the balloon. The device is then thrown away and replaced with a new one. However, the use of the device has revealed a high incidence (44%) of women suffering urinary tract infections and significant numbers (78%) reporting its use as uncomfortable and irritating.

Bladder neck support

A flexible ring which supports the neck of the bladder can be inserted into the vagina and the ridges then pressed against the walls to support the urethra. It is essential that the correct size is used for the device to be effective. It can cause infection of the vagina or urethra and there are significant numbers of users who report discomfort when using it.

Medications

There are a significant number of drugs available which can assist with urge incontinence. There is very little medication can do to improve stress incontinence, however drugs, such as anticholinergics, and antispasmodics, such as propantheline and oxybutynin, work by relaxing the bladder muscles to stop abnormal contractions. These are often effective in reducing urge incontinence by stopping the involuntary contractions of the bladder and allowing the muscles to relax so the bladder can fill and empty normally. However, there are side-effects with the drugs. Some people experience a very dry mouth, blurred vision and constipation.

Surgery

Stress incontinence in the case of women can be improved by different types of surgery.

The commonest is **Burchescolposuspension**. This has the highest rate of long-term success – 85–90 per cent success at five years after the operation. Essentially, all surgery for stress incontinence in women involves supporting or strengthening the pelvic floor muscles. Surgery is also available for men. Prostrate surgery often resolves the problems of incontinence which accompany an enlarged prostrate gland.

Many more surgical interventions are now carried out by laproscopic or keyhole surgery. This involves making very small cuts and using microsurgery techniques to correct the problem. This considerably reduces post-surgical complications and the length of stay in hospital.

Faecal incontinence

There are a range of ways faecal incontinence can be managed and improved.

Behavioural options

Exercises

Sphincter exercises are particularly useful for those who experience problems of urgency. The exercises, which are similar to those for strengthening the pelvic floor muscles, will strengthen the anal sphincter and assist in holding the faeces in the back passage. A specialist continence practitioner will be able to teach the exercises and biofeedback is often useful.

Changing bowel habits

Having a regular pattern of behaviour, such as regular meal times, going to the toilet 20 or 30 minutes after a meal, is likely to encourage the bowel to develop a regular pattern. The pattern also helps in planning to be near a toilet at the appropriate time. Sometimes people will feel more confident if their bowel is empty. This may be best done by inserting a suppository into the rectum. The client then needs to hold onto this for as long as possible, usually about 10 to 20 minutes, before going to the toilet. This should empty the bowel almost completely. The client can do this at a time that suits them. They can then feel confident that for the rest of the day, or at least for several hours, they will not need to rush to empty their bowels and are unlikely to have an accident.

Bowel training

This is a matter of the client learning to resist the urge to empty their bowels and feeling that they have to rush to the toilet at the first indication of a bowel movement. Many people who suffer from incontinence and who have had the humiliating experience of having an accident, are very afraid that this will happen again and so rush to the toilet the moment they are aware of anything in their back passage. This increases the problem. So, learning to break the cycle can help in training the rectum to hold onto faeces for a longer period.

Diet

Trial and error is the only way to establish if there are any foods which contribute to bowel incontinence. Very spicy or hot food can upset some people and food very high in fibre can cause difficulties for people who suffer from poor control and loose faeces or diarrhoea.

Devices

There are very few devices to deal with bowel incontinence, although an anal plug has been developed to assist with bowel leakage. It is designed to be worn inside the rectum and plugs the exit of the anus from the inside. It has to be removed in order for the bowel to be emptied and can provide some relief for those who suffer from leakage.

Medication

If a cause of incontinence is diarrhoea, or very soft or runny faeces, then medication, such as imodium or codeine, can be used to solidify the stools or reduce the bowel contractions.

Surgery

If the cause of faecal incontinence is external anal sphincter damage, it may be possible to correct this with surgery. The results of sphincter repair operations are good – 80 per cent of people report improvement two years following surgery.

Equipment to support clients in managing their incontinence

If all the options for curing incontinence have been tried and been unsuccessful or only partially successful, there is a wide range of products which can make the management of incontinence much easier, such as:

- hand-held urinals
- specially adapted clothing
- sheathes and body worn urinals
- catheters
- protection for beds and chairs
- protection for clothing
- pads.

Hand-held urinals

Hand-held urinals means that both men and women with restricted mobility can be continent and independent. It also means they can go out and participate in social activities where toilet facilities may not readily be available. A hand-held urinal can be used in bed, when seated or standing, much of which depends on the abilities of the individual.

Did you know?

A sachet of absorbent gel, such as the kind you use in hanging baskets of plants, placed inside a hand-held urinal will soak up most of the fluid and reduce the risk of spills.

Hand-held urinals for men

Men who use hand-held urinals when sitting down may find that extending the fly slide on trousers until it reaches the crotch seam will make the urinal easier to use. Male urinals come in various shapes to suit the circumstances in which they are to be used.

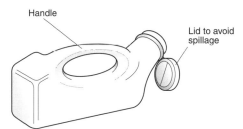

Non-spill valves will fit into the neck of most standard bottles

Hand-held urinals for men

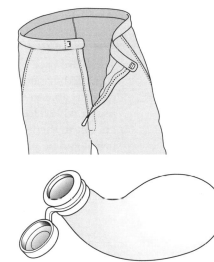

A snap-on lid helps to avoid spillage after use, as does a bedside or chair-side holder. A version with a flatter bottom is more stable and less easy to spill if placed between the legs in bed.

Non-spill valves will fit into the neck of most standard bottles

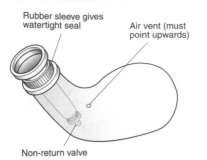

Rubber sleeve gives watertight seal

Air vent (must point upwards)

Non-return valve

The rubber sleeve fits snugly into the neck of the bottle with the air vent upwards. The valve allows urine to pass in but not to return out of the bottle. This is particularly useful for someone who tends to spill or drop a bottle.

This is useful for a man with a small or retracted penis, who has difficulty in using a standard bottle. The whole penis and scrotum can usually fit inside the bottle so that urine is caught at whatever angle it emerges.

Hand-held urinals for men

Single-use disposable urinals, made from lightweight plastic, can be carried in a pocket or bag for use when out.

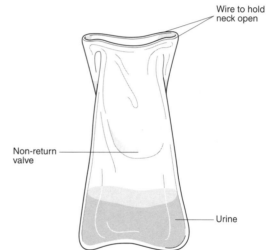

Wire to hold neck open

Non-return valve

Urine

Disposable urinal

Hand-held urinals for women

These are used by placing them between the legs from the front or they can be straddled or sat on. The choice of urinal will depend on the posture the individual client is able to use and their own circumstances. If you are supporting a client who uses a wheelchair or who spends most of their day sitting in a chair, then a u-shaped cut-out in the front of the cushion may be particularly useful. This means that the urinal can be placed in the space left by the cut-out, which avoids having to lift.

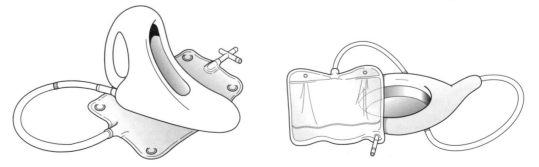

The bridge urinal can be used on its own or connected to a large capacity drainage bag.

Hand-held urinals for women

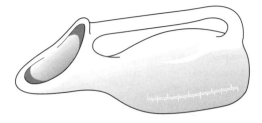

The female bottle-type urinal (Cygnet) can be used by a woman in a standing or sitting position or lying on her side.

A shallow triangular urinal can be used sitting or prone and has an emptying spout that doubles as a handle

Hand-held urinals for women

Clothing

Specially adapted clothing, such as split crotch knickers, wrap around skirts and similar styles, may help with the use of a urinal.

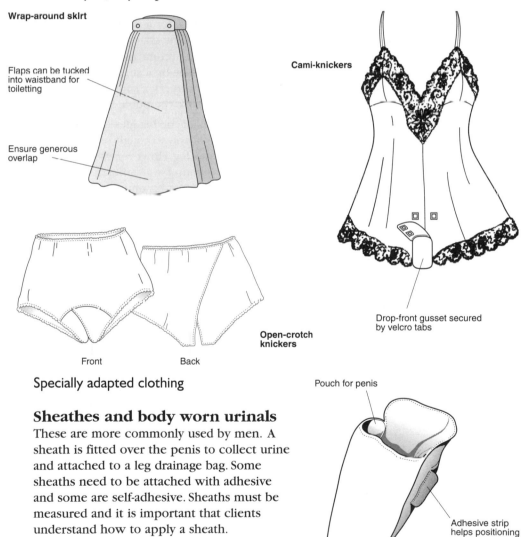

Wrap-around skirt

Flaps can be tucked into waistband for toiletting

Ensure generous overlap

Cami-knickers

Drop-front gusset secured by velcro tabs

Front

Back

Open-crotch knickers

Specially adapted clothing

Sheathes and body worn urinals

These are more commonly used by men. A sheath is fitted over the penis to collect urine and attached to a leg drainage bag. Some sheaths need to be attached with adhesive and some are self-adhesive. Sheaths must be measured and it is important that clients understand how to apply a sheath.

Body worn urinals are available in several designs and can be used instead of absorbent pads or penile sheaths. They drain into a leg bag or into their own reservoir.

Pouch for penis

Adhesive strip helps positioning

Sheath

Catheters

Catheters should only be used on medical advice and how they are used must be carefully explained to the client by a qualified medical practitioner. There are two types of catheter – an intermittent catheter and an indwelling catheter. An intermittent catheter is inserted into the bladder several times each day, emptying the contents of the bladder into the toilet, a jug or other convenient container for disposal. This can be done by somebody caring for a client or it can be done by themselves.

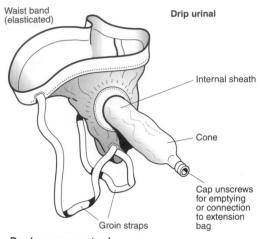

Body worn urinal

An indwelling catheter is kept in place for a longer period – a maximum of three months, by which time it will need to be changed and replaced with a new catheter. Normally, catheters are inserted via a urethra, in the case of both men and women, placed in the bladder and held in place by a small balloon which is inflated once inside the bladder. Sometimes after surgery a suprapubic catheter can be inserted through the abdominal wall just above the pubic bone.

Most catheters empty the contents of the bladder down a tube into a drainage bag. This can be supported in a range of ways, though usually by being attached to the client's leg. However, rather than using a bag some people prefer a catheter valve which fits on the end of the tube and is emptied every three or four hours into a toilet or suitable receptacle.

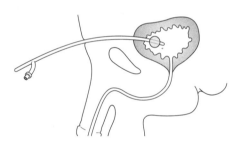

Indwelling catheter

A full drainage bag from a catheter or from a sheath is quite heavy, so it is important that an adequate support system is in place. For clients who are not mobile this is not such a problem, however for people who are able to move around there are a range of ways of supporting a drainage bag in place under clothing. Leg straps are often the easiest way to support the drainage bag, or a waist belt can be used.

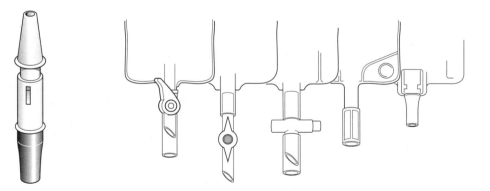

Catheter bags

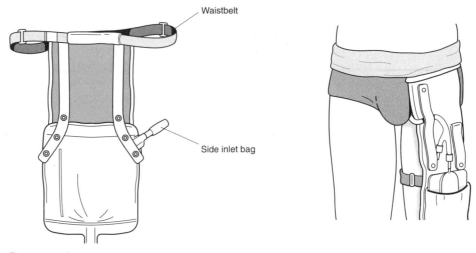

Waistbelt

Side inlet bag

Drainage bags

Another option is to use leg bag garments designed to hold a catheter drainage bag and to stop it slipping. Such garments usually have an opening to empty the bag.

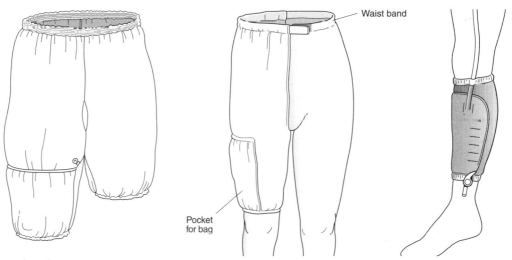

Waist band

Pocket for bag

Leg bag garments

Protection for beds and chairs

Covers to protect mattresses, pillows, blankets and duvets are available. They can be either disposable or washable and there are a range of advantages and disadvantages in both cases. There are different types of washable and reusable bed and chair pads. They range from basic plastic PVC covers to quilted and absorbent ones, which are much more comfortable to use. If disposable pads are used, they must be disposed of in line with the disposal of body waste procedures in your workplace. If they are washable pads, they should be washed separately and thoroughly dried before being replaced on the bed. Many of the current washable pads are designed to absorb large quantities or urine. If these are being used it is important that the client sleeps naked below the waist so the skin is in direct contact with the dry top surface of the pad. The urine will pass through this to a lower layer where it is held. This means that the skin does not come into contact with the urine, thus reducing the risk of skin irritation, rashes and bedsores.

Protection for clothing

Pads are the most popular product that people use to protect themselves against leaks of urine or faeces. Like bed and chair pads they can be either disposable or washable and reusable. Several factors need to be taken into account in deciding to use these, such as the degree of incontinence, the access to washing and drying facilities, and cost.

All-in-one disposable pads are suitable for either urinary or faecal incontinence, and are particularly useful for people confined to bed.

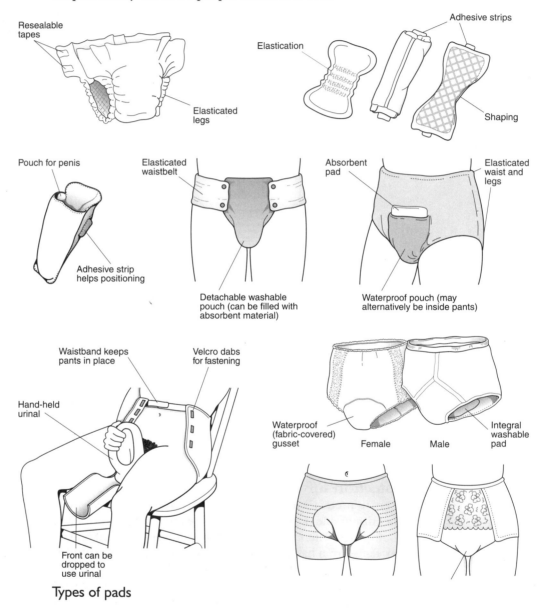

Types of pads

Disposable insert pads fit into specially designed pairs of knickers and can be disposed of after use. Male pouches can be disposable or washable and can be used by men with slight or dribbling incontinence.

Your role

Your role is not that of a specialist incontinence advisor, however it is useful for you to understand the ways in which incontinence can be effectively managed and to work alongside your client to improve their incontinence and to develop their own confidence in dealing with it. New products and treatments are constantly being developed and it is essential that you continually update your knowledge of what is available. One of the most useful ways of doing this is to attend exhibitions and to obtain literature on new developments from your local specialist continence advisor. The knowledge which you can pass on to your client will be invaluable in convincing them that suffering incontinence is not inevitable, and it can often be cured and always be improved.

Unit test

1 What are the main types of incontinence?

2 What are the commonest causes of each type of incontinence?

3 List the main approaches which can be taken to improving incontinence.

4 How common is incontinence? Can you remember approximately how many people in this country suffer?

5 How would you approach somebody who is too embarrassed to discuss their incontinence problem?

6 What could be done to assist faecal incontinence?

7 Plan an exercise programme for a women suffering from stress incontinence.

8 Consider what incontinence products you would advise for an elderly man who has dribbling incontinence and poor mobility.

Glossary

Abuse	Treating someone or something in a way that causes harm. Abuse may be directed at oneself (self-harm), at others, or at things. It may be emotional, financial, physical, psychological or sexual.
Aims and objectives	Targets and ways of achieving them.
Alcohol hand rub	Can be used to clean and disinfect hands where there is no access to soap and water.
Anaphylactic shock	A severe reaction to a substance touching or entering the body.
Assumption	An acceptance that something is true although there is no real proof of it.
Barium enema	Used to diagnose abnormalities in the stomach or intestines.
Burches colpo-suspension	A surgical procedure for women which creates a 'sling' to support the pelvic floor. Can be effective in dealing with stress incontinence caused by weak pelvic muscles.
Care setting	The context for health and social care services. These include hospitals, residential settings, day-care facilities, clinics and domiciliary settings.
Care team	All those with a formal or informal responsibility for care, whether paid or unpaid. The care team includes the client/patient.
Carer	A person who is delivering care in an informal capacity. A carer is someone who is responsible for supporting an individual through the provision of some form of care, be it physical, emotional or financial. The carer is usually a partner, relative or friend.
Cascading	A method of sharing knowledge, usually in a workplace, by one person accessing information and passing it on to colleagues.
Charter	A statement which sets out the rights and entitlements of users of a particular service.
Client/patient	The terms 'client' and 'patient' are used to describe the person who is the focus of health and social care activity and cover individuals of all ages. The term 'patient' is used only in matters specifically related to health care.
Clinical activity	Any treatments or investigations carried out by health professionals.
Clinical procedures	Clinical activities in which health care workers may be involved.
Communicate	Share information, ideas, views and emotions with people by speaking, writing, body language or through the use of equipment.
Confidentiality	The principle of only sharing information about individuals with those who have a need to know it in order to benefit the individual or when the safety of others may be at risk.
Consent	Agreement by the client, after being given information, for any procedure or clinical activity to be undertaken.
Data	The raw information obtained from any process of research or investigation.
Development plan	A document which includes targets and timescales for the planning and direction of your education, training and future career.
Discrimination	The practice of treating one person or group of people less well or less fairly than other people or groups.
Diversity	The different skills, abilities, language, culture, religion, values and beliefs which provide a rich and varied society.
Dynamap	Instrument for reading blood pressure and pulse.

Enable	To act in such a way that others will be able to do something through the provision of resources, information, encouragement or help.
Environment	The surrounding in which services are delivered, particularly the intangible aspects.
Equal opportunities	Offering services, without discrimination on the basis of race, sex, religion, disability, etc., which aim at ensuring everyone has equal access and equal treatment.
Ethics	Moral principles about right and wrong behaviour. An ethic of a particular kind is an ideal or moral belief that influences the behaviour, attitudes and philosophy of a group of people.
Facilitate	To make something easier or more likely to happen.
Feedback	Valuable information gained from others, such as supervisors, colleagues or clients on the way in which you carry out your work.
Group	A set of people who come together because they have something in common.
Hazardous waste	Medical, biological and human body waste, or waste from chemical and industrial processes which could cause a risk to human health.
Health and social well-being	All aspects of social, physical, intellectual and emotional/psychological health which contribute to one's health and social well-being.
Human Rights Act	Act of Parliament passed in 1998 but largely enacted in October 2000. The Act establishes a legal right to the provisions of the European Convention on Human Rights.
Individual	Any person who may be the focus of the activity concerned. This may be the person who is in receipt of the services but also may be other workers, managers or those in the vicinity.
Inequality	Different levels of opportunities to access the rights, benefits and routes to achievement.
Infringement of rights	An action or situation that interferes with someone's rights and freedom.
Internet	The interface between technology, e.g. computers, digital televisions, digital telephones, and the information on the World Wide Web.
Invasive clinical procedure	A treatment or investigation which involves putting instruments or equipment inside the body through the skin or through a natural opening.
Key worker	The person who has the main responsibility for relating to a client and is the main point of contact.
Life stage	Human development levels such as baby, infant, toddler, child, adolescent, adult, old age.
Manager	The person with direct managerial responsibility for the worker in the sense of allocating, co-ordinating and evaluating her/his work.
Materials and equipment	All types of supplies, consumables, sundries, instruments, equipment and machines. These may be clinical or non-clinical. 'Materials' refers to items which have a short life or single use. 'Equipment' refers to items which may be used many times.
Monitoring	The process of keeping a regular check to ensure that any significant changes are noticed.
MRSA (Methicillin-Resistant Staphylococcus aureus)	The most serious nosocomial infection which is resistant to all the common antibiotics.
MSSU (mid-stream sample of urine)	A urine sample which is obtained by asking the client to stop, or slow, their flow of urine and then restart into the collection vessel.
Mucocutaneous exposure	When potentially infected body fluids come into contact with mucous membranes such as eyes or nose.

Non-hazardous waste	Waste which does not pose a risk to human health.
Non-pathogenic	Micro-organisms which do not cause infection to humans.
Norm	Within the commonly accepted or usual boundaries.
Nosocomial infections	Infections which are prevalent in hospitals.
Package of care	The set of measures brought together to meet a person's needs.
Pathogenic	Micro-organisms which do cause infection to humans.
Percutaneous exposure	When potentially infected body fluids enter through the skin either because of injury, such as a 'needle stick' or broken skin.
Phenylketonuria (PKU) test	A test which can show the lack of an essential enzyme for breaking down phenylalanine. If undetected, this can lead to severe brain damage.
Plan of care	An outline of an individual's present and future needs and the ways in which these needs will be met.
Policy	Protocols, procedures and requirements to which the worker must adhere. Policies may be set at international, national, local or agency level.
Power of attorney	A legal process which gives one person, usually a relative or legal or financial professional, the power to conduct someone's financial and legal affairs. This power is only granted when someone is incapable of managing their own affairs.
Practice guidelines	Recognised good practice within agencies, including codes of good practice and recognised methods of working.
Pulseoximeter	An instrument for taking pulse.
Records	Electronic, written, diagrammatic, photographic or other information kept about an individual while in receipt of services.
Referral	The act of forwarding a case or issue to a person who is authorised or better qualified to deal with it. Referrals may be between workers in the same agency or across agencies.
Reflective practitioner	One who considers and thinks about their own practice, skills and abilities and takes steps to improve and develop their working skills.
Sharps	Instruments which could cause a penetrating injury such as needles, syringes, scalpels, razors etc.
Social stratification	A means of identifying society into different groupings according to income, occupation and lifestyle.
Socioeconomic deprivation	Consequences of low income and poor environmental conditions such as bad housing, education and local facilities.
Sphygmomanometer	A traditional instrument for reading blood pressure, which uses mercury and is being phased out of use.
Standard precautions	See **Universal precautions**
Stereotype	A fixed general image believed to represent a particular type of person or thing. If you stereotype people you form a fixed idea of them so that you assume they will behave in a particular way.
Sterile field	A treatment area which has had all pathogens removed.
Team leader	A person who is heading a team of workers to achieve common outcomes.
Universal precautions	Preventive measures which should be taken before being exposed to possible contamination by body fluids.
Values	The moral principles and beliefs that are considered important.
Venipuncture	The process of taking blood from a vein using a needle.
Visitors	Someone who goes to see a person or place who does not usually work there, live there or attend there.
World Wide Web	Almost unlimited source of information, accessible using information technology such as computers, digital televisions and digital telephones.

Index

abuse
adults 119, 123–4, 125–6
by care workers 124, 140
carers 121, 123–4, 134
children 118, 122–3, 125,
129–30, 138
dealing with 132–3,
137–40
definition 117
disabled 124
disclosures 131
good practice 141
inter-agency teamwork
137–8
legislation 122–4
perpetrators 120–21,
135–6
protection from 69, 137–8
reporting 69, 124, 127–8,
133–4
risk assessments 138–40
self-inflicted 119, 121
signs of 130–31
stopping 126
support for
carers 134
victims 134, 135–6
by visitors 121
abusers 120–21, 135–6
Access to Medical Records
Act 204–5
accidents
distress caused by 94–5
reporting 74–5, 94
addressing clients 55
advocacy, consent 238, 271
agencies see services and
agencies
allergies
anaesthetics 239, 272
anaphylactic shock 239,
272
clinical procedures 238,
239, 271, 272
latex 239, 240, 272, 343
Alzheimer's disease 144, 209,
305
anaesthetics, allergy to 239,
272
anaphylactic shock 239, 272
Apollo Syndrome 186–7
appraisal 104–5
asthma 262, 289, 335
Attendance Allowance 318

bacteria 158–9
barium enemas 230
beds
bridging 356–7

getting out of 355
naso-gastric feeding tubes
278
pressure sores 358–62
rolling over 356
behaviour, changes in 368
benefits
carers 321–2
child 318–19
claim forms 323–5
dental treatment 320
disability 318, 321–2, 325
entitlements 314,
317–18, 322
eye tests 318
fraudulent claims 324
low income 309, 319–20
payment methods 326–8
pensions 317, 318
prescriptions 318, 320
residential home fees
318
transport costs 318, 320
Benefits Agency 15, 317
biofeedback 393
bladder 380–81
bleeding 84–5
blindness see visual impairment
blood see body fluids and
waste
blood pressure
diastolic 259
systolic 259
taking 240, 258–9, 273,
286, 335
blood sampling
blood sugar test 255–6,
284
finger prick 255, 284
frequent 255, 284
phenylketonuria test 255,
281
precautions 240, 273
venipuncture 255, 281,
282–3
blood-borne viruses 162
mucocutaneous exposure
163
precautions 163–4, 240,
273
transmission 163
body fluids and waste
cleaning materials, dis-
posal 170
disposal 76, 170
eye protection 164, 240,
273
spillages 164, 170

universal precautions
163–4, 240, 273
body mass index [BMI] 261,
262, 288, 289
body temperature 257, 285
bowel action 381–2
bronchitis 254, 281, 335
budgeting 309–10, 311
Burchescolposuspension 395
burns and scalds 91–2

Caldecott Guardians 30, 31,
34
Caldecott Principles 29–34
cardiac arrests 85–6, 92
care environments, definition 117
care planning meetings
clients at 208, 208–9, 212,
213
preparation 207
proposals
client agreement
214–16
communicating
213–14
imposition 215
recording 212–13, 216
stereotyping 209
care plans 235, 268
abuse 127–8
changing needs 219
implementing 219–20
mobility 357
monitoring provision
217–19
review processes 220–21
carers
benefits 321–2
effect of distress 378
support for 330–31
case notes/files 235, 268
cash, security of 326, 328
catheters
bags 400–1
client procedures 333
hygiene 249
indwelling 249, 276–7,
400
latex allergy 239, 272
urine specimen collection
251–2
cerebral palsy 144, 151
Charters
Benefits Agency 15
Long-term Care 15
Patients 15
Child Benefit [formerly
Family Allowance] 318–19